"Just at a time when many are so near to despair at the sight of a rising far right, racist populism and the corporate capture of governments, Peter Beresford wonderfully gives us a comprehensive vision of how a new politics can be created to secure humanitarian solidarity and environmentally sustainable change."
Rt Hon John McDonnell MP

"Bravo! This book explains how personal politics and new social movements forge human connections that can be harnessed to transform society and shape a future beyond neoliberalism."
Peter Tatchell, human rights campaigner

"Charts a journey from destruction to renewal and alienation to inclusion. Invoking the spirit of others who have given us hope in the power to overcome, Beresford once again gives us an important book for our times."
**Sarah Carr, survivor researcher
and service user involvement champion**

"Peter Beresford brilliantly explains why we don't, won't and can't stop the power of the people."
Danny Dorling, University of Oxford

"Wholly original and timely, and steeped in the current moment, this is a book to savour slowly and to remain in frequent dialogue with."
Peter Barham, psychologist, historian and author

"In an uncertain world where political polarisation and raging inequality run like faultlines, The Antidote is a pressing and profoundly urgent book."
Mary O'Hara, journalist and author of *Austerity Bites*

"Beresford provides a comprehensive and thought-provoking analysis of the consequences of neoliberalism and offers a guide to how we can challenge its damaging social consequences."
Lee Gregory, University of Nottingham

"An accessible, masterful and critical analysis of the barriers to change and a meaningful doable strategy for their removal ... essential reading for students, researchers and anyone involved in the struggle for a fairer and just global society."
Colin Barnes, University of Leeds

THE ANTIDOTE
How People-Powered Movements Can Renew Politics, Policy and Practice

Peter Beresford

With a foreword by
Ruth Lister

First published in Great Britain in 2025 by

Policy Press, an imprint of
Bristol University Press
University of Bristol
1–9 Old Park Hill
Bristol
BS2 8BB
UK
t: +44 (0)117 374 6645
e: bup-info@bristol.ac.uk

Details of international sales and distribution partners are available at policy.bristoluniversitypress.co.uk

© Bristol University Press 2025

British Library Cataloguing in Publication Data
A catalogue record for this book is available from the British Library

ISBN 978-1-4473-7647-7 hardcover
ISBN 978-1-4473-7544-9 paperback
ISBN 978-1-4473-7545-6 ePub
ISBN 978-1-4473-7546-3 ePdf

The right of Peter Beresford to be identified as author of this work has been asserted by him in accordance with the Copyright, Designs and Patents Act 1988.

All rights reserved: no part of this publication may be reproduced, stored in a retrieval system, or transmitted in any form or by any means, electronic, mechanical, photocopying, recording, or otherwise without the prior permission of Bristol University Press.

Every reasonable effort has been made to obtain permission to reproduce copyrighted material. If, however, anyone knows of an oversight, please contact the publisher.

The statements and opinions contained within this publication are solely those of the author and not of the University of Bristol or Bristol University Press. The University of Bristol and Bristol University Press disclaim responsibility for any injury to persons or property resulting from any material published in this publication.

Bristol University Press and Policy Press work to counter discrimination on grounds of gender, race, disability, age and sexuality.

Cover design: Hannah Gaskamp
Front cover image: Stocksy/Neil Warburton

This book is dedicated to all those kindred spirits who have worked to enable others to have more say *and* control in their lives and the world we live in. I have been so lucky in my life to meet so many such helpful and altruistic souls, collaborating with some and making friends too. Thank you for helping me to keep going and for all the insights, understanding and help you have given me.

Contents

List of photographs	viii
About the author	ix
Acknowledgements	x
Foreword by Ruth Lister	xii
Introduction	1

PART I	Neoliberalism's destructive agenda	
1	Policing and a very neoliberal murder	11
2	Ideological damage – from the personal to the global	30
3	Fake news politics	42
4	The politics of disconnection	49
5	Divide and rule	59
6	Alienated even from ourselves	70
7	Betraying intimacy	76

PART II	New routes for a different politics	
8	Changing our approach to making change	97
9	Starting with our own lives	105
10	What the new social movements can tell us	116
11	A new watchword – 'only connect' on *equal terms*	125

PART III	Building a politics of inclusive connection	
12	What's wrong with the new communication?	139
13	Towards truly inclusive communication	155
14	Learning from what we know	173
15	Education for empowerment and change	192
16	Working together: building alliances, including everyone	205
17	Rethinking solidarity – extending connection	222
18	Conclusion and next steps	238

References	248
Index	284

List of photographs

Problems posed by neoliberalism

I.1	Environmental damage, weather disturbance	2
1.1	Gated community: cutting us off from each other	22
1.2	Commodifying housing 1	23
1.3	Commodifying housing 2	24
1.4	Even the Victorians seemed to do better: homelessness then and now	25
7.2	Grenfell Tower: the price of small state and privatisation	85
7.3	Public homelessness	86
12.1	The high street: made to fail	142

Pioneers pointing to another politics

7.1	James Baldwin	77
10.1	Audre Lorde	119
15.1	Frantz Fanon	199
15.2	Malcolm X	203
17.1	Fred Hampton	234

About the author

Peter Beresford OBE is Visiting Professor at the University of East Anglia and Co-Chair of Shaping Our Lives, the national disabled people's organisation, and has long-term lived experience of welfare benefits and mental health services. He is also Emeritus Professor at Brunel University London and the University of Essex and Honorary Professor at Edge Hill University.

He is a long-standing advocate of participation and empowerment as an activist, educator, researcher and writer. He has published over 30 books, and many chapters and journal articles, writing regularly for *The Guardian* and other mainstream and online media.

His previously published titles with Policy Press include:

- Co-editor (2011), *Supporting People: Towards a person-centred approach*.
- Co-editor (2014), *Personalisation*, Critical and radical debates in social work series.
- Author (2016), *All Our Welfare: Towards participatory social policy*.
- Co-editor (2018), *Social Policy First Hand: An international introduction to participatory social welfare*.
- Author (2021), *Participatory Ideology: From exclusion to involvement*.
- Co-Editor (2021), *COVID-19 and Co-production in Health and Social Care Research, Policy, and Practice Volume 1: The challenges and necessity of co-production*, Open Access eBook.
- Co-editor (2021), *COVID-19 and Co-production in Health and Social Care Research, Policy, and Practice Volume 2: Co-production: Methods and working together at a distance*, Open Access eBook.

Acknowledgements

I have a particularly large number of people to thank for making this book possible. First, for sharing their knowledge and experience to provide particular insights in their extended comments and quotations, thank you, Becki Meakin, Sally Witcher, Colin King, Helen Buckley and Karen Bunning. Second, thanks to all those who kindly responded to my requests to read and comment on drafts of this book including Catherine Beresford, Suzy Croft, Jennie Hutchins, Kathy Boxall, Susanna Alyce and Colin Slasberg.

Then I want to thank the anonymous reviewers who helped develop and improve the book for all the effort they put in. I hope they know how much they have helped.

I would also like to thank Lord Prem Sikka, Professor Shoshana Zuboff and Professor Sara Ahmed for their permission to use quotes in epigraphs. My thanks also go to Frederick T. Courtright, President of the Permissions Company, LLC Rights Agency for the James Baldwin Estate. We wish to credit James Baldwin for the excerpt from 'A talk to teachers' from *The Saturday Review* (16 October 1963) and excerpts from *Another Country: A Novel*. Copyright © 1962, 1963 by James Baldwin, renewed 1991, 1992 by Gloria Baldwin Karefa-Smart. Reprinted with the permission of the Permission Company LLC on behalf of the James Baldwin Estate. All rights reserved.

Peter Beresford of the University of East Anglia is supported by the National Institute for Health and Care Research (NIHR) Applied Research Collaboration East of England (NIHR ARC EoE) at Cambridgeshire and Peterborough NHS Foundation Trust. The views expressed are those of the author and not necessarily those of the NIHR or the Department of Health and Social Care.

Also, the many people at Policy Press who worked to get the book into production and had confidence in it, including Ginny Mills, Ellen Mitchell, Emily Ross, Anna Richardson and Kathryn King.

Next, more general thanks go to others who helped me develop both the idea and text, notably including my partner Suzy Croft and daughter Ruth Beresford. I also want to thank daughter Esther for the long-term insights she has given me into the development of child care and protection under neoliberalism in the UK, and, similarly, Rebecca for her professional insights into the destructive effects on education and mental health policy and practice it has had. Thanks also to grandson Charlie Hatton for reminding me of the significantly different ways in which young people use media compared to their elders.

Also, to my many Twitter/X friends for their helpful and generously given insights and ideas, who proved yet again that social media can be truly helpful and supportive – and challenge the problems we tend to hear more about.

Can I also thank Ruth Lister for the Foreword she wrote for the book, which perfectly catches its hope and intention and additionally makes the kind of connections which the book hoped to highlight and which are at its heart.

Over the years as I have learned more about participation and empowerment, which became the focus of my work and life, I have tried to share this. I have tried to delve deeper into participation and make new connections with it to bring about change. I hope I have helped readers in their efforts to do the same. In this book, I have sought to bring the insights I and others have gained to make broader connections between the key personal and political issues involved. I hope that just as my personal journey has been a helpful if sometimes difficult one for me, it may also be useful and helpful for others. We learn from each other, we work together and thus we can hope to achieve the change that is so much needed. Just as I have tried to explore in this book, we can see the personal and political intersect and cross over helpfully. Thanks to everybody who has been part of my journey, most of all, of course, my family and friends, but all who have helped make progress, especially those who were taken too early and who are still in our minds, if no longer present.

Finally, can I thank all the staff at the café at Waterstones Bookshop in Norwich where most of this book was written to the accompaniment of much tea, coffee and friendliness. Thanks for all your kindness and efficiency to me and other customers – and the endless Americanos with hot milk at the side which have kept me going.

Foreword

Ruth Lister

*Emeritus Professor of Social Policy,
Loughborough University, member of the House
of Lords and author of Poverty (2nd ed, 2021)*

Reading Peter Beresford's new book, especially Parts II and III, reminds me of the hope that so many of us had at the height of the pandemic that those dark days could lead to us 'building back better', as the cracks in our society became horribly evident. Debates about what a good or better society might look like helped to keep us going. Even the editorial board of the *Financial Times* wrote that 'Radical reforms – reversing the prevailing policy direction of the last four decades – will need to be put on the table. … Policies, until recently considered eccentric, such as basic income and wealth taxes, will have to be in the mix'. Referencing the Second World War and the Beveridge Plan, 'the same kind of foresight is needed today. Beyond the public health war true leaders will mobilise now to win the peace'.[1] Alas, it was not to be. Poverty worsened, public services became ever more threadbare, and the carers for whom we had clapped weekly during the pandemic did not receive any tangible recognition.

What this book does is not try to flesh out what a better society might look like but explore how we might do politics differently to get there. It emphasises the importance of means as well as ends, underlining that they are intertwined so that 'both need to be based on the same inclusive and egalitarian values'. It chimes well with the closing message of a recent pamphlet from Compass, the pressure group for a good society: 'We can't wait for the perfect government. We need to start making that society now and showing politicians what needs to be done'[2].

What both that pamphlet and Peter's book demonstrate is how myriad groups on the ground are starting to make that society. Inspired by the example of new social movements, Peter spells out the principles for a 'humanistic and inclusive politics' – what he calls 'a politics of connection'. It is a participatory politics which pays due attention to the obstacles faced by marginalised groups and recognises the value of different forms of

---

[1] Financial Times (2020), 'FT View' *Financial Times*, 3rd April.
[2] Sue Goss (2024), *The New Settlement for a Better Society*, London, Compass.

knowledge. This takes me back to when I first met Peter and he opened my eyes to the importance of a more participatory approach to researching poverty. It was a lesson I have never forgotten and it is encouraging to see today a much greater emphasis on recognising the value of the knowledge and expertise borne of lived experience, for instance through the Changing Realities project.

At the heart of the book is the feminist mantra that the personal is political so that the author's personal experience is interwoven through its pages. The aim is to unite the personal and the political in an empowering and emancipatory way in the belief that formal politics can learn from progressive developments in human relations. A striking example of this was provided by Jacinda Ardern, the former prime minister of New Zealand, who in responding to atrocity, evoked the power that lies in 'our daily acts of kindness'. Of course, not all informal politics is progressive and solidaristic, exemplifying the principles enunciated here. We need only think back to the hate-filled riots of summer 2024, fuelled by racism and xenophobia so that the ills of our society were blamed on asylum seekers and migrants. Marginalisation and despair can be exploited by the far right in pursuit of a very different sort of politics to that advocated here. However, as Ardern asserted in response to that Islamophobic atrocity, 'the answer lies in our humanity'.

This reminder serves to reinforce the importance of the kind of politics advocated here and the book's message that such a 'politics of connection, equality and inclusion' offers hope. Although our hopes of 'building back better' after lockdown were dashed, that does not mean hope should now be dismissed as Pollyannaish. The APLE Collective of individuals and organisations with experience of poverty work in the belief that 'from the tiniest seeds of change, we create gardens of hope'.[3] As Rebecca Solnit, who has written so persuasively about hope, argued in the context of the climate emergency and the need for solidarity with its main victims, 'to hope is to risk. It's to take a chance on losing. It's also to take a chance on winning, and you can't win if you don't try'.[4] And in the words of the doctor-writer Rachel Clarke, on the anniversary of the first lockdown, 'Hope is a leap of faith. It requires the willingness to act on the conviction that, for all the bleak facts of the present, a better future is possible'.[5] This book offers us a possible route towards that future.

---

[3] www.aplecollective.com.

[4] Rebecca Solnit (2022), 'Climate despair is a luxury. Those facing flood and fire can't afford to lose hope. Neither should we', *New Statesman*, 21–27 October.

[5] Rachel Clarke (2021), 'It's been a year of bearing witness to trauma. Call me a fool, but now I sense hope', *The Guardian*, 21 March.

Introduction

> It was the best of times, it was the worst of times
> ... it was the spring of hope, it was the winter of despair.
> <div align="right">Charles Dickens, <i>A Tale of Two Cities,</i> 1859</div>

> What we agree with leaves us inactive, but contradiction makes us productive.
> Johann Wolfgang von Goethe
(1749–1832) German poet and novelist

The paradox of our times

Charles Dickens was writing of a different age but prefigured the enormous contradiction of our own when there are so many reasons for hope, but presiding over it all is a doom-laden global politics. This book is inspired by that huge paradox, summed up by the widening gulf between the personal values we teach our children and the anti-social ideology that increasingly rules our lives. This book's vision is that the one may offer the key to transforming the other.

We are currently experiencing the full flood of this man-made disaster. It is blighting economies, dividing populations, undermining wellbeing and putting us and our planet at unprecedented risk through global warming and environmental damage. Its consequences dwarf pandemics like that of COVID-19 and yet many of us don't even know its name. It's the global catastrophe called *neoliberalism* – the deregulation of market economies and cutting back of state support for those they most damage. Offering short-term profit for the few orchestrating it, it brings insecurity, threat and disaster for most others. It has helped generate conflict within and between nations, created its own 'culture wars', forced mass migrations, reinforced hate and social divisions, divided Global North and South, created new kinds of colonialism and, most of all, it has concentrated power and wealth more narrowly than ever in a new 'overclass' without restraint or responsibility. It may be in its winter, but no clear end is in sight.

Yet, as all this has been happening, another much quieter revolution has been taking place in how we as humans regard and treat each other, other species and our endangered planet. This recognises our diversity, challenges discrimination and values us for who we are. As the existential impact of neoliberalism becomes clear, this book explores ways in which now at last, its antidote, the international people-powered movements based on lived experience, inclusion, equality and social justice, may offer an effective route

Photograph I.1: Environmental damage, weather disturbance

Note: Global warming and climate change have accelerated through failure to adopt and maintain sustainable policies because of the preoccupation of neoliberal politics and economics with production and profit.
Source: Marcus Kauffman/Unsplash

to ending neoliberalism's dominance and offer peoples and planet a truly sustainable future based on a renewal of democracy.

There is some suggestion that neoliberalism's days are numbered. The 2024 UK general election put a Labour government into power, the far right has apparently been defeated in France. But ' "hard-right" or "populist nationalist" parties are part of coalition governments in several EU countries, including the Netherlands, Italy and Finland' and Germany's anti-immigration AfD party has had huge success (Adler, 2024). However, the UK Labour government's 'tax and spend' first budget was not a break with previous neoliberal New Labour policy. Politics globally remain largely committed to neoliberal ideology and economics. It is difficult to see the re-election of right-wing demagogue and former President Trump in 2024 as signifying anything else. The big question for democracy continues to be how can we move beyond a situation where whichever party wins an election, neoliberalism stays in power?

The neoliberal threat

Neoliberalism, strongly evidenced to be seriously damaging personally and globally, has dominated international politics for half a century with no convincing alternative forthcoming. It's a form of politics which alienates us from each other and ourselves – at a personal and global level.

This book critiques the causes and consequences of neoliberalism's political success and sets out a road map to challenge it through a strategy of inclusive involvement. Drawing on the experiences of some of the most disempowered groups worldwide, this book highlights ways to disrupt neoliberal dogma through unified people-powered movements. The international Me Too, Black Lives Matter, Occupy and environmental new social movements (NSMs) all highlight the way such prevailing politics routinely marginalise and exclude great swathes of the population, making it possible for a small minority to take control, undermine democratic structures and traditions, exacerbate inequality and weaken social justice. They also offer key insights into how to challenge this situation through transforming and equalising our personal roles, relationships and identities.

The democratic alternative

For nearly half a century, a gulf has been developing between our personal and formal politics globally. As the former, sparked by NSMs have become more equal and inclusive, the latter, based on neoliberal ideology, have raised levels of inequality, poverty, disease, isolation, conflict and environmental threat. This text aims to help the reader make more sense of profit-driven neoliberal ideology and recognise its divisive and anti-democratic effects. It contrasts this with the trend to more equal roles and relationships in society and the growing value placed on diversity, highlighting the insights these may offer to build more liberatory policy and politics together.

This paradox of modern policy and politics offers a route to transformation, which is developed here. Traditional approaches to reform through big ideology and state welfare don't seem to be working. A conventional prescriptive paternalistic approach also gains limited support. This book centres and renews two key modern watchwords for transforming and democratising policy and politics to explore a different approach; the women's movement's 'the personal is political' and the modernist call, 'only connect'.

This text argues that the only way we'll transcend current politics and policy is by seeking to reconnect with ourselves and others equally and inclusively as both the goal of a new politics and the means to achieving it. It both sets out arguments and evidence for seeking such participatory political transformation and a route map for achieving it, building on the insights and lived experience of people more often seen as needing help themselves. It particularly draws on the insights of such disempowered people and groups to challenge the barriers they face, reversing the tradition of turning to the powerful to challenge powerlessness.

The structure of the book

The book is organised in three parts. Part I explores neoliberalism; its destructive personal and societal consequences and how such an elitist ideological approach has managed to capture and retain mainstream democracy, politics and popular support.

Chapter 1 introduces readers to neoliberal ideology through the appalling high-profile femicide of Sarah Everard by an on-duty policeman, highlighting the connections between this terrible act, neoliberalism and police, contrasting this with women's high-profile response, opening discussion about the wider ideological and international significance of these events.

Chapter 2 moves from the individual to neoliberalism's global consequences, focusing on four interconnected issues, all of which impact massively on our lives. These are (1) pandemics, (2) climate change and the future of the planet, (3) technological change, (4) war, conflict and terrorism. Each is highly controversial, all have life-changing implications for us all. While all have their own inherent major global effects, each in turn is related to and significantly influenced by neoliberal ideology.

Chapter 3 highlights the contradiction of how a politics – neoliberalism – which benefits very few, has achieved widespread support internationally. We see how this has happened, with consent and deception, through the manipulation of ideology and new technology. We introduce issues of communication, highlighting the growing gaps between formal politics and public understanding and political and personal values and moralities.

Chapter 4 reports on the sense of exclusion and disempowerment, increasingly felt under neoliberal ideology, which paradoxically, reinforces the attraction of populist, reactionary politics. What emerges is a systematic and innovative formal politics of disconnection and depoliticisation which effectively undermines democracy and leaves us isolated, uninformed, frustrated and powerless – as well as increasingly susceptible to the politics which disempowers us.

In Chapter 5 we look at the consequences of such neoliberal politics for us and our relations with each other. We are set against one another, using fear, snobbery, 'othering' and internalised oppression to divide and rule by encouraging a diversionary culture of blame, fear and suspicion among us. A range of out-groups are regularly stigmatised in right-wing ideology and media. Several disempowered groups are thus stereotyped, from refugees to disabled people; unemployed people to teenage mothers, undermining our fellow-feeling and increasing social dislocation.

Chapter 6 is concerned with neoliberalism's destructive capacity to alienate us even from ourselves. It explores its longstanding interest in 'aspirational politics', encouraging us to think of who we want to be, not who we actually are, thus misjudging our needs and political interests, with alienating and divisive results. We're encouraged to see ourselves as better than we are and others as worse. Finally, we return to neoliberal approaches to causation and solution and their individualistic, disconnecting and self-blaming logic.

Chapter 7 moves from the macro to the micro, while retaining a focus on connecting the personal and the political. Before looking at how the personal may change the political, we consider the impact of neoliberalism on intimacy as a case study. We explore neoliberalism's effects on emotions, including intimacy, how it uses them and responds to the emotional world. We see the consequences for intimacy of neoliberalism's reliance on the market, commodification and exchange relationships. We focus particularly on three international contexts where the two come into close relation; social care, pornography and a high-profile start-up company, OneTaste.

Part II highlights the failure of traditional approaches to change and the emergence of new routes out of the political logjam created by neoliberalism.

Chapter 8 looks at how people have tried to oppose neoliberal politics and ideology and why the traditional strategies adopted may have been unsuccessful, suggesting that a radically different approach is now needed. The big so far unanswered question is how do we get rid of neoliberalism? The suggestion here is that neither acquiescence, opposing it with grand theory, nor seeking support by returning to old welfare state ideas is likely to offer a way forward. More root and branch renewal involving us all is required and we focus on what that might look like.

Chapter 9 takes us from the harsh world of neoliberal politics to the more equal values, roles and relationships we are increasingly seeking in our *personal* lives. Over a similar period, new social movements (NSMs) have developed, challenging neoliberalism. Based on identity and lived experience, rooted in equalising roles and relationships, they have a transformative effect, impacting culture, law, policy and politics, highlighting issues of diversity and the need to treat them with equality. Just as NSMs have foregrounded the political relations of the personal, they now encourage us to explore how such rethinking and self-definition of our identities and relationships may relate to formal politics and help us reform and renew them.

Chapter 10 looks at how these NSMs are forcing our attention to a new emancipatory agenda, raising questions about what we might learn from efforts to equalise and humanise personal roles and relations that might help us develop more egalitarian and humanistic politics. This chapter addresses this question in more detail so it becomes, if instead of doing politics in the old ways, we try to transform them, as we are our personal roles and relations, could this bring about the change we've been seeking in formal politics and how do NSM values help?

In Chapter 11 we focus on a major theme in Western intellectual debate from the 20th century – the idea of *reconnecting* with each other. This enduring theme was explored through a series of key thinkers and has a continuing resonance into the twenty first century, not least because of the divisive effects of neoliberalism. While the latter's tendency is to disconnect, the NSMs, remind us that if such reconnection is to be helpful it needs to be reconceived for our age and rooted in a commitment to equality and inclusion.

Part III of the book offers a road map to achieve participatory politics that alone are likely to make a successful challenge to neoliberal ideology and halt the decline of democracy. It includes vignettes and case studies to do this.

Chapter 12 returns to modern communication, centring on its essential contradiction. While ostensibly there to bring us together, it raises increasing concerns about drawing us apart. The chapter starts with an examination of the new communication industries, their unaccountability, how they disconnect us from each other, and their vanguard role in neoliberal ideology – yet central importance at the heart of our lives. People who use social media offer a real-world example of the new communication, highlighting both how it objectifies us and offers us agency. We look at other ways forward to reconnect equally with each other in more direct ways.

Chapter 13 considers how communication can be made more inclusive and equal, given that effective democracy demands accessible communication if the political is to match the personal. The chapter focuses on politics and communication, surfacing the ideological and power issues involved and exploring how people's inclusive political participation has been inhibited and can be supported. We examine the 'digital divide', providing a detailed case study from a user-led organisation, Shaping Our Lives, and consider the additional insights offered by the COVID-19 pandemic.

Chapter 14 asks what counts as knowledge and highlights how neoliberalism perpetuates exclusionary approaches to knowledge formation. We move from privileging nineteenth-century scientism to revaluing lived and shared experience and experiential knowledge. We pay particular attention to including the knowledges of marginalised groups, and the discriminatory effects of not doing this (epistemic injustice/inequality) are explored. We learn about the key role in political reform of NSMs in challenging the damaging identities imposed on people, the importance of decolonisation and ways forward for sharing knowledge, making it collective and challenging traditional knowledge hierarchies.

Chapter 15 focuses on the need for more equal and inclusive education as part of our move to an inclusive and egalitarian politics. The chapter considers the importance of education for change framing it in terms of liberation and inclusion, which extend beyond school, to lifelong and emancipatory approaches to learning. The chapter offers a series of international examples of such a pedagogic approach, exploring the ideas of Freire, Fanon and James Baldwin.

In Chapter 16 we look more closely at developing more equal and inclusive ways of working together to challenge neoliberal politics effectively. We explore principles for truly inclusive alliance-building, essential if minorities are to combine to make the necessary majority. This includes the praxis of empowerment, self-organisation, coproduction, participatory organisational structures, and prioritising diversity and inclusion. We look at how user-led organisations (ULOs) have developed to enable the widest involvement possible.

Chapter 17 focuses on renewing our approach to solidarity in neoliberalism's hostile context. The NSMs' focus on identity and diversity has been criticised as weakening unity, but here it's suggested that this provides the basis for a different, more effective solidarity, based on inclusion. We see how traditional understandings of solidarity rested on the exclusion of some of the most marginalised groups and offer a case study highlighting how NSMs can help us develop more inclusive approaches by recognising the importance of addressing intersectionality.

Chapter 18 concludes the book, identifying key themes and outlining the next steps for renewal. While confirming neoliberalism's bankruptcy, it treats with caution growing suggestions that we're seeing its end. The book calls instead for us to work for and reconnect through a new participatory and sustainable politics. It sets out a series of principles drawing on ideas from NSMs, which offer means and ends for a reconceived participatory and sustainable politics, reconnecting us with ourselves and each other.

If you are reading this book, it is probably because its subject – neoliberalism – intersects with your life and experience, and probably not in a good way. That's because it is an ideology that seems to benefit few but to damage many. By a simple process of deduction, you are rather more likely to be in the second category than the first. That's why the purpose of the book – to enable us all to call a halt to this destructive philosophy and together build an alternative – hopefully, may enlist your attention and involvement. That is its fundamental aim.

PART I

Neoliberalism's destructive agenda

In the first part of the book, we chart the scale and wide range of destructive effects of neoliberal ideology and formal politics from the individual to the global. We can see its damaging influence behind both the rising and existential problems now facing us and the planet and our apparently reduced ability to be able to deal with them. Yet still, neoliberalism has managed to command wide support in democracies over many years with no end in sight. How has it performed this amazing conjuring trick?

1

Policing and a very neoliberal murder

> Now I'm a white heterosexual multi-millionaire, right (audience laughing/cheering). There's less than 1 per cent of us (audience laughing). But do I whine? No!
>
> Ricky Gervais, stand-up comedian,
> *Supernature*, Netflix 2022 (Spencer, 2022)

> Speak up! Now's the time. The good people are the ones that should have voice. They're the ones who should have power.
>
> Mina Smallman, campaigning following the murder of her two daughters and the abusive behaviour of two serving policemen, in: *Two Daughters*, BBC TV iPlayer, 2022, Director Jermaine Blake (2022)

Introduction

This book starts with where we are – with the politics and policies now shaping our lives internationally – the politics of neoliberalism and globalisation. If one very specific domestic event in the UK epitomises both the problems such ideology now faces us with globally and locally, and new ways of understanding and even liberating ourselves from them, it's the terrible murder of Sarah Everard on 3 March 2021. This is a murder that has become one of the global markers of the oppression of women and the collusion of the prevailing politics in it.

A defining femicide

I may surprise some readers by making this connection. Some may feel it is tendentious – elevating one woman's death to undue significance. I'd challenge this strongly – not only because of the Talmud's wise assertion that 'whoever kills one life kills the world entire' but because this is an age characterised by disconnection, a general reluctance to examine anything's social relations. It's a recurring theme. Yet as we see here, femicide links together wider structural inequalities and power imbalances and reflects on social control and the role of institutions in maintaining the neoliberal status quo. Connections between the personal and political are always critical. Exploring them may offer hope for future progress – this book's central concern.

In Sarah's appalling death, these connections – and disjunctions – are conspicuous. We see a polarisation between a police service stuck in a discriminatory organisational and *public* politics, and women and their supporters fighting for an emancipatory *personal* politics. It is the relation between these two and reforming it that is the inspiration for and the central focus of this text. For Sarah, it became a matter of life and death.

Sarah's murder became a defining event of 2021 in the UK and beyond, just as George Floyd's murder in the US was for 2020. By the time her killer had been convicted, seven months later, the names of 81 more women, murdered by men in the UK after Sarah, had been listed in a Facebook remembrance (Smith, 2021).

This murder of a white, middle-class woman became a force for challenging inequalities among women more generally instead of just highlighting them. It became such a symbol of the power and pervasiveness of male violence against women that it helped visibilise the issue for women everywhere, reinforcing their experience and testimony locally and globally. It resonated much further, highlighting the devaluing of women and gender-based violence. It made manifest their common oppression as well as surfacing prevailing inequalities based on race, class, nationality and sexuality. It triggered wider concerns about violence against women. Following her murder, the World Health Organization reported that about one in three women globally – about three quarters of a billion women – experienced physical or sexual violence during their lifetime (McBride, 2021). Sadly, almost every country has its equivalents: Pakistan and Qandeel Baloch; Ethiopia and Helen Lalango; Canada and Maple Batalia; Afghanistan and Farkhunda; Turkey and Özgecan Aslan, and so forth. (Wikipedia, 2024). Local examples came in for attention they might not otherwise have received. Sarah Everard's murder offers an extreme, international example of gender politics and their ideological consequences colliding.

She was walking home after visiting a friend when she was raped – and murdered – like George Floyd, by a uniformed policeman, Wayne Couzens. He used his warrant card to deceive and arrest her and his handcuffs to imprison her. However, despite official attempts to do so, this killing could not be explained away as a case of an isolated individual 'rotten apple'. It emerged that:

- three allegations had been made against him of driving naked below the waist from 2015 with no action taken;
- his police service nickname, the 'rapist' was known to senior officers;
- five other officers in a WhatsApp group were found sharing misogynistic and discriminatory messages, without intervention.

The institutional response was, to say the least, muted, with:

- the already compromised Commissioner of the Metropolitan Police, Dame Cressida Dick, widely pressured to resign, refusing – until later forced to;
- both the Home Secretary and Prime Minister initially ignored these calls;
- another police commissioner widely criticised for blaming Sarah for not challenging her arrest – and then forced to resign (Halliday, 2021).

This last tendency to blame women for the violence and other problems they encounter from men seems to be strongly entrenched in prevailing cultures – thus, the initial formal police response to the concern raised by women's organisations following Sarah's murder. Hundreds of women gathered for a peaceful vigil locally, demanding improved safety for women. The Metropolitan Police tried to ban the gathering, called on the women to disperse and trampled on flowers and candles, causing violent confrontations, with women arrested to chants of 'Arrest your own' (Graham-Harrison, 2021). A high court ruling subsequently concluded that the force breached the rights of organisers of the vigil and the Metropolitan Police were refused leave to appeal against this decision for a second time (PA Media, 2022).

What explains this

Thus, the police, ostensibly the front line to defend women from men's attacks, actually multiplied the threat. Different interpretations could be placed on this cycle of events (Dodd, 2021c). The conventional media approach was to individualise the issue as a 'human interest' story. However, what it most clearly signified, as with US police killings of Black people, was a representative of a system set up supposedly to protect people, routinely doing the absolute opposite. At another level, both affairs highlight issues of even greater ideological, political, structural and ultimately human importance. Crucially, these deaths concern the gulf between the political rhetoric and reality in a society and its political and policy structures – and the prevailing personal values of people and groups concerned.

The police are the arm of the state primarily entrusted with the notional role of maintaining the peace. Yet, as commentators have pointed out, the Metropolitan Police have questionable form in this area. In recent years, this includes:

- the Stephen Lawrence killing, with vindicated accusations of police incompetence, racism and corruption (Cathcart, 2000);
- cover-up evidenced over the murder of private detective Daniel Morgan and accusations the force was institutionally corrupt;

- the long-term use of undercover police to spy on peaceful organisations; the former exploited their role to form abusive sexual relationships with women involved (Chakrabarti, 2021).

We know that particularly little value is attached to some issues and groups. Therefore, if the police response to Sarah Everard's killing seems at best qualified, then for others it may be even worse. A well-documented example of this in the UK, which seems to combine much that is worst and most shocking about the Everard case, arose concerning the killing of Black sisters Bibaa Henry and Nicole Smallman, who were stabbed to death in 2020. The police failed to look for the missing women. It was only when their family searched that their bodies were found. Subsequently, two police officers took 'selfies' next to the dead sisters, sharing them on a large WhatsApp group and a further six police were investigated for failing to challenge or report this. Bibaa and Nicole's mother subsequently worked to raise awareness of police misconduct and condemned the police and media response to their deaths as racist and discriminatory (Dodd, 2020; 2021a and b; Blake, 2022). The two 'selfie' police officers received substantial prison sentences (Nicholson, 2022).

While the police are a powerful institution, which may not be greatly open to influence by the people it supposedly serves, its relations with governments tend to be close and co-serving ones. Thus, while women and women's organisations, post-Sarah Everard's murder called for greater control over the police, the UK government was planning to increase its powers, now extended to unprecedented peacetime levels to restrict protest (Mason et al, 2023). More general concerns have also been raised about the police service and:

- the low priority given to crimes against women;
- misogynistic and racist cultures;
- police officers and staff accused of domestic abuse still serving in law enforcement (Dodd and Haque, 2022);
- the under-representation of women, especially in senior roles;
- recruitment policies unfit for purpose;
- continuing evidenced reports of misogyny and sexual harassment in the Metropolitan Police (Ryan, 2022);
- the continuing unaccountability of the police, including the difficulty of funding legal actions against it in the UK with loss of legal aid (Vitale, 2017; Deivanayagam et al, 2021; Townsend, 2021; Dodd, 2021).

We see here inequalities in treatment between women and men, and Black and white people. We also see conflicts in beliefs, values and power between prevailing politics and political institutions and groups whose personal politics have been shaped by the oppression that they face. While I'm not suggesting that the UK police service is monolithic or that all serving in the police necessarily share the kind of values that are increasingly associated with it as an organisation and institution, there does seem to be a gap between its dominant values/culture and those now seen as more reflecting a modern democratic society – for example, in relation to women's rights and minoritised people – and that this has a significant bearing on the issues being discussed here.

Police, state and politics

Clearly, police history plays a part in this, but histories change. The British police have reactionary origins in opposing insurrection, like the American police, developed to stop runaway slaves. However, the British police have always come under some formal democratic control, whether adequate or not. The police service may have its own culture and ideology, but that is still subject to its political bosses. Ultimately, these can impose powerful pressure, as we've seen with recent UK Conservative governments, reminding us that governments can reduce as well as up the human and financial resources of the police. Indeed, a crude cycle of cuts and then rapid recruitment helped hide Couzens' criminality. While so far in the 21st century, the police have been overseen by Westminster governments of all major political parties, Labour, Lib Dem and Conservative, none has sorted out the problems under discussion here, although some arguably have made more determined efforts.

Also, governments committed to a small support state don't necessarily reduce the state's *control* role. Indeed, the longstanding association of 'law and order' arguments with the political right and rising political concerns about domestic disobedience and international terrorism mean that the state actually has an ongoing reliance on the police to regulate its population and the two – police and government/state – may be in a symbiotic relationship with each other. Thus, a small support state may actually mean *more* state control. This is reflected in the UK both in an increased emphasis on security services and the control role of welfare state services, from social work and mental health to schooling. The British critical theorist Mark Neocleous connects the discretionary violence of the police on the street to the wider administrative powers of the state and what he calls the compulsion of economic relations; that is the prioritisation of enforced wage labour (Neocleous, 2000).

In this interface between police and public, we can see a basis for the kind of collision of values played out in women's demonstrations to memorialise Sarah Everard – policing policy and practice based on reactionary personal politics and women demonstrators committed to equal rights and emancipation in theirs.

This dreadful unfolding of events continued while writing this book. Especially distressing was the news in January 2023 that another serving Metropolitan Police officer had been charged with multiple rapes and sexual offences over 20 years. This only emerged after numerous errors, as the Met was investigating more than 1,000 officers for alleged sexual offences or domestic violence. One woman he had attacked found the strength to report it after Sarah Everard's murder (Baird, 2023). Perhaps the final insult and definer of the gulf between oppressor and oppressed came with the publication of the Casey review of the Met in March 2023. It concluded that it was institutionally racist, misogynistic, homophobic, corrupt and in need of radical reform (Barham, 2023, p 184; Dodd, 2023). 'Also among those charged to hold the Met to account were a succession of Tory home secretaries' (Dodd, 2023).

All this leads us to this book's focus and thesis – the relationship between personal and formal politics and the impact each has on the other. Here, we have seen how the regressive personal politics of an individual in the police, unconstrained by the latter's organisational politics, resulted in murder, and how women's liberatory politics challenged it. We've also seen that there are equivalents the whole world over. What insights might such a contest offer us more generally for challenging reactionary and discriminatory formal politics which seem so resistant to conventional radical reform? That is a key question here.

Political and ideological contexts

Let's begin by putting this discussion in a political context, specifically concerning Sarah Everard's murder and then the book's broader focus – both heavily contested territory. The ideology currently dominating most, if not all the world's politics and economics, is *neoliberalism* – a controversial term, many of whose proponents are reluctant even to use. However, its critics have subjected it to frequent and far-reaching analysis. This doesn't mean it's a word often encountered in media headlines or that most of us necessarily feel confident to define (Harvey, 2007; Eagleton-Pierce, 2015).

With the ending of Soviet communism, a justifiable claim might be made that neoliberalism is the prevailing if not only global ideology. This was the precipitate conclusion of those, like Francis Fukuyama, who heralded 'the end of history' in the 1990s (Fukuyama, 1992). Some analysts even proclaim that mainland China as well as post-Soviet Russia is underpinned by neoliberal economics, although China rejects this because the state retains control.

While it has different strands and may have different 'flavours' in different national contexts (Larner, 2000), neoliberalism can be seen as a rerun of laissez-faire liberalism by updated means. From Friedrich Hayek to Ayn

Rand, it abounds with the same rhetoric emphasising individual freedom, consent of the governed and equality before the law. In earlier centuries, this was to be achieved through free trade, marketisation and restricting state 'interference'. Reincarnated in the later 20th century, we have additionally seen an emphasis on *globalisation*, pulling back the state and freeing the market. This is associated with privatisation, deregulation, free trade, austerity and an increased role for the private sector in society. The much-hyped theory rests on:

> two planks. The first is increased competition – achieved through deregulation and the opening up of domestic markets, including financial markets, to foreign competition. The second is a smaller role for the state, achieved through privatization and limits on the ability of governments to run fiscal deficits and accumulate debt. (Ostry et al, 2016)

In some versions, the state, in its much-reduced form still plays a key role, but one essentially concerned with supporting the market. As a theory, economic globalisation promotes the elimination of government-imposed restrictions on transnational movements of goods, capital and people (Harmes, 2012, pp 64–9). The argument that globalisation has developed because national governments can't stop it as a supra-national force ignores the potential challenge from supra-national organisations like the European Union, International Monetary Fund and World Bank, all of which operate on a world stage, and also the commitment of many neoliberal nations themselves to such economics and the advantages it's offered them, particularly in exploiting low-income nations (Yeates and Holden, 2009). Thus, the irony is that neoliberalism demands the engagement of the state to impose market dominance – nationally and internationally (Varoufakis, 2017).

Whether or not there is a causal relation between neoliberalism and globalisation, the two are certainly closely associated. As the first wave of liberal, market-driven politics and economics was linked with the rise of colonialism, the second has been encouraged by its commitment to globalising economics. This time around, the process has been advanced by controlling local economies and politics rather than necessarily settling and stealing their land – to the same effect – taking local/ indigenous people's resources to sell back to them (Barber, 2021, p 34 and following).

In principle what neoliberalism now means is:

- an extreme form of capitalism, the American political scientist, Frances Fox Piven called 'hyper-capitalism' (Goldin et al, 2014, p 125);
- advocacy of the 'minimal', 'small' state, rejection of Keynesian economics as failed and devaluing of state intervention;

- market fetishisation – as if it alone can deliver for societies;
- policies of 'economic liberalisation', including removing price controls, privatisation, deregulation, reducing government debt, lowering trade barriers and free trade;
- the racialised expansion of prison populations, replacing other institutional beds for those requiring support and perpetuating a source of no/low-paid marginal labour;
- massive tax cuts for the well-off, rising rents for the rest, restrictions on collective bargaining and the rights and power of trade unions and labour movement;
- the development of its own narratives through creating 'think tanks', influencing debate and taking on intellectual and research tasks formerly undertaken by independent academic organisations like universities (Eagleton-Pierce, 2015; Blakeley, 2024).

So, while there may be different strands of neoliberal philosophy, differently expressed across nations and societies, we should remember that neoliberalism is an ideology – not a political programme – and therefore infinitely variable according to the exigencies of politics and economics and how its proponents interpret it to deal with day-to-day realities. The most minor and least competent neoliberal politician has more say in shaping the actuality of neoliberalism than its most cited philosophers. The gulf between ideology and practice can be large. Instead of seeing this as reflecting neoliberalism's complexity, approach it as reflecting gaps between practice and rhetoric.

While Mrs Thatcher and her international neoliberal successors have sought to cut public spending, associating themselves with the so-called small or reduced state, this hasn't necessarily been matched with a reduction in spending on the social control aspects of state intervention; instead, these have increased with political concerns about internal unrest and social breakdown (itself a potential consequence of neoliberal public policies), as well as international terrorism. Additionally, while neoliberalism talks up the free movement of both capital and labour, where the latter may have what its proponents see as damaging consequences, notably by imposing pressure on local wages, then it's rapidly restricted. The resulting suffering, deaths and human rights abuse from such immigration controls are another real cost of globalised economics and politics (Schierup et al, 2015).

Liberal equals illiberal

While the term 'liberal' is popularly used to mean tolerant, free – and open – to new ideas and different opinions, its political meaning can be very different. Indeed, there seems to be an underlying tension in this, although this isn't necessarily apparent initially. The explicit philosophy of liberalism from the political thinkers Locke and Hobbes onwards highlights equality before the law and promoting individual rights, civil liberties, democracy and individual choice. It's been heralded as pioneering equality between the sexes, in relation to sexual orientation and in valuing animal rights (Huemer, 2012). But this is the same philosophy that actually gave us the oppression of utilitarianism, the terrors of the 1834 New Poor Law and the silent inhumanity of the prison panopticon, – where inmates were under constant inspection and control (Foucault, 1995). We can see the same cruelty and little of its rhetorical progressive force in its modern manifestations as neoliberalism. Thus, for example:

- In reality, the recent neoliberal UK Conservative government commitment to cutting state intervention has meant a significant reduction in access to legal aid and therefore to equality before the law.
- Cuts in UK welfare benefits and services mean reductions in the social rights of poorer, older and disabled people.
- The marginalisation of social care policy in England leaves increasing numbers of children and young people at the mercy of abusive adults.
- In 2020, two thirds of (then) Prime Minister Johnson's cabinet were privately educated and disproportionately few were women or from Black and minoritised ethnic groups (Cowburn, 2020).

This is where the rationales of neoliberalism's advocates and its critics' condemnations emerge as most polarised. While the talk is of rights and freedoms, the issue is of whose rights and freedoms.

The freedom from interference by the state of the advantaged in this arrangement is at the expense of the restriction of the freedoms of others (Harvey, 2007). Even if no causal relationship is imputed, it is the old distinction between freedom *to* and freedom *from*. *You* may be free to do what you like, but the rest are imprisoned by poverty and want. The benefits for one are at the cost of the other. This liberal ideology seems similar to a Ponzi scam or pyramid selling, where it's the people at the top of the chain or those who initiate the scheme who get the benefits, while the rest, whatever our high hopes, inherit the problems.

Trends in inequality and poverty

Free market economies have long been associated with material inequality and deprivation. This is hardly surprising as economists and politicians like Margaret Thatcher have seen the market as a driver for economic success (Lansley, 2021a). The statistics for inequality in UK income, pay and wealth, whose Westminster government has determinedly pursued neoliberal policies without interruption since the mid-1970s (including Tony Blair's

New Labour abandoning of the equality principle), are becoming more and more extreme (Dorling, 2018, 2019). Sadly, this doesn't make them any less true, although right-wing critics dismiss them. The UK became a much more equal nation post-war. Available data shows the income share going to the top 10 per cent of the population fell over the 40 years to 1979, from 34.6 per cent in 1938 to 21 per cent in 1979, while the share going to the bottom 10 per cent rose slightly. Since 1979, this process of narrowing inequality has reversed sharply. Inequality rose considerably during the 1980s, reaching a peak in 1990. (Equality Trust, 2021a). UK inequality in household incomes has remained at a roughly similar level since the early 1990s but is higher than during the 1960s and 1970s. While the share of income going to the top 1 per cent of individuals by household income increased during the 1990s and 2000s, there was some reduction in inequality among the rest of the population (based on incomes before housing costs) with the result that inequality overall appears fairly stable during this period (Francis-Devine, 2020). However, we've seen a dramatic increase in the income share going to the top, a decline in the share of those at the bottom and, more recently, a stagnation of incomes among those in the middle (Equality Trust, 2021b). The comment of the comedian Ricky Gervais at the beginning of this chapter ironically mirrored the slogan of the 2011 Occupy movement highlighting income inequality, 'We are the 99 percent' (see Wikipedia, 2025a).

The UK has a very high level of income inequality compared to other advanced Western countries. The top 1 per cent have incomes substantially higher than the rest of those in the top 10 per cent (The Equality Trust, 2021b). Levels of wealth (which often produces income) and income inequality in the UK are some of the highest among rich countries. Wealth in Great Britain is even more unequally divided than income. In 2016, the Office for National Statistics (ONS) calculated the richest 10 per cent of households hold 44 per cent of all wealth. The poorest 50 per cent, by contrast, own just 9 per cent (Equality Trust, 2021b). These figures are becoming even more polarised. Recent analysis by The Equality Trust revealed an extreme level of wealth inequality in the UK, which has spiralled since 2010. Thus:

- The five richest families own greater wealth than 13 million people.
- Over the last ten years, the number of UK billionaires almost doubled and their wealth more than doubled.
- The richest 1 per cent in the UK own as much wealth as 80 per cent of the population, or 53 million people.
- Fourteen million people, one fifth of the population, are defined as living in poverty. Four million are more than 50 per cent below the poverty line, and 1.5 million are destitute, unable to afford basic essentials (Equality Trust, 2019).

Such pressures also exacerbate other inequalities. People's economic positions are related to other characteristics such as gender, ethnicity, sexuality, disability and age – young and older people tend to face particular inequalities.

The trend to inequality is also an international (between countries) and global one (within countries). In 2016, the International Monetary Fund (IMF) researchers concluded that two key aspects of neoliberalism had led to increased international inequality. These include what is known as capital account liberalisation, that is removing restrictions on the movement of capital across borders and, fiscal consolidation, better known as the imposition of austerity policies (Ostry et al, 2016). In its 2020 World Social Report, the United Nations Department of Economic and Social Affairs similarly highlighted that income inequality has increased in most 'developed countries' and some middle-income countries – including China – the world's fastest-growing economy. The UN Chief Economist concluded that 'income disparities and a lack of opportunities', were 'creating a vicious cycle of inequality, frustration and discontent across generations'. The study showed that in the changing neoliberal global economy, the richest 1 per cent increased their income share between 1990 and 2015. The bottom 40 per cent earned less than a quarter of income in all countries surveyed (UNDESA, 2020).

If the increasing number of billionaires in the UK and internationally under neoliberalism highlights the trend of increasing inequality at the top end of societies, the growing number defined as being in poverty does the same at the bottom. As poverty analyst Stewart Lansley has argued:

> Poverty and inequality are critically linked. … Its scale is ultimately determined by (as the key architect of post-war prosperity, John Maynard Keynes, put it) how the 'cake is cut'. History cannot be clearer: high levels of poverty and inequality have gone hand in hand. It is no coincidence that over the last four decades, poverty levels have more than doubled, while the share of national income accruing to the top one per cent has surged. (Lansley, 2021a and b)

Impoverishing politics

Founding neoliberal thinkers like Charles Murray, writing in the second half of the twentieth century, advanced the idea of an 'underclass' fostered by welfare and state intervention which disrupted society's values and workings. This thinking, an early expression of the divisive thrust of neoliberal philosophy, gained major cross-party political support and media headlines internationally. There was never evidence of the existence of his heavily racialised group of disaffiliated poor people, who supposedly rejected society's values and threatened social cohesion, family and Protestant work ethics.

Photograph 1.1: Gated community: cutting us off from each other

Note: Three minutes from Grenfell Tower, the privileged residents of this estate are kept separate from and safe from the rest of us. Such gated communities like this one often have their own police or security service to protect them.
Source: Peter Beresford

Murray's social breakdown never materialised. In contrast, neoliberalism has undoubtedly encouraged the rise of an unaccountable *overclass*, preoccupied with its own power and interests, described by some as a 'feral elite' (Dorling, 2011; Beresford, 2012).

In Western societies like the UK, a range of new terms has been coined to capture the resulting financial insecurity: the 'pressed middle', 'precariat', 'new poor' and so on (Stiglitz, 2019). There is no one definition of poverty; absolute, relative and others abound, but the general trend of poverty statistics under free market conditions tends to be upward. In the UK, poverty was at its lowest as equality peaked in the late 1970s. As Lansley wrote, 'Barring the short post-war period, Britain has been a high-inequality, high-poverty nation for most of its modern history' (Lansley, 2021a).

Given it's generally the hunter rather than the hunted who's privileged in history writing, it tends to be 'the poor what gets the blame' for their misfortune. Thus, the dominant explanation for poverty has long been the deviance, pathology or idleness of 'the poor'. In 21st-century Britain, attributing blame to 'an over-empowered financial and corporate elite' – as would-be progressives like Lansley and Townsend before him – have done – carries little political weight. As historian R.H. Tawney wrote over a century

Photograph 1.2: Commodifying housing 1

Note: One of the extreme outcomes of the commodification of property is the development of zones like this. With concentrations of high-cost housing, offices and hotels, often 'dark' or unoccupied, they have been created primarily for profit and investment, while ignoring housing needs. This massive high-rise redevelopment stretches from Battersea Power Station to Vauxhall Cross in London and is one of the biggest in Europe.
Source: Peter Beresford

ago: 'What thoughtful people call the problem of poverty, thoughtful poor people call with equal justice, a problem of riches' (Tawney, 1913).

Estimates of global poverty are similarly discouraging. More than two thirds of a billion people are estimated to live in extreme poverty a 'slowdown in the pace of poverty reduction … observed over the last few years … the current COVID-19 pandemic is predicted to cause the first increase in global poverty since the Asian financial crisis of 1997/8'. Most of the new poor at the extreme poverty line, as well as the higher poverty lines, live in South Asia. This is followed by sub-Saharan Africa … and East Asia and Pacific … (Lakner et al, 2020; Schoch and Lacker, 2020). In 2020, the World Bank concluded, 'It was becoming increasingly unrealistic to expect that the goal of reducing extreme poverty to below 3 per cent would be attained at the global level by 2030 unless there was a widespread and sustained improvement in *inclusive* (emphasis added) economic growth' (World Bank, 2020). It analysed three additional factors whose convergence it saw as also driving the current trend: the COVID-19 pandemic, armed conflict and climate change. The scale and impact of all of these are also intimately related to neoliberal politics.

Photograph 1.3: Commodifying housing 2

Note: The former Battersea Power Station has become the focal point for a massive high-cost housing and retail centre despite early efforts by local people to develop it as a local resource and major source of lower-cost housing.
Source: Peter Beresford

Reducing poverty and inequality were two of the UN's global goals for sustainable development agreed upon by world leaders in 2015. However, the prestigious journal *Nature* concluded that most of these – including those for ending poverty and challenging inequality – are now 'out of reach', calling for them to be separated from economic growth, which is now recognised as both unachievable in the existing timescale and not equitably shared (Nature, 2020). So, while it would be simplistic to suggest that the only factors at work in current trends exacerbating inequality and poverty nationally and internationally are neoliberal politics and economics, what is clear is that such politics are closely associated with negative trends affecting both inequality and poverty and are failing to deal with emerging problems (Stiglitz, 2019).

While, rolling out neoliberal policies has been linked with numerous harmful socio-economic consequences globally, including greater poverty, unemployment and deteriorating income distribution (Rotarou and Sakellariou, 2017), it has also had many other hurtful human consequences resulting from the exigencies of the market, the prioritising of corporate and powerful interests and rolling back of support for those in need. Thus, as social insecurity and personal problems have increased, the infrastructure and supports to address them have been reduced. Small state philosophy

Photograph 1.4: Even the Victorians seemed to do better: homelessness then and now

Note: Rowton houses were set up by the Victorians for 'respectable' single men on a low income, offering them a cubicle or small room to live in to stop them having to live on the street or in lodging houses. This is the former site of one which became a charitable homeless hostel more recently.
Source: Peter Beresford

and privatisation mean cuts in support and a reorientation of services to bring profit to private suppliers rather than meeting needs. Deregulation and the commodification of services like social care, health, housing and planning make things worse. This is perhaps hardly surprising as public goods and amenities like energy and water supply become ever more harshly commercialised. All this creates a perfect storm of difficulty for an ever-growing number of people, realising more stringently than ever before the economist J.K. Galbraith's fears of a world of 'private opulence' and 'public squalor' (Galbraith, 1958). Neoliberalism might almost have been invented to achieve this with a return to Victorian conditions separating the well-off in their gated communities and privately policed neighbourhoods from the impoverished in increasingly damaging environments (Stiglitz, 2019).

Anti-personal ideology

Access to decent affordable housing, health care and educational opportunities has diminished, resulting in rising personal, social and community breakdown. Social policy, including welfare benefits support, has been reframed as a means of *disciplining* rather than supporting groups like disabled people experiencing discrimination and needing help with their basic needs (Harrison and Sanders, 2015). In the Global South, this is reflected in the reversal of improvements achieved concerning the UN sustainable development goals, for example, zero hunger, clean water and sanitation, gender equality and peace, justice and strong institutions (Nature, 2020). However, even in the Global North, in supposedly rich countries like the UK, there has been a reversal of trends to longer life and reduced morbidity and child deaths (prior even to COVID-19) and greatly increased levels of absolute poverty and abuse among children, with rising levels of mental distress and suicide reported. While increases in inequality and poverty associated with neoliberalism and globalisation may affect different parts of the world differently, they apply to both advanced Western industrialised countries and low and middle-income countries identified with the Global South. Thus, with market deregulation, workers are more likely to face weakened protection and worsened conditions in their own countries, causing increasing pressure to migrate and additionally, xenophobic reactions to such migration, increasingly linked with such economic change in stressful times.

Failed claims

While economic growth has been offered as a key justification for neoliberalism, the current conclusion of experts is that it is itself undermined by such pressures to inequality (Ostry et al, 2014). While neoliberalism was imposed with the support of international organisations like the World Bank, International Monetary Fund (IMF) and World Trade Organization, they have themselves begun to speak out against its failure to support economic growth (Ostry et al, op cit). The internal logic has had inequality as a driver for economic performance, pushing people to want something better. This may be true – few of us want to be poor or hungry. However, if poverty is endemic and there are only so many opportunities for upward mobility in a society, then all this is likely to influence is who goes up and down, not the scale of upward social and economic mobility possible or likely (Lansley, 2021b).

However, high inequality is linked with weakened economic performance (Ostry et al, 2014). The reality of neoliberalism is often far from its rhetoric. While the talk is of profit, global corporations avoid paying tax by creating paper debt and 'zombie companies' make a mockery of 'business productivity'. Banks and major corporations have been seen as 'too big to fail' and propped up by massive public subsidies, while small and medium-sized businesses at the mercy of extreme economic cycles have been left to the wolves. While the workforce is recast as a sacrificial lamb at the altar of free trade, arch capitalist nation, the US, has long privileged its own industries through protectionism (Mombiot, 2016). Not until European nations got together with Airbus was the US civil aircraft industry's near monopoly ended.

Neoliberalism's enthusiasts have long argued that theirs is not only a necessary philosophy but also in *all* our interests. Therefore, the more you privilege the well-off and powerful with incentives, redistribution and deregulation, the more their prosperity rubs off on the rest, including those at the bottom. This is in contrast to the more obvious idea that the better off we all are, then it will be better for us and the economy more generally. Since the US presidency of Ronald Reagan, this prospectus has been called 'the trickle-down' effect, supposedly benefitting everyone's wallets and purses. We had another catastrophic and short-lived experience of this under the 49-day administration of Liz Truss in 2022. As Galbraith reminds us, there's nothing new under the sun and this is 'what an older and less elegant generation' called the horse-and-sparrow theory: 'If you feed the horse enough oats, some will pass through to the road for the sparrows.' Not only is trickle-down counterintuitive, but all the evidence says it doesn't really happen.

More recently, neoliberal politicians like former UK premier Johnson have resurfaced the idea of 'levelling up' by which they seem to mean using neoliberal politics and economics to challenge local and regional inequality (Newman, 2021). This is a return to place-based ideas of challenging inequality on which 1960s US anti-poverty and UK community development policies were based. What's different is that while those policies were intended to ameliorate the consequences of market inequalities, levelling up has been offered as part of the same destructive package. Not only did area policies fail the first time round, but trying to reverse years of extreme social and economic damage done by neoliberal politics by pumping some public money into electorally sensitive areas seems an unlikely recipe for success (Toynbee, 2021; Editorial, 2023).

The debate about neoliberalism is complex and sometimes difficult to follow. No wonder that it's a dominating philosophy, as commentator George Monbiot has asserted, which many of us have never heard of. It's also reminiscent of long-lived arguments of the rich and powerful – that it's better to give to them than the poor, as they know best what to do with it. This author still awaits news of any significant body of rich and powerful people who have actually given up either of those advantages – unless held to ransom or at gunpoint. So far, this suspicion is borne out by the evidence, however much it's argued that working for equality and against poverty is in everybody's interests (Wilkinson and Pickett, 2010).

The redistributive reality of neoliberalism

As part of the process of negative redistribution under neoliberalism, welfare policy has not only been cut but also *redirected* – thus, the emerging praxis of 'welfare corporatism'. Instead of public policy being used to level up inequalities, it is actually used to *reinforce* them. At its most restricted, such corporate welfare may mean direct government subsidies to major corporations, but extending to more valuable tax loopholes, and regulatory and trade decisions which further free up the market, not only from state control but also as the beneficiary of public funding.

The British academic Kevin Farnsworth claimed in 2013 that the UK government was providing corporate subsidies of £93 billion, at a time when it was arguing that it couldn't fill a public spending gap in chronically failing social care policy, estimated at £2–3 billion (Whitfield, 2001; Farnsworth, 2013). While figures like his have predictably been challenged by such corporations and their representatives, such regressive transfer has been a key neoliberal development, demanding closer scrutiny by politicians and policymakers (Quinn and Turner, 2021).

Such state subsidies took extreme form in key UK and US markets following the 2008 crash (Ferguson, 2010; Sorkin, 2010). This strategy and associated handouts, headlined as 'privatising profits and socialising losses', accelerated with companies seen as 'too big to fail'. As CEOs and boards received multi-million dollar bonuses, millions internationally were losing their homes, and governments and taxpayers were paying out multi-billions to cover destabilising losses. This was indeed 'socialism for the rich and capitalism for the poor' (Sorkin, 2010).

It highlighted the development of a post-production, post-Fordist economy where the key goods for exchange were financial products, sold without restraint and increasingly based on unredeemable debt. As companies like Merrill Lynch made profits betting against the viability of financial derivatives, they were still hard selling them to each other and desperate, guileless consumers (Ferguson, op cit).

Such featherbedding of 'private enterprise' not only makes an increasing mockery of any assumption it's ruled by the surface stringencies of market economics, but it's also another reason why the much-vaunted economic efficiency of globalised/neoliberal economics has been widely questioned. Such inefficiency has increasingly been associated with the deregulated market as it is effectively subsidised and benefits from the easy profits associated with privatisation.

It is difficult to see the 2008 global economic meltdown as anything other than the consequence of a financial system based on increasingly unregulated schemes for short-term money-making, where restrictions imposed after the 1929 Wall Street crash were abandoned, government, regulators and bankers remained in overlapping, collusive relationship and successive warnings that the emperor was naked were ignored. There was no comeuppance for those who profited from this debacle and little if any help for those victimised by it globally. Ironically, this was not about profit or the competitiveness of the market, instead, it was about the selfish acquisitiveness of a small group of people, institutions and corporations allowed to run riot, largely concealed from the rest of us by routine reliance on big lies and deceptions (Ferguson, op cit).

The global financial crash was an ultimate expression of political and economic systems which prioritised short-term profiteering for the few at any cost (Reynolds and Szerszinski, 2012, p 42). Thus, 'the apparent return to health in the "boom years" of neoliberalism involved financialisation, economies of debt and a succession of speculative bubbles'. The post-2008 crisis shattered the mirage, 'suggesting an ultimate failure to escape the problems identified in the 1970s' (Reynolds and Szerszinski, 2012, p 43), which first gave force to the imposition of neoliberalism. Hopes that the excesses associated with the 2008 crash would give rise to more humanistic and egalitarian economics and call a halt to neoliberalism quickly foundered as the opposite largely proved to be the case (Castells, 2017). Progressive innovations were more likely to be incorporated into neoliberalism rather than herald its end (Gibson-Graham, 1996; Gregory, 2014).

We began this chapter by exploring the appalling murder of Sarah Everard by an on-duty policeman. We traced the chain of connection between this act and the institutions and prevailing ideology under which it took place. Such associations tend not to be made routinely. However, we saw evidenced collusion between such criminal and discriminatory behaviour and key institutions like the Metropolitan Police. This stood in sharp contrast to the kind of global anti-violence-against-women values subsequently mobilised on behalf of Sarah Everard and ultimately vindicated, which reflected increasingly widely held personal principles. Here, generally, we can see the case emerging for the international women's movement to be seen as a pointer towards a much-needed shift in social and political policy and governance. More specifically, we can see its significance concerning policing. By autumn 2023, Scotland Yard had had to apologise and pay 'substantial damages' to 'two women arrested during the vigil (for Sarah), in a major climb down following years of legal battles over the policing of the event' (Topping and Dodd, 2023). When the first of three official Angiolini reports into the Couzens' affair was published early in 2024, the enormity of his criminality against women, failure to deal with such behaviour and discriminatory police attitudes, emerged as far worse than initially appeared (Dodd, 2024). Yet, at the time of writing, *no significant political action* had been taken in response to the recommendations of the Casey Review for structural reform of the Metropolitan Police, apart from proposals to sack failing officers (Gye, 2023). Put simply, neoliberal governments seem to have a symbiotic relationship with unaccountable policing.

Next, having approached neoliberalism, its connections, disconnections and contradictions through Sarah Everard's murder and its wider ramifications, we look more closely at this ideology's broader relations and implications for all of us.

2

Ideological damage – from the personal to the global

> There is no such thing as a free market without government making the rules of the game.
> Richard Reich, US Labour Secretary under President Clinton (Kornbluth and Gilman, 2017)

Introduction

One aim of this book is to help us rethink prevailing assumptions, about what is and isn't possible in politics and policy and what the big issues are. Already, we've seen violence against women treated as peripheral. Even such violence meted out illegally by official keepers of the peace has been given little official priority. During my life, I've seen prevailing values move from the belief that only by the state controlling the market will we end poverty to the conventional wisdom becoming that only the market can achieve this and state interference makes things worse. The book began with an individual death, which I argue has much bigger ramifications for us and our politics. However, what happens to us as individuals is clearly on a different scale from what may befall us collectively.

Neoliberalism's big consequences

Neoliberalism and its bedmate globalisation are linked with phenomena that can cause individual suffering on a universal scale. It's such big-ticket ramifications of these economic and political developments that we turn to next. While they may seem more distant, we ignore them at our peril. We began with neoliberalism's relations with poverty and inequality. Now we consider a range of other global concerns associated with prevailing politics and economics which also have massive implications for all our futures. These are:

- climate change and the future of the planet;
- technological change;
- war, conflict and terrorism;
- pandemics.

All of these have a massive impact on *all* our lives. All have been seriously linked with global neoliberalism. Others may offer a different list, including say, the illegal world drug trade or pornography, associating their rise with unrestricted marketisation. We'll encounter them elsewhere in this book. However, first, let's look at the global issues I've identified and why commentators link them with these politics. These are indeed massive issues, commanding enormous attention. They are also highly contentious, dividing opinion. While I'll try not to over-simplify, for reasons of space alone, I'm likely to fail in my ambition. Readers should make their own enquiries to follow up this necessarily broad-brush examination. There are also two more general points to consider in the interests of accuracy.

The scale of human impact

The first point concerns the changing scale and impact of human life and technology throughout history. Once there were relatively few of us; now there are many. Once our lives and technology would have barely caused a flicker if there had been instruments to measure them. Now the situation is exponentially different and the impact is transformed. According to Wikipedia, while there are estimated to be about a third of a billion people in the world in the Middle Ages, now there are more than seven billion and the greatest increase in these numbers has taken place over just the last 60 or so years (Wikipedia, 2025b). If human beings historically have exaggerated their importance in the world, more recently the tendency seems to be to deny their effect. It's tempting to do this, as the sun still shines and the sky stays blue. Yet since the Western scientific revolution – 'the enlightenment' – our capacity to alter our environment has massively increased. Additionally, our increasing separation from the natural world through urbanisation/industrialisation has increasingly divorced us from the understandings of it that guided our ancestors and many indigenous peoples still.

Making connections

This leads to a second broader point, the issue of relation and connection. This was one of the key concepts that led me to write this book. However, here it needs to be considered in terms of *causal* connection. When we try to establish links between things, it becomes contentious. How can we prove, disprove or demonstrate causal relationships? This is not necessarily straightforward. Evidencing causation is not as clear-cut as showing their coexistence. The difficulty of proving smoking's damaging effects is a famous example. This held back action against smoking for a long time, not because it wasn't reasonable to believe smokers suffered greater morbidity/mortality – the coughing offered a clue. However, it was more because of the tobacco lobby's power to challenge any effort to prove the link. It was not until the 1950s when, for instance, 80 per cent of UK middle-aged men smoked, that epidemiologist Richard Doll was able to offer unpopular proof that smoking was a major factor causing lung and heart disease (Juren et al, 2012). Even after that, the international tobacco trade continued to question the evidence and ever since has maintained its profitability by securing new global markets and replacing old regulated ones. Since then, we have seen similar battles between research evidence and manufacturers concerning the damaging effects of sugar and fizzy drinks, with both fighting hard and effectively resisting responsibility and regulation (Yudkin, 2012).

Climate change

Climate change and the future of the planet are widely seen as the biggest single challenge now facing humanity, with global catastrophe impending if not adequately addressed. According to the scientific consensus gathered by the Intergovernmental Panel on Climate Change (IPCC):

> the answer is unequivocal. Human beings and our reliance on fossil fuels and generally unsustainable production methods are the fundamental driver of climate change. While it is true that the earth's climate naturally fluctuates due to a variety of factors, scientists have shown a direct connection between the current rapid rate of climate change and the start of industrialization. (IPCC, 2021)

Massive deforestation, industrial pollution, agribusiness, wasteful consumption models and massively expanded, subsidised air travel, all make matters worse. It is also associated with the loss of species and plant life and damage to diversity. Governments and industrial leaders have acted slowly as climate change and its effects worsen. Neoliberal preoccupation with profit and decontrolled markets undermines effective action and solutions. All else is subsidiary and regulation is a dirty word. Attempts to control developments most closely associated with climate change are strongly resisted under prevailing politics and economics. Emphasising 'scientific' rigour and reliability has been used mercilessly to exploit possible deniability (Bjornberg et al, 2017).

Technological change

The technological change taking place during the dominance of neoliberalism compares with earlier revolutions understood as:

- the industrial/agricultural revolution – the age of the scientific 'enlightenment' and steam, c1765;
- the age of mass production – harnessing electricity, mass communication, consumption, travel and the internal combustion engine, c1870;

- the digital age – the emergence of nuclear energy, rise of electronics, telecommunication, development of computers, internet, space technology, c1969.

We're now told we're living in a fourth equally far-reaching technological revolution, building on its digital predecessor – Industry 4.0. It is associated with a range of interrelated breakthroughs – nanotechnology, gene sequencing, renewables, quantum computing and artificial intelligence (AI) – interacting across physical, digital and biological domains. We don't know where these developments will take us, or with what problems, but we are told that their impact, speed and possibilities are even greater than previous technological revolutions (Schwab, 2017).

However we characterise these developments, the pace of change is accelerating., What would a Rip van Winkle waking from the 1970s make of the people he encountered walking about apparently talking to themselves on their mobiles? From his pre-sleep experience, he could only have understood them as distressed or deluded!

Artificial intelligence (AI)

Perhaps the most significant technological development – and most misrepresented and ill-defined – is 'artificial intelligence' (AI). Scientists like Allan Turing developed the term to mean machines that can mimic human responses, making independent decisions. Influenced by science fiction and films like *Terminator*, AI has come to be associated with popular fears and understandings, with robots taking over the world, computers ganging up against humans and a war between flesh and metal (which war has long been, as the 1914–18 poets reminded us!). But this is not the basis of current media panics. As the thinker, Yuval Noah Harari says:

> I talk a lot about the dangers of AI … as a warning. … The first thing to remember is that AI is the first tool in history that can make decisions by itself. … The second thing is that AI is the first tool that can create ideas itself. (Harari, 2023)

When, however, he says AI is taking power from us, as it is being used increasingly to make decisions, whether to give us a mortgage or job (Harari, op cit), he means that the people controlling those decisions are delegating them to so-called AI, not that it is making the decisions independently. There seems to be some confusion between machines' capacity to take on more traditionally human tasks and actual AI. The two aren't necessarily the same, although this hasn't stopped mass media from seeking headlines out of confusing them. Such decisions based on particular criteria or here 'algorithms' have increasingly been delegated in this way. What this may mean is not so much that AI will replace people/us, as that people in charge will use it to replace us/people. Predictably, this has emerged as a major popular concern about AI, where like the first industrial revolution it's cast as a great destroyer of roles and employment. On the other hand, upbeat commentators remind us how liberating AI could be, freeing us even further from tedious tasks and allowing us time for self-development and growth. We heard this all before with the automation of the 1950s and 1960s, and yet paradoxically many people are now working much longer hours than then, often commuting greater distances, with less collective support from state welfare.

The key point to remember about AI, as with any other major scientific or social change is that who it benefits and the consequences it has depends on who controls it (Zerilli, 2021). This is less likely to be a conspiracy of computers than whoever rules society.

Technology is neutral. Its effects may be good or bad, but what's developed and how it's used, depends on who controls it, their aims and when and if it's needed. Thus, the desperation of warring interests to 'win', created the cliché of war as technology's great accelerant.

The adage that technology serves the purposes of the dominant ideology holds true here as ever. In a neoliberal age, we can expect AI's masters to be narrowly based, powerful political and corporate interests, likely to use it in their own interests and to disadvantage ours. Such ruling elites may have to deal with a powerful tension between their desire to maintain peaceful control in society and the resulting reduced availability of work with which to discipline us. However, we can expect them to find solutions to this problem that will hurt us more than them!

While critics have argued that neoliberalism hasn't necessarily been the positive influence for technological advances once claimed, what there has been is powerful pressure to put such innovation before sustainability and majority world interests. This is true both of old polluting technologies and new ones. The preoccupation remains with enlisting new technology for short-term profit and political gain and retaining damaging old technology as suits. The public emphasis has mainly been on addressing short-term problems, like developing autonomous vehicles to make cuts in the number of drivers employed and using new technology including AI to replace paid 'carers', instead of more radical thinking challenging the over-use of road transport, or recognising the desire of older and disabled people for human company rather than just tech support. Instead of science offering promised routes out of the economic and ecological crisis associated with neoliberalism, too often it's been reduced to a product shaped by neoliberal values (Reynolds and Szerszinski, 2012, p 44).

War, conflict and terrorism

It's hardly surprising that neoliberalism, a philosophy based on privileging profit and inequality, is closely associated with rising world conflict. This has a range of expressions and is complex in causation. Much conflict is still best understood as a legacy of colonisation – a further reason why decolonising politics, international relations and knowledge, is wrongly trivialised. The World Bank highlights as key trends:

- conflicts in the 21st century sharply increasing from 2010;
- battle deaths largely concentrated in the Middle East;
- forced displacement on a scale unprecedented since 1945;
- conflicts increasingly affecting civilians;
- interpersonal and gang violence killing more people than political violence;
- interpersonal violence declining generally but is still very high in some regions;
- gender-based violence remains very high, with wider damaging consequences;
- violence and conflict affecting regions differently;
- violence and conflict are persistent and very costly;
- conflict and violence have multiple dimensions and drivers;
- poor people are increasingly concentrated in countries affected by violence.

Large-scale war has now reached Europe with the Russia-Ukraine conflict, with many nations providing weapons to Ukraine and with high casualties on both sides. The Middle East seems closer to all-out conflict than it has for half a century. The drivers and dimensions the World Bank Group data identify for major conflict and violence are all also associated with neoliberal and globalising politics (Marc, 2015). The relationship between war, conflict and neoliberalism is complex and two-way. An analysis of US military intervention policy under Bush and Obama highlights a process of post-war reconstruction harnessed to ambitious neoliberal economics aimed at transforming the host country's political economy, generating ongoing conflict. 'Each iteration of the cycle deepens the humanitarian crisis, and assures new rounds of local and sometimes national resistance' (Schwartz, 2011, p 190). It's as if a key purpose of such international conflict is to provide new markets to prop up otherwise unviable neoliberal economics.

The arms trade is also itself at the vanguard of neoliberal economics. Thus, Mrs Thatcher, refusing to support other UK manufacturing industries facing economic difficulties, supported the arms industry so that the UK became the second largest arms trader and one of the biggest manufacturers (Watts, 2016). Neoliberalism has greatly strengthened the military-industrial complex. In 2022, the seventh consecutive year of increased international arms spending was reported, supported by the Russo-Ukraine conflict (AP News, 2022). Things can only get worse with the Middle East conflagration.

As Gwynn Kirk and Margo Okazawa-Rey observe in their discussion of neoliberalism, militarism and armed conflict, the trend towards a neoliberal global economy and the prevalence of militaries and militarism worldwide have tended to be treated as separate, unrelated phenomena, despite this being widely challenged. They conclude:

> In critiquing and challenging neoliberal economic integration, it is essential to take account of militarism as an intrinsic element. Conversely in analysing militarism, war and armed conflict, it is also necessary to consider global economic forces and institutions. (Kirk and Okazawa-Rey, 2000, pp 1–2)

As Steven Staples similarly argues:

> The relationship between globalization and militarism should be seen as two sides of the same coin … globalization promotes the conditions that lead to unrest, inequality, conflict and ultimately war … globalization fuels the means to wage war by protecting and promoting the military industries needed to produce sophisticated weaponry. This weaponry in turn, is used or is threatened to be used to protect the investments of transnational corporations and their shareholders. (Staples, 2000, p 18)

The evidence inextricably links neoliberalism and militarism in numerous, complex, anti-personal ways, including:

- the prevalence or threat of war to resolve transnational and intranational disputes;
- bloated military budgets diverting resources from supporting people's wellbeing and challenging threats to it;
- the increasing militarisation of borders between global north and south to restrict workers' and refugees' movement encouraged by globalisation and conflict;
- connections between militarism and violence against women;
- the incidence of human rights violations in military conflicts;
- their reinforcement of systems of inequality based on gender, race, class and nation;
- the massive displacement of people through conflict – 90 per cent women and children.

What emerges are the historical and contemporary interconnections between economic domination, militarism, colonisation and imperialism.

Commentators argue for a radical redefinition of security *not* based on military security (Kirk and Okazawa-Rey, 2000).

The justification for militarism is that it's to protect us from internal and external threats. The same unsustainable argument has been the signature historic defence of Europe's imperialist kings, queens, emperors, Hitler, Stalin, subsequent dictators and the 1930s Japanese military elite. Western powers have maintained this pattern of military domination, developing sophisticated weaponry to restrict their own casualties, while imposing much heavier ones on weaker opponents. A key signifier of advanced modern neoliberal economies is being able to produce required main battle tanks, fighter-bomber jets, and nuclear and space weapons. It's only when one world power supplies dissidents to defeat another (for example, the US equipping Afghani rebels with Stinger ground-to-air missiles against the Soviets or in the present Ukraine-Russia conflict), that any real equalisation of arms takes place.

Such conflict is now badged as 'asymmetrical warfare', although the low-tech, guerrilla tactics involved have long existed – from the Peninsular War, through T.E. Lawrence and the Arab revolt, to the Viet Cong in Vietnam and Taliban in Afghanistan (Barnett, 2003). It's also presented as 'asymmetric' in terms, for example, of the barbaric beheadings associated with the 'Islamic State' and the supposed precision of US smart bombs on military targets.

War zones have become larger and larger and distinctions between armies and civilians become increasingly blurred, first by mass conscription and then with the latter targeted as 'collateral damage', further blurring distinctions between conventional warfare and terrorism. Big powers experienced this most sharply with large-scale attacks against them on civilian targets, like 9/11 and 7/7, disrupting notions of being at peace, even as they were waging war on what they conceive as aggression and terrorism, rooted in both nationalism and faith.

Modern understandings of terrorism can be traced back to 19th-century anarchism and the Zionist Irgun in pre-Israel Palestine. Terrorism is rooted in poverty, disempowerment and colonialism. Thus, it's easy to see global neoliberal politics and economics as fertile soil for its international development. In their text on neoliberalism and terror, Charlotte Heath-Kelly and colleagues explore some of the intersections between the two, using:

> two different but complementary approaches: the exploration of neoliberalism as terror, and of neoliberalism and terror: in other words, the 'neoliberal effects upon the production of terrorism discourse and technologies' (p 2). (Heath-Kelly et al, 2016; Bustelo, 2016)

They highlight a range of relations between neoliberal philosophy, terrorism and its modern reframing, including:

- manipulating public anxiety and insecurity to reclaim public support for neoliberal politics through exaggerated threats;
- further restricting domestic and international rights and freedoms to legitimate external aggression badged as 'counter-terrorism';
- the neoliberal marketisation of such counter-terrorism as a new expression of imperialist/colonialist control. (Heath-Kelly et al, op cit)

Pandemics

Writing five years into a global health crisis, the importance of the threat from pandemics like COVID-19 is undeniable. At other times, it's easier for richer nations to ignore them, especially as they affect the Global South. Even less attention is paid to their relations with broader politics and economics. Yet there's no question that neoliberal politics and economics have provided ideal conditions for their development and important barriers to their control. This is highlighted by the differential impact and distribution of pandemics like COVID-19. Predictably, poorer countries with restricted access to effective vaccines have fared particularly badly, but other factors have significantly affected rates of infection, morbidity and mortality.

Countries most enthusiastic about adopting market-driven, individualistic neoliberal values, like the US, UK, India and Brazil have had some of the highest death rates (Gutierrez et al, 2021; Hallett, 2024). Conspicuous among those with low death rates are nations committed to effective state-led, community-minded public health measures like Taiwan, South Korea and New Zealand (Malik, 2021). Also, it is the most disadvantaged in society, facing particular barriers and discrimination who have suffered most from COVID-19 experiencing the highest death rates, including Black, minoritised and Indigenous people, disabled, poor and older people (Beresford et al, 2021).

With their emphasis on deregulation, reduced state infrastructure, individualisation and consumerist choice, neoliberal politics sit poorly with effective, collective public health policy (Isakovic, undated). Neoliberalism's emphasis on profit and pressures to international conflict exacerbate the threat of pandemics in two further ways. The first relates to the treatment of animals. In a geopolitical context of increasing poverty, inequality, agribusiness and rising human impact on wildlife and its habitats, animals in the wild, for food, other production, medical research and even pets come off worse. The emphasis is on reduced production costs, and increased short-term profit at any cost, with minimal concern for animal, human or environmental welfare. As the virologist Nathan Wolfe has highlighted, pandemics thus tend to start with the transmission of an animal microbe to a human (Wolfe, 2011).

Most modern disease outbreaks can be traced to animals, including tuberculosis, BSE, SARS, bird flu and swine flu, and many involve poorly controlled animal treatment and movement (Levitt, 2020). It's been suggested without conclusive evidence that the COVID-19 outbreak is traceable to bats or local markets in China. Another unconfirmed hypothesis is that the pandemic arose from a leakage from a military laboratory developing biological weapons. This brings us to the second issue just referred to, the possible relation between pandemics and biological warfare (Felter, 2021). In the context of neoliberal and globalised conflict, this is not only seen in terms of direct militarisation of biological threats including pandemics and the use of biological weapons of mass destruction but also the development and use of destabilising misinformation techniques to magnify the threat of such pandemics and undermine public health responses.

As Rose Bernard and others have written, disinformation campaigns relating to pandemics are being weaponised to increase their negative impact on public health by increasing uncertainty, division, conspiracy theorising, distrust and dissent – normalising the anti-vax movement (Bernard et al, 2021; Quinn, 2021) – all encouraged and supported by neoliberalism's divisive, disempowering thrust. The effects can be far-reaching: institutionalising 'fake news', delegitimising science, reinforcing an anti-social role for social media and setting both internal and external communities against each other. Misinformation, conspiracy theories and COVID-19 denial have all had powerful, destructive effects under neoliberal regimes. China's lifting of draconian quarantine requirements was seen as reviving Asian markets, while massively raising infection rates (Guardian staff and agencies, 2023).

Connections

It quickly becomes apparent that all these issues – climate and tech change, war and pandemics – interconnect, magnifying their effects as well as being individually associated with neoliberal ideology. While they are all about interrelations, neoliberalism's inherent encouragement of individualistic explanations diverts our attention. We are discouraged from recognising such connections, instead, media headlines focus our attention on marginal issues like not using plastic bags and straws to improve the environment. Meanwhile, the interconnection of issues magnifies the destructive nature of neoliberalism and makes it even more difficult to deal with. Instead, we are diverted to individual gain and ambition, its moral imperatives.

The ramifications are endless – here we can just highlight some, like the continuing destruction of rainforests and massive subsidies on fossil fuel. They affect every aspect of our individual and collective lives, shaping every area of our experience, from the clothes we wear, what we read and how, to the toys our children play with. Developed for a neoliberal purpose, all have been identified as having damaging effects (Barber, 2021).

Just as we've seen that pandemics don't come out of nowhere, with subsidised mass air travel helping spread them, such travel is a key but often understated factor in undermining the environment and atmosphere. New technology is bound up with the unsustainable use of rare metals and dangerous elements while the world wide web (www) and cloud-based services – seen as cost-free – are becoming a major source of power consumption and heat generation (Greenemeier, 2013). The cost-saving logic of neoliberal production methods encourages centralisation and increases environmentally damaging transport and packaging costs. Greater poverty and inequality encourage low-cost, damaging production methods to accommodate the demands of profit and impoverished people who can't afford more.

As the 2008 crash highlighted, the neoliberal economy is no longer based narrowly on traditional production. Its financialisation has led to the massive expansion of financial 'products'. While this process may not be polluting in the same way as unrestrained production, its logic and priorities are the same and part of the overall pressure of neoliberalism to inequality, impoverishment and unsustainability. Conflict and the military generate their own huge, barely regulated economy that has a massive impact on the planet. This is hardly surprising since it is mainly concerned with exchanging enormous amounts of destructive, often poisonous energy to destroy infrastructure and built environments and to kill and harm human beings.

COP26: another case study

We began the first chapter with a case study – Sarah Everard's murder. We end this one with another to illuminate the present issues – COP26 (Conference of the Parties). This UN Climate Change Conference, which took place in Glasgow in 2021, is held annually. State leaders gather to agree on climate commitments and actions. It brings together many thousands, making international headlines and setting global environmental agendas for the future. It's all our business and unless you manage to live a media-free life, it's difficult to avoid awareness of it, however distant and vague that might be.

The Paris Agreement, reached at COP 21 in 2015, 'gave the world its first universal global agreement on climate change' (Hobert and Toft, 2021). One African delegate questioned the seriousness of the commitments made and the barriers facing participants from Africa like himself, stopping their voices from getting an equal hearing (Bazongo, 2021). Others there highlighted a parlous state of 'missed targets to support the South', 'the adoption of weak emissions-trading rules' and 'commitments that fall far short of what science requires' (Burelli et al, 2021).

We are left with the sense that even the supposed solutions seem constrained by the neoliberal, globalising politics that they seek to control. Significantly, as Indigenous women said at a COP26 rally, 'Femicide is linked to ecocide' (King, 2021). A year later at Cop27, some progress was reported. A fund was agreed to support Global South countries facing damage from extreme weather. However, as yet, there is no agreement on how the finance should be provided and where it will come from (Harvey, 2022).

There is also another link that should not be overlooked. As Richard Reich, President Clinton's influential Labour Secretary observed, quoted at the beginning of this chapter, neoliberal economics and ideology demand the acquiescence and collusion of governments and states to operate. The message from our two case studies seems to be that under the present, pervasive politics, at both an individual and global level, ideology trumps humanity; the personal is squashed by the political.

In the next chapter, we'll begin the process of analysing how and why this is.

3

Fake news politics

> We have a new Mafia in town (the offshore tax evasion system). It does not exactly shoot people. It doesn't put bullets in their kneecaps but its trade is just as deadly. It deprives people of opportunities to have healthcare, education, security, justice, and essentially a fulfilling life.
>
> Prem Sikka, Emeritus Professor of Accounting, University of Essex, speaking on *The Spider's Web: Britain's second empire*, independent documentary (Oswald, 2017)

Introduction

Neoliberalism's success is difficult to understand. How can an ideology preoccupied with the interests of a very narrow group regularly win democratic elections? This broader issue – of people apparently supporting politics that go against their own interests – has long commanded intellectuals' and activists' attention internationally. That hasn't stopped it but has certainly helped us understand it! Subverting democracy is an ever-developing activity – especially now in an age of major technological advances. New techniques have emerged as old ones continue. Psychological, sociological, economic, cultural and political strategies abound – whatever gains people's support.

False consciousness

Friedrich Engels, Karl Marx's collaborator, coined this term in the late 19th century to explain why a 'subordinate class' internalised the ideology and interests of 'the ruling class' (Engels, 1949, p 451)). Such consciousness was 'false' because it was antagonistic to the 'class interest' of those concerned, which they neither knew nor understood. He understood 'consciousness' as a class's ability to identify its interests and assert its political will.

Later thinkers like the Italian Marxist Antonio Gramsci (1891–1937) helped explain why people support regimes that go against their own interests (Gramsci, 1971). Gramsci developed the theory of 'cultural hegemony', or dominance. He described how the state and ruling class created particular norms, values and stigmas amounting to cultural institutions to maintain power in capitalist societies rather than just relying on coercion. A hegemonic culture propagates its own values so they become the "commonsense" values of all and maintain the status quo' (Jackson Lears, 1985; Eagleton, 2007, pp 93–125). Thus, capitalist societies enlist people's active support rather than just imposing structural constraints or enforcing their compliance.

The French Marxist philosopher Louis Althusser drew a distinction between the ruling class's use of repressive state apparatuses (RSA) to dominate (for example, government, courts, police, security and armed forces) and the ideological apparatuses of the state (ISA) made up of a range of social institutions and political realities unified by their commitment to control by dominant interests and ideology. These include educational, faith-based, sports and social clubs and media *institutions*, and are ostensibly apolitical and a neutral part of civil society. While the RSA operate based on repression and violence, the ISA work more subtly based on consent and internalisation of values – although ultimately it may be backed up by RSA (Althusser, 2014).

Exploring ideology

Althusser's definition of ideology is two-fold. First, is of ideology meant to conceal the exploitative arrangements to which the individual – or as he understood it – class – is subjected and which they carry within them. Second is ideology with its own independent existence. This may help us understand how we can be persuaded to support interests counter to our own, but it should also encourage us to explore the relationship between ideology and ourselves more thoroughly.

As I have discussed elsewhere, this can seem both close and tenuous (Beresford, 2021). Ideology is a concept few of us give much thought to or necessarily have much understanding of. It's not something most of us explicitly learn about at school. The term is often used in a pejorative way to undermine views as biased. On the other hand, ruling ideology's impact on us can be intimate and far-reaching, quickly becoming a matter of life and death. Thus, the UK government's small state approach to public health policy has resulted in the highest death rate from COVID-19 in Europe, with unknowable other consequences.

Our distant relationship with ideology

It's hardly surprising if, for many, ideology is an alien concept. It's complex, contested and rooted in narrowly expert debate. An ideology can be defined as a set of ideas intended to explain the world. However, such a neutral-sounding notion is only half the story. Crucially, behind political ideologies lie power and values. We may have our own personal ideologies but without the power to impose them all they may mean is the ability to kick the cat, or stop someone else from doing it!

My particular interest in politics, policy, occupational practice and research is public *participation*, or citizen/user involvement. There's increasing interest internationally in this in discussions about policy and democracy (Benner, 2024). There is also increasing consideration of ideological issues concerning participation, exploring participation's varied ideological roots. However, there's been little comparable discussion of participation in relation to ideology. Indeed, arguably, how participatory ideology's development should be hasn't been seen as an issue (Beresford, 2021). Given the influence political ideology can exert over us and the imbalances of power involved, this seems highly problematic.

That's particularly true of the ideology now dominating formal politics and political thought – neoliberalism – essentially a rerun of 19th-century market liberalism under 21st-century conditions – making its global operation even harsher. It's a divisive and polarising political ideology, putting issues of ownership at a particular premium. Not least, this is because it's such an extreme ideology which, the evidence indicates, benefits few and harms many. It is still a complex and ambiguous ideology, not to be approached in a simplistic, unthinking way, which operates in the context of yet another complex idea – ideology itself. This complexity and ambiguity, in the context of limited understandings of ideology, compound the difficulties and increase alienation from it. Additionally, few people seem to have any sense of or actual ownership of the ruling ideology or indeed of *counter*-ideologies, something we'll return to when exploring ways out of the present political impasse. There's a deep irony in having little say in political ideologies regardless of whether they challenge the status quo or perpetuate it!

What is particularly interesting about neoliberalism is that it is a relatively extreme ideology. Extreme ideologies, or at least ideologies with extreme consequences are not rare – for example, fascism and Soviet and Maoist communism – which bestrode the 20th century with the most terrible consequences. Nevertheless, most such political ideologies tend to have relatively short lives. Neoliberalism has been with us for about half a century with, as yet, little sign of ending.

The political disconnect

Neoliberalism is thus a harsh ideology, essentially based on the notion of 'winner takes all'. We assume the political world is brutal and harsh. Hobbes, the political philosopher, first wrote that life was 'nasty, brutish and short' in the 17th century (Hobbes, 2016). Many years before, when Machiavelli, the diplomat and author, was set the task of writing a political guide for a new prince, he wrote what has become known as the original primer of political cynicism and deviousness (Machiavelli, 2003). This was not, as the word *Machiavellian* suggests, because he was himself duplicitous and ruthless but because he wanted to distil the knowledge of *what would work* to preserve the prince from his enemies. He believed that private/personal and political morality had to be understood as two different things for a prince to rule effectively (op cit, pp 59–60).

We can perhaps trace from this point such drawing of distinctions between personal and political morality and the association of politics with nastiness and narrow ambition. Thus, people fall back on beliefs like 'all politicians are liars', 'they're all the same' and so forth. A small industry has developed subjecting political leaders to psychological analysis and finding their states of mind wanting (Beveridge, 2003). We may wonder what this says about those of us who vote for them (Maughan, 2013; Hughes, 2019). What we aspire to as virtues in our own lives, however, may not be the same as the characteristics we support in supposedly successful politicians (Primoratz, 2007; Flinders, 2020; Weinberg, 2020).

There's not only an expert history highlighting how political ideology can get us to confuse our own interests with dominant ones, but we have also seen how during the 20th century, new inventions and developments in mass media and communication, radio, TV and cinema, have all been used to influence mass audiences and electorates. Each has played a significant role in the development and popularising of political ideology, especially the extreme ideologies dominating much of the century. Now, in an age of IT, social media and networking revolution, we've witnessed the emergence of step-change methods to manipulate electoral systems and change electorates' collective minds. These have immense power to subvert the democratic process and undermine what people might want and value as citizens and human beings (Herman and Chomsky, 1995).

The recasting of formal politics

The scale and nature of the resulting problems were perhaps first highlighted by the 2018 Facebook/Cambridge Analytica scandal. The neoliberal-leaning, self-described 'global election management agency', Cambridge Analytica and its influential founders had close links with the British Royal Family, UK Conservative Party and the military. The company was noted for misappropriating digital assets, data 'mining', brokerage and analysis with strategic communication during elections. It was linked with the successful UK Brexit and first Donald Trump US presidential campaigns, and with manipulating elections violently in Global South countries. It used personal data illegally from Facebook to game voters in marginal constituencies to impact disproportionately on elections by psychological profiling of their digital footprint. Data from many thousands of Facebook users were stolen. It routinely used illegal methods and involved outside nations to manipulate domestic election results. While the hostile publicity caused Cambridge Analytica's closure, its signature methods have now been added to the electoral armouries across the political spectrum, especially on the neoliberal right (Amer and Noujaim, 2019; Wylie, 2019; Jungherr et al, 2020). In February 2023, an international consortium of journalists published their investigation results indicating that an Israeli-led team claimed to have 'manipulated more than 30 elections around the world using hacking, sabotage and automated disinformation on social media' (Kirchgaessner et al, 2023).

Reinforcing the status quo

While technology mushrooms and new crimes and deceptions proliferate, we shouldn't assume that such electoral manipulation favouring the political status quo is anything new. The documentary *Get Me Roger Stone*, offers a strongly evidenced reminder. Stone identifies as a political lobbyist and strategist (Bank et al, 2017). His career spans the last half century of US politics where he played a central role in Republican leadership campaigns from Nixon to Trump and had a transformative effect on modern politics. He first coined the slogan 'Make America Great Again' for Ronald Reagan long before Trump recycled it. Words like 'Machiavellian' are routinely used about Stone. What's most striking about him is his impact on politics, his ruthlessness and his cynical disregard for the truth. Lies he initiated like Barak Obama is a secret Muslim born outside the US; President Clinton is a rapist; crooked Hilary should be locked up (2017, op cit) have been repeated so often that they have entered the American psyche. It's difficult to overstate Stone's malicious influence on politics. As critics comment in the documentary:

> Roger is the ultimate insider, which makes him incredibly good at seeing how he can package someone as an outsider.
> He's very smart about anger. It's one of the things he understands best. It's angry, white working class voters whose resentments are being milked to push an agenda that's useful to some of the richest people in the country. (2017, op cit)

All this may help us better understand the counterintuitive effects of strategies like Stone's and indeed of President Trump and other populist neoliberal leaders, part of a powerful political elite that can command the support of disadvantaged groups like white working-class men and communities hit by globalisation and environmental reform – who then parrot their oppressors' rhetoric. The attack on the Capitol in 2021, which Trump encouraged, can be seen as the apotheosis of this development, stoking up violence, division and hatred, leaving the field free for those inciting it (Roberts, 2021). It's a frightening and anti-democratic strategy – reminiscent of nothing so much as the machinations of the Nazi propaganda minister Goebbels that led to the violence of Kristallnacht and greeted the premiere of the anti-war film *All Quiet On The Western Front* in Germany (Beresford, 2006). This is also reflected in Stone's own 'rules' for 'winning', which include:

- nothing is on the level;
- hate is a more powerful motivator than love;
- emotions cannot simply be erased or ignored, and to believe they can is a suicidally naive approach to political competition;
- the trick is being able to engage in negative campaigning without being successfully cast, or widely perceived, as running a negative campaign. (Stone, 2018)

These guides for action offered in plain sight are divisive and destabilising. Here indeed is a stereotypic Machiavelli. Stone's role as a long-term 'master of dirty tricks', might not matter except that he has undoubtedly played a destructive part in more than one presidential election and exerted an international influence over the democratic political process. His rules offer insights into populist neoliberalism's success. They do the very thing electorates hate having done to them. They follow the golden rules of propaganda – to sloganise, patronise, frighten, simplify, appeal to emotions, manipulate and lie outrageously. Their arguments are so blatantly dishonest, so conspiratorial, that paradoxically they become all the more difficult to refute. It's as if it is just too complex and too conspiratorial for people to believe! As a result, some marginalised groups seem prepared to fight to the death to support those most misleading them!

The political scientist David Runciman offers helpful insights into this increasingly significant paradox, highlighting the need to develop a different response to such political rhetoric. He has explored why so often in the US context there is such deep opposition to reforms of obvious benefit to most voters. Referring to the Obama health reforms, he writes:

> it is striking that the people who most dislike the whole idea of healthcare reform – the ones who think it is socialist, godless, a step on the road to a police state – are often the ones it seems designed to help. In Texas, where barely two-thirds of the population have full health insurance and over a fifth of all children have no cover at all, opposition to the legislation is currently running at 87%. (Runciman, 2010)

Of course, it could just be that Obama's opponents are very good at lying and misrepresenting their cause. Nevertheless, Runciman comes to a different, more worrying conclusion, asking:

Why are so many American voters enraged by attempts to change a horribly inefficient system that leaves them with premiums they often cannot afford? Why are they manning the barricades to defend insurance companies that routinely deny claims and cancel policies?

Keeping us on side

He concludes that if there's one thing impoverished electorates hate more than their poverty, it's being talked down to. He highlights the way advocates of right-wing policies bamboozle them with homely stories while progressives lose them with facts and stats. He cites the American political analyst Thomas Frank, who believes that 'the voters' preference for emotional engagement over reasonable argument has allowed the Republican party to blind them to their own real interests'. As a result, in seeking to strike a blow against elitism, they end up reinforcing the power of a super elite – the 1 per cent who most benefit from the neoliberal politics and ideology that they control and dispense (Frank, 2004; Runciman, 2010).

However, what both authors overlook is that the same alienated voters may actually feel powerless in relation to both Republicans and Democrats, Labour and Conservative parties – all traditional political elites – and are therefore all the more susceptible to any demagogue, from Thatcher to Trump, Farage to Putin, who seems to offer something different. This would explain the almost desperate images of alienated activists screaming for what they see as their cause on endless news items. They are not so much supporting this party or that, but whichever confused and symbolic policy they have come to identify with, from Brexit to building a wall against Mexicans. Indeed, many people seem more to be voting against something than for it.

We should remember that the populist politicians an increasing number have turned to are often at odds with their own parties just as much as with the oppositions they attack. It is this less often examined issue of people's sense of political exclusion and disempowerment we will be considering more carefully next as one of the cornerstones of this book's analysis.

4

The politics of disconnection

> No man is an island entire of itself; every man
> is a piece of the continent, a part of the main …
> any man's death diminishes me,
> because I am involved in mankind.
> And therefore never send to know for whom
> the bell tolls; it tolls for thee.
> John Donne, poet, 1572–1631, 'MEDITATION XVII'
> Extract from *Devotions upon Emergent Occasions*

Introduction

Neoliberalism, particularly where populist in nature, has shown a particular knack for isolating and turning us against our own best interests. It's given renewed force to the old conundrum, why would turkeys ever vote for Christmas – highlighting how they can be persuaded to. This is no small issue, suggesting Abraham Lincoln's famous saying: 'You can fool all the people some of the time and some of the people all the time, but you cannot fool all the people all the time' (attributed to President Lincoln, speech in Clinton, 1858) may need updating to 'you can fool *enough* of the people *enough* of the time'. How else can we explain how politicians have been able to inveigle us into supporting policies that only seem to serve their own narrow interests and to be increasingly distrustful of more progressive politics? We've seen how such politicians are increasingly skilled in manipulating the practicalities and imperfections of representative/indirect democracy and constantly developing new techniques and technologies to do so. They lie and use rhetoric and propaganda strategically. But how does it actually work? Much less attention seems to be paid to this more up-close, day-to-day aspect of their politics.

A different political paradigm

Perhaps this could be attributed to the fact that their opponents are still preoccupied with offering their own alternative explanations and proposals for change rather than with challenging what is essentially a very different political paradigm demanding a different response.

Populism plus

We're seeing strong pressures combining two major forces in modern politics: populism and neoliberalism, and the consequences. While not the same, each serves the other. Both left and right-wing populism damage democracy, but right-wing populism is an important ally of dominant neoliberalism (Muller, 2017). It offers neoliberalism a solution to its democratic deficit with its rhetorical emphasis on people versus elites. Neoliberalism creates the conditions for populism and they share an inherent commitment to division. Market fundamentalism and right-wing populism combine to support the development of new forms of authoritarian neoliberalism, reflected in its divisive and destructive social policy (Pühringer and Walter, 2017; Putzel, 2020; Joppke, 2023).

Former UK Prime Minister Johnson and US President Trump exemplify this development. Weekly Prime Minister's Questions (PMQ) is the setting for the former, where the opposition leader can challenge the prime minister. Here we regularly saw the Labour leader, a former barrister, described as a 'forensic cross examiner', outmanoeuvre him in debate. While this was much loved by critical columnists, its political consequences were minimal. At rallies and press conferences, Donald Trump's meandering statements, off-topic rants and 'unpresidential' behaviour were regularly condemned by journalists both in his 2024 campaign and during his first presidency. However, this did not faze him or his supporters. Both examples suggest not so much that the rules of the game had changed as that a different game was being played, which opponents and critics hadn't woken to.

The issue now is less about encouraging evidence-based voting behaviour than it is about triggering people's deep-seated fears and prejudices (Burkell and Regan, 2019). If historically, the three 'cleavage-based' factors for researching voting preferences were class, gender and religion, this is no longer so – not the way populist politicians play it (Brooke et al, 2006). We've seen two men become leaders of major 'Western democracies' on the back of their characters in major TV programmes: Trump, feisty billionaire business leader on NBC's *The Apprentice*; Johnson, self-parodying clown on BBC's *Have I Got News For You*. This is no accident.

A consumerist understanding of manipulating electorate behaviour – based on choosing between political 'products', rather than ideological commitment – also falls short. This isn't a rational process but has been transformed into a complex psycho-emotional one. Media news now plays the part for public information, that advertising has long had, selling conventional goods and services.

If the traditional political emphasis was on building connections – between party, leader and voter, from the individual to the collective – this politics is more about highlighting *disconnection*. It's a politics of division – against, not for something. Thus, Brexit, ending union with Europe, and Trump's presidencies – against migrants, opponents, 'fake news' and government. Voting may never have been about rational decision-making (Gorvett, 2015), but we're now in a step-change situation. Electorates are 'played' and the issue is as much about complex hidden psycho-social techniques as explicit programmes/ideologies. This situation of inflated promises and minimal returns is one any con artist would understand.

How it's done

Given politics' long and cynical history, this development is hardly new. However, it's now been adopted in a more innovative and structured way. In its current neoliberal iteration, it has special significance, and by harnessing new technological developments it has greater force. Nor does it have to work all the time for us all – just enough to tip the balance in a political system that's essentially hands-off for most of us. This political development has four potential expressions. All are about disconnecting us. That's how formal politics, nationally and internationally, can be controlled by and serve the interests of an ever-diminishing minority. They do this by disconnecting and alienating us from:

- prevailing politics and challenging them;
- each other;
- the origins of everything;
- ourselves.

We look at these in turn in the following chapters.

Disconnected from prevailing politics

In societies like the UK, politics is almost a dirty word. Seeing someone as political is more an insult than praise. Given that we have democratic political structures, some such involvement is to be expected. Here then is perhaps an essential tension. In the nature of democracy – rule by the people – there must be some public connection with politics, yet those so involved generate suspicion. This may be partly explained by the very restricted public involvement in UK mainstream politics. The limited nature of most people's political/civic involvement has long been documented (Beresford and Croft, 1989, pp 6–7).

The developing problem

In official UK reports, for example, the serious underrepresentation of women in parliament, in public bodies and as trade union executives is highlighted (Buchanan et al, 2024). While a record number of women, BME and young people entered parliament as a result of the 2024 general election, they are still underrepresented and the number of privately educated MPs is still disproportionately high (McKiernan and Miller, 2024).

To compound this, being a politician, both local and national, is increasingly professionalised, so the role of local councillor has been increasingly made a full-time one with the development of council cabinets. Increasingly, national politicians, previously recruited from a relatively narrow range of occupations, have become professionalised and increasingly separate from the rest of us, both by background and destination.

As the data still shows, public involvement is limited and biased, particularly in relation to protected characteristics. Thus, using the definition of political disengagement where people don't know, value or participate in the (formal) democratic process, in the UK we see the following:

- Young people, Black and minoritised people are less likely to register to vote, vote and be elected. 18–24-year-olds were least likely to have participated politically in traditional formal politics. They're more likely to have positive attitudes to politics and participate more in other forms of political life. The average age of councillors, candidates and MPs is over 50 (Uberoi and Johnston, 2021). The 2018 Census of Local Authority Councillors noted councillors' average age was 59.
- Gypsies and Travellers face particular obstacles to registration. They are often not regarded as being resident at any address. Other barriers identified included their mistrust towards politicians.
- Women are similarly less likely to register to vote or vote.
- Unskilled workers and long-term unemployed people are more politically disengaged than people from other occupational backgrounds, measured against all indicators.
- Women, people from white groups and older people were more likely to have negative attitudes toward politics and participate less (2021, op cit).

Some groups of disabled people experience additional barriers to political participation and some religious minorities have been identified as less likely to vote and participate politically, notably British Muslims. LGBTQIA+ people were found to feel inadequately represented and concerns about discrimination and abuse were a barrier to standing for office (2021, op cit, pp 8–9). Not much is known about the socio-economic backgrounds of councillors, candidates and MPs, although the number of MPs from a lower-skilled background has decreased in recent years. A picture emerges of distrust and reluctance to engage with UK politics, as well as in some cases continuing barriers, particularly relating to groups facing some form of discrimination, sometimes significant discrimination.

People in the lower C2DE socio-economic grades are more likely than people from socio-economic grades ABC1 to feel that the democratic system in Britain does not address their interests well. They are also more likely to hold negative political attitudes (2021, op cit). As the House of Commons report on political disengagement concluded:

- British politics is dominated by white, middle-class men. The associated masculine culture can discourage women (and other underrepresented groups) from seeking election.
- Women tend to take on most caring and household responsibilities. Combining the unsociable hours associated with elected office with family life can be challenging.
- Women are more likely to be in part-time and lower-paid jobs and, therefore, are less likely to have the finances required to stand for office.
- Political parties' inadequate candidate selection practices and a lack of access to networks, role models and information (2021, op cit, p 32).

When we explore formal politics in relation to personal politics, we will be drawn back to the issues this raises.

The worsening situation

Despite the emergence of new social movements (NSMs) and other anti-discriminatory pressures, such gaps generally persist. In recent years, as we have seen, the number and proportion of female and minority ethnic MPs has increased, although it's decreased for those with a manual labour background. The exclusionary trend has not been reversed despite government and other initiatives to reconnect people with formal politics. COVID-19 has also created its own additional problems. Prompted by concerns about levels of participation in elections, the Electoral Commission observed in a 2004 report:

> The most important factor in improving participation is persuading voters that the election (and the political process more generally) is relevant to them and that their vote matters. That is the responsibility of politicians – of all parties, and at all levels of governance – and, arguably, the media. (Electoral Commission, 2004, p 1)

This follows other attempts to increase UK electoral turnout using different measures to address political disengagement. These are often undermined by a similar misapprehension. The issue is not so much 'persuading voters' of the 'relevance' of the political process but *making* it relevant. It's not just a narrow public relations problem. *Relevance* extends both to what the process is concerned with and what impact the voter can make on it. If voters are unconvinced about either, it's hardly surprising if they stay unengaged.

Meanwhile, other political developments like the insistence on photo ID to vote have been highlighted as risking further disenfranchising groups, many of which are not supporters of status quo politics (Observer Editorial, 2023; Walker, 2024). Neither the ideology underpinning prevailing UK politics nor the personal behaviour of those who are powerful in the process are likely to have encouraged such unconvinced voters to think differently. First, neoliberalism serves a powerful but very narrow constituency. Second, the personal politics of many in key political positions highlight their allegiance to the status quo and distance from the electorate's interests. This was reflected in the parliamentary expenses scandal of 2009 (Eggers, 2014) and how many MPs, especially Conservative MPs, are landlords, while a large-scale housing crisis has affected the rising proportion of tenants under their administrations (Foster, 2016).

It's hardly surprising, therefore, that the age of neoliberalism has coincided with a time of narrowing involvement, with those who become politically involved coming under increasing suspicion. The 2021 House of Commons report uses the term 'political disengagement':

> broadly ... to capture a lack of participation but also disaffection or discontent with politics, as well as disconnection, alienation and apathy. (p 6)

Trends in political involvement indicate falling levels of voter turnout and trust in government. Younger people are less likely to vote than older people, especially since the 1990s, and older people tend to vote for the entrenched political right (2021, op cit). Significantly, the British Social Attitudes survey found that the proportion of people who believe they have a duty to vote has decreased from 76 per cent in 1987 to 66 per cent in 2015 (quoted op cit, 2021, p 9). Similarly, the Hansard Society Audit of Political Engagement shows a downward trend on three key indicators. Opinions of the system of governing are at their lowest point in the 15-year audit series. Beneath the surface, the strongest feelings of powerlessness and disengagement are intensifying. People are pessimistic about the country's problems and their possible solutions, with sizeable numbers willing to entertain radical political changes (Hansard Society, 2022).

Sadly, this trend is not confined to the UK. A 2018 study, part of an international consortium on Closing Civic Space, reported a large-scale survey to 'better understand public attitudes towards civic involvement'. Face-to-face interviews were carried out in 14 nations including countries from Africa, Latin America, Europe, the Middle East and Southeast Asia.

The study showed that beyond voting, relatively few people took part in other forms of political/civic activity. Some kinds of engagement were more common among young people, those with more education, on the political left and social network users (Wike and Castillo, 2018).

Growing the gap

While the received wisdom is that disaffiliated working-class people had a disproportionate impact in the UK Brexit vote (voting leave), the reality, as Ipsos Mori reported, was that people in social grades DE were less likely to vote in the referendum (64 per cent) than those in social grades AB (79 per cent), although most likely to vote Leave (64 per cent). *Age* was a stronger predictor of how people voted than social grade: 'the majority of 18–34-year olds in every social class voted Remain, while a majority of those aged 55+ in every social class voted Leave' (2021, op cit, p 28).

It would, however, be wrong to assume that wary attitudes towards formal politics immunise you against its worst instrumentality. The opposite may be true, with the most disempowered being the most susceptible. That's a lesson totalitarian politics have long played on, of which current populist policymakers are keenly aware. President Trump made skilful use of this with his 'fake news' soundbites and the successful Brexit referendum was essentially a case study (Grey, 2021).

Distrust of the political process discourages some people from getting involved and some from challenging it. Research suggests that while some people are unhappy with the way democracy functions and would like to have more opportunities to participate, others share their unhappiness but not their appetite for challenge (2021, op cit, p 4). The anti-vax movement – reemerging on a scale without precedent for a hundred years, and conspiracy theory responses to the COVID-19 pandemic, which particularly focused on disempowered groups – can also be read as signifying distrust with prevailing politics and policymaking.

Then there was the focus group

One of the electoral techniques that has blossomed under neoliberal politics has been the 'focus group'; a small group discussion heavily led by a moderator trained to keep people on track. Its success in this context is hardly surprising. As Liza Featherstone, the American journalist and academic has written:

> The story of the focus group is a story of the relationship between elites and the masses. The current culture of consultation has flourished and become more necessary in a period during which the actual power

of ordinary people relative to the rich – whether in the workplace or the political arena – has greatly diminished. (Featherstone, 2018a)

Thus, the focus group helps disconnect us from ideology and makes things seem more like isolated personal issues when actually it's a heavily ideological process that has been tied to a particular ideology – market ideology. From its beginnings as 'motivational research' in consumer testing, it has demonstrated its value in unpicking people's motivations. Then you can shape their choices, giving them a sense of importance while identifying and manipulating their desires and vulnerabilities. Ostensibly offering people a rewarding opportunity to participate, it's a testing ground to get people in line with what you want when you want it – which now is at the ballot box. As Featherstone says, a focus group 'is not what democracy looks like'. Instead, it reduces its possibility, alienating people from their political rights (Featherstone, 2018b).

The issue of intentionality

We don't know if it's part of the neoliberal plan to weaken people's connections with formal politics or to change it. We generally cannot evidence intentionality. But what we can say is that this seems to be a further commonplace consequence of such ideology. It happens in two ways. People become increasingly suspicious of mainstream politics and politicians; sometimes this encourages activism, but more often the opposite. It also makes some of us more susceptible to the blandishments of populist politics, although it's in their nature to over-promise. So, we are divorced from a key means of changing things – including such politics. Alienating us from conventional politics may not weaken them immediately, although there are fears it will in the longer term. It clearly weakens and divides *us*.

The process of disconnection beyond formal politics

First, though, this issue needs to be located in a broader context. The next two sites of disconnection with which this chapter is concerned – from ourselves and others – lead us to Karl Marx. It's difficult to examine such disconnections without reference to Marx, who developed this analysis, building on the philosopher Hegel's work. Marx identified four sites of alienation. Given his particular economistic and production-based starting point, two of these relate to the worker's labour, so that 'he' (sic) is alienated from 1) the product and 2) the process of that labour.

These dimensions of Marxist alienation have been copiously analysed and disputed. For Marx, real self-determination demands human control of the social conditions of human production. Alienation is important because it highlights why humans may only be free by regaining control of their material conditions. Under the 'free market' the results of their production are appropriated from them and transformed into capital (Gouldner, 1980).

It's two other expressions of alienation he discussed that concern us in our focus on ways neoliberal politics marginalise the majority – against whose interest many critics stress they operate. These are our alienation from self and others. Marx's primary concern with alienation was its capacity to disconnect people from 'human nature'. We won't address this vexed metaphysical concept here. Our focus is on people's separation from politics and their political interests. To do this we will draw critically on understandings from the human and social sciences – psychology, sociology and so on.

The context of disconnection

There's one more overarching point to make. Humans may be social animals, but we are not necessarily *political* ones, with a natural connection to the political, particularly the formal political. Whether we grow up in a one-parent, nuclear, gay, complex, extended or substitute family or residential alternative, we can expect to undergo some process of socialisation for adulthood in society. But few experience a similar process of *political* socialisation. We get little state schooling to become a political being. Of course, there's a spectrum and while some of us might even be denied citizenship or political rights as migrants or refugees, others may be much more effectively politically connected through their family, private education, personal interest and skills.

This is a poor basis for an effective, inclusive democracy, with its built-in inequalities and lack of preparation. On the other hand, it's quite a helpful breeding ground for populist and exclusionary politics – the prevailing politics we've increasingly been experiencing under neoliberalism. Thus, the starting point for understanding and interacting wisely with such politics will be a weak one for many of us. We should remember this, if only to make sense of how easily collectively as electorates, we may be swayed in directions antithetical to our own interests.

Where the messages come from

Prevailing attitudes change, including our own. Anyone who has lived a long life will recognise the truth of this. After much massive suffering, two world wars, inter-war depression, inflation, and economic and personal insecurity, the UK and much of Europe supported new welfare states to challenge the suffering, loss, poverty and inequality many had experienced. The conventional way of viewing this is that times and political realities change. What I'm suggesting is that behavioural change may have no less to do with how our political susceptibilities are manipulated.

Attlee's post-war government won a landslide victory promising nationalised services and created the NHS, free at the point of delivery and still much loved by the electorate. Without a doubt, the leftist Army Education Corps played a key role in influencing the returning 'khaki' forces vote. However, by 1979 Mrs Thatcher was able to win a memorable political victory promising to sell off council housing to create a nation of owner occupiers – which never happened.

This process of changing political allegiance is a two-way one, where we play a part in how we interpret and complete ideological and political messages through our interaction with them. Thus, our agency is involved – more or less – even if the 'democratic' process plays on unconscious attitudes, prejudice and misinformation. It isn't just a deterministic process. We cannot just discount having some ownership and responsibility for the resulting views we internalise – about ourselves and others. We may think our allegiance is superficial, but it's on the basis of such electoral preferences that massive political shifts and decisions are made. The point that modern political consultants, influencers and psephologists have learned is that it only requires a minority sign up to make a big difference.

Next, we look at what our present neoliberal politics encourage us to do to each other.

5

Divide and rule

> If you hate a person, you hate something in him that is part of yourself. What isn't part of ourselves doesn't disturb us.
> Hermann Hesse, German-Swiss poet and novelist, 1877–1962 (*Demian*, 1919) (Hesse, 2017)

> Life appears to me too short to be spent in nursing animosity or registering wrongs.
> Charlotte Bronte, novelist, 1816–1865, *Jane Eyre* (Bronte, 1992)

Disconnecting us from each other – introduction

Under neoliberalism, divisiveness operates at every level and while this may be true of all nationalist and tribalistic ideologies, neoliberalism majors in it at every level. There are many ways it alienates us from each other internationally.

Tourism – a case study of division

This is true of at least three of the dominant ways our paths may cross across nations and continents. These are war and conflict, international working, tourism, and often more closely linked with the latter than acknowledged, the 'gap years' of more privileged students. The rise of international working is a further expression of globalisation's neocolonialism – not to confuse with another – the plight of 'economic' migrants.

Modern international tourism is a perfect storm of all that's wrong with neoliberal ideology, politics and economics (Jeffries, 2022). Ultimately, its emphasis on the exotic may ultimately be as alienating as the other side of the coin; the neoliberal stress on the migrant threat. The Global North further exploits Global South impoverishment, encourages unsustainable tourism-based economies, and is key to expanding destructive trends like jumbo cruise ships and intense air travel. Neoliberalism's ruthless search for expanded markets may make the world seem smaller but sets us further apart from each other.

From personal, global and back

Neoliberalism's divisiveness starts much closer to home, with the pressures it imposes to distort and reject aspects of ourselves. This plays into the issue the writer Hermann Hesse articulated in his quote at the beginning of this chapter. It's a problem in itself, encouraging us to devalue diversity, but right-wing populist ideology also encourages more general hostility to people presented as different. Much more has been said about how we are set against each other than tends to be said about the equally important internal conflicts modern right-wing politics set up *within* us. What we don't like about ourselves we may find ourselves disliking about others. Such projection has been thoroughly explored in the psychological literature (*Psychology Today*, undated). It's the antithesis of 'empathy' which enables us to understand others' suffering from our own or different experiences. Internalising a negative mindset about ourselves may be used to set up the same revulsion of others. We project the negativity onto them rather than freeing ourselves of it. Here lies the poisonous potential of aspirational politics – of which more later.

Othering us

Thus, the idea and practice of *othering* people. We all know how easy it is to fear the unknown and for the unfamiliar to raise our anxieties. While many faiths encourage us to love and have a sense of responsibility for each other, with secular and faith-based philosophers and prophets saying the same, this is rarely the key message of political and ideological leaders (Turner, 2013, p 173 et seq). It certainly isn't at the heart of neoliberal politics. Instead, we see strong incitements to fear and hate. This may have always been true of politics and ideology, but it resonates particularly with neoliberalism. It makes special sense when we remind ourselves of the small proportion of people who actually benefit from such ideology. It therefore makes enormous sense to undermine any sense of solidarity and common feeling in the dispossessed majority – a routine strategy of such politics.

Developing a culture of fear and suspicion

Such a strategy certainly chimes with what we know about what motivates us from the psych and social sciences. We seem to fear the unknown – human and material. The Irish philosopher and activist Hubert Butler believed humans found it difficult to be close and trusting with more than small groups. He based this on the difficulties for us to 'know each other' in large numbers, writing of 'the ravages of second-hand experience' imposed by the mass media (Butler, 1985, p 2). This has been picked up on as 'profoundly relevant in the modern era of globalisation created and perpetuated by the mass media' (Gray, 2005, p 29). As his biographer in the documentary *Hubert Butler: Witness to the future* said (Gogan, 2016):

> It is sometimes said that human beings are almost biologically programmed not to be able to relate to more than the equivalent of a small community of other people. And Butler really believes instinctually we're not meant to relate to the world in the terms that the media and modern life demand of us. We can really only connect meaningfully with a relatively small group of people who we know and who we are in relation with and so one of his great concerns is that modern life places moral demands on us just in terms of scale which really are beyond our grasp. (Tobin, op cit)

Certainly, neoliberal ideology and its associated media seem to recognise this difficulty, but more to take cynical advantage of it than foster understanding.

Of course, it may be that politicians and leaders hate and want to destroy some people. Clearly, this was true of Adolf Hitler and other fascists. But it's also clear that for others it's a matter of what works for them politically. So, while Mrs Thatcher may have had some deep-rooted antipathy to LGBTQIA+ people, reflected in her introduction of Section 28 prohibiting 'the promotion of homosexuality', her party were happy when it suited, to support same-sex marriage, 'the pink pound' and so on.

Reasons to be hated

There are many reasons why particular groups or behaviours are demonised. However, crucially, debate tends to be constructed in the crudest headline terms with little place for the nuance of human life. The targets of right-wing opprobrium reveal a regular pattern. Overlapping groups under regular attack in recent years include:

- poor people
- people on welfare benefits (who may also be in employment)
- disabled people/mental health service users
- single parents/teenage mothers
- young people
- delinquents and people in the criminal justice system
- homeless people
- Muslims
- Black and minoritised people
- LGBTQIA+ (LGBTTTQQIAA)
- immigrants, refugees and asylum seekers
- foreigners

This is not an exhaustive list; some groups are perennial targets. Others, like mental health service users, may be high profile in the wake of tragedies following failure to ensure them the support they seek. Trans and transitioning people are currently conspicuous targets. However, claimants, disabled people and immigrants are regularly among the highest-profile victims of right-wing ideological attacks and the resulting violence and hate crime (Baumberg et al, 2013; Conzo et al, 2021; John, 2021; Waterson 2021; Ryan, 2022).

How division works

Mostly what demarcates 'us' from *them* is that *they* seem to be different to *us* – strange and unfamiliar. Critically, what converts neutrality about such differences are the messages we receive about them and what power they have. Twentieth-century history tells us the enormous power mass media and ideological leaders have in such circumstances (Herman and Chomsky, 1995). All this starts from assumptions about who 'we' actually are. Just as aspirational politics seek to divorce us from the real 'us', so in the context of 'others', neoliberalism distances the dominant 'us' from others by engendering some reimagined self of the purist ethnic and other origin. Neoliberalism appeals to such myths, however much reality belies them. In a nation like Britain, subject to so many invasions and migrations, who really expects to have some simple monolithic identity? DNA testing quickly confirms that for most of us. But the ease with which immigration still serves as a political crowd-pleaser highlights that reality has little part to play here.

The ultimate effect is to divide and rule. It's hardly surprising of a politics which is narrowly controlled and serves very narrow interests. How else, unless it divided us, would it be able to command enough support? That's the trick of right-wing politics, and populism is key to how it does it.

The language and imagery attached to these groups distances 'us' from 'them' and engenders hostility. They insinuate such groups:

- get something we aren't getting;
- take something from us;
- do something we wouldn't or shouldn't do;
- are different, threatening, weird, tainted or nasty;
- aren't suffering the same problems we are;
- do bad things – are immoral/amoral, downright criminal;
- are associated with violence, even terrorism (Tyler, 2014; Scambler, 2018; Mols and Jetten, 2020).

While political right spokespersons talk about 'the politics of envy' when left-of-centre commentators highlight the destructive effects of poverty and inequality, they often adopt such a strategy themselves to turn us against each other. They give us permission to despise and attack stigmatised groups, to fear, hate and misrepresent groups which can clearly be seen as:

- vulnerable
- distant
- powerless
- wronged, leaving us feeling guilt
- done things we may have done and aren't proud of (been poor and so forth)

While this may cause us some qualms, they can be attacked with impunity as there's unlikely to be much comeback.

Compare this with the way media and politicians treat individuals and groups who are publicly reviled but powerful or closely allied to them. Sir Philip Green, the UK multi-millionaire retailer was targeted for tax avoidance, hiding assets, sexual harassment and racial abuse. He made headline news calling for him to be stripped of his knighthood, but he never was. Prince Andrew, linked with convicted sex offenders Ghislaine Maxwell and Jeffrey Epstein and settling a sexual abuse case for a large sum out of court, continued in close company with his mother the Queen until her death. In both cases, political and media attacks ultimately abated, leaving Green with his huge yacht and Andrew still close to the King. Many disabled people, degraded by the cruel benefits processes of the Department for Work and Pensions, or driven to suicide by it, might have wished they'd come off as lightly, having done nothing wrong at all (Pring, 2024).

Community

Two other concepts offer helpful insights into our alienation from each other. The first is *community* which historically, was mainly used as a geographic term to delineate small, often unchanging groups. It was essentially a concept of exclusion, demarcating those who were 'in' and those deemed beyond the pale. Urban areas were enclosed by city walls which served to keep people out, as well as secure people within, and systems of welfare were localised and designed to control the threat seen from those who were mobile. Then, as perhaps now, the main pressure for mobility came from the search for work which was personally, socially and politically disruptive. It is not long since such fixed communities were commonplace. Researching people's understandings of community in the late 20th century, older people said they once knew everyone where they lived and strangers stuck out (Beresford and Croft, 1986, pp 78–101).

Since then, we have come to understand that there are many different communities: of interest, identity and now virtual communities created by social media. Current discussions of community, fostered by new social movements (NSMs), are also as much about *inclusion* and challenging past exclusions. Yet the contemporary dominant ideological discourse is more often based on traditional, fixed, excluding ideas – however much these may have been superseded. We can see such mythical notions of community in the rhetoric of Brexit and the flag-waving of royalism. No matter that the UK royals have their origins far from England or that Brexit harks back to a notion of sovereignty that has had little meaning since Victorian imperialism.

Talking inclusion, reinforcing exclusion

Neoliberal policies that supposedly are concerned with including people actually work to isolate them. We saw this with 'care in the community' in UK 'mental health' policy. Originally inspired to close down big Victorian institutions recognised as harmful, as introduced by Mrs Thatcher, community care was more concerned with cutting costs than de-institutionalising people. It failed to safeguard patients or the public, increasing risk and neglect and was heavily racialised, with Black and minoritised patients more likely to be subject to the psychiatric system's control provisions (Leff, 2001). Similarly, UK New Labour policies ostensibly to end 'social exclusion' were preoccupied with pressing people into employment rather than supporting them in society (Bell, 2006). Others, for example, to reduce single homelessness were also more concerned with control than support.

The 'underclass'

One highly significant example of right-wing efforts to 'other' people was the creation of the concept of 'underclass'. This brought together under one heading many of the out-groups attacked by neoliberals. The idea represents a rediscovery of equivalent Victorian notions of the 'residuum' or 'hard core poor'. It took the form of a disaffiliated and dangerous 'underclass' highlighted by Charles Murray (1996) and since has also been presented in terms of 120,000 'troubled families' (rebadged 'problem families'), regarded as costly and disruptive (Casey, 2012; Welshman, 2012, 2013). At the core of these concepts is the view that such groups reject mainstream morality and are shaped instead by dissident values. What's particularly interesting is that all attempts to identify such values have failed. Murray's predictions of the rise of such an underclass and its destruction of traditional society have similarly remained unfulfilled. This has not stopped continued interest in such apocalyptic social visions.

Neoliberalism is not just an ideology but a discourse which has gained enormous power and has pervasive effects on thought and political-economic practices. It has entailed the dismantling of institutions and narratives that had previously promoted more egalitarian, redistributive measures in societies, including the UK (Harvey, 2007b). This has happened through powerful alliances between politicians, media, think tanks and right-wing intellectuals and consultants. If it has reinforced their solidarity and unity, it has certainly undermined that of the rest of us.

Eugenics

A movement giving particular force to such pressures for exclusion, particularly in the first half of the 20th century, was eugenics. Based on pseudo-science, and particularly associated with Nazi Germany, the holocaust and the Aktion T4 programme to murder disabled people, it gained widespread support, particularly from the US and attacked immigrants, poor, disabled, Black and minoritised people (Novick and Burns, 2022). There has been a resurgence of interest in eugenics in this century with developments in genetic, genomic and assistive technologies. Such interest has been closely associated with neoliberal ideology, contrasting with pre-war interest which crossed ideological lines and reflected both its market and elitist preoccupations (Goodrow, 2019; Rutherford, 2022).

The divisive narrative

We can't know what effect the constant drip, drip of xenophobia and divisiveness has on us. It persists, however crisis-ridden right-wing politics may be nationally and internationally. While I've written this book, a UK prime minister (Johnson) has been found guilty under anti-COVID-19 legislation, the first British prime minister convicted of a criminal offence, and a hot war is underway in Ukraine, its flames fanned by a failing Conservative Westminster government seeking any diversion from its own calamities. At the same time, home secretaries were trying to send unaccompanied male immigrants identified as entering the UK illegally, to Rwanda to be processed, remaining there if accepted. Judging from Israel's failed experience with a similar initiative, this looks much more like a populist last resort than any kind of practical policy, although fortunately with the 2024 election of a Labour government, we will hopefully never know.

Hubert Butler's sense that human beings had difficulty relating to more than small groups helped him understand the importance of avoiding parochialism, while at the same time valuing the local. As the biopic about him said:

> This was very much a man who both acted and thought locally and globally, not being insular ... but making sense and gaining understanding from the local. (Gogan, 2016)

This is the antithesis of UK Brexit values inculcated by right-wing propaganda, which were used to convince some of the most marginalised groups in society that their situation was caused by other marginalised groups. They are much more likely to have things in common with them than with the powerful players who manipulated them and their opinions (Navarro, 2007). It's the civilianised version of underprivileged conscript armies drawn up against each other in the name of nationalism, belief or empire, to die for their over-privileged leaders.

Disconnected from the origins of everything

Neoliberalism's final alienating expression is how it isolates us from the origins of everything, particularly from the difficulties we experience and the part that wider factors and neoliberalism itself play in causing them. These are key questions about why things happen and indeed why neoliberalism now. They are massive questions for human beings and they raise issues about our part in what happens.

As humans, we seem to have a special curiosity about the origins of things that are distant from us, like the universe, black holes and the beginning of life – phenomena with little immediate impact on our lives. Similarly, there is much discussion encouraging us to wonder about inner space – our thoughts, motivations and dreams. However, that giant space in between the two, which plays a dominating part in shaping our everyday thoughts and lives, with which we are in constant interaction – the nature and impact on us of socio-political structures – apparently generates much less curiosity. Check out the TV listings; there are lots of costume dramas, uncritical cop shows and news as description rather than critique, but where is the political and especially the sociological lens? It's rare, however much it might be welcomed for analysing the soaps and 'reality' shows besieging us, supposedly as self-reflection.

If, as the political philosopher Immanuel Kant argued, 'every event involves a cause', then in the socio-political context, theories of human behaviour and behavioural change focus on structure and agency and the relationship between them. This is where *structure* is the recurrent patterned arrangements which influence or limit the choices and opportunities available and *agency* is individuals' ability to act independently and make their own choices (Barker, 2005, p 448).

Very different understandings of causation and ideological differences underpin such theories. While left-of-centre ideologies historically seem interested in making the connections between structure, behaviour and experience –for instance:

- the relationship of poverty and unemployment with economics/economic policy;

- outcomes for Black and minoritised people relating to the discrimination and inferior opportunities open to them;
- major differences in health status and mortality rates according to social class.

Neoliberal ideology is much more closely associated with individualistic explanations of people's circumstances, behaviour and opportunities – and of course, individualistic solutions. Thus, the right-wing clichés of:

- poverty and unemployment as lifestyle choices; work hard and you can get on;
- any child can get the benefit of private education if their parents make that choice in their spending;
- saving the planet is down to each of us – switching off lights, walking or cycling instead of driving.

It is a solipsist world vision, where whatever our difficulties or whatever goes wrong, it is either our fault or our personal responsibility to put right. However little the evidence chimes with such an analysis – that we can resolve socio-economic and political problems – each of us, one at a time, such explanation is now the dominating one, shaping understandings of many personal and social issues. It also currently carries enough resonance to convince enough of us enough of the time. Also, significantly, it carries a logic which encourages us to blame both ourselves and each other for what goes wrong and which diverts attention from any political or ideological origins it may have.

This is clearly important for neoliberalism, as well as our discussion. It disconnects us from the origins of everything, with doubly damaging effect. It reinforces neoliberalism's divisiveness by encouraging us to see the causes of our difficulties as within ourselves or particular out-groups. It also helps get the prevailing politics off the hook for its failings. Our disassociation from politics extends beyond being distanced from active engagement to being divorced even from any understanding of what part they play in damaging our lives and the world. For the many who may feel we have little say in 'the big picture', it's not surprising we're also left feeling we have little understanding of it. In this way, the effects of neoliberalism can be hidden while in full public view.

We are encouraged instead to accept the 'little picture' of small state politics, which emphasises our individual causation and culpability for the difficulties we encounter. We are encouraged to internalise *social* problems as our individual limitations. This ranges from being made to feel bad about being poor, unemployed, disabled, old or homeless – the whole litany of social problems – even to being a woman, Black or LGBTQIA+. We can feel guilty about ourselves and rejecting of others – isolated and ultimately powerless. This may not be a neoliberal intention, but it's certainly a key atomising consequence. All is made worse by the routine operation of neoliberal economic and public policy to:

- worsen employment conditions;
- weaken trade unions;
- reduce public provision;
- reduce services like social work on which people become more dependent with cuts in mainstream provision.

All these flow from neoliberalism's commitment to individualised explanations for social problems. All leave us further fragmented and alienated from ourselves, each other and from understanding what's happening to us. Meanwhile, neoliberal politicians secure our support on the basis that they alone can sort things out, performing the conjuring trick of convincing us that it's all our fault when they are unable to do so!

The UK COVID-19 pandemic is a tragic case study of this process under neoliberal ideology.

- Government interventions are inadequate because the infrastructure is lacking, science and experiential knowledge are devalued and small-state thinking rules.
- Health and care services have been so run-down that they are unable to cope with the run on their services. Pushing people out of the NHS to free up beds for COVID-19 cases results in massive mortality through the social care system.
- Weekly clap-ins for the NHS and the creation of Captain Tom, as a massive focus for charitable giving, provide a populist diversion from the developing disaster.
- Track and trace systems fail, protective clothing is inadequate, costs soar and waste rises because of overreliance on inexperienced, high-profit and profiteering private sector organisations.
- Control is regained through a successful publicly funded and state-led vaccination programme.
- Poor information, inconsistent policy and low public participation all encourage conspiracy theory-building and low levels of vaccination take-up among marginalised, high-risk groups.
- Government enthusiasm for individualising responsibility and rejecting state intervention means policy reverts in 2022 to one of individual responsibility with the massive increase in infection, morbidity, hospitalisation and long COVID cases.
- High levels of public concern and instability of the UK prime minister diverted by government refocus on the Ukraine war.

The pandemic posed neoliberalism with even bigger questions. Countries with more extreme neoliberal regimes like the UK, US and Brazil tended to be those with the least effective approaches to COVID-19 and have among the highest casualty rates. The number of UK deaths by May 2023 is estimated at nearly 227,000 (*triple* the civilians killed in the Second World War blitz) (BBC Data Journalism Team, 2023; Hallett, 2024). There was no great focused outcry against government policy or calls for a general election. Yet in the media campaign against the left-wing Labour leader Jeremy Corbyn in the 2019 general election, much was said about his unsuitability and how disastrous his election would be. The Conservative government avoided any such public reaction to its chaotic response to the pandemic. Instead, public anger was focused on 'partygate', concerns that the PM ignored public health restrictions, which extended even to people not being able to be with their loved ones when they died or attend their funeral.

In some ways, the UK public reaction to COVID-19 has been as if it were an act of god. The focus on 'partygate', rather than the massive unnecessary loss of life and economic damage done during the pandemic through poor political decision-making, further reflects this. Yet the momentum of neoliberal ideology has long seemed unstoppable. We next look at perhaps its most immediate and far-reaching effect: – its ability to alienate us from ourselves.

6

Alienated even from ourselves

> Always remember that you are absolutely unique, just like everyone else.
>
> Apocryphal

Introduction

The most obvious way in which neoliberal politics disconnect us from ourselves is by encouraging us to think less about who we are and our actual interests than who we want to be and with what interests we identify. This is framed as 'the politics of aspiration'. Instead of focusing on where we actually are, the emphasis becomes what, who and where we might want, or be led, to believe we can be.

Like many other ideas which started with progressive aims, like *cultural capital* (Bourdieu, 1986), the idea of aspirational politics is often used to reinforce the status quo, although it also has origins in challenging it. The broadest sense in which the idea has developed relates to setting aspirational political goals, like the United Nations Sustainable Development Goals to eliminate poverty and hunger, or the UN Conventions to safeguard the rights of children and disabled people. Aspirations in this sense are lofty goals 'that exist without being fully realised, and towards which one progresses by means of change' (Roosevelt, 2012, cited in Finnemore and Jurkovich, 2020, p 760). Our reach may always exceed our grasp, but they help by providing targets for politicians and for people to press for. They carry risks; identifying targets isn't the same as achieving them. Electorates can grow weary of such a process and become open to manipulation if their politicians can't be held to account (Finnemore and Jurkovich, 2020, op cit).

The term has also been used to suggest that if people's aspirations are raised, they can be helped to improve their situation, and social mobility can be increased by raising people's expectations (Griffiths, 2007). There's no question that when people are disempowered, their expectations may be crushed, and raising expectations is a routine part of most understandings of personal empowerment. However, this is not the same as challenging the barriers that crucially undermine people's expectations, barriers which we know are perpetuated within disadvantaged families (Calder, 2016).

That leads to the third sense in which this idea of aspirational politics is used – our focus here. This is where the approach is to emphasise shared identities and values to mobilise people by highlighting common aspirations for political and social change. As Stephen Reicher and others have put it, politicians:

> use aspirations to create a 'consonance' between themselves and their followers based on collective identities that in turn allows them to shape the goals of the group they lead. (Reicher et al, 2014, p 155)

But this 'consonance' can be a false one. There are obvious examples, as when Prime Minister Cameron told the British people 'we're all in it together', when clearly at a time of rising inequality and poverty this just wasn't true for most of us and multi-millionaires like him and his cabinet. Similarly, when wartime leader Churchill told the blitzed East End, 'London can take it', he was quickly told, 'We're taking it, not you!'

Self-aspiration

This expression of aspiration politics is concerned with shaping our voting and decision-making. It encourages us to identify as the kind of person who supports a particular policy or proposal. There are significant similarities between such an approach to political engagement and aspirational branding in consumer marketing. There the goal is to raise interest, profile and, of course, *aspiration* and desire for a product or service. However, this is from an audience who might want it but can't afford it, although they may like to think that they could at some future point. Thus, there's an aspirational brand strategy, celebrity endorsement and associated fashion models. The premise of such marketing is that purchase decisions are made at an emotional level to enhance self-concept (Hunter, 2017). We have seen something similar emerge with the development of online 'influencers'.

In the UK Conservative leadership elections of 2022, the right-wing candidate, Liz Truss, drawing on a longstanding right-wing tradition, promised an 'aspiration nation' as a central part of her successful campaign 'where every child, every person has the best opportunity to succeed' (Stewart and Allegretti, 2022). What this actually meant, given that she was a key part of a government which presided over reduced equality and social mobility, is open to question, but it was a clear culmination of long-term neoliberal leanings across all major political parties.

Mind the gap

Such thinking underpins targeted aspirational politics, where the aim is simply to get voters to sign up, even if it runs counter to their interests. Such politics play on and obscure the gap between the individual's reality and the fantasised outcome. It works on the same unrealistic hopes and dreams that the UK Big Lottery has invested in, with slogans like 'It could be You' or 'You've got to be in it to win it', with the same casual disregard for mathematical odds and likely outcomes.

It is not difficult to see how playing on the gap between people's reality and hopes – actual situation and desired destination – would work to the advantage of neoliberal politics which have redistributed power and resources away from the majority to a narrow elite and increased the risk and uncertainty facing most of us. We're encouraged to imagine ourselves as better off, more important, even more desirable than we are. We're encouraged to sit in judgement rather than be judged. We're made to feel as though what we have to say matters. Remember the endless vox pops during Brexit when TV news singled out some of the most disadvantaged supporters of the leave campaign to parrot the words of anti-EU leaders against immigration and regulation and for nationalist 'sovereignty' and isolation? What we should also remember is that this is a process of *alienation*, distancing us from our actual selves. This is in sharp contrast to left-of-centre narratives. These have highlighted rising inequality and poverty, which was dismissed, as we have seen, by neoliberals as the mean-minded 'politics of envy'.

The downside of such *aspirationalism* is that at some serious inner level, it means engaging in politics as who you feel you should be, not as you are – which truly is *alienation*. Voting against who you really are and your actual interests bodes badly for your psychological and material wellbeing. It's more likely to reinforce internal tensions than resolve them. It's hardly a basis for loving ourselves, which, as we're frequently told, is the first step towards being able to love others. Such a political version of 'keeping up with the Joneses' is a high price to pay for aligning yourself with unrealised personal and social ambitions rather than acting to realise them.

Under neoliberalism, with reduced social mobility, increased inequality, poverty and insecurity, this is happening with greatly reduced chances of such ambitions being met. Such aspirational politics may have made sense under the American Dream when each generation could expect to do better than the last. But that dream has ended in the US (Chomsky, 2017).

One issue highlights how divisive politics and ideology alienate us both from others *and* ourselves. We're encouraged to devalue and distance ourselves from some scapegoated out-groups, but if we sense overlaps within ourselves, then that alienation extends to us. This happens with many identities; one pre-eminent example is disabled people – constantly under attack from neoliberal welfare policy. Traditional tragedy and dependency models of disability encourage us to devalue disabled people, and if we become disabled ourselves, encourage us to internalise such negativity about ourselves (Cameron, 2023a, 2004a, 2024b). In this way, we can see the complicated relations that may exist between hate for others, self-hate and projected hate – all of which neoliberal ideology encourages.

Pups we are sold

The prospect of home ownership for council tenants under Mrs Thatcher exemplifies this. Before Thatcherism, the dream of home ownership had little resonance in the UK, although it's easy to see how her flagship right-to-buy policy served her interests. Council house sales raised massive capital, transferred repair bills at a stroke and created a new class of discount homeowners indebted to the ruling party. What's interesting is what's happened since. Now at least four out of ten council homes sold under Margaret Thatcher's policy have reverted to private landlords, with their tenants paying more than twice the rents councils charged (Collinson, 2017). Nonetheless, homeowners have boosted Conservative electoral success as their property values have increased. Many such 'homeowners' were actually only mortgage-holders, owing big debts with rising numbers defaulting, unable to make their repayments (Eaton, 2021).

One of the controversial issues particularly highlighted under UK neoliberal politics has been people's reliance on benefits. A welfare rights worker described views she frequently encountered from new claimants.

> They say they've worked all their life, or never claimed before and are judgemental about other claimants. 'I've always stood on my own two feet, nobody's ever helped me'. They'll tell me about the high benefits a neighbour gets, which I know can't be true. They highlight how the system is defrauded – as if they are unusual in not doing this. I asked one woman what level she thought this abuse was. 'Oh 50 per cent of cases', she said. 'No that's too much', said her husband, 'Maybe 25 per cent'. In fact, fraud overpayments were officially calculated at 1.1% in 2018–19 and underpayments also at 1.1% (DWP, 2021). By contrast HMRC reported a loss of £31 billion in 2018/9 from tax evasion, representing 4.7% of total tax liabilities. Yet much less media and public concern is generated by the latter and far fewer staff devoted to overcoming it. (Cannon, 2021 and see *The Secret Welfare Rights Worker*, 2021)

The siren pressures

Even when people have negative experiences of prevailing neoliberal politics, the effect may be divisive rather than encourage solidarity. It's a further reminder of the gap between how we live and how we're encouraged to understand our experiences. We're encouraged to align ourselves with an identity we don't share, which may be antithetical to our reality. We're encouraged to play that down in pursuit of uncertain hopes and promises.

Standing in the cold, we press our faces against a window as if we're part of the excitement within. We:

- read endlessly about the lifestyles and luxury goods most of us can't ever expect to afford;
- are the audience for distorting 'reality' shows which have created a new sub-genre of 'celebrities' while supposedly feeding us and our possibilities back to us;
- vote on endless 'talent' and wannabe shows, the low-budget replacement for star entertainment, as if our say matters;
- check out the shelves of celebrity magazines which imply we're equal with the famous names we are encouraged to diss;
- instead of 'giving to charity' hope to profit from the proliferation of lotteries they now offer, promising wonderful new life chances.

It's a new world of faith, hope and charity, where possibilities of imagined change are dangled before us instead of any real prospect of improvement. We're encouraged to see ourselves as special, as change is depoliticised and commodified. How does this work when for many of us our day-to-day reality is of reduced state support, longer working hours, and poorer and deferred pensions? The gap between our daily diet of worsening services, costly utilities and the advertised world constantly increases. We may believe the Andy Warhol slogan that we'll all get 15 minutes of fame, but it certainly hasn't happened for most of us. Neoliberal ideology seems to work because people have so successfully been discouraged from making political connections. However, discouraging us from understanding our interests in this way makes it all the more difficult to sort them out.

Snobbery

One further expression of neoliberalism's disaffiliating effects is *snobbery* and the particular UK or perhaps English preoccupation with it. Snobbery is a perfect bedmate for neoliberalism, arising from a deep-seated sense of inferiority, just what the aspirational aspects of neoliberal ideology cultivate. Snobbery, as Wikipedia puts it, is about seeing a correlation between social status and human worth. It's essentially about hierarchy and valuing yourself over others – which chimes with the aspirational aspects of neoliberalism. The self-confessed Bloomsbury set snob, Virginia Woolf, offered a definition which helps us to understand why snobbery and neoliberalism work so well together:

> The essence of snobbery, is that you wish to impress other people. (cited in Morgan, 2019, p 4)

Sociologist David Morgan was right to stress that snobbery matters, becoming more pertinent as inequality grows. Under neoliberalism, this extended to 'making the right [aspirational] choices', whether that was in relation to food, body shape or voting for Brexit – which he offered as a case study of snobbery (op cit, pp 56 and 106).

Snobbery isn't just about wanting to think you're *better* than others but that they are *worse* than you! That draws us back to the other defining characteristic of neoliberalism that we explored – how it isolates us from *each other*. Even this may not match its ability to alienate us from the very core of ourselves. Next, we look at where such politics can have some of the most corrosive and undermining consequences, yet where, equally, some of the most profound insights can be found for challenging it. This is human intimacy.

7

Betraying intimacy

> Terrifying, that the loss of intimacy with one person results in the freezing over of the world, and the loss of oneself! And terrifying that the terms of love are so rigorous, its checks and liberties so tightly bound together.
>
> James Baldwin, American writer and civil rights campaigner, *Another Country*, 1962[1]

Introduction

I only realised this chapter needed to be written after finishing the book. I should have understood sooner that if I wanted to explore what we can learn from our personal roles and relationships to develop more helpful formal politics, then ultimately, I would have to think about *intimacy*. I've been helped by the new social movements' (NSMs') constant reminder that the two Ps – politics and the personal – are inseparable; each connects deeply with the other, whether we recognise it or not and however antagonistic they might seem. James Baldwin is one of the most powerful messengers reminding us; counter-pointing his writing of hate with the writing of love; cruelty, with kindness, encompassing the biggest and smallest things and making us rethink which is which. He has been an essential guide in thinking about the kind of *connection* in which I have been especially interested here. As we saw at the beginning of this chapter, Baldwin never fights shy of reminding us of the importance of love and intimacy any more than he underplays their cruel US context (Baldwin, 1962).

Intimacy is a benchmark for the personal, demarcating one of its highest expressions. Googling 'intimacy' tells us it means:

> closeness between people in personal relationships. It's what builds over time as you connect with someone, grow to care about each other, and feel more and more comfortable during your time together. It can include physical or emotional closeness, or even a mix of the two.

---

[1] *Another Country: A Novel.* Copyright © 1962 by James Baldwin, renewed 1991, 1992 by Gloria Baldwin Karefa-Smart. Reprinted with the permission of The Permissions Company LLC on behalf of the James Baldwin Estate. All rights reserved.

Photograph 7.1: James Baldwin

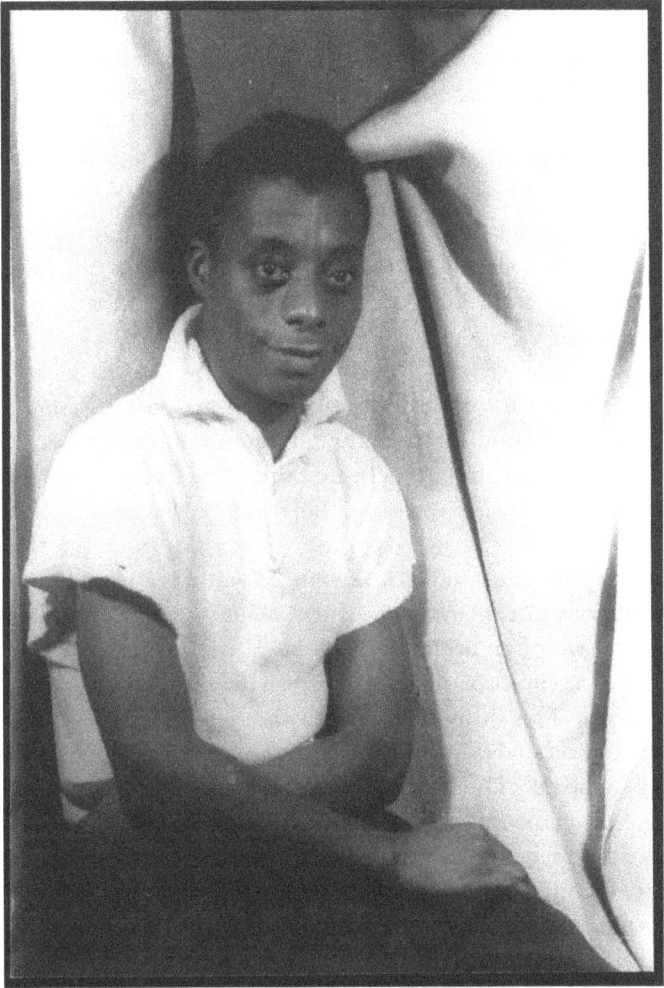

Note: African American writer and civil rights activist, 1924–87. Identified as a voice for human equality.
Source: Portrait of James Baldwin, Library of Congress, Prints & Photographs Division, Carl Van Vechten Collection [reproduction number LC-DIG-van-5a51683]

There's also an earlier stage, – getting closer to *ourselves*, mind and body. We are most vulnerable to external pressures if we haven't addressed any internalised difficulties. With intimacy, as beyond, we need to check within ourselves. It's associated with the most powerful emotions: desire, love, fulfilment – as well as when things go wrong, loss, jealousy even hate. Intimacy is perhaps the apogee of the personal and yet often we think of it as almost the antithesis of the political. It is perhaps what most of us hope for in our lives and that generally means other people. They can offer us the closest of connections – that word again – by shining new light on us and helping us be the person we aspire to be. Intimacy is a highly personal but also social idea. We can have our intimate thoughts, but intimacy implies connecting with others. Frequently, intimacy is understood in terms of a sexual or loving relationship, although it needn't be. Friendship and camaraderie can also offer it.

The instrumental world with which politics are associated sits badly with ideas of intimacy. Yet, collective action for a common cause can generate just such roles and relationships, where commitment and loyalty are key. I've had just such experience in service user organisations, but have equally experienced some of the dreariest encounters in conventional community/political action.

Intimacy is where we may bare all of ourselves – not just literally, which may be easiest – but metaphorically – our fears and secret thoughts. There are few things my partner doesn't know about me after many years together, but there will be some, just as there are things that I don't know about her. Openness is important, but no one should live in someone else's pocket. It's in intimate relationships where some of the most brutal acts take place – often because intimate tends to be equated with private. Here exists the hidden world of abuse, marital rape and violence – where personal roles and relationships have often been seen as political no-go areas.

However, it's connections that still concern us here, particularly the insights intimacy offers. This book started with the highlighting by the women's movement and other NSMs of the political relations of the personal – 'the personal is political'. Discussion of intimacy should do the same, adding insights exploring the implications for formal politics of the major equalising changes we have seen in personal roles and relationships brought by NSMs. These movements have also challenged dominant understandings of sexuality and gender – which imposed moral and even criminal constraints on permissible expressions of intimacy – have sometimes overshadowed.

Neoliberal intimacy

So, how does neoliberalism come at intimacy, given the impact of the political on the personal? The international picture emerging in this first part of this book is not encouraging. The effects of globalised neoliberalism have been increased insecurity, poverty, inequality, mortality, disability, ill-health, alienation, disconnection and conflict.

This is no basis for optimising relationships and intimacy within them. This structural context puts great pressure on both, reducing public and other resources to deal with them, as international evidence highlights. But there are contradictions here. We shouldn't rely on a simplistic assumption that good only comes from good or vice versa. We've had helpful evidence since the French sociologist Durkheim's findings on suicide, that levels of a social problem not only relate to the pressures operating on an individual but also to other social forces, like religion, class and culture (Durkheim, 2002). Hardship can bring people closer together and strengthen social bonds – and its antithesis – do the opposite. Those of us who have escaped such consequences can only imagine the emotional effects of being displaced as a refugee, caught up in war, being treated as an outsider, impoverished and traumatised – all of which have burgeoned globally under neoliberalism.

We should think very carefully about intimacy in relation to neoliberalism, what effects neoliberalism may have on it and what part it plays in shaping understandings. First, though, we need to remind ourselves of the founding principles of neoliberalism and put it in the broader context of the emotional world. Following on from the early 20th-century liberalism of Von Meses and Hayek, it was based on an unconditional commitment to the free market to 'create well-being' and opposition to state intervention. This contrasts sharply with the post-Second World War welfare state-based ideology's emphasis on state intervention to restrict the market (Hayek, 1944; Delboy, 2018).

Neoliberalism and intimacy

We can understand neoliberalism's relationship with intimacy in how it connects with the emotional world, which it does in three ways:

- affecting emotion
- using emotions
- responding to the emotional world

Effects on the emotional world

Neoliberalism is associated with:

- raised levels of fear and uncertainty;
- fear of, and actual social isolation;
- increased problems of mortality and morbidity;
- problems facing growing numbers of refugees and migrants;
- raised levels of madness and distress. (Wilkinson and Pickett, 2010; Hertz, 2021)

Neoliberalism's emotional manipulation

Emotional manipulation is at neoliberalism's heart. While its proponents have little interest in the metaphysical and an emphasis on instrumental and economic roles and relationships, they have long shown a skilled understanding of the centrality of emotion for its success:

- giving more weight to emotional than evidence-based judgements;
- using our own (defensive) emotions against us to alienate us from ourselves and others;
- fear, fantasy and snobbery are all central in neoliberalism's efforts to confuse us about our own best interests and divide us;
- it explicitly uses policies like education, welfare, housing and social care to perpetuate antagonism;
- its use of discrimination in the guise of racism, transphobia and so forth, as emotionally-based political weapons.

As a system of formal politics, this extends from its stated objectives to how it maintains power. We have seen the latter with the UK Conservative Party's increasingly subtle use of consultants like Cambridge Analytica and the dishonest Brexit campaign, both of which played heavily on emotional antagonism. Neoliberalism tends to be sold on 'efficiency' as a politico/economic system that 'works' and is 'evidence-based'. Its supporters contrast this with Keynesian and welfare statist ideologies, which are presented as wasteful. Yet a repeated electoral lesson is that neoliberalism is sold on feelings, not facts.

Neoliberalism encourages us to respond not on the basis of knowledge but of the feelings it engenders. Given that it encourages our dislike of 'others', it also reinforces this by seeking to keep us divided from them and misrepresenting them. This is not about a division between intellect and emotion, experiential knowledge and feelings, but rather between feelings it encourages and a frequent lack of actual knowledge. This becomes a vicious circle, weakening possibilities of connection and trust, with us being encouraged to fill in the gaps. For example, we know we are restricted to low-paid jobs or poor-quality housing, but powerful voices happily tell us why – because 'others' are doing well on welfare benefits or council housing we don't get. Neoliberal mass media and policymakers perpetuate these dishonest messages.

While 'textbook', evidence-based knowledge might be what is most valued in Western science/research, for many, it counts for less than what we know from our 'lived' experience – which is readily dominated by powerful others' interpretation. Sara Ahmed, the feminist academic offers analyses of the role of emotions in debates on international terrorism, asylum and immigration, reconciliation and reparation, based on reading the 'emotionality of texts' (Ahmed, 2014). She helps us to question neoliberal rhetoric and reminds us that emotions are culturally constructed rather than tied to particular groups and we can change them.

Dividing the collective

It is important to draw the distinction between individual and collective expressions of emotion. The former is where our deepest feelings may be held and expressed; the latter is where the lowest common denominator of feelings can be expressed – chauvinism and aggression – ultimately leading to mob logic and action. We saw that in the 2024 summer riots where refugee accommodation was violently attacked.

While such reactions may make for exciting crowd shots, they have much more divisive outcomes in the political arena, raising levels of hate crime, fear and loathing. This is bad enough when it's engineered against other nations and potential enemies like the tub-thumping recently from the UK and US against China and Russia. However, when it's encouraged domestically, setting up large segments of the population as an 'enemy within', then it's real cause for concern. We have seen this in the UK and beyond, where successive right-wing governments have dumped large numbers of asylum seekers in disadvantaged towns and areas they have neglected, leaving local populations feeling ignored and rejected. These have then been violently mobilised with the connivance of extreme right organisations against such refugees (Azhar, 2024).

Given that historically reactionary ideology has highlighted the supposed over-emotionality of constituencies it devalues, from women to Black people and Jews, its own reliance on emotional appeal is a significant reflection of its essential contradiction. This reflects extremist politics more generally, using the crudest collective emotion to generate prejudice.

After the divisive UK Brexit vote, new terms of abuse were coined for the nearly 50 per cent who lost the vote: remoaners, project fear and bremoaners. It's been a time of hardening antipathies and abuse, stoked up by neoliberal media and politicians, with critics dismissed as the 'chattering classes' and the *Daily Mail* singling out judges as the 'enemy of the people'. In English-speaking countries like the UK and the US, proponents of neoliberal ideology have prioritised developing a lexicon of attack against their opponents firmly based on emotional rather than rational appeal (see, for example, Murray, 2020).

This takes its most developed form in the so-called 'culture wars' promoted under neoliberalism. Framed in heavily polarised language, to set us against each other as 'woke', 'the blob' and so on. What is different about this populist strategy is that it represents an aggressive, pre-emptive attack on the values and institutions of both mainstream and new forms of democracy, like NSMs, in defence of neoliberalism's own divisive, minority interests. This is Goliath presenting himself as David – elite as outsider, perpetrator as victim.

If there's one thing neoliberals have learned it's that our responses to formal politics tend to be emotional rather than intellectual, based on feelings rather than evidence. Neoliberal politics have played mercilessly on this, harnessing the most tested and innovative techniques to achieve it. To make explicit a constant theme we have encountered, they rely on:

- division
- fear
- uncertainty
- insecurity

All are based on emotional appeal. None stand up to independent examination.

Isolating the individual

I'm not saying that by relying on our emotions in politics we necessarily behave irrationally. Sometimes it's only feelings of empathy that limit neoliberal propaganda (as with the front-page photo of a drowned child refugee). Rather, that neoliberal ideology encourages a biased response to control us.

This isn't a difficult approach to adopt since historically, politics – meaning how people are governed – has relied heavily on control not consent. Formal politics might seem far removed from deep emotion, but the two have close links. Totalitarian politicians seem particularly wary of strong emotions, particularly intimacy. In his dystopian novel *1984*, George Orwell highlighted how Big Brother and the Party determinedly undermined loving relationships among family, friends and lovers to secure complete control. To ensure its authority, the Party must counter all loyalties derived from love, sex, and family and redirect them into itself (Orwell, 1949). Such ideology has historically seemed reluctant to allow intimacy to stay with its traditional host, the family. The historian Lisa Pine has shown how the Nazis converted the family into a vehicle for their own aims. 'They aimed to shatter the most intimate human group, the family, and to place it as a breeding and rearing institution completely in the service of the totalitarian state', emptying its relationships of their emotional content, removing its role in socialisation to youth groups, 'stressing independence from parents, as well as exploiting inter-generational antagonisms' (Pine, 1996, pp 294–6). Such politics use emotion enthusiastically to set us against each other; the emotion and feeling neoliberalism majors on isn't intimacy but fear.

The neoliberal response to the emotional world

The ultimate claim of neoliberalism's proponents is that it provides for our wellbeing – through the free market. At this point, our aim is not to critique this claim but rather to explore *how* they say it does it. Three key elements they say enable it to, are:

1. it offers the most efficient economic system to meet our needs;
2. it converts our needs into commodities;
3. it makes it work through economic/'exchange' relationships.

Efficiency

According to our ideological allegiance, this is either the market's great achievement or its supporters' big lie. It's the claim long made for market-driven ideology and greatly reinforced by the Soviet Bloc's collapse – its only large-scale enduring competitor. As most of us have been socialised in and have internalised this system, it has the strengths of any status quo position, magnified by the assertion that it's 'the only game in town'. While some call for neoliberalism's reform, few outside NSMs, seem able to think beyond the box. It has become a taken-for-granted parameter for most discussions, including those about our emotional and intimate lives and feelings.

Commodification

In essence, commodification means transforming a need (or right) into a good or service with market value. Marx believed everything eventually became a commodity: 'the things which until then had been communicated, but never exchanged, given, but never sold, acquired, but never bought – virtue, love, conscience – all at last enter into commerce' (Marx, 1847). Arjun Appadurai, the Indian American anthropologist, sums commodification up as 'anything intended for exchange' or any object of economic value (quoted in Ertman and Williams, 2005, p 35). This is both its strength and weakness. There's been much discussion about human needs over the years, as theoreticians have struggled to work them out, to identify 'objective' ones, often imposing their own values in the process. Needs identified range from fundamental ones like food, shelter, sleep, clothing and warmth, to other more complex, value-laden ones like belonging, safety and esteem (Rowntree, 1901; Maslow, 1943; Doyal and Gough, 1991).

It all depends on how we think we should treat our fellow human beings. A key issue is that the market value of such needs doesn't necessarily coincide with what resources people have. Thus, the spectacular rise in homelessness and inadequate housing since the extreme marketisation of housing and UK council housing sell-off from the 1980s. Whatever benefits are claimed for this, with the sale of other public goods and services, it has increased their cost to consumers and highlighted that the needs of lower-income consumers are at particular risk of going unmet. Thus, converting our needs into commodities may inhibit our ability to meet them. That's why commodification is challenged and the commodifying of some things rejected, like water, knowledge, human and animal life – although it doesn't stop it from happening.

Commodification also introduces a new factor into the equation – focusing attention on purchasing things to meet our needs. Doing so influences our understanding of those needs and how and why to meet them. It develops needs because this generates a bigger market – which is what the market and its supporters always want. Ultimately, this can leave us mistaking the commodities for the needs we hope to meet rather than the (manufactured) needs we have been encouraged to associate them with. Thus, we learn to 'want our own home', have our 'own car', buy the latest smartphone, trainers and so on. These become our needs because they signify the meeting of our needs. The commodification of need also generates signifiers of success and failure – being better or worse, having a bigger house or car and so forth. So we become as much commodity-driven as needs-driven (Schimank and Volkmann, 2012). Similarly, such commodities can become mementoes and symbols for our emotions.

This is a materialist approach to wellbeing – we meet our needs by paying for them. This can extend to all aspects of our lives: ideas, information – in some societies – and even our organs and women's eggs. We may feel uncomfortable; we try to think of some things as being beyond consumerism, but as the street artist Banksy has highlighted, even art is largely commodified. Commodification perpetuates hierarchy rather than supporting equality and inclusion. As market logic maximises the range of needs to meet, responding to the market differences developing between us, commodification perpetuates the unequal roles and relationships highlighted here. Pursuing commodities to meet our needs has the incidental effect of reinforcing neoliberalism. If we want them, then we have to have the money to pay, so we sign up to the ideology – in practice if not in spirit – it's difficult not to!

Just as commodification serves as a material means of meeting our physical needs – for food and water – it also extends to our emotional ones, like love, affection and ultimately intimacy. This brings us back to this chapter's focus. There is a certain irony in this – that we should turn to the market with all its instrumentality – to respond to our most sensitive and *intimate* emotions and acts. However, unquestionably we do just this. Why is more complex, although in a world increasingly dominated by neoliberalism's unboundaried impact, the answer may be simple. We do not know of other ways of meeting our emotional needs; the market becomes the default position. It demands that role.

Photograph 7.2: Grenfell Tower: the price of small state and privatisation

Note: In 2017, 72 people died through uncontrolled fire resulting from the poor design and dangerous external cladding of this 24-storey council residential tower block. Many similar buildings are still unsafe as a result of inadequate regulation and cost-cutting public policy.
Source: Peter Beresford

The point is not that commodification is wrong, but when it ignores the environment, distorts our needs or responds to them unequally – consequences of unbridled market expansion – then we may justifiably feel concerned – and this is the situation under neoliberalism. It puts our commodified needs at odds with the planet.

Photograph 7.3: Public homelessness

Note: A common sight in UK streets, inseparable from the commodification of housing, are the sleeping bodies and bedding of greatly increased numbers of homeless people rough sleeping in all weathers.
Source: Peter Beresford

Exchange relationships

Commodification is only one of the key changes taking place under a market-based ideology like neoliberalism. The latter is not only associated with a changed relationship with our needs but also with *each other*. Here's a simple example from the UK experience, although I should say it isn't necessarily easy for people coming from other cultures and economies like the US readily to understand. My sister moved to New York from the UK to become an au pair. She was involved in a minor traffic accident as a pedestrian. When the ambulance arrived, the first question she was asked, while she was lying on the ground, was, 'Do you have health insurance?' That seemed so strange to us as what we'd have expected from the NHS would have been, 'Are you ok?' or 'Where does it hurt?' Many years later, as a UK academic, hosting some American social work academics, they similarly found it difficult to make sense of the NHS. 'But who pays for it?' they asked.

The difference is that healthcare in the US is a commodity; in the UK it is primarily an entitlement. The US paramedic who was operating in an economic relationship in an insurance-based system, first needed to know who was paying. This is the essential difference. Thus, the relationship we have over purchasing a commodity is an *exchange* one, where the purchaser gets the commodity and the seller the payment. It's a commercial transaction. This is the exchange on which their relationship is based. Exchange relationships have mushroomed as neoliberal ideology has become entrenched. Where once the student/academic relationship was based on learning and teaching, now as the student pays for their education, it is also an exchange one. This has been highlighted when academic staff have taken industrial action through the worsening of their employment terms, and right-wing media have routinely condemned them for failing to fulfil their side of the transaction or 'bargain' with students.

Thus, in an exchange relationship, it's not the 'relationship' that's its own reward, it's the *exchange* of goods and services. Such exchanges are also dignified as social interactions, with particular etiquettes and rules. Rules relating to honesty, quality and fairness have developed to offer some protection to parties in the relationship. Neoliberalism's preoccupation with profit qualifies this, as does the weak bargaining position of poorer consumers. When one of our daughters as a student nurse had to work in an NHS private ward, every test and procedure had to be logged to be paid for. There was a different relationship between nurses and private patients. However, the invidious aspects of the market are most closely associated with those working at the top of the pyramid – they profit disproportionately.

This is the case because many of us are simultaneously consumers and workers in the market – employed by and reliant on it to buy things. We also have other relationships with each other. So, at a day-to-day level, we are generally relating to people like ourselves, and the routine mores of everyday life readily seep into our commercial transactions. It's only likely to be when service is bad, workers are overloaded or the inequalities between workers and consumers are pronounced, that we're reminded that this is an instrumental relationship, primarily based on serving the market and shareholders. It perpetuates division and inequality, even if allowing for some social mobility within it.

It's not that the market doesn't engage with our emotions or necessarily makes a poor job of it. However, that's not its *primary purpose*. Similarly, an exchange relationship may not first be concerned with emotions or meeting our emotional needs – but that's not to say it doesn't. Equally, humans are complex, especially those who fit bills like 'emotionally intelligent' or high in 'social skills'. Both we and such relationships are nuanced and multifaceted.

Selling emotion

It's still difficult to be persuaded that the market and its commodification and exchange relationships don't degrade its ability to respond appropriately to our emotional needs and not demean or distort them. These processes undoubtedly impact on understandings of and responses to our needs and emotions. Something has to be sold – sometimes oversold – and that affects everything. Emotional response is both the medium and the product.

A key way emotion comes into it is in the selling of commodified goods and services. The use of emotions is central. A whole domain has developed to meet this demand – 'emotional advertising' – and while other emotions are also employed, happiness is the most common one. As the marketeers themselves acknowledge, 'Many purchasing decisions are influenced by the … emotions we're experiencing at the time',

> you can harness the power of desire to feel moved, compelled or connected to others through the stories told in ads. (Welbourne, 2022)

This is a very sophisticated area of human endeavour which taps into the psych sciences and world of social media and is a close cousin of the dark arts of electoral manipulation. They converge in 'stealth marketing' and 'dark advertising' (Hilson, 2021). None of us can feel confident that we stand above them and their capacity to confuse and demean our intellect and emotions.

Sentiment or sentimentality

One way commentators suggest that the market corrupts our needs is by substituting sentimentality for sentiment and emotionalism for emotion. This distinction has long been drawn. Wikipedia defines sentimentality as relying on 'shallow, uncomplicated emotions at the expense of reason' and, 'the tendency … to invest strong emotions in trite or conventional fictional situations' (Wikipedia, 2023a). A branch of advertising has developed to exploit such a sentimentalist approach – 'sadvertising'. The 'heart-warming' aim is '… (to) foster a sense of goodwill and strong emotional connection' (El Kaliouby, 2015) – to manipulate our emotions, feeding them back in a palatable, profit-seeking way. This seems a superficial response to emotional needs and is unlikely to meet them. Oscar Wilde defined a sentimentalist as 'one who desires to have the luxury of an emotion without paying for it' (Wilde, 1905). The modern irony is that paying for sentimentalism in the guise of emotion is what you often have to do in the commodifying market. The sentimentalism associated with the market and its commodities is even less than watered-down emotion. Again, as Wilde put it:

> the sentimentalist is always a cynic at heart. Indeed, sentimentality is merely the bank holiday of cynicism. (Wilde, op cit)

Happiness

Policymakers have become increasingly interested in the idea and emotion of 'happiness'. It has begun to be used as a societal measure for 'wellbeing', where its strength and weakness is its essentially normative nature. It does give us some idea of how populations feel at any given time, although we must also take into account experience, history, culture and so on. While its limits and that of its measurement must be recognised, the data is interesting. This challenges any assumption that strongly neoliberal societies are happy societies, just as rates of wellbeing, and physical and mental health, seem to be in inverse correlation with them. Impoverished, conflicted and colonised countries score badly, with Nordic countries scoring noticeably higher. However, neoliberal nations like the UK and the US do not score as highly as their economic and international significance would suggest. Equally, their much-touted wealth isn't matched by their happiness quotients, raising questions about how much the commodification of needs and access to its products actually make it possible to buy happiness (Sanchez and Deck, 2019).

One way we may seek to, in a commodity-based society, is through the illegal drug trade, with its unique selling point of altering our state of mind. This is a global industry, estimated to constitute about one per cent of the world's trade. The UK and US are among the top five illegal drug-consuming nations (Wikipedia, 2023b). This suggests that while such drugs may not make you happy, despite their apparent neoliberal economic 'success', such nations include many people searching for something different to what they get. The harsh conditions such ideology imposes on some in relatively rich societies give a taste of the brutal economic conditions it imposes on Global South societies.

Three case studies

When we try to meet our emotional needs through the market, we may get less than we bargained for. How well does the market perform this function? Three case studies all connecting closely with intimacy highlight the problems. They all highlight the shortcomings of the consumerist model advanced for meeting needs and securing rights privileged in neoliberal ideology. The first is UK social care, the second is the global pornography industry and the third is a major modern US start-up, OneTaste.

Social care

Key to neoliberalism's advance has been the market takeover of public services. This has been particularly developed in the provision of UK social care, the policy directed at supporting older and disabled people needing help with daily living tasks and to live in mainstream society. This is a policy uniquely concerned with connecting the personal and the social. It is also the domain, where our physical needs and emotions intersect, where we may need to turn to strangers for help with our most intimate living tasks. It includes residential, domiciliary and day-care services, largely provided by the private sector in the UK (Hudson, 2021), although this is an international trend. While the NHS is still primarily free at the point of delivery, social care is means and needs tested, with a large and growing proportion of service users not getting the help they are entitled to. Provision is inadequate, scandal-ridden and widely recognised as being in a long-term crisis, demanding radical reform (Drakeford and Butler, 2005; Hudson, 2021; Humphries, 2022). If the social care market is over-reliant on institutionalised care and ill-equipped to support people at home, its funding system is at the cutting edge of modern global financing. As expert Allyson Pollock has observed:

> crucial is the loss of accountability for the enormous public expenditure since outsourcing became prominent … it is virtually impossible to track where our public money is going. … Companies and their shareholders have squeezed spending on services and staff and found myriad ways to disguise and conceal profits. (Pollock, 2021)

Such companies often pay less than the minimum wage while continuing to dispense large dividends to shareholders (Pollock, op cit). The predominantly women and BME workforce is poorly paid, trained and supervised, and insecure, with working conditions compared unfavourably with supermarket shelf-stackers. It's expected to support people facing some of the biggest difficulties that can face us: dementia, loss, isolation, reduced mobility, insecurity and impoverishment. All this is in the context of continuing and institutionalised disablism, heterosexism and ageism in most societies. It is no surprise that it falls far short in addressing developing issues concerning gender, homophobia and belief (Nash and Stewart, 2002; Stonewall, 2019).

What surprises me is less the occasional examples of abuse that emerge in this field, usually to be traced to the inadequacy of the organisations involved, than the amazing commitment that this devalued workforce is repeatedly identified as showing. We see workers demonstrating kindness and respect, doing their best for service users, often against the odds (Beresford et al, 2011; Beresford and Slasberg, 2023). The face-to-face care people receive can be amazingly positive, addressing their physical and emotional needs, but the market model system is a defective one, failing the rights and needs of service users and their loved ones (Butler, 2022).

Pornography

Pornography is a massive international industry. Porn tends to be defined in terms of stimulating sexual excitement through description or display of sexual activity. Now it's mainly associated with online products. Identified as the largest online industry globally, governments want to control it, but this is increasingly difficult because it operates beyond borders. Attitudes about porn are polarised, although this is changing with the recognition of its diversity and performers' and women's increasing involvement in its production, the complexity of feminist perspectives on the subject and recognition of sex workers' perspectives (Murphy, 2015). It has mushroomed under neoliberalism, yet one of the contradictions is that now you don't have to pay for it – you simply open your device. Yet porn for both performers and producers (who may be the same) is about making money. It's recognised as a form of sex education, albeit often a distorting one. Research indicates that porn is implicated in sexual violence against women (Bergen and Bogle, 2000; Vera-Grey, 2021). The mainstream porn industry is dominated by men, poorly regulated, exploitative at many levels and often ridiculed for its poor quality and low standards (Ditum, 2016).

However, any discussion about intimacy, neoliberalism and pornography, demands caution, as porn is such a clear expression of sex and selling sex, both of which are heavily stigmatised in our world. The industry mirrors neoliberalism, however, under a different politics it could be different. We should be wary where pornography is dismissed crudely as a negation or corruption of intimacy because not all porn is the same and not everyone is comfortable with the idea of people filming themselves having sex and selling it. A conversation is needed about how intimacy, porn and neoliberalism relate to each other. However, caution is needed in how porn is positioned in that – whether we're suggesting that the kind of porn that is now made reflects neoliberalism, or that the very notion of porn does, as some of its strongest critics suggest. Judging from history, there is always likely to be porn, and simplistic judgements about it won't be helpful. There are different pornographies with different histories and literatures. There is increasing interest in sex worker-centric approaches to porn which offer the chance of getting beyond crude moralising responses. Some porn critics take an almost Marxist approach without necessarily realising it. They highlight people's exploitation, selling their labour as sex workers, but they don't apply it to other jobs nor indeed their own. Yet as sex workers say, many of the issues they experience in their workplace are similar to those of other workers – like issues with your boss, not having control over your own labour or receiving all the proceeds from it (Fox, 2018).

OneTaste

The 2022 Netflix documentary *Orgasm Inc.* offers an insight into an extreme expression of market exploitation (Gibson and Klevin, 2022). It covers the rise and fall of OneTaste, a multi-million dollar US start-up which 'promised spiritual enlightenment and community through 15-minute female orgasms' and 'orgasmic meditation'. This system of high-priced workshops, recruitment and training sessions, described by critics as a cult and investigated by the FBI, usually involved at its heart:

> a man using a gloved, lubricated fingertip to stroke a woman's clitoris for 15 minutes, touching only the upper-left quadrant of the clitoris in an up-and-down motion. (Miller, 2022)

Promises of liberation were among its unique selling points since overshadowed by legal filings of sexual abuse and participants' accounts of trying to recover from damaged lives (Huet, 2018). OneTaste highlights how the sophisticated selling techniques of big business can influence us to act in ways which may actually be antagonistic to our rights and interests. It's a reminder of the subtlety of neoliberalism's similar ability to manipulate our political choices.

What's also interesting about this example is how it turns what would ordinarily be an act of significant intimacy into something public – women having their clitorises stroked with a crowd interacting around them. This is intimacy in one sense, but perhaps not as we have understood it. It's a topsy-turvy world in which the entrepreneur/cult leader can make people act as they probably never ordinarily would – or imagine they would. However, this also mirrors the political consultants who can apparently persuade many of us 99 per cent to vote in the interests of the one per cent who are the actual beneficiaries of neoliberal politics. A subsequent Netflix docuseries focused on Twin Flame Universe (TFU), which claimed to find people's life partners for them. The series concluded that TFU assigned such partners to people, assigned their gender and functioned like a cult, one of the 10,000 it identified currently in the US (Peck, 2023).

Conclusion

These case studies provide an insight into the complexity of the relationship between neoliberalism, emotion and intimacy. They confirm neoliberalism's power to damage but not its absoluteness. English social care is perhaps the most shocking example. Neoliberalism has reduced such emotional labour to menial work, but it can still engender respectful relationships and intimate activities undertaken with sensitivity by a devalued workforce. We can marvel at their commitment while fearing for them and those they work with under sometimes appalling conditions.

Both the other two case studies illustrate neoliberalism's potential to divorce sex from intimacy, although both mainstream and other pornographies have experienced positive challenges to this from the feminist and LGBTQIA+ movements. In the context of sex, we understand intimacy in terms of societal values relating to love, romance and relationships, Pornography provides graphic depictions of sex, as opposed to cultural ideas of intimacy. The gap between the two seems to be porn's province under neoliberal ideology. Yet one of the latter's ironies is that its moralistic rhetoric tends to be antagonistic to such porn, while the socio-economic conditions it perpetuates encourage it. The same also seems to be true of our last case study, where deregulation and small-state, light-touch approaches to control highlight inherent contradictions between anti-libertarian right-wing values and public policy in practice. It results in workers and consumers being put at risk of abuse.

These findings confirm the view of cultural theorists like Lauren Berlant that intimacy involves the relation between public and private spheres and is helpfully understood as a private/public nexus (Berlant, 1998). Norms about intimacy are also bound up with hierarchies of race, nation, gender and sexuality. This brings us back to this book's initial discussion and our focus on the personal as political – the one influenced by the other and in turn that the formal political can and may be influenced by the personal – with this last offering hope and insight for challenging neoliberal ideology.

It also brings us back to our initial focus on connecting. Neoliberalism may not prevent people from connecting, or the existence of intimacy, but it throws big, increasing barriers in the way of both. We have seen its capacity to distort such connection, the way that the market's commodification of our needs and imposition of exchange relations impose hierarchy and inequality in our roles and relationships. Also, to judge from the OneTaste example, connection may have very different meanings for us. Clearly, OneTaste was seen by its supporters as making meaningful connections possible – but others may be less convinced.

In light of these examples, it's difficult to avoid concluding that overall neoliberalism works against us connecting with each other, particularly on equal and inclusive terms. Paradoxically, OneTaste's founder Nicole Daedone made a particular claim for her company to do so. Her opening words in the Netflix documentary were:

> The only thing that ever heals; the only thing that ever awakens is – connection. Our world is getting hyper-connected but human connection is beginning to dissolve. I do think that there is a cure and that cure is female orgasms. (Gibson and Klevin, 2022)

Such unlikely claims are perhaps best summed up by the epitaph on Sir Christopher Wren's tomb in St Paul's Cathedral, his masterpiece:

> Si monumentum requiris circumspice
> [If you seek his monument, look around you].

Neoliberalism's monument is similarly all around us in the conflict, isolation, uncertainty, poverty, disease and environmental threat that extend over the whole globe with increasing force. There is a final irony here. While neoliberalism has done everything it could to divide and isolate us from each other, one of its major accusations against its critics is that this is what *they* seek to do, thus the attacks on 'de-' and 'no-platforming', where supporters of NSMs have challenged the neoliberals' right to attack others' rights (Murray, 2020; BBC News, 2021).

In her exploration of *Radical Intimacy*, Sophie Rosa concludes that capitalism's recipe for life leaves people feeling 'atomised, exhausted and disempowered'. Her examination of its failure extends to the 'wellness industry … the mental health crisis and racist and misogynist state violence. Under capitalism, she says, 'Making connections' means networking for work', while our aspirations for intimacy are diverted and undermined (Rosa, 2023).

As we report in Chapter 11, this world of isolation which neoliberalism has given us is also the focus of the latest iteration of E.M. Forster's watchword, 'only connect', in Noreena Hertz's best seller, *The Lonely Century, 'a call to reconnect'*. This highlights the loneliness and isolation that neoliberalism has imposed on us internationally (Hertz, 2021). The truth is that these are just the emotional tip of an existential threat posed by neoliberalism, which we ignore at our peril. Yet this momentum of neoliberal ideology can still seem unstoppable.

In the next chapter, we'll look more closely at how people have sought to combat neoliberalism's threat and why the traditional routes adopted seem to have been so unsuccessful. We need to look in new directions if we want to break the current socio-economic impasse, building on prefigurative practices and experience. That's the aim of the second part of the book.

PART II

New routes for a different politics

Having highlighted the apparent unstoppability of neoliberalism, **Part II** of the book moves on to explore insights for a different political future. How could we bring about this change? This section offers a bridge between the present widely experienced exclusionary politics and a changed, more participatory politics many, including this author, aspire to. We see how traditional approaches to opposition no longer seem to work. We also examine counter forces developing at the same time as neoliberal ideology, with a very different emphasis – on sustainability, participation, reconnection and the valuing of diversity and inclusion. We consider how we might build on the different politics they envision and move towards them.

8

Changing our approach to making change

> I am your voice.
> Donald Trump to an applauding crowd, 2016 presidential campaign

> Today, I am your warrior, I am your justice … I am your retribution.
> Donald Trump, 2024 presidential campaign speech (Panorama, 2024)

Introduction

While neoliberal politics may contain the seeds of their own destruction, only serving minority interests, they keep going – on and on! They seem to be self-perpetuating, with their capacity to divide, misrepresent and create misunderstanding, reducing effective opposition. In his own book on the subject, Mark Fisher, the political theorist reminded us of an earlier phrase, 'it's easier to imagine the end of the world than it is to imagine the end of capitalism' (Fisher, 2009, p 2). Neoliberalism appears unstoppable. Internationally, whatever the outcome of elections, neoliberalism still seems set to win. Important advocates like Trump retain the confidence its populism has given them (www.youtube.com/watch?v=ehvUQrRDyyU). How and why? – these surely should be the dominating questions of our times. And yet they largely go unasked. There may be concerns about politicians' behaviour, political morality and the merits of a particular policy, but somehow these do not get laid at the door of dominant ideology. Instead, they are seen in abstraction. Perhaps this is another expression of neoliberal ideology's power to isolate and disconnect. There's little mainstream thinking outside its box. Whatever the case, neoliberalism has a remarkable capacity to misdirect our attention, so that for many, or at least enough of us, this is not a question we seem to be asking.

Hopefully, this text will mobilise people by evidencing why it's so important to ask such questions. It's not that there isn't much dissatisfaction with rising uncertainty and threat. But there's still a gap between people's experience of formal politics and their response to it, for example, in the 2023 English local elections. Bludgeoned by inflation, facing new tax rises and massive increases in utility prices, opposition was still muted. Psephologist Sir John Curtice saw Labour's result as, 'no better than its score in last year's local elections' (Curtice, 2023). The Lib Dem Party maintained its progress – the same party that propped up Conservative neoliberal politics after 2010 and enabled its return to power in 2017. While the UK Labour Party had a landslide victory in the 2024 general election, it still presented as a party strongly committed to neoliberal values. The crypto-fascist and populist neoliberal Reform party gained a worrying 14 per cent of the vote. Thus, the electoral response to neoliberalism's depredations still seems less a bang than a whimper.

The outcome of the 2022 French presidential elections reinforced this conclusion. While the centrist standing candidate Emmanuel Macron secured a second term, there were more worrying underlying trends. Turnout was very low and the far-right candidate Marine le Pen significantly increased her vote with the rallying cry of speaking for marginalised voters, gaining support from younger voters – hardly indicating neoliberalism's end in Europe (Bland, 2022). While a determined New Popular Front ultimately defeated the far right in the 2024 French elections, the longer-term threat of them gaining power remains unabated (Chrisafis, 2024).

How might we at least interrupt this dominant thrust of neoliberal politics, even if we can't end it? What have people done to achieve this and with what success? It's not as though there haven't been many opportunities for challenge over the last 50 years, given all the problems and conflicts neoliberalism has generated, starting with the original Chilean test bed (Dattari, 2022).

There have been at least three major political/ideological responses to neoliberalism in formal politics historically:

1. a rising acceptance that it is essentially unreformable, possibly the norm, perhaps only ameliorable;
2. a continuing reliance on grand political/economic ideology and theory;
3. persistence with would-be traditional welfare state-based approaches and responses.

The logic of 2 and 3 seems to be to try and undo what neoliberalism has done. All these strategies can be spotted, often in varying combinations. A further effect is the way neoliberalism has encouraged broader right-wing reaction to emerging social, economic and political problems, exacerbating conflict and division and strengthening racist movements internationally. Let's now look in turn at each of these three responses.

Neoliberalism is for keeps

In the UK, this response was epitomised by Tony Blair's approach to Labour's historic 1997 victory. Instead of seeing this as evidence of the electorate's weariness of years of neoliberal cuts and regressive redistribution, he reshaped

Labour in the same image. Thus, the ending of Clause 4, deregulation of banks and the Bank of England and the extension of privatisation and marketisation of public policy. He spent much more on the NHS and social policy but based on increasing outsourcing, pressing people into low-value employment and subsidising low private sector wages. New Labour's 'third way' perpetuated the principles of neoliberal ideology, yet it is still often seen as successful, with Blair the longest-lasting Labour PM (Price, 2007). What we'll never know is what would have happened if John Smith, the previous Labour leader hadn't died prematurely and had governed along old Labour lines as expected. Then we might be starting from a very different political history!

It's interesting how quickly neoliberal politics became entrenched as the 'new normal'. By the mid-1980s, a few years after Thatcher came to power, a new term had been coined, 'welfare pluralism', to disguise the ascendency of marketised public policy and retreat from state intervention (Beresford and Croft, 1984). It wasn't only supporters of New Right ideology who internalised it. It seems to have affected us all, almost by a process of osmosis. As it happened over a period of massive scientific development, the two have been closely linked. We can all find ourselves spending long periods on our phones listening to grating music and being told 'no operative is currently available', as if this resulted from a world 'operative' shortage rather than the market maximising profits and minimising staff.

As utilities like water suppliers have sold-off reservoirs, and water loss has massively increased through infrastructural neglect, we unthinkingly accept hosepipe bans and even water rationing, as if every problem really does demand an individualised solution as the neoliberal mantra wants us to believe! As fewer of us have had significant experience of, or grew up under any other politics, we just don't know how it was, what's been lost or what to judge things by. Even as oil and electricity prices shot up in 2022, creating demands for state subsidies, the utilities were reporting massive profits.

We may come to understand the reality of what we experience, for example, with disproportionately high rents, but then it's generally too late and we can expect little change from prevailing small state politics in the wake of a massively costly pandemic. We don't have to believe in neoliberalism, but it seems to have made enough of us accept it. Thus, for example, we are routinely told that changing the situation would cost too much in tax hikes, which people wouldn't tolerate, or, as I have reported elsewhere, to believe in the possibility of real social care reform in England, I must believe in Father Christmas! (Beresford and Slasberg, 2023).

The idea of looking again at neoliberalism's actual economics gets ruled out. Progressive tax redistribution is off the agenda. Assumptions that the only remedy is cutting public spending and services have become ingrained in our understanding as 'the only game in town'. Orwell's Big Brother would be proud of the way so many of us seem to have internalised Mrs Thatcher's slogan: 'There's no alternative' (Berlinski, 2011). It's the mirror image of Fukuyama's 'end of history', and while both clichés may be untrue, both have gained enormous power and psychological investment.

It's all the more shocking when we read that the people who spearheaded the latest iteration of UK neoliberalism – the governments from 2010 onwards were a narrow group of Oxford University 'chums' who gave us three failed prime ministers, one of whom opened the door to Brexit, another presided over draconian immigration law and a third, Boris Johnson, was uniquely convicted of a criminal act as PM (Kuper, 2022).

Perhaps the real problem is not so much acceptance of, or acquiescence to neoliberalism, as a broader failure to recognise it as a coherent value system, increasingly driving the direction of our society and shaping our lives. This lack of understanding of ideology and denial of having a say in it seems to pass most of us by (Beresford, 2021). We don't necessarily recognise its many expressions – the curtailed supportive state, increasing restrictions on our lives and rights, and the ways we are divided. These are all closely linked with neoliberalism and are its proponents' stock-in-trade.

Continuing reliance on grand theory and ideology

There's certainly no shortage of critiques of neoliberalism even if its advocates still claim there is no such specific belief system! It's not surprising that a key source of opposition to neoliberalism has come from the left, from Marxian to Keynesian perspectives (Saad-Filho, 2007). Predictably, a heavily ideologically-inspired world view would be most determinedly opposed by its ostensible polar opposite. First time round, the most radical challenge to capitalism came from the overlapping forces of socialism and communism. Last century, this capitalism was the enemy to be defeated. Nothing less than a portmanteau value system like socialism or fascism was seen to offer the possibility of broader change. However, this has changed. The left no longer seems to have the power it once assumed. In this narrow sense, there has perhaps been an end to history.

Neoliberalism has been widely criticised from the political left and right – by economists, philosophers, linguists, environmentalists, feminists, and the anti-globalisation and Occupy movements. The 2008 recession also gave rise to new scholarship which rejected neoliberalism and sought policy alternatives.

Such significant developments rooted in the old and new left and traditional left/right politics have made surprisingly little impact on dominant new right politics or thinking. The most determined dismissal of neoliberal ideology from the statist left has been readily dismissed as 'they would say that wouldn't they'. It is not linked with the same powerful praxis it formerly had, with its army of unionised workers and broad-based community organising. As formal politics and economics internationally have moved consistently to the right, the discourse has stayed the same, as though future elections will be fought as elections were before this long-ago seismic shift to the right. It's like the compulsive gambler who convinces themself that the next throw of the dice will be different – which just hasn't happened.

It's hardly surprising then if Marxist critiques of neoliberalism are among the most convincing, given the massive impact of Marx's analyses of capitalism the first time around (Jipson and Jitheesh, 2019). However, they've been readily shaken off by neoliberalism's self-perpetuating structures, now deeply embedded internationally. In the Global North, at least, leftist ideology has been unable to generate political power against them or mobilise the grassroots enthusiasm their predecessors once commanded. It no longer has the infrastructure of an international political force. The reactionary nature of state socialism, epitomised by the defunct Eastern Bloc, undermined its oppositional potential. People's negative experience of the state's regressive role under neoliberalism has paradoxically reinforced their sense of disaffiliation from the state. It has more clearly become the ally of neoliberalism, not people, as a force for social control rather than social support.

However powerful the intellectual critiques of neoliberalism, advocates have deflected them by acting as if 'sticks and stones may break my bones but words can't hurt me'. That's why neoliberalism's emerging economic failure is so important, causing some of its most important and closest advocates like the World Bank and IMF to distance themselves from it. But this has been more to discipline than fundamentally challenge it.

Many people's disassociation from traditional left-of-centre ideology means this now lacks the same potential to rally opposition. While it may have been a vanguard of opposition, this is now easier to isolate. Relying on others to negotiate the complex world of political ideology, rather than developing our own involvement, puts us at risk of another problem. This is the massive capacity neoliberal politicians and populists have demonstrated to emphasise the fault lines between us and advantaged and supportive allies, using a cynical rhetoric stressing inequality and paternalism.

Summing up, continuing reliance on grand theory to oppose neoliberalism feels like relying on one outmoded economistic theory/ideology to fight another apparently more powerful one. While neoliberalism still manages to carry conviction as new politics, however much it's actually rooted in the past, leftist ideology is increasingly dismissable as anachronistic. This doesn't mean that neoliberalism has it all its own way. There are numerous campaigns to rally around, as we'll see in the last part of the book, when we hear about many current single-issue struggles directed less against neoliberalism than the many problems it faces us with, from poverty and racism to climate change and colonialism. However, these are often approached in isolation rather than associated with neoliberalism. None alone has enough traction to stand up against grand theory backed up by big power on the scale of neoliberalism. It's this which seems to be needed for real change. Currently, there's little sign of it. Neoliberalism seems unstoppable and fundamentally unreformable, as the next response highlights.

Welfare state-based responses

These have formed perhaps the most visible opposition to neoliberal politics in the UK and other Western democracies. They have highlighted the loss of old welfare state protections and the wisdom of restoring them. While framed in policy terms, like all policy, this strategy is tied to ideology. While it is a policy expression of an ideological position, the emphasis is less on underpinning values than on the practical benefits offered by it. If Tony Blair epitomised a UK Labour Party acceding to neoliberalism, his successor but one, Jeremy Corbyn, was closely associated with resisting it and restoring Labour's post-war welfare state principles. As his 2019 manifesto made clear, this included:

- increasing public spending;
- a green economic strategy;
- cutting private provision in the NHS and creating a national care service;
- renegotiating Brexit;
- redistribution through raising low wages;
- nationalising key industries, utilities and services;
- increasing council housing stock;
- providing free internet.

This is a radical reformist agenda committed to restoring mainstream state-controlled public services with increased funding, based on the universalist principles and progressive redistribution of the post-war Labour government's welfare state (Prince, 2018), while also being committed to the greening of economic policy. In the US, Bernie Sanders occupied a similar position, challenging the mainstream neoliberal position of both Donald Trump and Hilary Clinton in his presidential election campaigns, campaigning for:

- more progressive taxation and a raised federal minimum wage;
- more public and not-for-profit housing;
- universal government-run health insurance;
- increased state investment in infrastructure;
- breaking-up big tech;
- a green economic 'new deal'.

Sanders drew parallels between Corbyn and himself, both trying to revitalise their parties and democracy, bringing more people into politics (Rabin-Haft, 2022). He saw himself as a social democrat, just as supporters of Corbyn highlighted that, while presented as hard left, Corbyn was actually closer to mainstream European left-of-centre parties. Certainly, their supposed association with extremism has been central in campaigns to discredit them.

The brutal truth is that hostile campaigns against them succeeded and both leaders were prevented from achieving office or reforming party policy. Both had large, committed bodies of supporters – and succeeded in increasing involvement in mainstream politics, particularly of young people. Nevertheless, neither represented a successful challenge to neoliberalism despite closely reflecting the interests of many voters. Both had strong political track records – Corbyn as a much-valued constituency MP and campaigner and Sanders as a respected senator in the Upper House.

The two leaders stayed committed to traditional welfare state values under neoliberalism. These may still be found at the heart of the UK's left-of-centre media, as well as among such intellectuals and commentators, even in disciplines like social policy, where neoliberal public policy is still often discussed as if it were a short-term aberration from Fabian welfare traditions. Yet there is little sign of neoliberalism ever being dislodged by such appeals to old collectivist values. Why does this challenge to Scrooge-like neoliberal politics, a challenge which appeals to our self-interest and has a much better track record than privatised utilities or care, appear to offer such a modest challenge to the new private enterprise politics? How has it been so easy to write off its advocates as 'dinosaurs of welfare', preoccupied with the past?

There are several reasons for this. All relate to the power of right-wing propaganda, the strength of its media and the increasing sophistication (and deviousness) of populist techniques used. However, all connect with the believability or otherwise to electorates of the old welfarists. At least four explanations can be identified. All relate to the longevity of neoliberal regimes and their effective impact on people. Summing up, they include public acceptance:

- *of prevailing political agendas/dominant discourse about change;*
  The political right's consistent message is that welfare state approaches are obsolete. Market is much more efficient than state. Whatever its relation with reality, this message now seems to be widely internalised and accepted.
- *that such amelioration of conditions is no longer feasible* – especially with the rise of 'risk society' (Greve, 2020);
  People seem to have accepted that generally, they should make their own arrangements and anything else would be wasteful. The key exception in the UK is the NHS, which has become a totem.
- *that conditions have changed and state welfare no longer makes sense;*

Society and social relations are now fundamentally different to 1945. This repeated policy message ignores how welfare state responses themselves developed and responded to social and attitudinal change (see Beresford, 2016).
- *that governments might have done it post-war, but not now.*
The enormous expenditure, for example, incurred and found in response to the failure of the small state response to the COVID-19 pandemic is ignored by this widely used argument.

As well as:

- *weakening of experience of the welfare state as a supportive and equalising institution;*
After many years of neoliberal cuts, most people do not have direct experience of the original, helping welfare state based on universalism, so don't necessarily judge it by such criteria or identify with it for themselves.
- *that instead, people have much more experience of welfare as a marginalising and regressive force.*
This neoliberal welfare state is a residualised one, associated with stigma and control. It is no longer primarily an equalising institution to help people in difficult times or facing additional difficulties and is not seen as such. This links with the re-emergence of Victorian 'welfare chauvinism' – based on hostile populist arguments against immigrants and refugees (Mény and Surel, 2002).

In societies like the US and UK, where Obamacare can be presented as communistic and Corbyn as a hard-line 'red', it's hardly surprising that neoliberalism seems to have met with as little opposition as it has. In the next chapter, we turn to so-called 'new social movements' (NSMs). We suggest they can offer key insights into how we may challenge the unstoppable dominance of neoliberalism.

9

Starting with our own lives

> Politics have no relation to morals.
> Niccolo Machiavelli, 1469–1527,
> *The Prince* (Machiavelli, 2003)

Introduction

So far, this book has largely focused on the formal politics we live under. It's a harsh story of rising difficulties for many and excessive power and wealth for a few. Such neoliberal ideology has privileged the unprecedented accumulation of power by elites globally. It's a politics tied to rising poverty, inequality, morbidity, conflict, division, exclusion and discrimination. It is a highly instrumental, hierarchical, alienating and exchange-based politics, creating an unaccountable 'overclass' with unprecedented power, significantly freed from the moral and legal constraints imposed on the rest of us.

Every so often a chink in the curtain lets us see the gross abuse of freedom this has allowed those who are privileged by resulting wealth and power. Thus, the criminality of Russian oligarchs hidden until conflict with Ukraine, the serial child sexual abuse perpetrated by billionaire Jeffrey Epstein and his accomplices, the sexual abuse of women by Roger Ailes, head of far-right Fox News and Hollywood producer Harvey Weinstein revealed by the #MeToo campaign. More routinely, we see the frequency of workplace bullying, discrimination, hate crime and sexual harassment under the poorly protected, grossly unequal conditions of neoliberalism.

Neoliberal ideology is hardly alone in formal politics in having such extreme attributes and effects, but it's a particular outlier in the field. Here we see the antithesis of the morality most of us have been encouraged to live our lives by, whether within faith-based, spiritual or humanistic belief systems. From the Jewish Talmud, through the Muslim Koran, via the French Revolution and modern socialist belief systems, there is the same emphasis on justice and freedom – liberté, égalité, fraternité – on looking after the worst off, respecting parents and elders, caring for each other, all conspicuously absent from neoliberal *political* ideology.

However, political logic often appears at least amoral if not immoral. Politics as realpolitik, that is to say, based on instrumental rather than moral priorities, seems to be what prevails (Davies, 2000). Socio-political institutions may abide by moral principles their leaders set, but it's difficult to see how they themselves can possess them unless we anthropomorphise them. This is a fundamental mistake we may too readily make about politics and political choices when we should be thinking more about our human responsibilities engaging in them.

A conflict of values?

The values and relationships associated with formal neoliberal politics seem distant from the more equal ones and mutual acceptance most of us increasingly aspire to in our personal lives. A vision of parents, guardians and primary schools instead teaching youngsters ruthless boardroom ethics – the eat-or-be-eaten values of private equity companies – points us to a world, riven with conflict and driven to hate and disaster. Yet that's where formal politics now seem to be taking us, with rising international conflict and the prospect of environmental catastrophe linked with the long-term dominance of globalised neoliberalism.

As billionaires at the cutting edge of these developments, like Elon Musk, preach a gospel of privatised space travel and colonies on Mars, the rest of us, unlikely to afford the ticket for such an escape, can only contemplate our children's, children's future on an earth they've ruined.

That's what gives such urgency to the questions I'm asking here, which aren't just about the particularly short-term and extreme politics that now prevail internationally, but perhaps about 'liberal' democracy more generally. We may feel reassured that we live in a 'democracy', but our lived experience of democracy may be rather less evident. Few of us are likely to feel our schooling in the state system was democratic, nor our workplace, and for some of us, even our families may not hit the mark. Schools and universities have become increasingly competitive. Thus, we may have little practical equipment to negotiate supposedly democratic politics.

And it is here that getting to grips with what's happening politically becomes a difficult, even unmanageable task for many of us. We're not greatly helped when we turn for understanding to the dictionary. There's still a strong tendency to offer face-value, consensual definitions of politics that are as likely to add to the confusion as resolve it. Thus, on Wikipedia, we are told:

- The British political theorist Bernard Crick argued that 'politics is a distinctive form of rule whereby people act together through institutionalized procedures to resolve differences, to conciliate diverse interests and values and to make public policies in the pursuit of common purposes'.
- The American political scientist Harold Lasswell described it as 'who gets what, when, how'.

- The German sociologist Max Weber described it as the sphere of activity involved in running a state. 'The state can be defined as a human community that successfully claims the monopoly of the legitimate use of physical force within a given territory'. (Wikipedia, 2022)

Each may offer some insight, but I doubt any will greatly increase the confidence of any Ms or Mr Average trying to understand the worsening impact of daily politics on every aspect of their life, whether they recognise it or not. Having just watched the BBC documentary *The Rise of The Murdoch Dynasty*, I feel that such consensual definitions of politics offer me minimal equipment to understand how this one advantaged newspaper proprietor could exert the disproportionate influence he had over UK and international politics and culture for 40 years. Public lack of political understanding has to be an underlying reason for the unstoppable success of such neoliberal ideology. Yet new right politics also have much in common with the politics that preceded them.

They generally share the same narrow demographic base, routine exclusions and discriminations. However contradictory it may seem, dissatisfaction with such traditional politics has given impetus to current right-wing populist ones. There is both continuity and discontinuity in such politics. And while neoliberalism may be strongly associated with extreme ideology – the narrow pursuit of profit and ruthless personal ambition – the instrumentalism and amorality more generally associated with politics have long been a cause of public disaffiliation. We should not focus over-narrowly on neoliberal politics if we want to end it. Its seeds can be found in liberal democratic ideology more generally and beyond that.

We can see the impact that neoliberal politics have on social and personal relations, roles, behaviour and values. This is a helpful prompt to dig deeper and examine the broader politics of our roles and relations. We soon see that just as 'no person is an island', these connections are affected by much bigger forces in society: social, economic, political and cultural. This includes all the links people have as partners and family members, in learning, work and recreation, as adults and children. These may change over time and place. Sociologists and historians have told us about the different patterns of roles and relationships operating in feudal, mercantilist, capitalist and post-industrial societies, as well as their different bases, from fiefdom through exchange to service relationships, as well as cultural differences. These can help us understand who we connect with, how and why. They also encourage us to explore underlying equalities/inequalities in such roles and relations, their ideological origins and shifting understandings of and responses to them. We may have common-sense understandings of them in our own lives, but we also benefit from examining them more closely.

Some roles and the relationships that go with them may offer us particular insights, not necessarily because we have experience of them, but because they encourage us to think particularly carefully and critically more generally about them. They also remind us how harsh and unequal direct personal relations between us can actually be and to avoid any romanticising of them in relation to political relationships. Such suspect relations include:

- Slavery: where one human being is owned by another, the relationship is as property and there is no freedom except that allowed by the owner (no freedom at all).
- Sex work: traditionally known as prostitution where people, particularly (underprivileged) women, sell sexual services (to more privileged) men, as workers, generally with high risk and little protection.
- Heterosexual marriage: the formal union of two people in a personal relationship with codified rights and responsibilities, which historically and still internationally has privileged men.
- Employment: work undertaken in return for payment, where ultimately, one person controls the time and labour of another.
- Landlord/tenant relations in the provision of housing as a commodity.

All are historically important, all contentious. None is narrowly associated with one particular ideology. All can help us unpack roles and relationships and their connections with wider structural issues. All raise questions about equality, some can be seen as inherently damaging and unequal, for example, slavery, and others unequal and discriminatory in certain cases, like heterosexual marriage under patriarchy, or employment and landlordism, unless coupled with particular rights and entitlements. Slaves in the US southern states were less likely to gain their freedom than those in ancient Rome. All these examples remind us that the nature of roles and relationships varies according to context and, in some senses, all relationships, including formalised ones, are also ultimately personal relationships, and we need to remember the larger forces that shape them. We become aware of the particular purposes they serve in their societies and cultures, as well as for the individuals involved in them.

The significance of New Social Movements

Over the same period that neoliberalism has been achieving global dominance, a parallel development has flowered. Its significance here is that it has been headed in exactly the *opposite* direction to neoliberal politics and ideology. It's been concerned with challenging division, opposing narrowly profit-based developments and working for egalitarian and sustainable goals. This is the emergence in the second half of the 20th century of 'new social movements' (NSMs) and NSM theory.

What is the relationship between NSMs and neoliberalism? Are they a reaction to it or part of a more enduring challenge to dominant values? Are culture wars neoliberalism's counterattack? It's difficult to be definitive. Clearly, neoliberalism's extremism encourages opposition, but the NSMs were already emerging before its rise. The women's and Black civil rights movements can be traced back to the 19th century at least. NSMs challenged traditional statism no less than market-driven ideology. Whether there is a causal or other relationship between the two remains in question (Bieler, 2011). What we can say is that NSMs and their values have certainly thrived and impacted effectively on values under global neoliberal ideology.

Neoliberalism has encouraged a particular focus on the individual and self, reflected in the appeal to consumerism and personal empowerment. If this has diverted attention from its undermining of collectivity, it has also incidentally refocused attention on individual rights and personal agency – like NSMs – a dialectic that demands more attention.

NSM theory suggests that they are significantly different from past movements in goals and focus. Unlike other political ideologies we have considered, their primary relation is not with economic systems. Instead, they first highlighted the routine discriminations in societies beyond class, developing theories to understand them (Buechler, 1999).

Buechler argues that there is no single NSM theory but a set of variants on a general approach to 'something called the new social movement', which he defines as a 'diverse array of collective actions (displacing) the old social movement of proletarian revolution' (Buechler, op cit, p 46). Many such movements have been identified based on experience and identity, like the women's, lesbian, gay, bisexual, transgender and queer (LGBTQIA+), Black civil rights and disabled people's movements, as well as movements focused on social and rights issues like the climate change/environmental, animal rights, peace and anti-nuclear movements. These movements operate at local, national, supra-national and global levels. They are not narrowly concerned with economic issues, like the labour movement, focused on socio-economic reform or revolution, but on achieving individual and collective rights within a context of social and cultural change. They remind us of the large numbers marginalised by conventional political developments, including oppositional developments. They highlight how many groups have been spoken *for* and excluded by prevailing institutions, interests and groups – often ones they see as oppressive.

They also highlight issues of 'intersectionality', which acknowledges that identities are interrelated and multifaceted. Many people within marginalised groups face further discrimination and barriers. Such insights have often been devalued because of the crude tendency to treat difference hierarchically (Hill Collins and Bilge, 2016).

I've long been actively involved in the mental health service user/survivor movement and closely linked with the disabled people's movement. More recently, I have also formed close links with the international Mad Studies movement, which challenges traditional discourses about madness and distress. All identify as NSMs. I've also developed links with other NSMs. These affiliations can be interpreted as biases. I see them instead reflecting the value of such movements and the importance of gaining experiential knowledge of and through them.

NSMs are particularly relevant as they enable us to understand inequality as referring to more than poverty and material inequalities. We can better see how it limits the part some groups can play in the development of discussion, policy and ideologies. NSMs show that such inequalities follow from more than traditionally understood differences in political power based on socio-economic status.

What distinguishes movements based on identity and experience is that they grew out of the sense of oppression felt by those who established them. Social theorists identified the emergence in the late 20th century of a wide range of groups, which they conceived of as NSMs (Touraine, 1981; Oliver, 1996). Characteristics associated with NSMs include that they:

- remain on the margin of the political system;
- offer a critical evaluation of society;
- imply a society with different forms of valuation and distribution;
- raise issues which transcend national boundaries and have an international perspective. (Oliver, 1996, p 157; Oliver and Barnes, 2012, p 173)

The Canadian philosopher Charles Taylor developed this discussion, trying to analyse the move by such marginalised groups in Western societies to make claims for recognition of their identities and experiences based on gender, race or ethnicity (Taylor, 1992). The American feminist philosopher Nancy Fraser argues that such a 'politics of recognition' 'covers a range of approaches to group identity'. She identifies three expressions of this, which she favours uniting, saying:

> To reduce status harms and value hierarchies, one could assume a deconstructive approach aimed at destabilizing current identity categories ... other ways of transforming the status order [include] the kind of liberal universalism which tries to affirm universal humanity and, the kind of politics of difference which tries to revalue the undervalued identity. (quoted in Alldred, 1999, p 134)

While NSM theory is strongly grounded in the work of sociologists and philosophers, like Touraine, Offe and Castells, and Habermas and Guattari, it has also come in for criticism, questioning the distinctness and significance of such movements, suggesting their weakening of solidarity and devaluing of materialist issues and economic relations (Bagguley, 1992). According to Kendall, NSM theory focuses on movement culture; it also pays attention to identity and its relations with culture, ideology and politics (Kendall, 2005, p 533).

Some commentators argue that the most noticeable feature of NSMs is that they are primarily social and cultural and only secondarily political (Scott, 1990; Pichardo, 1997). This may be to misunderstand their approach to politics and the political. It ignores the fact that part of their mission is to redefine the political, as we'll see.

Connecting the personal with the political

It's the connections NSMs make between us, our lives, relations and broader ideology and formal politics that define them for many of their advocates. Thus, their stress on the rallying call of the second-wave women's movement from the late 1960s, 'the personal is political' (Hanisch, 2006). This challenges assumptions that women's traditional role as providers of sex and childcare, to be 'feminine', homemakers and supports for men, are inevitable, narrowly private issues, highlighting them also as political issues. To escape the male domination imposed by the patriarchal trap demands recognition of prevailing relations and political action to change it. Women's lives can be traced to the politics that they live under. Thus, the 'personal' problems women face have political origins and political consequences. Hanisch took part in women's therapy groups and she argued that they were a political solution, not as was suggested, apolitical, and women discussing their lives and difficulties was a political act (Hanisch, op cit). While feminists have identified different relations between the personal and political, all highlight the importance of their interconnection. This includes as political issues:

- women's restriction to the private sphere;
- women's shared, collective experience of oppression;
- the impact of politics on the personal sphere to which women tend to be restricted;
- the resulting routine restriction of women's rights – human, civil and social.

This discourse has been criticised on the grounds of its heterosexism, eurocentricity and blurring of conventional political boundaries. It's also important to acknowledge issues of intersectionality already touched on. We are talking here about the prevailing ways in which people are treated in society according to who they are and how others relate to them. Built into these relations are assumptions of worth and associated with these are attributes of status and power. These have long been hierarchical but are often structured in more complex ways than acknowledged. We know, for instance, that societies like the UK tend to be ageist, with older people frequently facing routine discrimination. Yet, it's very different for members of the House of Lords, who may be older but of privileged class, status and power.

Similarly, women may have been denied the vote in pre-1918 Britain, but any working man would have known his (inferior) position in relation to an upper-class woman, even though he might feel able to mock her under his breath. She knew she was her husband's legal property but actually lived a highly independent life beyond the experience of her working-class female equivalent. Those economically and politically powerful might be able to bend the rules, but there would be little hope of that for most ordinary people trapped in an imperialist nation-state and its prevailing value system. Those with the least power and resources, who tend to be 'the poor' are almost always the most vulnerable when it comes to conformity with prevailing values, facing the biggest barriers in self-organising (Beresford et al, 1999). That's why we shouldn't over-simplify the issues NSMs raise, and instead recognise their complex context and fully address intersectionality.

NSMs have played an invaluable part in opening up the meaning of political, encouraging us to make connections and rethink ignored or taken-for-granted relations. The interest of NSMs in identity, lifestyle and culture is rooted in concern about their political relations – how the politics we live under affect how we are regarded according to who we are in society – the power we're granted and the value given to us.

Revaluing diversity

More generally, NSMs have pioneered the recognition of the value of diversity and the importance of treating it with equality rather than perpetuating division. They've made a step difference in helping us understand that we are all different and to defend such difference. None of us is positioned outside that difference, and diversity is not something to judge. The only people and institutions that profit from devaluing diversity and resulting division are those seeking individual or collective advantage from it to advance their own excluding agendas. NSMs provide an opportunity to challenge the received messages we have been subject to – to be honest about ourselves and others instead of projecting our fears and encouraging antipathy. They help us resist pressures to judge, reject, demonise or misunderstand other groups and stay separately entrenched. They have helped us to trust our experience of others rather than what we hear about them and to value the solidarity that can come from recognising our shared interests and common struggles for our rights.

The impact of New Social Movements

The impact of 'the personal is political' and the NSM ideologies it has grown from has been far more than rhetorical. They have given us all the opportunity to reassess our lives in relation to the politics that have ruled and often constrained them. This has enabled us to question and revalue how we have been treated – and socialised to understand and treat others – from childhood onwards.

From personal experience…

This makes sense in my life, as it may in yours. We can begin to work out what has shaped our lives and attitudes. We may not live under a political tyranny, but as a child, I certainly felt subject to a personal one. This was not primarily patterned by my family but by my interactions with state and other systems. Initially, this meant state school where I quickly learned the importance of obedience and conformity – having been on the receiving end of routine injustice and bullying. For this little boy, fear was the dominant emotion. The dominant culture appeared to be based on toxic notions of masculinity, reflected in a preoccupation with competitive sport and rooted in some expectation that like previous generations, we would be conscripted into another global conflict. Indeed, barely a year has passed since then without British service people being killed in some imperial conflict, from Korea through Northern Ireland to Afghanistan.

I internalised many of the prejudices of my age. Instead of controlling childhood bullying, school seemed to harness it to keep us divided and subdued. Boys were separated from girls and any 'softening' influence they might have had, from 'infants' onwards. Nowhere since have I been force-fed as I was at primary school, nor subjected to legitimated physical violence as I was with caning at secondary school (Beresford, 2016, pp 83–4). Life has been a journey of unlearning the discriminatory lessons we were taught, trying to free myself from their damaging impact on my own understanding of myself, and working to decipher their political relations. I, like many others, have been greatly helped by being involved in NSMs.

…To broader change

NSMs have not only enabled us individually and collectively to challenge our own understandings of human roles and relationships but have also resulted in broader political, social and legal change. Thus, as Wikipedia records, the centrality of the feminist idea that the personal is political has meant that it has been 'the impetus behind many policy and law changes, including the following in England':

- legalisation of abortion (1967);
- access to NHS contraception (1961);
- access to NHS contraception regardless of marital status (1967);
- criminalisation of rape in marriage (1991, 2003);
- Married Women Property Act revision (1964) (Wikipedia, 2022).

The pressure to challenge discrimination, for equalising change in roles and relationships in society, has been an international, not to say global one across the different identity-based movements. Many caveats have to be offered:

- More progress has been made in some parts of the world than others.
- Issues of patriarchy, heterosexism and white privilege can hardly be said to have been overcome, even if significantly challenged.
- Achievements towards equality in law don't necessarily reflect achievements in reality.
- Progress is vulnerable to counter-pressures from neoliberalism's continuing economic and political power.
- In some societies, issues identified as rights in others are still illegal and severely penalised, for example, criminalisation for being gay or transgender.
- In some societies, outlawed discriminations, for example, based on caste and against Indigenous peoples are still operating.
- There is a continuing gap between outlawing discrimination based on identity and ensuring the full and equal rights of all groups.
- One consequence of liberatory progress is that the ending of one set of formal/official restrictions is replaced by the creation of others, for example, terrorism, gang violence or hate crime.

Nonetheless, NSMs' achievements are real and far beyond legislative change. Their positive impact may be uneven, especially for oppressed groups in the Global South. However, NSMs continue to have an impact on how people live their personal lives. They challenge existing inequalities and demand we re-examine them. They are changing attitudes and realities, encouraging change in understandings of self, family, gender, sexuality and ethnic relationships. They have:

- raised markers for change, highlighting issues of oppression and the need for reform;
- created new liberatory understandings of inequality and exclusion;
- internalised change in people, which is difficult to calculate and tends to be underestimated, although ultimately crucial;
- raised resistance, grounding these issues intellectually and ideologically;
- provided a basis for effective, innovative collective action;
- extended legal protection to marginalised groups in many places.

The opportunities to challenge pathologising stereotypes and rethink ourselves, encouraged by NSMs, have brought massive possibilities. They put us in a more equal position to understand the existing political system because we can escape its psychological control and achieve harmony with ourselves. Also, we don't have to devalue others to feel OK about ourselves. The neoliberal plot to divide and rule loses its power; we see things better as they are.

The actions of NSMs have encouraged a process of change, enabling progress. They had done this through both parliamentary and extra-parliamentary action. The results are embodied in national laws, international courts and global charters. They offer some safeguards that affect day-to-day practices and realities, influencing individual and collective understandings and behaviour. Such NSMs have highlighted and challenged the persistence of unequal roles and relationships in our lives, the exclusion from and marginalisation of some groups in the public sphere, and the moral panics raised against some groups. In the next chapter, we look more closely at other key NSM values and their central role in helping us change ruling politics.

10

What the new social movements can tell us

> The term 'politics' shall refer to power-structured relationships, arrangements whereby one group of persons is controlled by another ... although an ideal politics might simply be conceived of as the arrangement of human life on agreeable and rational principles from whence the entire notion of power over others should be banished ... this is not what constitutes the political as we know it, and it is to this that we must address ourselves.
>
> Kate Millett, American feminist writer and activist, *Sexual Politics*, 1970

Introduction

We live in very uncertain times. While the UK has sought to isolate itself from Europe, the damaging consequences of Brexit have highlighted our interdependency at every level. Gaza is aflame in the Middle East, but much closer to home there's a hot war in Europe between Russia and Ukraine, with no real end in sight and, like the conflict in former Yugoslavia, reflecting unfinished business relating to the Soviet Union's creation and collapse. All this takes place in the broader context of the large-scale global political and socio-economic damage done by neoliberalism's global dominance. The gap between such political values and those demanded of the general public under lockdown was brought into sharp relief by the UK 2022 'Partygate' scandal, with senior politicians laying down one law – while practising another – partying, while nationwide, families had to leave loved ones to die alone (Elgot, 2022).

The emerging struggle

These are also contradictory times, given the increasingly liberatory direction of travel of the new social movements (NSMs). As formal politics have become more antagonistic, unequal and divisive, these movements have been developing alongside as a rising challenge to inequality, division and exclusion in our personal roles and relations, and as a force for sustainability in our world. The resulting gulf between our formal and personal politics seems to be getting bigger and bigger.

In the UK it's difficult to think of any time where this same trend has been so strong, except immediately after the Second World War, when there had been much freeing of personal roles and relationships with regard to gender, ethnicity and sexuality. Think of the radically changed wartime roles of women, the arrival of many Black Americans and their significant cultural impact, and the temporary liberation of gay men and others under the emergency conditions of war. Post-war, politicians, church leaders and associated social commentators led a massive reaction, anxious to reimpose discriminatory values and force the emancipatory genie back into the bottle. Thus, the moral panic against divorce and gay men like scientist Alan Turing and the re-emergence of Mosleyite fascism (Beresford, 2016, p 97).

The widening gulf in values

While initially, this book focused on the unstoppable dominance of neoliberalism, what we can now see is another equally significant struggle. This is manifesting itself in an increasing gap between the personal and the political reflected in the discrepancy between the values and behaviours associated with each. This gap is generating increasing conflict. It isn't a helpful basis for stability in either the political or personal arenas, the private or public spheres, or for cohesion between the two as they jostle uncomfortably.

This conflict can be seen as a further negative consequence of neoliberal ideology's dominance, with the rise of the NSMs at least partly a reaction to it. However, they should also be seen as a radical development in their own right – going far beyond the routine preoccupations of our formal daily UK politics which seem to have lurched from one firefighting activity to another, whether it's unsafe cladding on high-rise buildings, jeopardising the UN rights of disabled people or ministers accepting freebies. The same pattern of political short-termism has predominated.

The NSMs, however, have been the inspiration for sometimes breathtaking change. This includes forcing our attention on:

- *Decolonisation*: for example, of education: rethinking and reconstructing curricula and research that preserve the Euro-centred, colonial lens … challenging the institutional hierarchy on knowledge and Western framework (London Metropolitan University, undated a and b).
- *Trans issues*: helping all to understand what these mean and securing people's rights who might identify in these terms … including someone who feels that their internal sense of their own gender doesn't match their assigned sex at birth. … 'Transgender' is also an umbrella term for diverse communities whose gender doesn't match their assigned sex, including those who occasionally wear the clothes of a different sex but don't take steps to medically transition and who don't feel their gender can be

categorised. ... This includes non-binary people who don't subscribe to the binary notions of gender – that is, that humans should be organised into either male or female categories, with prescriptive roles and identities based on external genitalia. That's not to say being non-binary means placing your gender identity somewhere between male and female; there's no one single way to be non-binary (Burns, 2020).
- *Mass extinction*: Extinction Rebellion is an international movement that uses non-violent civil disobedience to try to halt mass extinction and the risk of social collapse (Extinction Rebellion UK, 2022).

Reversing the telescope

Just as neoliberalism has pushed us towards more unequal, disempowering roles and relationships and damaging the planet, NSMs have been pulling us in the opposite direction towards more equal roles and relationships and sustainability. As Kate Millett's quote at the beginning of this chapter highlights, NSMs like the women's movement have redefined the boundaries of politics to include the personal (Millett, 1970). Neoliberalism is unremarkable in advancing alienating, unequal roles and relationships. It's a broader problem linked with formal politics more generally. While we have seen neoliberal politics seek to divide and alienate us from each other, the NSMs have challenged judgementalism as a disempowering and divisive form of self-defence.

What can we learn from personal roles and relationships and efforts to equalise and humanise them that might help us develop more egalitarian and humanistic politics? If often inferred, this question is infrequently asked. Yet, it's at the heart of Audre Lorde's famous comment that, 'we will not rebuild the master's house with the master's tools'. That's to say, a politics based on discriminatory values is very unlikely to achieve its antithesis. She thought it was problematic to have 'any discussion of feminist theory without examining our many differences, and without a significant input from poor ... Black and Third World women, and lesbians'. To do so, she wrote, 'weakens any feminist discussion of the personal and the political'.

She had been asked to speak about difference at a conference where the input of Black and lesbian feminists was marginalised. For her, it was as if this was a natural consequence and a 'sad' and unacceptable outcome of living in a 'country where racism, sexism and homophobia are inseparable'. As she put it:

> What does it mean when the tools of a racist patriarchy are used to examine the fruits of that same patriarchy? It means that only the most narrow parameters of change are possible and allowable.

She saw differences among women as crucial to forging their personal power:

Photograph 10.1: Audre Lorde

Note: A self-described 'black, lesbian, mother, warrior, poet', a pioneer of the women's movement, writer, activist and intersectional feminist 1934–92.
Source: K. Kendall, Flickr https://www.flickr.com/photos/42401725@N00/2733757260 available under creative commons CC BY 2.0 licence

> Only within that interdependency of different strengths, acknowledged and equal, can the power to seek new ways of being in the world generate, as well as the courage and sustenance to act where there are no charters. (Lorde, 1984)

Given the impact neoliberal politics have on personal relations, behaviour and values, Lorde's comments raise a further question. Wouldn't it also be helpful to explore this relationship from the *opposite* end? What might we learn *from* personal roles and relationships and current NSM pressures to equalise them, to transform formal politics and roles and relations associated with them? What can NSMs teach us about this? Not only is the personal political, but the political is personal.

Audre Lorde's quote offers an unparalleled insight. It demands we look again more closely at that defining mantra of the women's movement, the personal is political. She seems to be saying that it works both ways – the political is also personal. It's a two-way street, but much less seems to have been written about this. Yet, if formal politics' superstructure affects the nature of our relationships with each other, then surely the latter relationships also have a bearing on such politics? If we want to transform these politics, won't we need first to transform these relationships with each other? Otherwise, how will we escape the master's house?

Perhaps this has been too difficult a question to be asked widely. Maybe it has, but been drowned out by the power of conventional politics and the noise from neoliberalism's proponents. That's hardly an argument to ignore this path. Instead, it may highlight the importance of adopting it more determinedly.

If we subject political roles and relations to the equalising pressures NSMs have to personal ones, what might we achieve? Put differently, if we focus on doing politics differently, trying to transform them, as we have our personal roles and relations, could this help bring about the change being sought in formal politics? Could it halt neoliberalism's apparently unstoppable progress?

There are already signs of a growing interest in and activity around such a move. We can see it in the discussions already touched on, which have increasingly foregrounded ideas of 'wellbeing' and 'happiness' in politics and as measures of societies' success. For example, in his book, *The Kindness Fix*, educator Jason Wood, drawing on the work of many pioneers, makes the case for greater *compassion* in public life, highlighting the growing international movement for more humanity in public policy and politics (Wood, 2024).

We can't predict outcomes, but surely it would be worth exploring an approach based on working to equalise politics' social relations as a strategy for political change. Arguably, this is what many NSMs have been doing. This would not only focus at a macro level, as some grand theories and ideologies have done historically but at a micro one, up close and personal. It could also explore bringing together the different struggles of such NSMs on the same basis of equality and anti-discrimination, challenging traditional hierarchies.

There are two continuing concerns here. First, how might we move towards such a new politics, and second, what might they look like?

We start with the lessons we have learned from recognising that *the personal is political* and the way that the two are interlinked. Then we explore more carefully the implications of the fact that the political is also personal, in the sense that it's rooted in our understandings of personal roles and relationships. If we're committed to relationships that are truly anti-discriminatory and egalitarian, how would we reconcile our formal politics with this? How might we renew them by drawing on what we've learned and are doing to challenge inequality and disempowerment in our personal roles and relations?

Key New Social Movement values

Two more value-based characteristics closely linked with NSMs demand attention. These are their association with:

- participation and participatory approaches to their activities and approach;
- sustainability and the future of the planet and its environment.

NSMs highlight these principles to different degrees and in different ways. The second is central to the anti-nuclear and environmental movements. The two principles tend to interact with each other, influencing NSMs' processes and goals. These are not isolated movements – they all connect – but not necessarily as much as might be hoped or expected. All their principles, discussed in the last chapter, treating diversity with equality, participation and sustainability play a part in their distinct politics and in their methods to achieve them.

These last two principles help us make better sense of NSMs' potential for bringing about change in traditional politics. We will develop this in the book's third part when we focus on key ways for making political change. To start, let's consider participation.

Participation

Many people with marginalised identities have united within NSMs to fight for equality and speak for themselves. Historically, others have spoken for them, often reinforcing their exclusion. We've seen women patronised and psychiatrised, LGBTQIA+ people rejected and criminalised, older and disabled people marginalised and institutionalised, and Black and minoritised people infantilised and oppressed. This time around, through their own NSMs, they have been able to act for themselves. Sometimes for the first time, marginalised peoples and groups have been able to work collectively to develop their own understandings of themselves, each other and their place in the world to challenge dominant narratives perpetuating their disempowerment.

We have also seen a regular pattern in the emergence of such NSMs, first of the most empowered members of groups raising their issues and then being challenged by others facing multiple oppressions, demanding the opening up of agendas to include their perspectives to make possible truly inclusive and diverse involvement. As Audre Lorde put it in her famous paper:

> Within the interdependence of mutual (nondominant) differences lies that security which enables us to descend into the chaos of knowledge and return with true visions of our future, along with the concomitant power to effect those changes which can bring that future into being. Difference is that raw and powerful connection from which our personal power is forged. (Lorde, op cit)

Participation for members of NSMs means having a direct, effective voice to effect change. People talk about 'making a difference', 'having a real say', rejecting 'tokenism' and their demands being 'rubber stamped'. These aim to be democratic movements and organisations, working for democratic change, frequently based on a model of participatory democracy (Martin, 2004; Beresford, 2019). Those primarily concerned with challenging people's oppressed identities have placed particular emphasis on such direct involvement compared with others with more issue-based concerns like [the] peace and environmental movements. This is because they are in every sense demanding to 'speak for themselves', rather than issues that might seem to be external. Thus, we see the special insights and developments in theory-building in this area from the Black, women's, disabled people's, survivors' and LGBTQIA+ movements. This compares with the increasing daring and experiment in how the environmental and anti-nuclear movements have sought to generate impact, even if essentially retaining the traditional paradigm of using mainstream media and exerting pressure on the public and representatives. But that doesn't mean there aren't significant cross-overs between such movements and major overlaps in their memberships (Jordan and Lent, 1999; Todd and Taylor, 2004; Meyer, 2021).

What's also interesting is that while such NSMs are poles apart from neoliberalism, when it comes to participation there initially appears to be a meeting point. Participation is a core concern of both neoliberal ideology and its mirror opposite NSMs. However, they place very different interpretations on it. The goal of NSMs is a radical redistribution of power and a push for participatory democracy. For the political new right, similar rhetoric conceals a continuing commitment to the market. It is not the balance of power or its redistribution with which it's concerned, but the old market rhetoric that the 'consumer is king'. Such involvement as there is, is that which free marketeers preach as forthcoming from our role as consumers, not as citizens. The interest here is more in the marketisation of public policy than any extension of control to the citizen as a public service consumer.

A common language conceals radically different understandings. This has led to much conflict and distrust over the extension of provisions for popular involvement in public policy. A market model of consumer involvement is very different from a struggle for citizens' say and rights. This is another expression of the massive gap between NSMs' commitment to involvement and that of populist neoliberal politics. Perhaps most important here is articulating this difference to avoid continuing misunderstanding. It is difficult to see how Kate Millett's definition of politics, set out earlier, which highlights the imposition of power over others will ever be challenged without the inclusive participation that enables people, individually and collectively, to challenge other people's and institutions' power over them (Millett, 1970, chapter 2).

Sustainability

Sustainability is not just a goal of NSMs specifically dedicated to it; they've done much of the advanced thinking about it in association with progressive university departments, not-for-profit organisations and related think tanks. As has already been highlighted, sustainability is a core commitment *across* NSMs. Values are not siloed here, as becomes clear. This is exemplified by ecological feminism which seeks to connect the demands of the women's movement with those of the environmental movement. The aim is to develop a world view and bring about a world which challenges prevailing socio-economic and conceptual structures of domination (Warren and Cheney, 1991).

While by now many of us may have a sense of what's meant by sustainability, it's helpful to get a clearer picture of where the debate has got to. Notions of sustainability rest on three pillars: its environmental, economic and social dimensions. The environmental movement has generated public concern about the human impact on the environment, climate change, loss of biodiversity and pollution. Dominant commitments to 'economic growth' stand at odds with the commitment to sustainability, and usually this has been presented as a conflict between 'us' and the planet rather than the consequence of a free-for-all for the most powerful at the expense of the rest of us, particularly the Global South.

Like most big ideas, 'sustainability' has come in for criticism. One is that it is an impossible goal to achieve because of the detrimental impacts of humans on the environment. The other is that it's a vague portmanteau idea. Neither of these objections really holds against the environmental movement's demand for a more urgent response to the worsening, strongly evidenced problems identified. It's also difficult to see how NSMs, committed to diversity and participation, could ignore such an overarching issue as sustainability and stay true to their other defining values. On the other hand, as has been seen, neoliberal politics and economics have made it increasingly difficult to progress the 2030 Agenda for Sustainable Development with its 17 sustainable development goals.

Our examination of personal politics, the struggles and aspirations of people and groups to be revalued for their lives and achievements in the context of NSMs, highlights the gulf that's developed between them and the formal politics that rule over us. We raised the question of how exploring more equal and inclusive personal politics may help in the renewal of formal politics dramatically shaped as the latter has been by neoliberal ideology. The challenge of the NSMs: rejecting unequal, excluding roles and relationships, addressing inclusion and diversity, changing and democratising forms of collective action and building from the bottom up, has been our starting point for trying to work out what a different politics might look like and how we might move towards it. Forms of collective action committed to change in process and aims, the feminist, Black civil rights, LGBTQIA+, disabled people's and Mad Studies movements, therapy groups, empowerment processes and self-organisation, all offer insights for ways forward. Both concerns – change in political process and objectives – currently seem enormous issues, possibly even unattainable, as personal, social and international tensions rise in our world and its future seems increasingly uncertain. However, we have no alternative but to address this task, and the major changes that seem to be taking place in our understanding of and relations with each other offer some hope of making progress. We'll turn in the final part of this book to explore possible next steps in attempting such a rethink. First, though, in the next chapter, we consider the importance of developing truly *equal ways* of reconnecting with each other if we're to transform policy and politics.

11

A new watchword – 'only connect' on *equal terms*

> Have you ever been a leaf and fallen from your tree in autumn and been really puzzled about it? That's the feeling.
>
> T.E. Lawrence (Lawrence of Arabia) writing to (his friend, the artist) Eric Kennington about being retired, May 1935

Introduction

This book has highlighted several political, ideological, social, economic and cultural themes. These have included pressure to rising inequality and poverty, to short-term personal profit, environmental damage, disempowerment, colonisation and alienation. We have also heard about powerful counter-themes: valuing diversity and treating it with equality, struggling against discrimination and for sustainability, for equal individual and collective rights and recognition, and for more say in what happens to us in society. If the politics over us has become harsher and more individualising, the personal politics between us seems set in a kinder direction, with more emphasis on egalitarian roles and relationships. Bottom-up movements continue to challenge top-down formal politics. Pressures for participation battle with the most powerful rekindling of populism since the days of pre-war fascism and state communism.

The plea to connect

Current pressures are also reminders of much earlier calls for change and of one particular form they took. Here we may find clues for achieving change for the future. One enduring strand has been framed in terms of *connection* and *reconnection*, highlighting separations and inequalities of their own times. During a period, as now, when the gulf between personal and formal political values seemed ever to be widening, that past precedent may offer insights worthy of reconsideration. That's not to say times are the same – although some similarities are to be seen – but they may help us find our own 21st-century insights, building on earlier ones.

One of the broader effects and expressions of neoliberalism is the way it seems both accidentally and deliberately to disconnect us from each other. This takes many forms. Neoliberalism restricts international movements.

Its commodification of housing limits where and with whom we live, its marketisation of education shapes who we grow up with and how we are socialised, and the restrictions it imposes on social mobility limit who we will work with, get to know and even form intimate and partner relationships with. We've seen the powerful lines of division neoliberalism creates in a place like the UK, between citizens and non-citizens, between rich and poor, disabled and non-disabled people.

This theme of reconnection is worth checking out. Connection has been described by the literary critic Alan Jacobs as 'the great task of modernist aesthetics': Discussing translation, he quotes poet T.S. Eliot:

> The ordinary man (sic) falls in love, or reads Spinoza, and these two experiences have nothing to do with each other, or with the noise of the typewriter or the smell of cooking; in the mind of the poet these experiences are always forming new wholes. (Jacobs, 1997)

E.M. Forster

This theme of reconnection is to be found more in Western arts and social sciences than politics and political theory. Thus, it's been associated with fields of activity particularly interested in exploring relations. The first and perhaps definitive use of the idea 'only connect' takes place in novelist E.M. Forster's 1910 key work, *Howard's End* (Forster, 1910). This is perhaps not surprising given the essential concern of the novel form to make connections between the personal and the political. It's also relevant to note that as a gay man, out only to his friends, just 15 years after Oscar Wilde's imprisonment for sodomy, Forster can himself be seen as coming from a heavily threatened perspective. What he said was specific:

> She would only point out the salvation that was latent in his own soul, and in the soul of every man. Only connect! That was the whole of her sermon. Only connect the prose and the passion, and both will be exalted, and human love will be seen at its height. Live in fragments no longer. Only connect and the beast and the monk, robbed of the isolation that is life to either, will die. (op cit, p 184)

However, his meanings went much further. While the central issue of the novel is the connection of two different families, as critics have commented since it meant much more:

> The idea of 'only connect' can be traced throughout *Howards End*. Forster employs personal relations to emphasize the importance of connection and mutual understanding, but does also, on a more

abstract level, write about the connection of the past and the present. (Schuller, 2001)

Indeed, connections and disconnections were increased by the decline of the British empire, tense relationships in Europe and emerging clashes with changing moralities. It works at different levels – personal and political, 'highlighting the need to connect what has become disconnected' (op cit, 2001).

It's these antagonisms which also give this theme of reconnection particular resonance for our own age. Significantly, the period when Forster was writing was to be dramatically ended by the cataclysm of the First World War and also was associated with massive scientific innovation and social change – like our own times. As the US sociologists Mary Virnoche and Gary Marx have argued, in *Howards End*:

> Forster and his characters struggle with the dilemmas of making connections in a Victorian liberal-humanist period that preceded the First World War. While the epigraph 'only connect' suggests a positive imperative for making ties, it also implies despair for the difficulties of making those connections. His story weaves in and out of the tension between ideological visions of connection and the obstacles created by an often hostile world. (Virnoche and Marx, 2024)

T.S. Eliot

The next conspicuous apostle of connection was the American poet T.S. Eliot who painted a bleak picture of its antithesis in his epic poem *The Waste Land*.

On Margate Sands.
I can connect
Nothing with nothing.
The broken fingernails of dirty hands.
My people humble people who expect
Nothing (Eliot, 1922, p 301)

He wrote this at a time of particular personal difficulty in 1921, while he was recovering from a 'nervous breakdown' (Moss, 2009). It's a poem about disillusionment, lack of human relationships, dystopian war and politics. It's difficult to pin down exactly what it's about, 'but the sense of dislocation and despair ... is tangible' (Adams, 2014). Eliot is decrying the lack of connection and pleading for something else. When, almost a century later, Margate residents were brought together to produce a collectively curated exhibition about the poem, the writer Mae Losasso concluded cautiously that a buzzword for the exhibition 'would be fragmentation. Universally the term seems to have become a bye-word for modernist art' (Losasso, 2018). This rings powerful bells with our postmodern focus and brings us to a third key discussion.

Richard Hoggart

This comes from the English sociologist Richard Hoggart. There's a direct continuity here. Hoggart references both Forster and Eliot in his 1957 text *Uses of Literacy*, described by the *Observer* as 'A vivid inside view of working-class culture and one of the most influential books of the post-war era' (Hoggart, 2009, end cover). It's difficult to overstate its significance in UK socio-cultural life, from A-level set text to praise as a 'truly essential (book) about British society' (Hanley in Hoggart, 2009, p ix).

If Forster and Eliot aspired to be forward-looking, this is a perspective that is undoubtedly looking back, setting the author's best-selling vision of the 'close-knit values of Northern England's vanishing working class communities' against his paternalistic fears about the 'arrival of a new, homogenous, US-influenced "mass culture"' (op cit, end cover). We should remind ourselves that he was actually writing just six years before the Beatles' US 'invasion', Mary Quant-inspired fashion and the UK-born 'swinging sixties'. He was also writing under conditions familiar to his predecessors (and us) – the shadow of war, economic decline, social division and fast technological change. He shares Eliot's doom-ridden vision without Forster's sense of possibility. Thus, he wrote:

> 'Only connect' said E.M. Forster, thinking of the conflict between the claims of the inner and the outer life. 'Only conform', whispers the prevailing wind today … the majority are probably right, and you ought to go along with them. … The strongest argument against modern mass entertainments is not that they debase taste … but that they over-excite it … and finally kill it. (op cit, pp 172–3)

I'd again remind readers of John, Paul, George and Ringo, Aretha Franklin, Bob Dylan, Dusty Springfield, Stevie Wonder, and so on, and in what a creative period Hoggart was actually writing. There seems to have been little critical re-evaluation of Hoggart's book since, although it is long overdue. The historian Tracey Loughran concluded that such scholarship, while claiming 'to speak for the subordinated and dispossessed … replicated the messages of dominant cultural forms and therefore unwittingly reinforced elements of existing power relations' (Loughran, 2016, p 46). Stuart Hall, the Jamaican-British sociologist and cultural theorist identified *The Uses of Literacy* as a founding text of cultural studies (Hall, 2007). However, its companion text, published in 1971, Hoggart's BBC *Reith Lectures*, even more directly entitled 'Only Connect', offers greater insights into his mindset (Hoggart, 1971). They emphasise Hoggart's limited viewpoint. The book's sexist grammar and limited consideration of difference give it an antediluvian feel.

Hoggart looked at differences between national cultures when it would be helpful to look more closely at intranational differences beyond class – Hoggart's particular focus – at least extending consideration to what have become the 'protected characteristics' (EHRC, 2021). He talked about our 'common life' (p 99), but that seems more illusory as each year goes by, epitomised, as we have seen, by former Prime Minister Cameron's 2012 assertion that 'we are all in it together'.

At one point Hoggart noted that:

> It would be pleasant to think that all the talk about communication today reflected and respected this diversity and richness, but it rarely does. (op cit, p 99)

His own analysis didn't seem to either. He referred repeatedly to men and 'he' 'him' and 'his' in his text, which generally meant white men. He focused on national positions, without investigating differences according to status, power, ethnicity or other expressions of diversity. He asked if 'we are really more in touch' now (p 100), but left the 'we' with all its exclusions and assumptions unexamined. Is it really possible to talk of Britain as a whole society that can 'talk within itself as a whole'? He seemed ambivalent.

This seems all the more anomalous when we remind ourselves that by 1971, when he was giving his Reith lectures, the second-wave feminist movement was well underway, the US Black Civil Rights movement had already achieved high visibility, gay liberation movements had begun to emerge and there were already the first flowerings of the disabled people's and mental health service user/survivor movements. It seems amazing that so little attention was paid in these lectures or his 1957 book to issues of difference and the oppressions related to them – especially given the brief he set himself:

> To look at the great variety of ways we have of getting in touch with each other, and at the assumptions which lie behind those efforts to get in touch about what our relations to each other should be. (Hoggart, op cit, p 13)

This seems to prefigure the preoccupations of NSMs with equalising our roles and relationships and at one with this book's ambition to renew formal politics by learning from such insights. Nevertheless, while Hoggart addressed broader structures of communication, education and economic development, these were distant from the heavily loaded structures like the think tanks, electoral consultants, and the media proprietors and influencers we now have to deal with. We'll have to find ways of getting beyond them if they are not to mediate our conversations.

Renewing our thinking for the 21st century

Hoggart was emphatic:

> We can connect, we have to connect; not by ... the solemnities of most attempts at 'international understanding' but by a fully-faced and felt realisation of common qualities, the ribs of the universal human grammar. (Hoggart, op cit, front fly leaf)

Such insistence on connection may be a necessary but certainly not sufficient condition for the change sought by Hoggart and here. It's clearly important under neoliberalism to highlight this issue of reconnecting rather than being divided and isolated. But it's unlikely to be enough to talk of 'only connect'. We have seen neoliberalism pulling us apart, increasing horizontal and vertical inequalities between us, and NSMs working to bring us back together more equally. This is something different. Maybe what we should be saying for this age is 'only connect – trying to challenge exclusions and inequalities' encouraged by our present politics. We need an *inclusive* approach to connecting that:

- builds on NSMs' concerns with addressing difference with equality;
- reveals how electoral processes can seek to misdirect us;
- challenges ways in which dominant structures of power and communication undermine our relations with others.

It's a massive aspiration, but one we can see beginning to happen within and between NSMs. A crucial lesson learned from them, which now needs restating, is that the personal is political and the political impacts on the nature of the personal. So, while Hoggart reminds us of the importance of 'how we get in touch with each other', he has less to say about how prevailing communication structures affect this, and critically, how we can deal with them.

The lives of all these three men, Forster, Eliot and Hoggart, highlight contradictions between them and their messages:

- Forster's privilege meant his reality was of routinely unequal relationships.
- Eliot highlighted connection, but his epic was obscure and he was bigoted (Kaveney, 2014).

- Hoggart spent his life escaping the working-class culture he ostensibly venerated.

This highlights the limits of their personal politics. By contrast, Forster's friend T.E. Lawrence spent much of his adult life living humbly in the military to compensate for what he saw as his imperialist betrayal of the Arab revolt. His efforts and experience even led to official reform in RAF recruits' conditions (Lawrence, 1955). As he wrote to his friend Eric Kennington, enforced retirement felt like a severing of the connections he so much valued, and with it, purpose (Garnett, 1938).

Those three major 20th-century figures may help point us to a way out of the political logjam of the early 21st century by focusing on reconnecting with each other, but they don't offer a detailed road map. We have to work that out for ourselves, not least because 'only connect' needs to be reconceived for our times in terms of social inclusion and equality. We need to pay much greater attention to:

- the increased pressures to disconnection and challenging these;
- who we try to connect with, how and why;
- challenging exclusions and inequalities in connection.

Each of our three thinkers, the novelist, poet and sociologist, was writing at a time of massive change. These were watersheds in communication technology. All were times of change affecting people's contact with each other for better and worse. It's hardly surprising that discourse about better connecting took place at such times of conflict, change and technological innovation. The picture book emphasis was on Boys' Own inventions, increasing mobility, speed and the bridging of distance – express trains, ocean liners, intercontinental passenger planes, rockets – breaking records, connecting empires. Also supposedly making the world a smaller place, communication developments – corresponding to the periods of our three pioneers – were generating enormous change. First film, telephone and telegraph, then talkies, radio and television. Now it's smartphones, internet, email, social media and AI changing everything. The pace is constantly accelerating, with these developments supposedly 'bringing us closer together', yet suspicions have been growing that this isn't really so. This, we saw earlier, is picked up in the latest expression of interest in *reconnecting* from US 'thought leader' Noreena Hertz, who connects increasing concerns about people's isolation with neoliberalism and new technology (Hertz, 2021).

Such suspicions of technology were earlier fed, sometimes paternalistically, by commentators like Hoggart, concerned about the homogenising, imperialist culture imposed by US media. He warned against accepting their messages uncritically, advising us to 'reinterpret those readings for ourselves' (op cit, p 25). As he warned 'talking to others begins with talking to yourself and with being yourself in talking' (p 29).

It's a welcome caution for our times, when, neoliberal media have gained so much skill in alienating us from ourselves, our experience and each other. Now the issue has gone beyond the *influencing* that bothered Hoggart and his contemporaries to a more far-reaching process of external mediation. Our views are not so much affected as *reshaped* by new structures of communication and control.

The consequences are extreme. As our lives are damaged by rising prices, working hours and public health problems, reduced public services and wages, enough of us in the UK, for example, seem to have been persuaded to see the solutions narrowly in terms of voting 'Brexit', imposing anti-immigrant policies and attacking those even worse off than ourselves. If anything, these 'remedies' have made things worse, weakening the economy, narrowing the labour force and increasing division. So, in the UK's 2019 general election a 'red wall' of longstanding Labour voters in Northern constituencies, for the first time turned 'blue' and helped return a Conservative government, which, with its associated media and consultants had manipulated their vote. This can only be a cause for concern for anyone with a commitment to democracy, and at the time of writing, its legacy continues with the scale of the popular vote for the fascistic Reform party.

Challenging racist exclusion and discrimination

Perhaps two of the most contentious developments that have taken place challenging traditional assumptions about identity and understanding, subjecting them to particular scrutiny, have concerned issues of *white privilege* and *decolonisation*. Neoliberal ideologues and media have attacked both with particular vehemence and dismissed their advocates as 'woke' or 'snowflakes'. Both are particularly important for challenging oppression, building alliances and connecting with each other equally. Speaking in the context of madness and existing approaches to 'mental illness', but with much wider relevance, Colin King, a Black survivor research activist and founder of the Whiteness and Race Equality Network, talked with me about them:

> White privilege is important because the notion of whiteness doesn't really exist, it's a mythology, it's been constructed historically, and what comes with whiteness is a set of values that makes one race inferior to another. It's embedded in our political systems, in the dreadful impact of hundreds of years of slavery. It took away from African people their ability to define their reality, their social system, their own psychiatry. So, the legacy of that is that they were defined by a 'reality' that actually dehumanises 'the other' and puts them in a role of subservience.

I'm not criticizing white people, I'm criticizing the process of 'whiteness' and it's not necessarily only white people, but also other communities that can buy into that system of domination. It leads to entitlement – people feel entitled to claim ownership to a system, that their reality is the only reality looking at the world. As a practitioner and someone who was sectioned under the Mental Health Act, I see it vividly in how people activate those privileges and you're not able to challenge whiteness. It's not visible, not claimed, not named, it's part of the madness. To see it and name it, makes you the victim, the disorder. They exercise their control over you through this notion of white superiority.

Most of our (psychiatric) founding fathers believed very strongly in eugenics. So, I'm really angry we're currently culturally blinded not to see that there are opportunities not just to decolonize, but to deconstruct and destroy the legacies of those things that had a major impact on the psyche of Black communities, but also the psyche of white practitioners unaware that they are practising racist things because of the systems, science and values which they accept. It's also legalized in our legislation as part of our neoliberal approach to 'mental health', when Thatcher came in and produced a commercialized system which re-enacted the power of whiteness to make Black people a slave again, by making calculations of what we were worth. It's embedded in our counselling, our psychological theories, our child care. Black people are much more likely to be diagnosed schizophrenic, to be admitted to psychiatric hospitals, to become part of the criminal justice system – as if there's something about us as the dysfunctional person unable to adopt those white values. Whiteness pathologises Black people.

Now it's a privilege to be white, but it's also a privilege to use your whiteness in the right way. It's not about things being white, it's about things constructed as whiteness. Whiteness constructs reality. That's the problem we've had. White people get offended when I talk about white privilege. They are white so they think you are talking about them as privileged. They are white so they have privilege – but they do. You can't get away from that. Being white doesn't stop people having experiences of discrimination others may suffer. But they have the privilege of being white, which means you can use that to reinforce cultural differences.

That's the great problem that (Frantz) Fanon talks about, privileging whiteness, makes you want to be white to fit in. And I think that's where the madness come in, when you are trying to fit in, where I believe you adopt a whole system of dehumanization – want to be bleached, etc., adopt the values of whiteness.

I want to work across the colour line, it's important, to see how these processes are affecting us when we work together and we look at each other and make decisions about each other. That's the challenge. Can we come together and look at how racism is being activated, when one is privileged and one is not; when one is black and one is not. What are the implications?

Some people will have to get to the first stage to understand what whiteness is and how it affects them and may give them privileges. They may have to sacrifice some of their privileges, to go across and work across that line, which can be very difficult. Not many white people I know understand what the notion of whiteness is in their lives. So, what do white people need to do to challenge white privilege when they work with other people? That's why I set up the Whiteness and Race Equality Group. It's for white people to all sit down and begin to look at that and before we interrogate race, we have to interrogate how we construct each other.

It's also about reshaping generations of people and all those racialized perspectives. It's very difficult. It's not just a challenge for white people, it's a challenge for us as Black people, if we are really going to change things and I think it is the same around gender and class.

As a lived experience Black man, I'm at the bottom of the class system. Sometimes being a lived experience person (as a mental health service user) is worse than being Black. If I say lived experience, automatically I am relegated to dysfunctional, someone who has been sectioned. If I say Black, I've still got the possibility that people will hear me as an individual. Put those things together, it's a recipe for disaster! I was a social worker, a manager, a commissioner, a researcher – all those attributes are relegated when you identify as having lived experience – they are no longer important.

White privilege for me is people standing up at a meeting and saying I think that's racist. That's a white privilege. The real privilege is that you can use your whiteness to challenge how other people are treated in the system and I don't see many white people using that privilege. And that makes it easier for me as a victim of those processes, to work in that colour line. The responsibility of white privilege is to stand up for people oppressed by it. Privilege is a very complex thing, held and given to different people according to their status.

I think decolonization is realizing the way in which certain people have adopted values, decisions and political perspectives based on views of the world that become scientized; how this emerged at one particular time of slavery and the colonial period when western society – the Enlightenment – produced a set of ideas about cultural other, about cultural superiority, which validated their position in the world.

> What we really need to do is look at what things are really important to decolonize that will have the most effect and are most damaging for Black people's lives. Also, to explore ideas that may be useful to reconceptualize race – things like the unconscious with Fanon – and understand it – in a liberating way, ideas about shared ideas and values – which I think is very difficult. Do we have the power to decolonize schizophrenia, the definition of 'mental disorder'? No. I think if we as people with lived experience were able to decolonise them, then that would be the biggest outcome for race inequality. One last thing, how the economic framework reinforces white privilege. The 1960s are for me a really important period to get back to. I think now we are at the worst moment in the history of neoliberalism. We are in an economic slave system now. (Personal communication with Colin King, November 2023)

Colin King's message is powerful but nuanced and complex. It's also clear. Centring these two ideas to challenge the discriminatory status quo has a key role to play both in surfacing and countering inequality and in building equal alliances to overcome it.

Beyond communication

The 20th-century call to connect and its 21st-century successor suggested here, to connect equally and inclusively, aren't just about revisiting communication but a much bigger task. A much broader set of forces are at work dividing and undermining us, which demands we work to:

- decipher if and how formal politics divide and make us unequal;
- find our own ways to connect, not relying on existing/'their' channels;
- explore our different and unequal potential and opportunities to reconnect;
- challenge exclusions and treat diversity with equality;
- listen to ourselves and each other, not just 'them' and their versions of 'us'.

Next steps

To bring down 'the master's house', we must use different tools. What would this mean if we develop our own processes to achieve our self-defined aims and objectives? It is likely to include:

- critiquing contemporary communication, highlighting its limitations and exclusions;
- working towards inclusive, equal communication and language;
- moving towards inclusive learning and education;

- developing our own inclusive knowledges;
- finding better ways to work equally together;
- renewing our understandings of 'solidarity';
- moving to inclusive action: building from the bottom, challenging the top.

That means equipping and supporting *everyone* to be an effective part of democracy rather than ignoring the inequalities and barriers now facing many. To do this, in the book's third and final part, we draw on the experience of many NSMs and struggles, mindful of their intersections, drawing on experiential knowledge and campaigning for involvement, inclusion and equality.

PART III

Building a politics of inclusive connection

Part III of the book focuses on bringing about change in the politics and ideologies that shape our lives by finding ways for us all to reconnect with each other. What might be needed to make that possible and where might it take us? We can expect to find ourselves needing to rethink almost all the ways we do things if we are to achieve our aims and include everyone. Here the book takes us through a range of key, often neglected issues, where we need to do this if we are to challenge the taken-for-granted exclusions of both mainstream politics and attempts to change them.

12

What's wrong with the new communication?

> Our societies have faced other institutions that imposed catastrophic consequences on people and society, such as human slavery and child labor. It was understood eventually that there is no bargaining.
>
> Shoshana Zuboff, social psychologist and Harvard professor (Zuboff, 2022)

Introduction

That 20th-century mantra, 'only connect' is about many things but, ultimately, it has to be about *communication* – at least initially.

The paradox of current communication

Ironically, in a period headlined an 'age of communication', in an 'increasingly interconnected world' (Edwards et al, 2019), 'bringing us together', where innovation has been breathtaking in scale and pace, we're still talking about the problem of connecting. Why? I'm suggesting that at its heart is the increasing 21st-century aspiration to connect on inclusive and equal terms and that our communication systems are failing to do this and may actually be obstructing it. This is the starting point for our examination of reconnection as key to renewing formal politics. Generally speaking, 'we' – the majority – don't own the means of communication and may be unable to change that, but we can rethink how we might challenge this in future.

This draws us back to the issue at this book's heart: the growing gap between our personal and formal politics, specifically between our need to communicate and the prevailing politics of communication.

The technological leap

At one level, the capacity for human communication is unparalleled. In a world of laptops and smartphones, mass intercontinental travel, Zoom and Teams, most of us have an unprecedented capacity to be in touch with each other. This applies globally – to a small village in Africa – just as it's taken for granted in the Global North. Niger, for example, has one of the lowest levels of telephone coverage in Africa, with only about half the population covered by mobile broadband. But now the World Bank has supported its 'smart villages for rural growth and digital inclusion project' to increase access to cell phone and broadband services in rural areas. The bank is proud to announce that 'Increasingly, the data demonstrates that digitalization helps to reduce poverty in rural communities', saying:

> For the predominantly young people in those villages, the ability to make their first phone call, record their first social media video, or to join a class on the internet, will mark a huge step forward for future life opportunities. But for older people too, whose children may have moved to the city, the chance to talk to them live by video-chat, or to receive instant payments from them using mobile money, could be truly transformational. (World Bank, 2021)

Communicating isn't necessarily the same as connecting though. We should look more closely at the massive new communication structures that have developed and acknowledge our limited understanding of them. We can't rely on our common-sense assumptions. Many of us may have some naive notion of the internet as a kind of benign connector in the sky. It's actually an enormous series of data centres and vast servers needed to support the internet and store the content we access. These are now contributing significantly to global warming (BBC, 2022). Fortunately in some countries, like Denmark, efforts are being made to harness this energy to heat homes instead of just damaging the planet (Jones-Casey, 2022).

The problems of ownership

It's not just the science of modern communication that's complex and difficult to grasp. Its organisation and ownership are also opaque. There's probably never been a golden age when personal communication has been secured from interference, with the Secret Service and other official agencies stopped from monitoring our post, calls, and even homes and bedrooms. However, new science and ownership structures create new problems and threats. This includes, as we have seen, the UK phone hacking and Cambridge Analytica scandals and Facebook's personal data selling, Russian manipulation of the UK Brexit vote and US election, collusion between tech companies, and security organisations, and political and lobbying consultants. Spy agencies have defeated internet security (Ball et al, 2013). Amazon's Alexa records private conversations, warning us against locating them in bedrooms (Wolfson, 2018).

Five 'tech giants' are currently identified in the IT industry – GAMA: Alphabet (Google), Amazon, Apple, Meta (Facebook) and Microsoft. All relate to communication but with much wider remits. Social media like

TikTok, Instagram, YouTube, LinkedIn, Amazon and the rest are interactive digital channels that facilitate the creation and sharing of information and other forms of expression through virtual communities and networks. As Wikipedia references:

> Big Tech companies typically offer services to millions of users, and thus can hold sway on user behavior as well as control of user data. Concerns over monopolistic practices have led to antitrust investigations (in the US and Europe). … Their impact on privacy, market power, free speech, national security and law enforcement (has been questioned). … It has been speculated that it may not be possible to live in the digital world day-to-day outside of the ecosystem created by the companies. (Wikipedia, 2022)

Thus, for example, in 2023 the US Federal Trade Commission and 17 US states alleged Amazon was illegally using monopoly power. The Commission Chair said big tech 'has skirted regulatory scrutiny for decades' (BBC, 2023). Increasingly, our personal, even most intimate communication, is being mediated by some of the biggest ever corporations. Technology is now much more complex and difficult to understand. It's the new magic, which we just use.

These corporations' power reflects their vanguard role in neoliberalism. Each is worth trillions of dollars, all are closely associated with deregulated neoliberal agendas and their leaders have their own free-market goals. They have outstripped traditional systems of accountability and taxation.

Scott Galloway, the American author and entrepreneur, has condemned the companies for 'avoid(ing) taxes, invad(ing) privacy, and destroy(ing) jobs' (Pisani, 2017), while the academic Nicos Smyrnaios has described the group as an oligopoly, dominating the online market through anti-competitive practices, ever-increasing financial power and intellectual property law. He argues that this follows from economic deregulation, globalisation and politicians' failure to deal with technological developments. He has recommended developing an analysis of the internet's political economy to critique its methods of domination to encourage opposition to it (Smyrnaios, 2016).

These corporations are at the cutting edge of neoliberal values and far from us in wealth, process and purpose. They are among the richest, most powerful market organisations, making their leaders some of the richest men on the planet. Herein lies a massive contradiction.

The paradox facing us

What's fascinating is that *such* organisations are central to our *personal* communication. Through them, we share our personal lives (Facebook),

Photograph 12.1: The high street: made to fail

Note: The collapse of UK high streets and their shops tends to be presented as an inevitable economic fact. This ignores the high levels of taxation they tend to face, compared with massive online companies where the opposite is the case, the lack of infrastructural support for their development and the high profits to be made from city centre housing instead.
Source: Peter Beresford

happy moments (Instagram), political opinions (Twitter/X) and so on. We can't pretend we stand outside them – we use them. Indeed, we may do so to condemn the ideology they represent. It's a fearsome updating of Orwell's *1984*. I enjoy using Twitter/X, although its takeover has led many to leave it. I check out Facebook with those close and share messages with WhatsApp.

I can't pretend I'm not involved and not conflicted. The irony of social media, whose politics I hate, isn't lost on me and doubtless on many others too. There's a big rift between what we want from social media and what they want from us.

Big Tech is part of the broader collusion between neoliberal states and big corporations within the framework of globalisation, with little serious effort made by governments to control it. As American filmmaker Jeff Orlowski said of his social media documentary, *The Social Dilemma*:

> Our social media platforms are powered by a surveillance-based business model designed to mine, manipulate, and extract our human experiences at any cost, causing a breakdown of our information ecosystem and shared sense of truth worldwide. This extractive business model is not built for us but built to exploit us. (Orlowski, 2020b)

As the Cambridge Analytica scandal highlighted, once they've found out our innermost desires, then they can manipulate them for their own purposes, economically and politically. Now the references shift from Forster and Eliot to Orwell and Huxley, from how things might be, to the dystopian vision that some see as already having arrived. Orlowski wrote of us trading 'our subconscious preferences for memes, our social cohesion for instant connection, and the truth for what we want to hear' (Orlowksi, op cit).

But when Orlowski refers to 'instant connection', he's not talking about the egalitarian vision of 'only connect' that we are exploring. His version is much more about how many 'friends' we can say we have on Facebook, or how many followers on X. Also, while social media are ostensibly about connecting, what they equally seem to be about is *dividing* – which lines them up with the bigger neoliberal agenda we've discussed. Divisiveness is both the intention and the effect of social media.

Damaging democracy

Orlowski's documentary, based on the views of critical pioneers and insiders, is disturbing. The industry business model is very distant from one primarily concerned with communication. They want your sign-up so you will look and act. They seek to change your behaviour so you will buy from their advertisers. The latter are the customer. You are the product! Their business is mainly selling their users to advertisers and politicians. As Jaron Lanier, the computer scientist says: 'Changing what you do, who you are, how you behave, is the product (for advertisers)'.

They harvest money and data and ultimately change behaviour. They have developed the most sophisticated behaviour modification techniques to manipulate our attention, extending this to manipulating real-world behaviour, like our voting, party allegiance and even attitudes towards each other. The 'connection' they are primarily interested in is our sign-up, attention and use. Governments and others are 'weaponising social media, which were massively used by Russia in the 2016 US presidential election and to incite violence, for example, in Myanmar with the killing of Rohingya Muslims' (Orlowski, 2020a, op cit). Social media are serving the neoliberal aim of disconnecting us from each other. As Mario Rubio US Senator for Florida said:

> We are a nation of people that no longer speak to each other … who have stopped being friends with people because of who they voted for at the last election … who have isolated ourselves to only watch channels that tell us we are right. (Orlowski, 2020a, op cit)

When I asked people on Twitter/X why they used it and Facebook, there was a big response. They said:

> I wonder if there is a space for an ethical platform, with mutual ownership that could show how social media could be different, in content, transparency and algorithms?

> Twitter users are highly heterogeneous in their motivations, although the core drive is to feel 'I matter' – the all-consuming unmet need of our individualistic society.

> I'm here purely to start or contribute to conversations that change perceptions around mental health and neurodiversity. I see it as part of my work. How can I advocate for clients if I won't lobby for change?

> How else do people have connections if they're mostly housebound, living alone?

> Because it gives us a platform to connect with others. To tell our story, to share our experiences Many of us have been thru horrific systemic failures. It's empowering to connect with others when we have been isolated Most importantly it evidences [and] exposes serious corruption.

> I agree … I resisted getting a social media account for years … joined twitter last year … helps me to keep up to date with news on the move and can be a good extension of the classroom … with the occasional pic of my dog thrown in for good measure;) Good servant … bad master!

> Open question I think Peter. It's used 'against us' commercially and politically, but it's also a way of learning, sharing and combatting the truly awful mainstream media in the UK.

Such comments highlight that these media are complex and ambiguous. People emphasised connecting and connecting for particular purposes. Many who use social media and networks are well aware of their inadequacies. Whatever these platforms' aims and ambitions for themselves, some subscribers certainly seem to understand them. Whatever their agendas for us, we are not necessarily passive partners in the process and may have our own active agendas for them. This offers hope when we look at playing a more agencied role in connecting with each other.

In and against big tech

Few of us can stand outside big tech. It underpays tax and workers and is thus advantaged compared with traditional businesses, particularly the shops and high streets that are still important parts of many people's social lives and mental maps. The new social movements (NSMs) that challenge its neoliberal values can no longer escape it. Indeed, it can offer some groups, notably disabled people able to get on line, particular benefits. But these often seem to be double-edged. Thus, in the UK, Pat's Petition, bringing together disabled people and family carers, grew from 'the realisation that many disabled people and carers could not take part in demonstrations ... or even get out easily to meet in groups' so that a virtual e-based approach could make possible the campaigning they were otherwise debarred from. However, 'the joy of making contact' was (soon) replaced with 'a toxic and tribal' atmosphere, 'where groups jostle for power'. The organisers never found a way of resolving such destructive effects but remained committed to virtual campaigning and felt it was imperative that:

> we all get together and find ways of recovering friendly, co-operative ways of working together to achieve the aims of supporting all disabled people and carers. (Onions et al, 2018, p 334)

Some social networking problems are endlessly rehearsed on public forums, but not necessarily to do anything about them. The greatest concerns have been raised about social media damaging children and young people's 'mental health' (Siddique, 2019).

Googling the right-wing *Daily Mail* under the heading, *social media damaging children*, produced a long list including:

- Just an hour a day on social media can make kids LESS happy
- More children are self-harming due to social media –
- Leaked Facebook Papers reveal social media giant targeted children as young as SIX years old to generate bigger profits. (Google, 2022)

Platforms once seen as opening new doors to contact, are now under attack for isolating children, now more often alone in their bedrooms and absent from parental supervision. This has created headlines about them being isolated and cut off from others by being addicted to games, social networks and screens (Jones, 2018). Although these problems are regularly highlighted by mainstream media, little has been done to control them. An early message from the Labour government elected in 2024 was that it would do more to safeguard children, but we have heard this before from neoliberal administrations (Selman, 2024).

Our dependence on big tech

What's interesting is how dependent so many of us have become on social media, how intimately they connect with our lives and how much we entrust them with. This has become a major moral panic but resulted in very little effective action. Big tech has made little attempt to regulate itself and the government in the UK, for example, has imposed minimal regulation (The Guardian, 2019).

Many of these findings should be treated with caution. It's not only the social media companies that want us to use them; media, think tanks and charities all want our custom. Putting it crudely, we're clickbait for them. They want us to spend time with their messages, pass them on and help them go viral. What's emerging is that social networking/media offer little confidence that we are connecting with each other on equal terms. We may gain skills in using them and sometimes mitigate their agendas because of our growing skill in advancing our own, but this is no simple journey to unmediated connection with each other. We have already seen here how other ruling communication channels affect our communication with each other. As one of the experts said in *The Social Dilemma*:

> Social media are not just a tool wanting to be used. It's got its own goals using your psychology against you.

This is another warning to listen to Audre Lorde and steer clear of 'the master's tools'. We began the book with neoliberalism's apparently unstoppable power and then signalled the importance of reconnecting on equal terms. This chapter has highlighted how limited progress will be if we rely on the tech giants for that. Having established their role in advancing neoliberalism and damaging democracy, we now turn to possible next steps to achieve more equal and inclusive communication.

Ways forward

However many problems e-technology is linked with, equally we can't overlook the amazing gains it's given us. We can keep in touch with those close to us anywhere and at any time simply and economically through our devices. Without Zoom and Teams, working through the pandemic would have been a very different kettle of fish. The 1950s fantasy of colour TV phones, one of few to be realised, has become so routine that we barely give it a thought. We really *can* keep in better touch.

In this sense, there has been some realisation of the goal of connecting. But all this has happened in the context of hard-right politics, reinforcing central control and relaxing market regulation. Social media have played a significant part in extending the politicisation of the personal in new reactionary ways. As I write this in a café, two older white men at a nearby table are condemning our 'snowflake society' preoccupied with safety (better to have unguarded factory machinery?) and how they're offended by Muslim women wearing niqab (they don't wear the clothes they choose?). Why is this on their minds rather than the loss of local jobs and amenities and the rest?

I've discussed social media at length because ostensibly they could do much to bring us together, but they have their own costs. They offer contact but on *their* terms. Some commentators think they seriously threaten the future of democracy globally and there's already disturbing evidence of this, if little formal political response (Henderson, 2018). Our urgent question remains; how can we connect equally and inclusively with each other when so many pressures push us in a different direction?

Nor can we easily escape social media, however worrying they are. Computer scientist Jaron Lanier argued that if he could 'get a few people to delete their ... accounts (that would) create a space ... to have a societal conversation' (in Orlowski, 2020a, op cit). How many of us would really do this? Social media, like online shopping, have convenience appeal – when life's increasingly complicated – even if you don't like their values. They can force down prices, critical if you're poor, accessible if your mobility is restricted. No wonder Orlowski's documentary talked of our 'pact with the devil'.

What else is there? So far none of the alternatives to X set up to challenge Musk's hard-right restructuring of it seems to have gained much traction, particularly not globally. 'Alt-tech' is a group of websites, social media platforms and internet providers that began as alternatives to more mainstream providers, but it has since become home to the political right and associated discrimination. Distributed social networks are decentralised networks, typically based on free and open-source software (FOSS) that aim at community moderation of content. They are intended to provide an alternative to the 'walled gardens' of big tech social networks (Holloway, 2018) along the lines of a public utility. Sadly, initiatives like these and the US Center for Humane Technology (www.humanetech.com), which offer a different vision for the future, are at the margins, with limited impact on big tech.

The need for a new communication strategy

To connect with each other on an equal and inclusive basis and reverse current trends to fragmentation and exclusion demands the development of a radical new communication strategy which puts the reform of big tech at its heart, but recognises that much more may be needed. Essentially, we need to address the political and the personal. We need to make personal and political changes, and the latter is only likely to come through working on the former. We must build on the positive ways we connect with each other in our personal lives, counteracting the inequalities and exclusions of formal politics.

Regulation

So far, proposals for big tech reform, as discussed in *The Social Dilemma* revolve around improving its regulation. This highlights the chicken and egg problem. The reason regulation is inadequate is that governments are unwilling to impose limits on the enormous power of these huge corporations while they serve their interests. There may be some wriggle room here concerning high-profile problems of suicide and mental distress among young people highlighted by mainstream social media critics. This could be a way to improve regulation.

But 'regulation' rarely seems to be an effective means of controlling such corporations. In the UK, we've seen the regulation of public services, utilities, and broadcast and press media being increasingly ineffective over the years, as other political safeguards have been curtailed. The strengthening of controls over the private sector is equated with a strengthening of the state. Thus, the creation of arms-length bodies with often limited power, as well as the bureaucratisation of regulation and a worrying two-way traffic between regulators and the regulated.

What's really needed is for this issue of the nature, role and governance of communication industries to be given much greater priority and attention. This demands greatly increased corporate accountability, which won't happen without much more political control. There are currently powerful pressures against this for obvious ideological reasons. This would be presented on neoliberal platforms as the reactionary state attacking the wealth-creating market. A more helpful way forward might be to frame reform in terms of *democratisation*, with a programme of change committed to increasing the participation and effective voice of big tech users, individually and collectively, involving them explicitly in its governance. This again would meet with resistance, but it offers a way forward which is at least consistent with the consumerist rhetoric of neoliberal ideology, which could give it some traction.

Changing communication structures to make them more inclusive has to be central to any communications strategy committed to equalising power in society. What's suggested here ultimately demands political change, and here, of course, is a chicken-and-egg problem. Politicians generally seem remarkably un-tech savvy, and this has long been shown in their failure to address new scientific challenges and instead form mutually profitable alliances with them.

Making our own change

Any reform programme dedicated to equalising communication can't only be about formal political change. That just takes us back to the problem of the chicken and the egg. What will create the impetus for such change? It almost certainly has to be *us*, and it's about more than reforming existing structures. It also means exploring different ones. It also has to extend to making personal change, individually and collectively. *We* have to find ways of achieving change. We will have to act differently – *ourselves*.

'We' will need to review our own actions and consider what changes we must make in them to bring about big change. If there's one golden rule, it would be developing our own channels of communication, not relying on 'theirs' – that's to say the ruling ones – 'the masters". So, here's a more general point. We need to speak more and listen to each other – directly. We are merely markets and intelligence to the communication giants. They encourage what was once called 'Chinese whispers'. We need to cut them out.

Our primary effort surely should be on cultivating our *own* channels and processes of communication. We can't rival or match the scale and power of new technology, but we can take a more active role in shaping our own communication. This could mean trying to develop our own news sources, our own online groups, chat lines and lists, and our own alternative information resources. Of course, this is already happening. We know that some groups are turning to different news and other media sources than mainstream ones. NSMs have been developing their own histories, archives and recorded cultures. However, it would mean a more focused, integrated, explicit and determined commitment both to developing and using these. We know that younger people are already investing more in doing this than perhaps the rest of us.

Reconnecting with each other

It could mean doing much more to be in *direct* communication with each other rather than relying on mediated arrangements. The latter have characterised the way that prevailing politics have operated to misrepresent and divide us. They have come between us with their traditional and social media. There is one thing we can do that no one else can and that's to initiate *first-person* contact. We can reach out and go out of our way to make contact with others to share our own accounts, our own perspectives, our own experiential knowledge and our own narratives. We can do this instead of being conduits for the second-hand stories that are passed on to us by politicians, so-called experts and influencers and their mass media and social networks. We can do this knowing that speaking directly to others still has a power beyond other media, just like any live performance.

It represents a powerful counter to all those vox pops on radio and television that still find someone in the street, for example, when Prime Minister Johnson was dumped as PM, to tell us he did a good job, never following up with, 'What did he achieve for you?' We have seen repeatedly, the skill and determination with which right-wing governments have successfully divided us. Donald Trump was right, the media, and not just social media, do spread 'fake news', but it's neoliberal fake news.

It's sometimes as if I can't be in a public place, such as a café, check-out or train, without encountering a barrage of prejudice and hate. The drunk away-football fans abusing women and BME passengers on trains, older people bad-mouthing immigrants and youngsters, fit young men taking seats from pregnant women and disabled people on the overcrowded London tube. I was always taught to confront racism and other overt discrimination, but it's becoming a more demanding job. We may see this as part of our strategy for connecting with others more equally. However, such a strategy will have to be much more comprehensive and thought-through if it's to help reconnect us on safe and equal terms.

We can draw on models like 'street epistemology', and public 'conversation with random people, to find out if they have good reasons to believe their claims' and beliefs (Axellson, 2020). The aim is not to win an argument but to encourage others to think about their beliefs and assumptions:

> How confident are you that that is factually true? What do you think is your biggest reason for thinking that is the case? If that reason wasn't available to you, would you be just as confident that it's true? How did you conclude that that is a good reason? (Axellson, 2020)

Such a technique developed by Anthony Magnabosco in the US, to challenge conventional wisdoms, follows from the 'Socratic method' of questioning that was developed by the ancient Greeks to foster critical thinking. This can help people rethink taken-for-granted views without creating conflict (Farnsworth, 2021).

We can try and do these different things in our:

- personal and social life;
- working life;
- activism in NSMs, and beyond.

Equalising relationships

In day-to-day life, this could be no more than extending the idea of every day/random acts of kindness to everyday acts of *connecting*. I am just suggesting that in the most obvious, everyday ways, we all seek 'to connect' more, on equal terms. We start small. We develop our own lines of communication, recognising that they may always be marginal. We do it with people we do and don't know, acquaintances and colleagues in queues and crowds, buses and trains, passing in the street. We reach out to have conversations with a purpose with people we might not ordinarily connect with. We set up our own chat rooms, lines and groups. Where they may have thrived to explore personal matters, here they can grow to personalise political ones. It does mean talking to strangers and exposing ourselves to views we might normally seek to avoid. It does mean securing people's safety. It's something we can do too in more structured ways in our NSMs, our service-user and other grassroots organisations – no longer just trying to communicate via prevailing media. This seems an important strategy to develop as part of our repertoire of collective action.

It's something I've been doing for some time. I make a point of talking to strangers, saying hello, being friendly, trying to interrupt the pattern of divisive assumptions and discussions, of challenging racist and discriminatory background chat. It can be hard work. We have to be sensitive in how we do it, not abuse inequalities of power and try to avoid making things worse!

We talk to others, speaking from direct experience, challenging our own and other people's prejudices. We try to tell things as they are, highlighting realities and offering alternatives to the dominant news agenda. We make that agenda explicit. This is the opposite of mass communication. It's the articulation of first-person experience. It may need its own ground rules. The aim is not to persuade but to enable ordinary truths to be in the ring with all the other feeds out there, jostling for attention. Our only agenda should be to share what we know from lived experience instead of amplifying and reproducing 'our master's voice' or staying in our own comfort zone.

Of course, there's nothing new about this, except its purpose. It's what moral crusaders, like the 19th-century Women's Temperance Movement did, challenging drunkenness and male violence against women at its meetings, knocking on doors, marching through the streets, in its newsletters, tea shops and so on. It's what happened in the left-wing cycling clubs that abounded between the world wars. This time, it would be spreading the word to challenge neoliberal narratives. It's what political parties do now, canvassing at election times or Jehovah's Witnesses when they knock on your door. The difference is that the motivation here is to connect us (on equal terms) with our realities rather than to sell a bill of goods.

Across groups

If we're serious about connecting with others in equal and inclusive ways then we'll need to do this across our different movements, identities and experiences. This raises a wide range of issues which we must also address. Communication is not a level playing field. It raises bigger issues for some than others. It must always prioritise staying safe. We can't expect people to connect with each other who may feel vulnerable or discriminated against by doing so. It may be awkward and embarrassing for some of us. We don't all have to do it, but it can make a significant difference and it can be the route for some. We may need confidence-building and assertiveness training. Having said this, it is interesting how much groups facing disempowerment have become ambassadors and high-profile advocates for challenging conventional prejudices in societies like ours. This includes disabled and trans people, mental health service users/survivors and other so-called 'user groups' facing some of the worst marginalisation in society. If we are disabled – or blind like one of my friends – we seek help if we need it, not to highlight our 'dependence', but to familiarise non-disabled people with the realities of disabling environments and societies. Telling our own stories and setting the record straight, has become central in rewriting our identities, roles and relationships and reshaping public understanding.

Challenging discrimination

A particularly pertinent discussion here is that initiated by journalist Reni Eddo-Lodge in her best-selling, *Why I'm No Longer Talking to White People About Race*. She highlights the inability of white people to recognise structural racism reflected in the way Black people who speak out about it are vilified (Eddo-Lodge, 2017; Evans 2018). Others have picked up the issue. It raises the point that if Black and other disempowered people are to challenge such issues, then they have a right to support from the rest of us against resulting attacks. This emphasises the importance of building alliances between different identity-based movements rather than expecting those victimised by discrimination to challenge it alone. It's a reminder of the commonality of oppression as a unifying force in calling it out.

The effectiveness with which racist agendas have been pursued through neoliberal Brexit/immigration policy has increased divisions in the UK along race, class, gender, age and disability lines. To bring about change, we have to challenge the discriminatory views that people have been encouraged to hold. Those views won't change without intervention. We have to challenge people to decouple themselves from such internalised discriminatory attitudes. We must draw on what we've learned in the personal sphere to counter this legacy of public sphere politics. This is a task that shouldn't be left to those victimised by discrimination. If we are to confront it as part of our determination to connect more inclusively and equally, then we must support each other across the boundaries of identity and embrace intersectionality in relation to identity and experience. Foregrounding intersectionality helps avoid crude hierarchising of difference and tendencies to isolate groups in separate silos instead of acknowledging our many overlaps. Equally, just because we experience one kind of oppression, doesn't mean we necessarily understand others. We may need help to do so.

As poverty and inequality have increased under neoliberalism, so more of us have experienced marginalisation and discrimination. Many are not used to seeing themselves in this way and retain negative attitudes about those they previously associated with such stigma, distancing themselves from them and denying the commonality of their situation. All these are issues to explore together if we are to challenge the divisions imposed on us and remake equal basis connections that have been undermined. This is part of a broader process of anti-discrimination. We help each other understand the discrimination we challenge and get to understand facing other people and opposing broader discriminations.

Reconnecting our movements

Much more needs to be done to connect our different movements, to emphasise our overlaps in terms of securing rights, working for sustainability, ending conflict and countering the threat of nuclear war. Instead of NSMs falling foul of the longstanding criticism of them as single-issue campaigns, this will achieve much greater solidarity and impact. NSMs that cross over different experiences and identities have a particularly helpful role here.

We often badge our allegiances and identities. The red ribbon is the universal symbol of support for people living with HIV. Pink is a symbol of support for people with breast cancer, the white poppy of remembrance for victims of war and supporting non-violence. The purple ribbon signifies disability, equality and support. Perhaps it's time to find ways to make visible our wider solidarity for our rights and against inequality more generally.

'No-platforming'

There's one last point to raise in the context of unequal access to the media and the divisive role it plays. It's especially important, given our concern with connecting with each other – *on equal and inclusive terms*. In recent years, some groups, students and campaigners have been attacked by neoliberal media and politicians for challenging discriminatory 'hate speech' on public platforms. This has come to be known as 'no-platforming' or 'deplatforming'. The UK Higher Education (Freedom of Speech) Act 2023 was introduced to impose controls on universities and students' unions in this context, although it is still not in force.

Framed by the political right as censorship and anti-free speech, no-platforming is defended as challenging hate speech and attacks on minority rights, for example, those of Muslims and trans people. The reality is that these are complex, normative issues, often a matter of where a line is drawn or how comments relate to the law. Few would support the right of a modern-day Hitler to be allowed 'free speech'.

These are typical of the comments I received on Twitter/X when I asked people about this.

> There are a lot of people who seem to get a massive amount of media coverage to talk about how they're not allowed to talk about the things that they're constantly talking about and it's just ridiculous.
>
> In general, I'm against it but if speakers are promoting hate and prejudice or inciting people to violence against vulnerable groups, then I do approve.

Such comments reflect my own take on the issue and sense that supporters of neoliberal ideology are unhappy with any challenge to their point of view. In other words, dissent is not acceptable and they are happy to demand their own democratic voice while curtailing other people's. I experienced this issue when I organised a conference at Brunel University about the future of the welfare state, including the right-wing media columnist Katie Hopkins on the panel. I thought it would be helpful to expose and answer her views. As was heavily reported at the time, Brunel students gave:

> the rest of the world a masterclass in how to deal with (her): don't silence or threaten her – just turn your backs and then quietly walk out of the hall (with her wrongly claiming in the *Daily Mail* that this author was involved in organising it all!) – to the applause of the rest of the audience. (Media Monkey, 2015)

In the next chapter, we explore what might be needed to build truly inclusive communication.

13

Towards truly inclusive communication

> Much unhappiness has come into the world because of bewilderment and things left unsaid.
>
> Fyodor Dostoevsky, Russian novelist and writer, 1821–81

Introduction

It's hardly surprising that a book starting with the exhortation 'only connect' should pay so much attention to communication. Here we pick up the discussion on the part played by new technology. It's also difficult to see how we can challenge the divisive pressures of neoliberalism without such an emphasis on communication. In this chapter, the focus shifts determinedly to developing more *inclusive and equal* communication prompted by the sharp realisation of how excluding and unequal communication so often is routinely in our world.

We regularly communicate in ways that leave out large swathes of the population, taking for granted that many mainstream communication approaches, old and new, are riddled with barriers. This can be for historical, social, cultural and political reasons. It's not restricted to particular 'out-groups' – although these have often been the most helpful in raising such issues. As a mental health service user/survivor, at work, I have been able to secure 'reasonable adjustments' under equality legislation to overcome some of these communication access difficulties. Yet I know that similar problems apply much more widely to people without such recourse.

The disabled people's and Deaf people's movements have challenged this and made progress. However, it remains a problem for many, excluding them in various ways. We must work to remedy this if we're really committed to a renewed politics which are truly democratic. Struggles for personal politics help us understand the direction that formal politics need to be moving in.

All communication is ultimately personal – if it's to work. That's to say if it's to convey a message accessible to recipients. There's no excuse for communication to exclude anyone in the 21st century. Generally speaking, we now can avoid that. Inclusive communication may sometimes have cost implications, but it's difficult for governments and corporations to plead ignorance convincingly, yet typically many people still get left out.

We've already heard a lot here about communication in relation to renewing formal politics and changing our relations with them. This is to be expected, given that communication is essentially about sharing messages with each other and moving from the individual to the social; from the inner to the outer world – what connects the personal and the political. Human communication is a massive issue both as a universal phenomenon and as a discipline. More accurately, it relates to several disciplines ranging from information theory to semiotics – the study and theory of signs and symbols. Paradoxically, communication is an issue few of us reflect on much and least of all explore with each other.

Language

Spoken language is central in communication, but once we start thinking about equal and connecting communication, we realise how such language can perpetuate rather than overcome barriers (Anderson, 2012). We probably think of spoken language first when thinking about communication, but it's a mistake to stop there. Even spoken languages are associated with non-verbal cues, including facial expressions and body language.

Of course, language issues may create barriers for ethnic, linguistic and cultural minorities, for indigenous people whose language is discriminated against and so on. My Jewish refugee granny never learned to speak, read or write English. What did that mean for connections beyond her own community? What's it like beyond home and family for UK refugees with cuts in support and an engineered tide of xenophobia against them? Of course, language issues are only one of the factors perpetuating inequality in general and in political communication.

The complexity of communication

To find out more about communication, I spoke to Karen Bunning, a speech and language therapy academic whose work focuses on communication. She said:

> Communication's something taken for granted, but often what people think about when they try and define it are the surface level features, the words we string together, not some of the deeper issues to do with experience, the understanding you bring to it.
>
> I favour a model of communication (Fogel, 2007) as a mutually socially coordinated process, not just a sender and a receiver. That doesn't cover it. You can end up thinking this person has problems in understanding the information I give them in the written format, so all I have to do is change the format of that and then they'll get it. That's your sticking plaster model. What we do in life is work together as communication partners. Each party brings their own

experience, knowledge and you work together to co-construct meanings throughout the conversation.

It's a messy business. Intentions and interpretations can be different. That's to say, it's about communicative intentions – what we're trying to achieve by the act of communication. It's also about how we make sense of the communication acts of another person. But this mess develops some form because we co-construct a message together. It goes wrong all the time in human communication. If you've got someone who has dementia, autism or a learning difficulty, you've got a mismatch in the code system that you're using. So, you have to rearrange what you input to this co-constructed process. So, it's not about giving a message – it's about connecting, making sure we're connecting.

There is no such thing as someone who doesn't communicate. There's *atunement*. Communication's a social thing. We have to atune to someone's natural repertoire. You open yourself to hearing, observing this person and you select your skills and create a ramp. It's always possible to co-create so long as we try, by deliberate selection of our communication skills. You tune them to this person. So, this person understands when I use really concrete language. That person is really supported when I use a lot of facial expression and whole-body movement. We've all got to learn. (Bunning, 2022 personal communication)

Communication and inequality

Karen, in her comments, drew us back to 'connecting'. Yet communication seems to be characterised by inequality. These inequalities operate in all areas of difference highlighted by NSMs, but particularly disability and Deafness. There are inequalities in the skills we bring – our access to and familiarity with different means of communication and the confidence we have in communication. The effects are pervasive. Thus, it's long been known that middle-class people do better out of the UK National Health Service because they're more skilled in how they use it. Equally, older people are less likely to access all the welfare benefits they're entitled to.

Every communication innovation brings new exclusions as well as new benefits. However, already many people are disadvantaged in communication. Nearly nine million people in the UK have very limited literacy skills ((NLT, 2022). More than a third of staff in UK small and medium businesses identify failure to communicate effectively as their biggest cause of stress (Microsoft, 2019).

My partner Suzy works as a welfare rights adviser with a voluntary organisation for people aged 50 plus. COVID-19 and lockdowns highlighted communication differences because now she couldn't visit people but instead had to speak with them remotely. As she reported:

> Government has been anxious to make the benefits system on-line. But many people don't have equal access to the internet. Even working in a modern western city as I do, few people use a computer to complete their forms. Generally, they can't fill them in themselves. So, I fill them in with them on the phone, but they mostly use a landline; many don't have smartphones which makes it more difficult. They don't have the advantages of raising volume etc. Mostly people want to explain how much they can do, despite their difficulties, because of their honesty, when what the government Department for Work and Pensions is interested in, is how *little* someone can do – to qualify. However carefully medical staff may have tried to explain, many don't really know what's wrong with them, or what medication they've been prescribed and why. (Personal communication, 2022 and see *The Secret Welfare Rights Worker*, 2021 op cit)

Things can go really wrong in communication. In war, non- and miscommunication are routine hazards. That's where actuality collides with intention and serious adjustments have to be made. The phrase 'fog of war' is used to describe how readily communication goes wrong in battle conditions – most famously perhaps with the Charge of the Light Brigade!

But deliberately confusing meanings or making communications difficult to understand can seem like the essence of political communication. The terms we have developed for political communication and communicators like 'spin', 'spin doctors' and 'spinmeister' are all about misrepresentation. As the Ricky Gervais film, *The Invention of Lying*, highlighted, a world without lying might be a difficult place to inhabit, but one full of lies is untenable. That's why the search for more honest, inclusive *political* communication is likely to benefit from learning from personal communication, where ultimately the primary purpose tends to be to *connect* – and where constant liars have few friends. In a political world where inequality is the rule rather than the exception, we might expect communication to be shaped by such discriminatory structures and political communication to epitomise this. That seems to be the case.

Communication and ideology

An issue emerging here is that communication is ideologically loaded – explicitly or implicitly. People tend to communicate in ways consistent with their ideological objectives. This means that communication can be *weaponised*. This affects why, how and with whom they communicate – the means and ends of their communication. In the context of neoliberal politics, we've seen modern electoral communication techniques intended to distort democratic outcomes, focused on marginal groups to swing a vote, tailoring messages to their idiosyncratic preoccupations, without necessarily any intention to honour such messages.

Even the three figures most associated with connecting, Forster, Eliot and Hoggart, however global their concerns, were actually only talking to small albeit significant minorities. Until filmed, Forster's work was largely confined to elites and academic syllabuses; Eliot was primarily a highbrow poet and Hoggart's key texts were clearly for men, not women. While all these *men* wanted to connect with others, their understanding of what this might mean was narrow, conditioned by their times.

Small groups can exert a disproportionate impact through the power of their communication systems, while, large groups can be marginalised. This is both because of the damaging effects of anti-democratic politics and the limited political understandings of the rest of us. This brings us back to power issues in communication and ideology. The political sociologist Steven Lukes identified three dimensions of power; the third was concerned with getting people's consent to, or at least acceptance of domination. It's not difficult to see how communication put to an ideological purpose plays a role in this (Lukes, 2004; Beresford, 2021, p 72). Even though communicating is something most of us are expected to do routinely, it's something we aren't necessarily well-equipped to deal with. My experience of this as a state school student – since reinforced as the curriculum has become more politicised – was mostly of learning to *answer* questions, more than being encouraged to *ask* them. This is a training likely to put many on the back foot in communication in later life. We may not even be in the best position to make the most of what power we actually have (Gaventa, 1982). Many self-improvement books focus on improving our communication skills. However, given that structural issues also apply, this may offer limited opportunity to equalise communication.

Politics and communication

I want to focus here particularly on communication issues which weaken democratic politics and perpetuate the inequalities associated with them. These are particularly important in the context of political communication, when as now, the dominant politics privilege the voice of the powerful. However, they also have wider implications through restricting others' life chances. So long as people's chances of connecting politically are qualified, it will be more difficult to reverse such trends.

Political communication is a special case and, in that context, what you see is not what you get. Right-wing US President Ronald Reagan famously articulated this, saying: 'If you're explaining, you're losing'. Journalist Sonia Sodha powerfully made the following point, as she laid bare the logic of neoliberal economic rhetoric with the headline: 'Drastic public sector belt-tightening is not an economic necessity but a political decision':

> It's why stories that chime with people's instincts about how the world works are more persuasive than ... carefully constructed facts that don't ... particularly ... in economic policy, where the narratives of the political right are more compelling because they are more intuitive. (Sodha, 2022)

Routine inequalities

Communication reflects broader patterns of discrimination (Barr and Topping, 2021). In the workplace, we know that gender bias impacts communication and leadership (Sarkis, 2019). Stereotypes about social class also undermine communication. While NSMs have sought to challenge such inequalities, they still exert a powerful influence. What's particularly concerning is that in a society like the UK, where snobbery, xenophobia and being 'aspirational' have been encouraged in formal political discourse, these issues largely seem to pass without serious notice. They are the insidious taken-for-granted currency of the conditions under which we relate to each other in most public spheres we engage with. Some of these inequalities apply more generally to communication; some apply particularly in the context of formal politics.

They apply especially powerfully in the context of political communication. We've already touched on the biases that operate there, restricting the range and depth of political participation and meaningful communication in political debate. How possible any real democracy can be, as long as communication is so qualified, is questionable. It signifies the perpetuation of elites and hierarchical structures of formal politics, where the only change may be in the composition of the powerful. A key route towards change must be examining existing communication systems and seeking to equalise them, drawing on particular examples where some of the most extreme exclusions apply.

Technology and the digital divide

As we've seen, new technology has only recently created a communication revolution. The first 'hand-held' cellular or mobile phone was launched in 1984 when Orwell's 'newspeak' was set. By 2012, one billion smartphones – a portable computer device that combines mobile phone and computer functions into one hand-held unit – were in use worldwide. This step-change in communication has been closely associated with other major developments like the internet, worldwide web and battery development. It's a truly revolutionary development, affecting all our lives, whether or not we have access to it, and it has created a new social problem.

This is the *digital divide* and reflects the unequal access groups have to computers, the internet and so on. The uneven way in which digitalisation is happening globally reinforces existing inequalities and exclusions. At the end of 2021, the UN's specialised agency, the International Telecommunication Union (ITU), warned that almost half the world's population didn't have internet access. The digital divide is estimated to affect 52 per cent of women and 42 per cent of men globally. It reflects other inequalities. As of December 2021, in Africa, only 43.1 per cent of inhabitants had internet access, compared to 88.4 per cent of Europeans and 93.4 per cent of Americans. While digital reach is extending fast, digital literacy is taking more time globally (Iberdrola, 2022). The global divide has numerous consequences including:

- access divide – infrastructural costs penalising poorer countries;
- use divide – because of restricted digital skills;
- quality of use gap – denying some in some societies the full benefits.

Effects of the divide include increasing isolation in both urban and rural areas, perpetuating barriers in the way of study and knowledge sharing, gender discrimination because women are more disadvantaged than men, accentuating social differences by restricting access to employment (Iberdrola, 2022).

Gypsies, Roma and Travellers

The barriers to equal and inclusive communication are legion in societies rooted in inequality. They relate to who we are, our resources, how we see ourselves, our relation with each other, history and culture. We often seem to take for granted communication's stratification – how we more readily communicate with people with similar demographics, for example. Yet all social divisions can create major barriers to connecting with each other.

A report supported by the UK National Institute for Health Research highlights how damaging such poor communication can be. The project consulted with travelling communities, focusing on access to healthcare to identify their concerns and stated:

> the relationship between Travelling communities and health providers continues to be characterised by poor communication and misunderstanding, including limited staff cultural competency and

limited skill in ensuring patients understand. The COVID-19-led move towards more digital forms of health care is adding to already numerous intersecting barriers to access. (Burrows et al, 2021)

The authors concluded:

> There is a sense of fear and distrust in the system, and until more inclusive modes of communication are routinely offered … communities are likely to miss invitations to health checks, immunisations and outpatient appointments. (Burrows et al, op cit)

COVID-19 has exacerbated these problems, reinforcing digital exclusion and distrust at times of conspiracy theory, particularly within groups like European Roma who have long experience of official oppression.

COVID-19 and lessons for communication

During the COVID-19 crisis, we saw some of the transformative positive effects of new technology, as well as ways, without radical reconsideration, it can create new divisions leaving many people behind.

The lockdowns, imposed internationally because of the pandemic, resulted in radically different ways of living, working and communicating. These could only take the forms they did because of the new technologies discussed here. Indeed, it's interesting to contemplate how far we would have been able to adapt our working lives in a pre-personal computer/internet age. As it was, much communication and work could now be done in safe, efficient ways remotely. Arguably, we were developing ways of working and connecting that were more efficient and sustainable. This was particularly true of international working where instead of people routinely relying on air travel to get together, they learned to work together online. They reduced the damaging environmental effects, cost and time-wasting of unnecessary travel, particularly flying.

New cultures grew up around the novel, routine use of e-communication. We saw people in the informality of their own space, humanising working relations, sometimes with their children and pets providing diversions on and off-screen, homemates in the background, or people providing their own attractive backdrops to keep some privacy. We began to see some convergence of personal and wider worlds as each borrowed from the other, with remote family-based pub quizzes, parlour games and the rest.

Some of the most intimate, life-enhancing and life-ending moments were worst affected in such circumstances because of the need to isolate, with people left alone in crisis and death. The reassuring rituals of loss and mourning were attenuated, and even new life was not welcomed as it ordinarily would be. I met babies who'd spent the first months of their lives locked down, with loved ones unable to share much of the joy ordinarily experienced. People with dementia, supposedly 'in care', often had to be left alone and unsupported with their low-paid, poorly protected carers, particularly vulnerable to COVID-19. Not only was this a pandemic which hit the most disadvantaged most often and most badly. They were also likely to have the least resources to deal with it. So, they were more likely to be locked into small, substandard housing, perhaps in one room, with no garden to escape to, in the highest-risk areas (Beresford et al, 2021; Hammond, 2021).

The pandemic has offered unprecedented opportunities to rethink the personal and political, and our roles and relationships with each other. If ever there was a time when we experienced our personal roles and relationships being restricted and our work/public roles being freer because of the difficulty of imposing conventional control on us in our own spaces, COVID-19 was it.

Significantly, those at the top of established political and ideological structures still seemed able to behave differently from the rest of us. This was symbolised in the UK and other neoliberal regimes by them conspicuously ignoring the law. Yet while these powerful people might have thought they could sidestep restrictions imposed on everyone else, the public opprobrium they encountered for travelling, partying, congregating and breaking the rules, for once, may have matched the real constraints the rest of us experienced.

We saw some of the alienation associated with the public/work sphere being transferred to the private relational sphere and also perhaps more significantly, vice versa – some of the more humanising and egalitarian influences overlaying our work life. Who was to know at a meeting whether you had to switch the camera off because the internet was unstable or if you were just having a breather or spending time with your children. Of course, the regressive direction of most technology was quickly reasserted and apps were developed to monitor online performance to control home working, just as if you were in a factory or office. The consequences of COVID-19 and lockdowns have been complex and ambiguous, but they offer some insights for equalising communication in the future.

The pandemic has highlighted both the barriers and benefits associated with old and new communication approaches. It emphasises that any desire post-COVID-19 to go back to the old days is likely to be exclusionary, while simplistic assumptions that upgrading to new technology will be inclusive are likely to be mistaken. Instead, we see the value of learning carefully from the experience and creating fresh mixtures of old and new, remote and face-to-face, developing the best from both and developing new hybrid models. There are prefigurative insights here for inclusive change.

Unfortunately, during the UK lockdowns, little if any attention was paid to the lived experience of those with the most familiarity with the conditions many more of us now had to cope with. This included people with impairments, long-term conditions and mental distress who are routinely restricted long term to their homes, and in some cases, their beds. Where health research had begun to take user involvement more seriously, this was now put on hold as though it wasn't important in an emergency (HRA, 2021). These groups' involvement had much to offer from their knowledge of isolation, insights which highlighted the importance of the emotional/psychological costs of such separation, what helps to deal with them and the importance of including this in any calculations about the actual costs of isolating people (Hammond, 2021; Williams et al, 2021).

We all, however, gained prefigurative experience. Disabled people who'd faced travel barriers now saw non-disabled people having to adapt to the same constraints. Suddenly, after being told for years that it wasn't practical for them to be involved remotely, they were seeing everyone having to make the same adjustments, and quickly realising they were workable, even if not what they were used to.

Disabled people

It's no accident that we're now focusing on disabled people - the group most obviously, historically and routinely marginalised in communication. It's a broad and complex category, which tells us much about communication barriers and ways of overcoming them more generally. It's therefore one that's likely to be particularly helpful as a case study.

In the UK (excluding Northern Ireland), disability is defined by the Equalities Act 2010 (Gov.UK, 2010). It's based on an individual medicalised model, *not* the social model developed by the disabled people's movement. Thus, it's defined by what you *can't* do, rather than the barriers you may face. For the Act's purposes, a person is disabled, 'if he or she has a physical or mental impairment and the impairment has a substantial and long-term adverse effect on his or her ability to carry out normal day-to-day activities'. It can include a physical, sensory, fluctuating, progressive or life-limiting condition. It includes long-term conditions like HIV infection, cancer, multiple sclerosis, stroke and heart disease or auto-immune conditions. The impairment can be physical or mental, thus including people diagnosed as having learning difficulties, 'autistic spectrum disorders' and/or 'mental health problems'.

Physical impairments include people who are:

- blind/have a visual impairment;
- have always been deaf (Deaf/part of the Deaf community) or acquired a hearing impairment (known as small d deaf);

- Have lost limbs or limbs do not function ordinarily (Office for Disability Issues, 2011).

There are exclusions as well as inclusions. Such a definition is complex and normative, but it provides a significant ballpark for considering issues of communication. There are other issues too. Being disabled can mean being disabled from birth, having a separate education and growing up as part of a distinct group developing its own identity. It can also mean acquiring an identity as a disabled person and encountering a set of new issues, problems and barriers. The largest group of disabled people in societies like the UK tends to be older people. Already often facing ageist discrimination, many seem reluctant to take on this additional, often stigmatising identity, and are often left isolated as older disabled people. They are less likely to be involved in organised activism.

Issues relating to disabled people also extend to disabled children, disabled parents and parents of disabled children, as well as all other areas of intersectionality discussed here. All make for an invaluable case study of communication issues. Also, because of the conspicuous achievements of the international disabled people's movement, they offer many invaluable insights into how we can challenge barriers to communication, which not only damage and invisibilise particular groups but leave the rest of us without the benefits of their insights.

The social model of disability developed by disabled people has a particular relevance to communication. Readers may recall that it distinguishes between people's impairments or perceived impairments and the disabling social response to them. Significantly, this is also sometimes known as the *barriers* model of disability – as it highlights the barriers disabled people experience in society. Such barriers may be attitudinal, based on prejudice; environmental – not offering an accessible environment; cultural, ignoring the particular culture of the disabled people concerned – or indeed and central to this discussion – relating to *communication* – imposing barriers on the communication of and with disabled people.

Of course, it isn't only barriers directly relating to communication that are relevant here. As countless disabled people continue to argue, if you can't get into a space to communicate, from a TV studio to a voting booth, then you can't contribute your opinion. Baroness Jane Campbell, a wheelchair user, had to have adaptations made before she could contribute equally in the UK House of Lords!

We must remember how important communication is to human beings. As social animals, we largely live in social settings and have developed sophisticated systems to govern these. If we can't be part of such processes, we're powerless to influence them and have little control over our lives. That's why political communication is important.

Some disabled people communicate in their own languages, including signing (British Sign Language – BSL – in the UK for Deaf people); Makaton – signs and symbols used by children and adults who are deaf-blind and Braille by some blind people for reading. Understanding of these issues is limited. While it's estimated that 11–12 million people, and rising, in the UK have some degree of hearing loss (one in five of us), BSL is used by 150,000, a sizeable linguistic/cultural minority, but still a minority (RNID, 2022). One study has shown that less than 10 per cent of people in the UK know more than two words in BSL and more than half don't know any (O'Dell, 2019). More than a third of a million people are registered blind in the UK, yet only a tiny, declining proportion use Braille, the communication system most lodged in the public mind. This latter development relates to the mainstreaming of blind students and the development of revolutionary new technology.

Such misunderstandings are perhaps a measure of public ignorance about communication issues, but also of the unconsidered assumption that it's for others to remove the communication barriers they face, rather than the rest of us, for example, by children routinely learning to sign from an early age at school. Similarly, 'guide dogs for the blind' are heavily advertised to raise funds, yet according to Wikipedia, only about 4,800 blind people currently have them in the UK.

Disabled people are a highly diverse population, and issues of intersectionality apply, further marginalising some groups within the population and increasing the discrimination they face in communication and beyond. Earlier, we focused on the barriers facing Travellers. Recent research highlights how these are even greater for disabled people within Gypsy, Roma and Traveller (GRT) communities. While Deaf and Disabled people's organisations seek to be inclusive, the evidence indicates that 'in reality ... only a tiny minority of GRT members were involved in such organisations, and the voices of Disabled GRT members are not heard in policy debates'. As the report concluded:

> Fruitful communication is necessary if we are to find ways to understand and embrace cultural differences. Literature and policy are essentially silent on issues of disability within UK GRT communities and the voices of their Disabled members are absent. (Unwin et al, 2020)

As this highlights, disabled people face some of the biggest communication barriers. These relate to sensory impairments, learning difficulties, mental distress and neurodiversity. Yet despite this, or perhaps because of it, they and their supporters have pioneered some of the most radical innovations to overcome the barriers that they and the wider population face.

Shaping Our Lives: A case study of inclusive communication

We can get some idea of this from hearing about the communication – comms – strategy of a UK national disabled people's/user-led organisations, in which I am involved, Shaping Our Lives. Shaping Our Lives has been in existence for more than 25 years. It's run by disabled people/service users, is structured as a community interest company and is committed to increasing the say and control of service users/disabled people over their lives and services to support them. This is what its former comms worker, Helen Buckley had to say on the subject:

> It's about finding a way for an organization to talk to people. So, what do we want to say and what's the best way to reach out to various audiences? Because of our focus on inclusivity, there's a lot more to consider when delivering communications; all aspects of the message, the language we use and the ways we deliver that message. For example, what format we use and that might be an ebulletin or on-line, on a website or social media, but also trying to think about people who don't access those forms of communication and will this work with a screen reader; have we used alt (alternative) text for images. There's an increasing move to visual media, which is hugely popular; but if you're doing that you are missing out a whole range of people who aren't able to engage with it. Even if you do use an image, you can also put alternative text so a screen reader can describe what's there. But even charities aren't using those very basic things. We do reports, in word doc formats or accessible pdf formats, others won't, automatically excluding people. We're trying to reach a wide range of people, who have valuable lived experience to share, who could make a real difference to how services are designed and delivered – it might be a disabled person, someone from a minoritized community, plus people running involvement, people working for councils, the NHS, researchers, universities etc. A lot of our work is helping people do involvement more inclusively – there's cross-over there – but there's distinct messaging aimed at particular groups of people.
>
> Access needs aren't always cut and dried – they might fluctuate or depend on what you get involved in. It may not always be easy to advocate for yourself – or if you have brain fog, a lot of people do, if they have an energy-limiting illness, or long Covid. There may be people who are neurodiverse who find it difficult who need a quieter space, and we'll have one. There are so many facets to communication. The words that you use and how you phrase them, are important to

people. Words have power, how we talk about things can affect how we approach them.

Listening is important. It's important to be learning all the time. From a comms point of view, that's a big thing. When you add it up these things can affect a lot of people and sometimes it's just small changes that can make a big difference. Why should a disabled person constantly be teacher on what they need? Why isn't there more understanding generally? You can't be expert on everyone's access needs, but there are basics. Different access needs can conflict with each other. We ask everyone what their access needs are and try and meet them. (Personal communication, 6 October 2022 with Helen Buckley)

Becki Meakin, the highly experienced former involvement lead for Shaping Our Lives, who is blind, also had a lot to say about communication. The complexity of the issues she raises rarely seems to get an airing beyond the worlds of disabled people, as though these can be seen as unrelated to the rest of us. She began, speaking from a personal perspective:

As a blind person, what I find frustrating is the way people create information to share, but don't necessarily think about the end user. They create what they think's going to look really good, or using language that's maybe familiar to them – but not to other people – and that's where lots of the barriers come – not so much the way it's presented – but understanding what it is that's being presented to you and being able to absorb and work with it.

I'm a great fan of short information because listening to it – as a blind woman and retaining it, gets more difficult as you get older. The thought that goes into what will people get from the information is equally important to presenting it in a format that's actually accessible.

I realise increasingly one of the skills we have as an organization is being able to put ourselves in the position of the other person we're trying to communicate with and thinking about their barriers, whereas a lot of people don't have that sort of insight. Various different access technologies are available – that's great and there's a lot of development going on – but how it happens now, people put it out for 'live testing', so it's not necessarily a good product when it comes to a handset or laptop. They let people complain when it doesn't work very well – and improve it over time. So, things are tested by the users, who naively think they are using something quite good! If you can use your phone well, there are endless apps now, mind you the time you waste is phenomenal, finding and trying to make an app work for you. (Personal communication, 28 October 2022 with Becki Meakin)

Addressing access issues not only has significant implications for the communications policy and practice of a disabled people's organisation like Shaping Our Lives, but it also fundamentally influences and shapes *how it works*. This is what Helen, Shaping Our Lives' comms worker said:

> It's been very different working for Shaping Our Lives, as a user-led organization. It's a much more collaborative space than other organisations. I've worked for charities that are much more top-down; the structure is you have your managers – it filters through. With Shaping Our Lives, it's much more a collaborative group. I've particularly enjoyed the meetings we have with the National User Group (NUG) because it feels like space to discuss things together – as if you're making decisions informed by all different life experiences. You don't normally engage with trustees. They tend to be a very removed board of people who are quite mysterious! With our NUG I've met most of them, talked individually and as a group, there's a real rapport, it feels equal, not like a top-down structure – very open communication.
>
> How we work together has to be different because this is what we set our stall on, being inclusive. There are things we can't compromise on, if there's a video we're producing and it needs to be captioned, to BSL interpretation, that has to be in the budget. It's about trying to highlight those issues in a transparent way. It has implications for how we work and to encourage others to work in the same way. We're drawing on 20 plus years of expertise, involvement and lived experience – that's the value anyone working with us is getting – their way of working should be changed by it. There are all sorts of barriers – resources, access –You don't know what you don't know and it's important to share that with people and hope you get a response back that's equally honest and willing.
>
> When you aim to be a collaborative organization, things might be a bit slower, that's not a negative thing. I think often there's a wrong perception that disabled people are a burden and it costs more to accommodate them. Getting on a bus, being able to travel, are basic human things, but I know from just navigating a buggy with two small children that loads of things won't work for a wheelchair user. There are so many barriers and when you've got cost-cutting going on across organisations, things like getting BSL interpreters or thinking about the technology on your website and making sure it's accessible, are falling to the wayside. Everything is moving to digital, even parking – and charities using chat bots online. It's got pre-programmed responses on. And that isn't working. There are all sorts of things that are being done that are putting up new barriers. People are getting left behind in the calls for great efficiency, cost-cutting, whatever you call it. Everything

is moving to digital and that's not working for everybody, it's very excluding. Communications moving on-line is leaving people out. (Personal communication, op cit with Helen Buckley op cit)

This is what Becki said about inclusive communication for a disabled people's organisation as a user involvement lead. She has taken a strategic role in advancing inclusive working in Shaping Our Lives:

> We work hard as a ULO (user-led organization) to be as accessible as possible. Quite a bit of that is thinking about the nature of the information we share and trying to provide it in an accessible format – not just the nature, but the content of the document.
>
> Sometimes I think universities think we're a bit unsophisticated with our work, because we try to produce something easy to use for as many people as possible. I always say it's best to start with the simplest version you can – plain words, simple formatting. Start with that version – as your base line. Don't start the other way round, with a simplified version for people who can't absorb your complicated version. That's the wrong way round.
>
> To make everything accessible is expensive. Thinking that creating a simple Word document meets everyone's access needs is not so. It's a good starting point, but then you've got all the variations of creating a BSL, an 'Easy Read' version, etc. I'm not a great fan of 'Easy Read' (which usually combines short, jargon-free sentences with simple, clear images to help explain content), but it's helpful for some people. Lots of people need someone to talk through the concepts; they may not be able to read the words and the pictures are meaningless on their own. If people don't read, then they won't read Easy Read. They need someone to help, else Easy Read may be pointless for them.
>
> Someone needs to sit down and explain to participants to get that understanding across. We could use a lot more voice texts and memos, where you can actually explain something. On WhatsApp I get quite a lot of people who record their message rather than writing it out. It's much clearer if someone does that. I use a screen reader on my computer and voiceover on my phone. One of the difficulties with that in terms of access, people will be trying to talk to me while I'm listening to the device talking – they forget – I can't do both!
>
> Inclusive communication is much bigger. A lot of the barriers people experience, are about more than making a document accessible. It's about communication *intention* – and government intentions sometimes clearly are to deceive people or provide insufficient information to make a good judgement.

People don't realise what it takes to have better access, so they struggle with what they know. It's this idea unless you have had support, opportunities to work – education and funding – you don't necessarily get to try different ways of doing things. So, you get left behind, just doing things the way you know. If you had support to know how to use your I-pad, you could become more independent in communications and have a lot more access to things. We're moving on to these new IT systems with access technology and as a small ULO, we don't have the luxury of an IT department, of training, support. It's really difficult to find trainers who know how to use all these new IT systems. The trainers, they need time to work things out.

With communications, we are limited by people's access to equipment etc. Issues of inclusivity are not high on policy and cultural agendas. With Traveller communities, for example, they've got loads of attitudinal barriers, but before they get to those, they can't even access information, or get an address so information will get to them and most of them will struggle to absorb any written information and the younger people coming through are learning language much more than the older generation and they are dependent on very young people to interpret information for them. That's a complete communication barrier for them. The time and effort we need to make communication accessible is considerable and sometimes the cost is substantial and should be a *right*.

Communication is a cultural thing which means you have to spend time, sit down with people, get to know them, before they can be comfortable with communicating. And you probably need an intermediary for that to happen. We can't just walk in there. For that work, we had people who knew those communities, introduce us, build up trust, why we were there. The first thing's always got to be asking someone, what works for them and not using language that's exclusive to you, your sector, or what you're used to. We were talking in Shaping Our Lives about what equality and equity mean; difficult words to use. You could be pushed out of a conversation quite easily by not having the confidence to use words like that, or 'diversity' or 'inclusion'. It's that fear of 'I'm not sure I really understand – have I got the authority to use these words which are associated with a certain level of expertise'. So, we must avoid using jargon and find out what that person needs – and adopt that. We must think about the people we're trying to communicate with. When you think of the population as a whole, all the young people, what they might need to understand, much older people – the rising difficulties as we get older – our eyes, ears, mobility, and confidence. It's a very small group left behind when you take out all the considerations for communication that we should be thinking of. (Personal communication, op cit with Becki Meakin)

None of us can appreciate all communication access issues that may affect disabled (or indeed other) people. We can only be sensitive to their possibility and constantly try to be proactive and responsive to them. Support technology is also constantly improving. People take in information in different ways. We know that there are particular issues for people who experience dyslexia or identify as neurodiverse. What works for one person may not work for another. A sensitive approach based on listening to people's self-defined needs and reaching out to check options is essential. None of us can know the whole gamut of needs or helpful responses. The background colour to print, print size and font, and speech-to-text computer programmes can all have a helpful impact. Inclusive communication is everyone's responsibility.

The sometimes extreme communication barriers facing disabled people highlight the importance of recognising the routine exclusions facing many other groups. They emphasise the need to investigate and address such barriers if the rhetoric of political democracy and the achievement of social, economic, civil and human rights is to become real. Not surprisingly, inclusive communication lies at the absolute heart of any possibility of us all having a real chance of connecting with each other to enable real change – at personal and political levels. This brings us to the *subject* of our communication – what we want to share – and challenging longstanding inequalities in relation to such knowledge.

14

Learning from what we know

> Time spent in reconnaissance is seldom wasted.
> British army adage originally attributed to the Duke of Wellington

Introduction

We've talked a lot about communication, connection and information. All have a key part to play in gaining wider support against the reactionary formal politics that have been dominating our lives for too long. Now we turn to knowledge and knowledge production; how they've been captured by neoliberalism and the pioneering progress being made to reverse that and reconnect them with our lives and experience.

A personal word first

I should perhaps start by saying that Trumpian ideas like 'post-truth' and 'fake news' don't really feel new to me. My father killed himself when I was four and left my older sister and me with a mother who could be terrifying. She never told us he'd died. I didn't discover he had killed himself until I was an adult! Among the things she did tell us was, 'If I say something's black and it's white, then it is black'. It was really only when I was grown up and talked about this with my partner that I began to realise the magnitude of what she was doing. While I would resist statements like this at the time, challenging them with her and in my own head, for a small child it was pretty difficult to escape their power! I don't think I really did. The issue was more about being able later to break away from the power exerted over us. I don't think my poor sister ever could. However, I got an early apprenticeship in understanding broader issues of knowledge manipulation!

I am talking about the capacity of one individual, or indeed group, to impose their meanings on another – to have sufficient control to force that person to understand something as they tell it. I think the valuable term that's developed to help us see this is 'gaslighting' (Thomas, 2018). This comes from the film *Gaslight* where a murderous husband seeks to drive his wife mad by manipulating the gaslight in their home to make it flicker, then telling her this is her delusion (Cukor, 1944). What's important here, which I came to understand, was that someone was trying to impose damaging meanings on lived experience, conflicting with the individual's own understanding, or telling them they are imagining things, to undermine them. What some of us have realised is that mass media often are like this too, to support their ideological investment. When Donald Trump coined the term 'fake news', he was destabilising our beliefs to give himself free rein to fake news.

At one point as I was drafting this text, with UK inflation rising, energy bills multiplying, social care close to collapse – denied workers by Brexit – and more strikes threatened, the message from neoliberal media was very different. We heard Conservative leadership candidates telling us of the successes achieved, the currently absent Prime Minister Johnson making a front-page promise, 'there's a golden future ahead' and contender Liz Truss saying: 'I will keep UK safe' (Sunday Express, 28 August 2022). This was intentional deception on a massive scale, soon exposed by both candidates being rejected. And, of course, who knows better about lying than a liar?

Gaslighting as we've seen, means making someone question what they know. It's a particular sort of knowledge this is often concerned with – what they think they know from their own experience. This is very close to home for us all. It relates to knowledge we particularly trust and rely on – *experiential knowledge*. We will come back to this. Clearly, my mother sought to destabilise the trust we children felt able to place in *our* own experiential knowledge.

Neoliberalism and knowledge

A key way neoliberal politics do this is by manipulating what we know about the world, ourselves and others. That's why it's crucial to subject the issue of knowledge and how we know something to critical consideration. It's a building block for how we connect (or don't) with reality and each other. A politics like neoliberalism that serves so few interests yet enlists the support of so many raises questions about our knowledge and understanding of it – where these come from and how they seem to chime so little with what may be in our best interests. Turkeys are not noted for their intelligence, but we readily talk about our love affair with neoliberalism as an instance of 'turkeys voting for Christmas', because it's so clearly against our and their best interests.

This discussion of knowledge is not narrowly situated within neoliberalism; it also draws on knowledge's broader history and politics. However, the knowledge specifically associated with neoliberal ideology, giving it authority and validity, does offer us a helpful starting point. In neoliberalism's case, it's the knowledge created by its ideologues and pioneers, like Hayek, Friedman, Thatcher and Pinochet, advancing its principles of economic liberalisation, marketisation, globalisation, monetarism, public sector cuts and privatisation. As discussed in Chapter 1, neoliberalism has varied origins and meanings. The state plays an active role in supporting market dominance, extending it to the public sector and offering it resources and legitimation. The knowledge generated by neoliberals, like that associated with any ideology, is value-based and normative, but this is a helpful reminder to be cautious about any assumption of neutrality relating to knowledge. Neoliberalism has been such a powerful force that it's done more than generate its own body of self-serving knowledge. It has also, even more significantly, had a big influence on the global restructuring of knowledge and education (Ward, 2014).

The legacy of scientific knowledge

It's no coincidence that the age which first stressed the importance of *scientific* knowledge was that which gave us the idea of ideology and an associated corps of ideologues, with the credentials to analyse and develop it (Beresford, 2021, pp 20, 42). This is the Age of Enlightenment, the 18th-century period, also known as the age of reason, associated with Western 'scientific' discovery, that is to say, the systematising of knowledge, a preoccupation with measurement, experiment and invention. For me as a child, this meant visiting the London Science Museum and seeing the wonders of steam engines that made possible the first industrial revolution. Or walking a bit further along Exhibition Road to marvel at the dinosaurs first discovered around the same time which challenged biblical timetables for creation. But these are just the visible expressions of a fundamental intellectual change. All grew out of the Western shift from faith-based belief to the search for provable, 'objective' truths.

We may have moved a long way since, to a more complex world of relativity, nanotechnology and string theory. Yet many still associate science with values of objectivity, neutrality and distance. These are still privileged values in research and scientific projects. It's the most traditional kind of quantitative research, based on the positivist values referred to previously, which is still the 'gold standard' in health and social research. Thus, randomised controlled trials (RCTs) and systematic reviews based on them are still counted as the definitive basis for the most rigorous research for knowledge production (Glasby and Beresford, 2006). Such research approaches still often privilege individualising explanations of the psycho-social phenomena they investigate, consistent with neoliberal ideology.

In her groundbreaking study of how natural science number-crunching has been misapplied to our bodies and lives, researcher Sarah Chaney shows how we have internalised crude statistical notions of 'the normal' and these have been transmogrified to create notions of abnormality with appalling discriminatory consequences, even providing a pseudo-scientific justification for eugenicism's horrors (Chaney, 2022).

An unhappy alliance

The Enlightenment was also an accelerant for new global imperialism. The freedom, justice and liberty it proclaimed were essentially restricted to privileged European men, while it helped provide the conditions for inequality, derestriction of trade and transfer of wealth, which notably impacted Indigenous peoples and included the continued enslavement of African Americans and genocide of Native Americans. Decolonising scholars challenge the Western knowledge system for still seeking to determine what should be considered scientific knowledge and continuing to 'exclude, marginalise and dehumanise' those with different systems of knowledge, expertise and world views (Dreyer, 2017). The concerns of those committed to decolonising knowledge are that the Western knowledge system has become a norm for global knowledge, with its methodologies alone acceptable for knowledge production. They seek to support and legitimise other knowledge systems. According to the Peruvian sociologist, Anibal Quijano (2013), the decolonisation of knowledge is necessary to create new avenues for intercultural communication, the exchange of experiences and meanings, with a vision of an alternative rationality that may rightfully claim some universality. We should remind ourselves that neo/liberalism, the science of the enlightenment and colonialism are the three legs of the stool long dominating our conflicted and unequal world. We can see that as we seek to liberate ourselves from this, we can also begin to decolonise knowledge.

How we know

Knowledge can be produced in many ways and has many sources. As Wikipedia reminds us, the most important source of knowledge is perception, based on the five senses. Other sources identified include introspection, 'memory, rational intuition, inference and testimony' (Wikipedia, 2022). These all originate within us, our individual minds and cognition – 'the mental action or process of acquiring knowledge and understanding through thought, experience, and the senses'. These may seem enough to us, living our lives and negotiating the world we live in. But as Chaney reminds us, the scientific imperative that came into ascendency with 18th-century Western secularism prioritised the acquisition of knowledge through the scientific method based on repeatable experimentation, observation and measurement (Chaney, 2022).

It's such knowledge, incorporating the assumptions of its age about the inferiority of Indigenous and BME people, women and others, that has helped give us the discriminatory context of modern human life. It has artificially imposed a narrow range of what counts as reliable knowledge and indeed knowers. It has also long been used to legitimate and perpetuate inequalities between different groups. As we've seen, this has long been powerfully reflected in the structures of research, historically dominated by privileged white men (and sometimes women) (see Beresford, 2016, pp 14–153). All this sits uncomfortably with claims that research is neutral and objective.

Researchers themselves have additionally highlighted the powerful effects of neoliberalism on research, its ownership, focus, methodology, results and impact (see, for example, Besley and Peters, 2006; Nicolescu and Neaga, 2014; Vohland et al, 2019).

The challenge to traditional research

The positivist research tradition has been increasingly challenged over the years. Its logic is that reliable knowledge is gained through the senses by a process of observation and measurement and all the researcher does is collect data and interpret it in an 'objective way'. This has long been questioned, particularly in social and human research, even where supposedly 'rigorous' research methods were applied (Boaz and Pawson, 2005). A key challenge came from new social movement (NSM) members who were re-evaluating the negative identities imposed on them, based on ruling prejudices and stereotypes, still often embodied in the research of racist, patriarchal societies.

During the second half of the 20th century, identity-based NSMs challenged such identities attached to them, first by developing their own movements and organisations, and then by expanding their own knowledge production to question existing research approaches and their evidence. This was true of all such groups. In 1969, Nathan Hare, the African American sociologist and activist, identified as the father of Black studies, wrote:

> On the shoulders of the black scholar falls an enormous task. He (sic) must de-colonize his mind so that he may effectively guide other intellectuals and students in their search for liberation. … The connection between white colonialism and its scholarship has always been apparent to black and other victims of it. However an examination of this relationship is in order. (Hare, 1969, p 58)

In the last quarter of the 20th century, gay and lesbian studies gave rise to Queer studies, and in the early 1990s, Queer theory developed from this. This has broadly been associated with the theorisation of gender and sexual practices outside heterosexuality, which challenges the notion that heterosexual desire is 'normal' (Warner, 2011). The discipline of transgender or trans studies emerged in the early 1990s in close connection with Queer theory. The ultimate goal of transgender studies is to provide knowledge that will benefit transgender people and communities, and challenge their negative presentation and treatment (Beemyn and Goldberg, 2021).

It is now nearly 50 years since the British sociologist and feminist Ann Oakley published her longitudinal study of women *Becoming a Mother* (Oakley, 1979). It was much cited as helping to establish a new paradigm of feminist research. In a subsequent book chapter, she wrote of social research interviewing:

> the mythology of 'hygienic' research with its accompanying mystification of the researcher and the researched as objective instruments of data production (in a feminist methodology is) replaced by the recognition that personal involvement is more than dangerous bias – *it is the condition under which people come to know each other and to admit others into their lives.* (emphasis added, Oakley, 1981, p 58)

Reviewing the research more than 37 years later, Oakley elaborated on this challenge to the possibility of people encountering each other objectively, suggesting that:

> the complex political and social relationship between researcher and researched cannot easily be fitted into a paradigm of 'feminist' research, and that the concepts of a gift and of friendship as components in this relationship deserve more attention. (Oakley, 2015)

Equalising relationships within research

This concern with the relationship between the researcher and the researched also characterised the research emerging from disabled people around the same time. Mike Oliver, a pioneering disabled academic and activist, made it clear that the emancipatory disability research he and other disabled people developed was politically committed rather than supposedly neutral, based on a different set of roles and relationships for research. The key characteristics he associated with it were that it was based on:

- equalising relationships between researchers and the researched;
- research committed to supporting the empowerment of research participants;
- research committed to making broader social and political change in line with their rights and interests. (Oliver, 1996)

A bigger pattern emerged: first members of NSMs wanted to have a say in existing research, then to undertake their own, rather than be the subject of other people's or partners in collaborative research, and then they wanted to develop research based on their own experiential knowledge (Barnes and

Mercer, 1997; Sweeney et al, 2009). Most recently there's been increased official interest in coproduced research, where the whole process of research production is one where, for instance, service users and their organisations and service providers and theirs', work equally together.

Pressure for change

The positivist research paradigm is contrasted with an *interpretivist* one. This holds that humans construct knowledge as they interpret their experiences of and in the world, rejecting the objectivist notion that knowledge is simply there to be identified and collected (Hiller, 2016). This is a framework which helpfully fits the research approaches adopted from NSM perspectives.

The issue though is not just about research production; it's about *knowledge* production. As the present discussion highlights, research cannot be treated in isolation, and knowledge and research should not be treated as synonymous. For those of us seeking to challenge the barriers we face, research is unlikely to be the starting point for change, even though it may have an important part to play. We will reflect on our own experience. We may have the confidence to challenge – at least in our own minds – what happens to us, how others see us, our status in society. But crucially, it is when we have opportunities to explore our lives with people with overlapping experience, especially if they are further down the line of thinking them through than we are, that we can really think afresh and come to new understandings about ourselves, how we have been understood and why that might not sit comfortably with our own understandings and indeed rights, interests and needs.

There are few things that can be more personal than our emotions and experience. What's significant is how, historically, they have been mediated by the politicised processes of analysis, interpretation and, ultimately, understanding that take place in societies. Social research, as part of the dominant system of knowledge production, has been bound up with this process. Thus, we have variously been allocated our value and status as women and men, Black and white, heterosexual and LGBTQIA+, young and old. So, who we are and what that means, have all historically been set for us by the societies in which we live. Thus, we know ourselves and others. I can clearly remember as a child having a clear idea of what 'masculinity' entailed, hating it and feeling I wasn't much of an exemplar. I wasn't good at most sport, I couldn't understand why most boys seemed to want to hurt each other. Pretty quickly I concluded I was a natural born coward and there was no war I'd want to get killed in!

The irony was that it was 'going mad' in my 30s that really helped me make more sense of myself and question the messages I'd internalised about myself. I am not saying I hadn't started on that process, but what felt like the extreme difficulties I experienced as a 'mental health service user' – including new levels of fear, confusion and incapacity, created a powerful impetus, first, to deal with what felt like their terrifying effects, and second, to understand it all at a more fundamental level. The treatment I received from NHS psychology services was ultimately helpful. But it was also what felt like the extremity of my situation that led me to get actively involved in one such NSM, the psychiatric system survivor movement, which had a profound effect on my thinking (Beresford, 2010).

However, all this flies in the face of traditional research values. If RCTs and systematic reviews are rated as the research 'gold standard', views from research subjects like disabled people are seen as having *least* validity. This has been an official medical view, reflected in a hierarchy offered by the UK Department of Health (Department of Health, 1999, p 6). Yet in our ordinary lives and the research developed by NSMs, these latter approaches have assumed particular importance. Also, as the research work of the Service User Research Enterprise (SURE) at the UK Institute of Psychiatry highlights, the battle is not between quantitative and qualitative research. Both can be empowering/disempowering, participatory and excluding. SURE has evidenced that RCTs/systematic reviews are not as 'rigorous' as assumed, and much more can be done to make them participatory (Rose et al, 2003; Papoulias et al, 2014; Wykes et al, 2018).

What's concerning is that both knowledge models we have been discussing here were often disregarded by the UK government during the COVID-19 pandemic. Neither pre-existing arrangements nor policy responses to the pandemic were consistently based on either traditional expert scientific research or the insights emerging from service user knowledge. Senior health officials who war-gamed the impact of a coronavirus hitting the UK warned four years earlier of the need to adopt preventive public health measures, but this was not done (Booth, 2021). The director of public health who commissioned this exercise also advocated public and patient involvement in research. The Health Research Authority concluded the pandemic had:

> exacerbated the lack of resilience of the place of public involvement in UK research. ... The lack of shared, high quality information about all aspects of public involvement limits its ability to become a core part of the way research is conducted in the UK rather than something which is 'nice to have'. (HRA, 2021, p 5)

In retrospect, this seems a victory of ideology over evidence, consistent with small state thinking and low public spending approaches to public policy. But for everybody affected by the pandemic it also meant a failure to include their knowledge, and we will never know what its real cost may be. Given that this pandemic impacted especially heavily on disadvantaged groups, this is particularly important since the burden has been experienced especially unequally. It has also raised a bigger, exclusionary issue highlighted by service users, user researchers and research.

As part of their/our own knowledge(s), service users and other NSMs have placed an increasing emphasis on lived experience and the experiential knowledge derived from it. It's this experiential knowledge and the research building on it that has enabled marginalised groups to develop their own understandings of themselves and the world, and critique existing exclusionary ones. However, such knowledge has long been devalued by positivist research criteria as inferior because it's explicitly political in purpose – its goal of bringing about personal and political change – and because it clearly fails the neutral, objective and distanced test applied by positivist science.

Challenging knowledge discrimination

Because of this issue's importance and its centrality for this book's core concern – reframing our formal politics – I must be transparent about my own involvement with knowledge issues. I first wrote at length about them in 2003 because of my increasing concerns. I had a privileged education in conventional terms (even if I didn't much enjoy it!) of secondary school until 18, and then going to university. I was as well-equipped as anyone to make sense of things, understand how the world worked and its impact on me. However, based on principles of competition and elitism, that's not necessarily state education's purpose. While I don't doubt there may be many far worse equipped than me, when I experienced serious distress, living long term on benefits, the support I gained from other survivors was especially important in offering a way forward.

However, I began to see what little value was attached to their experience and viewpoint. Mental health service users like me mainly figured in psychiatric research as a data source. We'd mainly be asked about our symptoms and state of mind, for this information to be fed into highly formalised tests and inventories for others to interpret and be able to allocate us to diagnostic categories and associated treatments. There seemed little interest in what *we* thought was happening, what problems *we* thought we had and *our* ideas for doing something about them. No matter that our thoughts grew out of direct experience – not only of what was going on in our heads but also in psychiatric and other systems we were sucked into, how they really worked, what it felt like using them and what their outcomes felt like to us and those close to us.

The devaluing of lived experience

Generally speaking, little weight was formally attached to our views and experience. There might be a scandal, say about inpatient treatment, and then our views might be sought, but this was the exception, not the rule (Beresford, 2016, pp 111–14). We can also see specific reasons why the knowledge of mental health service users/survivors might be discredited. It's a group:

- long devalued in society;
- associated with other devalued groups (women, Black and minoritised people, LGBTQIA+ people);
- defined based on its perceived irrationality;
- seen as potentially dangerous, untrustworthy, unpredictable.

The same tends to be true of other, overlapping groups facing oppression who are also the subjects of public policy, including disabled and indigenous peoples, children, young and older people, people identifying as neurodiverse, homeless, poor and criminalised people. Thus, people with learning difficulties have often been seen as lacking the intellectual ability to provide reliable information, and people without verbal communication, the capacity to express their preferences. So, putting those two points together, what we see is that groups facing particular exclusions and discriminations can also expect that they as knowers and their knowledge will both be called into question. Let's take stock now:

- Some groups are seen as inferior knowers and their knowledge as inferior.
- This is based on such groups being seen as inferior, defective or deviant.
- These groups experience discrimination, disempowerment and negative stereotyping.
- Their knowledge has generally been based primarily on lived experience rather than on research evidence.
- Prevailing 'scientific' positivist research privileges knowledge it sees as objective, neutral and distanced.

This clearly works to the disadvantage of the groups discussed here. They fail on all the criteria associated with such positivist research. They cannot claim their experiential knowledge is:

- neutral – by definition it has personally happened to them;
- objective – the knowledge in question is based on their subjective experience;
- they are close to the knowledge in question having gained it through direct experience.

All these values concern the *relationship* of the individual finding things out with what they are finding out about. The emphasis in all is that what's best for 'scientific' knowledge is that the person should be disassociated from the object/subject of their attention. Clearly this is the antithesis of the situation in relation to 'experiential' knowledge – knowledge gained by direct or 'lived experience'. This helps us understand why historically the evidence of groups who are marginalised and devalued is granted less value. It's only if such knowledge is interpreted or confirmed by a valued researcher or other 'expert' that is seen as having authority.

Revaluing experiential knowledge

Through history, some oppressed groups have managed to spread their knowledge. Doubtless, they've challenged conventional accounts of them and their actions, and on some occasions managed to exert a bigger influence and reach a wider audience. But we can expect that it's only if and when their power increases, for example, when American slaves were freed, or soldiers came back from the frontline in 1918, that they were really able to challenge the prevailing discourse.

The emergence of NSMs and the increasing emphasis on involvement in public services have provided a similar impetus for change. At its heart is the implicit recognition that positivist research principles are essentially discriminatory. By their logic, ruling white heterosexual men have the right to pass judgement on women, Black, minoritised and LGBTQIA+ people because they can claim to be distanced from the latter's experience and therefore better placed to interpret it. This has colluded with a history of discrimination against such groups, essentially legitimated by research. As I wrote in 2003:

> If you have direct experience of problems like disability, hardship and poverty … of oppression and discrimination, when such research values are accepted, what you say will always be seen as having *less* value – *less* credibility. Because you will be seen as 'close to the problem' – it directly affects you – you cannot claim that you are neutral', 'objective' and 'distant' from it. So on top of the discrimination you already experience. … You are likely to be seen as a *less* reliable source of knowledge. We can see how this worked for a long time against women and children who were subjected to sexual and violent attacks. … (Their) knowledge and experience … were not listened to or valued. (Beresford, 2003, p 13)

Summing up:

> if you have experience of discrimination and oppression you can expect routinely to face further discrimination and be further marginalised by being seen as having less credibility and being a less reliable source

of knowledge. This fundamentally and additionally invalidates people who are already heavily disadvantaged. (Beresford, 2003, pp 14–15)

Double discrimination

In other words, you can expect to face *double discrimination*, making it all the more difficult to overcome oppressive reactions to your experience and identity. This discrimination against disempowered people extends beyond research. The same devaluing of them as knowers often happens in legal/quasi-legal situations, which are meant to offer them redress. They can expect less weight to be attached to their accounts than of those more powerful. Thus, traditional approaches to the production of knowledge have tended to reinforce people's powerlessness.

They have also privileged the knowledge of others, making the problem doubly difficult. The values of positivist research advantage those without direct experience, as they can claim to be 'objective', 'distanced' and 'neutral'. 'In this sense, their ignorance is seen to make them better knowers or sources of knowledge' (Beresford, 2003, p 15). We can see how this can exacerbate the problem, so that it's only when researchers say something is true that it is. If research attention hasn't been paid to an issue, then it's that much more difficult to get it addressed. We've already seen how this has applied to violence against women, but historically it's been true of many other concerns, including, loss of species, climate change and hate crime.

The myth of neutrality in research/knowledge production has long been challenged – in the natural as well as social sciences. The source, funding, focus, nature and dissemination of research can all create bias. It's a human activity which brings its own biases (see, for example, Rose and Rose, 1971; Conolly and Troyna, 1998; Dancy, 2004; Rathbun and Turner, 2012).

Rethinking knowledge assumptions

My 2003 hypothesis challenged the routine devaluing of experiential knowledge, calling into question conventional research values and proposed instead:

> The greater the distance between direct experience and its interpretation, then the more likely resulting knowledge is to be inaccurate, unreliable and distorted.

In other words:

> The reliability and accuracy of knowledge and the distance there is between direct experience and the interpretation of that experience

upon which such knowledge is based, are likely to be in inverse proportion to each other. (Beresford, 2003, p 22)

Of course, we may be distanced from our own experience if we're alienated from it or accept others' interpretations rather than developing our own. In *It's Our Lives*, I showed how the distance between experience and interpretation could be both increased and reduced (Beresford, 2003, pp 41–56). Thus, we see how neoliberal ideology, by alienating us from our experience, can undermine the knowledge that comes from it. But this is still different from an outside researcher imposing their own meanings on such experiential knowledge. Even when user involvement in research has been encouraged, we still find conventional researchers doing this. They, like all such external interpreters, are at a disadvantage, seeking to offer a last word on the experience of others – which they don't share. However, this does not necessarily stop them from doing it!

Different meanings and intentions

We've been talking here about involvement in knowledge production. It may be helpful to remind ourselves of an important distinction that's emerged in the discussion about participation recently. This is the use of the same terminology to mean quite different things, based on different, often opposed ideologies. Service user movements struggled to develop a different research that was democratic, based on equal relationships and committed to advancing their knowledge(s) and bringing about the broader change they were seeking. Governments and research institutions, however, were more concerned with a consumerist, market-style approach to involvement that was informed by service user and citizen perspectives, but whose aims and control remained essentially as before. These have been contrasted as the liberatory/democratic and supermarket/consumerist approaches to involvement. It reminds us that our agendas, as powerholders and power-seekers, may be different and that while they may overlap – for example, between research, researchers and researched, that can't be assumed. A distinction is increasingly drawn between so-called health and care research 'public, patient involvement' or PPI and the effective user involvement patients and service users seek (Madden and Speed, 2017; Beresford, 2019; Colder Carras et al, 2022). While the former seeks to draw in the perspectives of research participants to existing research, the latter is concerned with changing the power relations and purpose of research.

Coproduction

We haven't yet discussed the latest attempt to transform knowledge production, which aims to overcome the division discussed earlier. This comes under the heading of *coproduction* and seeks to break down the barriers operating in research and other approaches to knowledge creation between producers and recipients. There's now a rising political and policy interest in this idea and an emerging literature, although in my experience, rhetoric has tended to outpace reality. The increasing talk of coproduction and pressure to demonstrate its existence comes when progress even on basic user involvement has been hesitant under neoliberal politics. There are many structural and other inequalities, particularly of power, status and resources to address before we can have routine confidence in such coproduction policy and practice. These can only be isolated to a degree from broader and increasing neoliberal constraints and barriers (Beresford, 2019; Rose, 2022, chapter 5). I've been involved in projects which have been consultative in ambition, but where the insight and commitment of their initiators has meant they have come closer to being coproduced in reality. Equally, I've been involved in self-badged coproductive efforts that have resembled basic consultations. I currently place more confidence in developing effective user-controlled research and knowledge-creation initiatives than over-optimistic attempts to coproduce, which too often fail to address structural inequalities which readily undermine them. This does not mean that we shouldn't pursue opportunities for coproduction (see Beresford et al, 2021), but equally, I'd be wary of putting them at the centre of the agenda for countering overarching neoliberal politics, which can insidiously undermine their potential.

Knowledge discrimination

A similar issue is also emerging in relation to experiential knowledge and the status granted it. Two discussions seem to have developed, ostensibly about the same thing, although it may be helpful to look at them more closely to check this. First, as we've seen, is that developed by the welfare user movements. Second, and more recently, an academic discourse has emerged in relation to these issues of knowledge, experiential knowledge and the imposition of inequalities on knowers.

While the user movement discussion has mainly been framed in terms of discrimination and oppression, this new academic discourse has tended to be discussed in terms of *epistemic injustice* and inequality (Kidd et al, 2017). The British philosopher Miranda Fricker is particularly associated with this and her book *Epistemic Injustice: Power and the ethics of knowing* as a foundational text (Fricker, 2007). It hasn't so much built on devalued knowers' viewpoints, like the service user movement, as instead asserted its own academic analysis of such experience. The emerging literature, which, at the time of writing, has given rise to special issues of two academic journals and an international edited handbook, has been presented using the neologism, 'epistemic injustice'. Fricker identifies two aspects to this;

first, testimonial injustice – or unfairness – devaluing what someone says, based on their identity and, second, hermeneutical injustice – or how people interpret their lives (Fricker, op cit).

This suggests the two overlapping discussions, activist and academic, have very similar focus and concerns. The activist discourse seems to have come first and can certainly be traced to the beginnings of the UK Disabled People's movement, where there were major discussions related to collective action and research about non-disabled people speaking for disabled people (for example, UPIAS, 1976). This raises the question of whether the academic discussion of epistemic injustice aids or substitutes for the activist one. The first doesn't so much reinforce the viewpoints of devalued knowers, as assert its own academic analysis of their situation. I published *All Our Lives* in 2003 and it has been heavily cited (over 200 to date) but, for example, it's not referred to in Fricker's book, which was published four years later. Nor is much service user-led material cited in the Wikipedia entry for epistemic injustice. When I tweeted about the different discourses about epistemic injustice, the response I got highlighted the overlaps between concerns about discrimination and injustice. But people were also concerned about the use of language like 'epistemic' as off-putting and an unlikely basis for effective campaigning. After contributing to a seminar with Fricker, I asked her if she:

> might be interested in supporting the development of discussion around this issue which more fully involves people identifying as psychiatric system survivors, or indeed others who feel the consequences of epistemic injustice.

She wrote back saying she didn't think she had any more to offer on the subject (Beresford, 2014). This sums up the difference between these two discourses; one is tied to action for change, the other to the demands of the academy, highlighting why academic interest in activist issues can be a double-edged sword, reinforcing the difficulties facing activists as knowers, as well as highlighting their struggles. Already, discourse about epistemic injustice in the context of psychiatry is coming in for adverse questioning from survivors for being 'discussed more widely by clinical academics than by authors with personal experience of psychiatrization' (Russo, 2023).

From individual to collective knowledge

This revaluing of experiential knowledge is now beginning to be mainstream. We're seeing it in first-hand accounts to help others in similar circumstances, highlighting lived experience beyond either the traditional self-help approach or misery memoirs. Such a text is the young comedian and actor Joe Tracini's, *Ten Things which I Hate about Me*, which announces on its end cover:

> If there is even the smallest chance that me telling you how I live with me helps you live with you; if it opens up a space for someone, somewhere to be more honest about their mental illness, it will have been worth it. Please don't kill yourself. (Tracini, 2022)

While it's still located within a mental health model, it's written with such wit and realism, confronting suicide and wretchedness, that I certainly found it helpful. Its commitment to lived experience is now particularly developed in the new NSM and discipline of Mad Studies and the debate it has prompted.

Yet, still often our lived experience and the resulting knowledge are dismissed as anecdotal, no more than individualised stories of questionable value and reliability. Even where there's recognition of their value in relation to individual experience, having a kind of testimonial value, they still tend to be devalued as limited to the individuals they come from, without broader value. This is to ignore the potential connections between individual and collective experiential knowledge.

Not everybody who has the same or similar experience interprets it in the same way. That's why it's important to move beyond relying on one person's reading of an experience – although this has its own validity. It's helpful to include as wide a range of interpretations of people who've been through the same or similar circumstances. This also challenges the argument frequently raised in relation to 'user involvement' that the people who get involved are 'unrepresentative', as if other stakeholders are of anything more than themselves.

Traditional research-based approaches clearly can offer opportunities to aggregate individual responses through quantitative and qualitative methods. They can also make it possible for individual views to be negotiated and synthesised with others through group discussions and other collective research methods. But this is no less true in the production of experiential knowledge. It may start with the exploration of individual experience and self-interpretation. Each person may place their own interpretation on such experience, according to their circumstances and identity. And even that interpretation may not be a constant, changing over time and with altering situations. These interpretations and understandings will also be influenced by each person's relation with diversity and intersectionality. This is a strength not a weakness.

However, most important, critical interpretations of our experience, especially of oppression, discrimination and exclusion, tend to find their most fertile ground in the self-organisation and collectivity of traditional and especially new social movements. As we have been seeing, the challenge to traditional and current neoliberal formal politics and ideology has particularly come from NSMs, which have especially focused attention on challenging ruling stereotypes, discriminatory roles and relationships.

There's no need to stop with people's individual interpretations of their lived experience even if we start there. It's possible to move from individual to collective experiential knowledge. As I wrote in 2003:

> We can share our experience with others and relate our different interpretations ... of experience to each other. In this way, it becomes possible to develop knowledge which synthesizes people's different understandings and perspectives on their common (and varied) experience. (Beresford, 2003, p 39)

We can do this through our own NSMs and self-organisations, getting together with others with related experience in groups that we control. Working together, we can develop our own shared understandings, views and goals, learning from each other how on an inclusive basis we can best make sense of the diversity of our experience.

This makes possible a truly social and inclusive process of generating our own collective knowledge based on shared experience. This has been happening with NSMs like the psychiatric system survivors and disabled people's movement where we've been able to explore and negotiate common themes, differences and the multifaceted nature of our identities. It has also made it possible for us to develop our own participatory and emancipatory research which pulls together our 'user knowledge' in a systematic way. This has enabled people to develop their own discourses to:

> Set next to and sometimes challenge prevailing views and understandings. These may be expressed in written materials ... as well as through electronic media, our own websites, arts and culture. What starts as people's own analysis of their experience, can become sophisticated and influential forms of knowledge, impacting on and fundamentally transforming popular understandings. (Beresford, 2003, pp 30–40)

Democratising knowledge

We've seen how the institutions associated with producing knowledge, from universities and research organisations, through to mass and social media, academic publication and research assessment, have increasingly been restructured in line with neoliberal ideology and politics, in the UK and globally, with an increasing intolerance of dissent. Yet the challenge has continued to grow.

Perhaps it's not surprising that some of the most disempowered groups – disabled people and mental health service users – have been among those most determinedly developing their own counter-ideas and knowledge.

All, over time, have highlighted the crucial need to be inclusive of diversity in their struggles, and though this can be doubly difficult because of their limited resources, it has become an increasingly important commitment in their struggles to redefine themselves, their relations with others and place in the world.

The knowledge production inspired by NSMs and beyond offers an alternative to consuming the news and information fed to us through neoliberal politics, ideology and their associated media. We can build on and extend the work that has been going on for years now, pioneered by such NSMs to develop understandings built on our own experience and ideas, to work out how we want to conceive ourselves and others rather than primarily internalising the often divisive and discriminatory versions fed to us by formal politics and ruling ideology.

The whole process of developing our counter-knowledge is based on collective and inclusive processes. We turn to, and value our own and each others' personal lived experience and learn to treat the knowledge handed down to us by neoliberal ideology and its institutions with corresponding caution as we come increasingly to appreciate its distorting versions of us and others. Instead of accepting the assertions offered to us by ideologically-bound politicians and knowledge-makers, we can check it out against the test of our own experience. Is what they tell us how it actually is for me in my little corner of the world? We do not have to accept 'their' big picture but can continue to build our own – in the plural rather than the singular.

The approach to knowledge production highlighted by NSMs, notably those of welfare service users and their concern about the exclusion of their lived experience, reflects a commitment to the valuing of the personal and their determination to connect that with social justice and inclusive politics. They reject the dominance of neoliberal politics that reinforces poverty, inequality, disempowerment and insecurity in shaping our understanding of the personal, for a personal shaped by commitment to treating diversity with equality, inclusion and participation and anti-discrimination.

What the NSMs have shown us is that even oppressed groups can counter neoliberal claims through the production of their own knowledge. There are, of course, more and less subtle barriers in the way of this, but a strong tradition already exists to build on. Put simply, by seeking to create knowledge based on our commitment to equal and inclusive roles and relationships, that starts with our personal politics, we develop the knowledge base to counter the formal politics that continue to undermine, divide and exclude us.

Spreading the knowledge

We have begun to share and disseminate this knowledge both among ourselves and beyond. We have done this through our collective working in and beyond our organisations and movements, through our newsletters and magazines, online and through dedicated and more general social networks and media. We have also engaged with mainstream media, academic and professional texts and begun to develop and alter the terms of the debate within their pages. Members of NSMs have established their own academic journals, generated special issues of others and even changed the processes of publication and peer review in such journals (for example, Beresford et al, 2023; Hughes et al, 2024). We have seen members of NSMs gain academic skills, undertake PhDs and develop participatory ones, gain academic roles and develop their own new areas and forms of study, from Disability, to Queer and Mad Studies. New forms have also emerged, like human, living libraries or libraries of lived experience, where such knowledge is shared between people directly 'lending people rather than books', sharing conversation and recording and valuing their oral contributions in the same way that written materials have historically been shared and valued through quotation (Prospero, 2017; Lancaster University, 2023).

In this chapter, we see the important part that traditional values relating to knowledge production play in reinforcing inequalities between us. We see the whole issue contested by NSMs unfold, of how oppressed groups have negative identities imposed on them and then these may be internalised. I certainly internalised the negative identity my mother sought to impose on me, and I had to spend much of my life dealing with and trying to escape from it. Knowledge control and false knowledge have thus long been used to undermine and devalue us. The transformative role of NSMs has been to help give us permission to reinvest confidence in our own understandings of our identities and our lived experience of them and the oppression we may experience. This has been a critical contribution to meaningful human reconnection and a formal politics renewed by it. In Chapter 15 we will look at the important part that a renewed approach to education can similarly play.

15

Education for empowerment and change

> The paradox of education is precisely this – that as one begins to become conscious one begins to examine the society in which [one] is being educated.
>
> James Baldwin, American writer and civil rights campaigner[1]

Introduction

Many of us spend much of our lives trying to sort out things that caused us difficulties in our childhood. If we're lucky, have good support and relationships, we make positive progress. This is the kind of education that can truly be thought of as lifelong learning, embracing our emotional and intellectual development. But sadly, for many of us, it's not the kind of formal education for life we receive. Nor does our state education greatly help in making sense of formal politics, which may be why, so many of us find ourselves increasingly alienated from them.

Education has constantly come up in this discussion of formal politics and personal roles and relationships; the gaps between them and the insights this may offer us for political change. In this chapter, we focus specifically on education because of its centrality to this issue and its both retrograde and liberatory potential. If, as we'll suggest, formal education has often served as the handmaiden of regressive politics, it's also key to its democratisation and reuniting formal and personal politics in a liberatory direction. However, the kind of education were talking about to help develop more emancipatory politics, tends to be very different from what we're familiar with from school. It's this paradox and reality we turn to now.

Education and change

Education is important in any process of change. It's long been a route out of poverty, a way that Western working-class literary characters, like those

---

[1] "A Talk to Teachers" from *The Saturday Review* (October 16, 1963) 1963 by James Baldwin, renewed 1991, 1992 by Gloria Baldwin Karefa-Smart. Reprinted with the permission of The Permissions Company LLC on behalf of the James Baldwin Estate. All rights reserved.

of the radical thinker H.G. Wells, could escape their narrow destiny in stratified societies like early 20th-century Britain (Sherborne, 2011). More recently, progressive debate focused in the UK on the 11 plus exam, how it discriminated against working-class, Black and minoritised children, limiting the social mobility all major UK political parties have electorally committed themselves to. Similar concerns were raised about the powerful 'public school' system with frequent failed demands for its abolition. Significantly, the high point of upward social mobility in the UK is now almost 50 years past in the mid-1970s as we have seen (Li and Devine, 2011). Since then, it's been moving in the *opposite* direction, with rapidly rising levels of neoliberal sponsored inequality.

Left-of-centre educationalists have long seen education as a route to liberating society and have been condemned as 'social engineers' for doing so. Yet it's probably been right-wing ideologues who've done most to line up education for their own political projects – particularly neoliberals. Education is not only a way individuals can improve their circumstances, it's also key to broader social change. We have seen how the post-war Labour Party pioneers sought to shift from 'selection' to 'comprehensive' education to widen educational opportunities. The first Education Act in 1870 was similarly based on social engineering principles. Then though, it was to impose compulsory education between ages five and 12 for Britain to compete in imperial manufacturing-based economies (Norman, 2022) and to fit the needs of modern mass armies.

The neoliberal turn

Education reform has been central to the UK neoliberal agenda. It has perpetuated the ruling reactionary political order, reinforcing its discriminations with increased segregation, privatisation and heirarchising of knowledge through radical reform in how:

- schools are built, increasingly through costly private/public partnerships;
- governance operates, increasingly taken out of local authority to private, less accountable control, such as academies;
- schools are managed, with additional layers of new managerialism, shifting control further from professional educators and increasing controls over them;
- school students are taught, with new national curricula, imposing central control and ideological conformity;
- schools are funded, with reduced government support and increasing responsibility for fundraising to parents and governors;
- schools relate to each other, with increasingly competitive relationships and parents left to 'choose' the 'best school' rather than being able to rely on high standards;

- further and higher education increasingly expected to compete and fend for themselves financially and students to pay more for their studies.

Teachers could once aspire to work as professionals in the state system. However, in its neoliberal consumerist iteration, they're almost powerless, buffeted between their political masters' ideologising and the perceived self-interest of parents. Once state primary schools were left to educationalists to become sites of innovative child-centred learning. Now they have joined their secondary equivalents within the neoliberal project. I've just watched a video of one of our granddaughters. She's a lively five-year-old and recently went into year one class. Her granny asks, 'How are you getting on at school?' 'Bad, I hate doing the work, I can't play', replies my granddaughter. 'Say something positive', says her seven-year-old sister. 'No, I don't like the work', she says.

First, came a national curriculum – in 1988 – micromanaging what teachers taught and revised as governments changed. Tests, exams and assessments became increasingly important, with SATs for seven, 11 and 14-year-olds, and AS levels. Ofsted, the new regulator, was introduced, imposing bureaucratised targets and rigidly imposed syllabuses. All of this is in line with the new neoliberal managerialism (Hanson, 2018). Then came political pressure for more children to learn Latin and, in 2023, to do much more maths, 'to 18', without any evidence as to why this needed to happen.

As UK education investment has declined, private/public schools have become more important. This is one of the earliest sites for our disconnection and alienation from each other. As inequality has increased with neoliberalism, so the importance of a segregated education system, advantaging some children at the expense of others increases. As the writer Alan Bennett said, private education 'isn't fair' and that's its point, to reinforce privilege (Green and Kynaston, 2019). This operates at every level. A friend who taught at Eton, the most prestigious UK private school, said to me, 'I was the servant of the rich'.

The British education system is two-tiered, equipping the privileged few to be the ruling class, or at least to acquire the networks, culture and status to perpetuate their advantage. For the rest, we're there to fill what's left for us. Whatever our talents or qualifications, that's increasingly insecure and devalued.

Don't assume the public school model is any more liberating than the state one, despite the massive privileges it confers. Its purpose is to fit the ruling class's children into the roles required of them. There's a history, from Tom Brown's *Schooldays*, through autobiographies like those of George Orwell and Cyril Connelly, reminding us just how unpleasant this experience may be (Leith, 2014). Serious problems of sexual abuse continue to be reported. What the rest of us often inherit from the public school system are the destructive effects of being on the receiving end of its damaged alumni who rule us. Certainly, the role it serves is to prepare us to be leaders and followers – based on privilege – and little else.

The limits of meritocracy

There's long been some rhetorical consensus among UK political parties on the virtues of equal opportunity, if not of equality itself. But it's perhaps time also to re-examine simplistic assumptions that meritocratic education – education based on ability – is simply a good thing. What it actually often does is alienate us from our life of origin, while not necessarily enabling us to belong to a more privileged adopted status.

Crucially, meritocracy isn't really about changing society. It's about changing who rises in the existing hierarchy. A classic British instance of a meritocratic model was Second World War officer selection. Following early defeats employing the traditional self-perpetuating system based on recommendation, War Office Selection Boards – Wosbees – were introduced, based on testing. This had much-improved results, but not necessarily for the 'temporary gentlemen' so created, who frequently faced later problems of adjustment in their families and society (Allport, 2009). Anyone who watched the sitcom, *Are You Being Served* will remember Captain Peacock's sad figure, reduced post-war to a pompous floorwalker in a crumbling department store.

Education and socialisation

A distinction is sometimes drawn between education and socialisation. The US sociologist John Clausen defines socialisation as encompassing both learning and teaching and 'the means by which social and cultural continuity are attained' (Clausen, 1968). Put another way – how society prepares us for the roles it has for us. Education is a significant contributor to socialisation, alongside other influences like family, peer group and media. We can quickly see how different political regimes seek to shape education to serve the socialisation purposes they require.

Thus, post-war UK Labour administrations worked for comprehensive education, with all children (still excluding disabled children) in the same school. Subsequent Conservative governments restored the old 'grammar' schools and more recently reformed education in line with their neoliberal thinking and 'trickle-down' philosophy. Meanwhile Blair's 'New Labour' sought a third way, reprioritising education with slogans like 'Education, Education, Education', while attempting to mitigate the pressures of impoverishment by balancing neoliberal economics with tax credits and increased welfare benefits.

These shifts in the intended aims of education reflect a values battle waged from governments' competing ideological positions, many framed in polarised terms. These range from prioritising state or market intervention, rights or responsibilities, collective help or individual responsibility.

Inclusive education

The term 'inclusive' is used here to signal a determination to include all on equal terms. We've particularly focused, in this book, on inclusivity and equality in connection with roles and relationships. Specific meanings are also attached to 'inclusion' in an educational context. These follow from the historic tendency to regard disabled people either as ineducable or requiring separate education. So-called 'special education' has tended to be inferior education. Until the latter part of the 20th century, children with learning difficulties (labelled as 'severely subnormal') were seen as needing 'training', not education, and sent to 'junior training centres' rather than schools. Once this was reversed, the next struggle was to challenge segregation, first under the banner of 'integration' and then *inclusion* (Tuckwell and Beresford, 1978).

UK social policy has mainly been directed towards 'notions of locational, social or functional integration' rather than inclusion based on the 'wholesale restructuring of education … relating to human rights, social justice and … the politics of recognition' as campaigners have demanded (Flood and Kikabhai, 2018, p 103). The inclusive education movement, led by disabled people, is a longstanding one, but the resistance it's encountered, especially under cost-cutting neoliberalism, has been remorseless and growing. Pressures against inclusion have also grown as schools have become more competitive, preoccupied with their regulatory status and seeking more advantaged students. This has been compounded by the increasing use of school exclusion in response to students seen as problematic. Thus, the irony that children needing particular support are particularly devalued in a consumerist system, with some Black children facing particular discrimination (Adams, 2018; Weale, 2020; McIntyre et al, 2021).

Theories and philosophies of education

There are different theories and philosophies of education and different understandings of how it works and what it's for. There are strongly competing interests, most significantly of those who shape and those who receive it. Education concerns us all, but it tends to be thought about mainly for children, which creates problems because predictably, it's adults, not children, who shape it. The latter largely lack the power or position to determine their education. Thus, education is perhaps the policy inherently most based on inequality and unequal relationships, historically extending to inequalities concerning so-called protected characteristics, perpetuating further hierarchies of inequality.

Yet, there's long been a movement for child-led education, enabling children to have a real say in their learning and schooling. There have always been educators imbued with such a commitment and particular kinds of schooling associated with it, plus periods when it's been in the vanguard. For example, the Steiner schools emphasise the balanced development of 'head, heart and hands'; the Montessori approach is based on the goal of self-directed learning; and A.S. Neill's Summerhill School of the 1920s foregrounded democracy and personal happiness (Wikipedia, 2022). I learned this from my history teacher Mr Witcombe who told us we should always be asking *why* – probably the most important lesson I learned at school and I'm not sure many are so lucky. We can see why; it's perhaps the most insurrectionist lesson to impart and could encourage us to question everything. It certainly had that effect on me!

Unfortunately, much 'progressive' schooling tends to reinforce privilege as it's largely only available to those who can pay. It's an approach often restricted to the more advantaged and enlightened, who are better placed to make choices about their children's education. Significantly, such schooling tends to connect the personal and political, with its emphasis on holism and more egalitarian roles and relationships – at least between learners and educators, encouraging individual thought for a more humanistic and connected world. It reflects the aspiration explored in this book, to bring reactionary formal politics more in line with progressive developments in human relations and understanding. While progressive education offers insights to move in this direction, sadly this has been limited by its association with privilege and class interest.

Filling buckets and beyond

The most common theoretical approach to education is the 'bucket theory' or 'banking model' of learning. This essentially consists of trying to fill 'the heads of pupils with knowledge' – the knowledge that the state decides they need (Titcombe, 2015). Not surprisingly, rote, dates, battles, nations, kings and queens all figure large in this educational approach. The current Westminster-imposed national curriculum has relied heavily on such notions of 'education', which serves a political purpose in the modernist tradition of equipping us for work, war, traditional social reproduction, gender roles and so on. It's the antithesis of person-centred education.

Liberatory approaches to learning

It's in strong contrast to emancipatory person-centred approaches to learning that have developed internationally. These have adopted a different ideological approach; one which isn't trying to bend the individual or group in a particular ideological direction. It's not based on the traditional educational model of seeing our heads as something for the educator to fill, to ensure ideological conformity and avoid challenge and dissidence.

A constellation of approaches has given force to such developments. While these have relevance to all of us, for childhood as well as whole-life learning, they have largely developed in the context of adult education – where the aim is generally to correct and challenge the disempowering consequences of previous socialisation and politics.

Frantz Fanon

Two key names in such developments are Frantz Fanon and Paolo Freire, both of whom had their own histories of oppression and exclusion. Frantz Fanon (1925–61), born in the French colony of Martinique, is remembered as a political philosopher, psychiatrist and anti-colonialist. His particular importance here is that he saw education in several senses as at the heart of democratic change. He saw it as a means both for the development of renewed subjective understandings through collective involvement and towards democratisation. As he wrote in his final book, *Wretched of the Earth*,

> To hold a responsible position in an under-developed country is to know that in the end everything depends on the education of the masses, on the raising of the level of thought, and on what we are too quick to call 'political teaching'. (Fanon, 1963)

Much earlier in his *Black Skin, White Masks* (Fanon, 1952), Fanon analysed the destructive consequences of colonial subjugation for Black people. Judged as inferior by white colonising populations based on their identity and language, they sought to mediate their situation by the performance of 'whiteness'; a strategy doomed to failure and alienation. As we discussed earlier, alienation refers to the condition of being estranged from oneself and others. While its meaning varies in the Marxist and psychoanalytic traditions, Fanon used it to describe how Black people were made to exist in relation to others and to identify with whiteness rather than their own blackness. He placed an emphasis on the lived experience of Black colonised peoples, emphasising the raising of Black consciousness to bring about change and decolonisation. His idea of Black consciousness has been widely influential. Fanon's understanding of political consciousness extends to the personal and political context in which people live, the place and time of birth, class affiliation, nationality and race – a significant issue in the context of this book's focus on inclusion and diversity. While he saw colonialism as subordinating Black people, he still believed in their ability to challenge this.

Photograph 15.1: Frantz Fanon

Note: A French African Caribbean psychiatrist, political philosopher and Marxist, influential in post-colonial and decolonising studies, highlighting Black consciousness, 1925–61.
Source: Fanon, Frantz (1925–61), Institut Mémoires de l'édition contemporaine archive, reference: 178FNN/1 – 178FNN/9 https://collections.imec-archives.com/ark:/29414/a01145371565 2qDUJ2p/daoloc/0/1

Paolo Freire

Fanon's work was a key influence on the Brazilian educator Paulo Freire (1921–97), whose work in turn connects several international radical movements, including liberation theology, decolonisation, anti-poverty and critical pedagogy, influencing teacher training and grassroots movements internationally and drawing on Marxist thinking. His philosophy was one committed to self-empowerment, social justice and bottom-up collective action. For Freire, education was not neutral. It either reinforced social control or became the 'practice of freedom', by which women and men deal critically with reality and discover how to participate in the transformation of their world (Jane Thompson, cited in, Mayo, 1999, p 5). He saw education as one way in which oppressed people could be active in their own liberation. For him, liberatory learning – pedagogy – must be owned by those seeking liberation: 'The oppressed must be their own example in the struggle for their redemption' (Freire, 1971, p 39). Freire also believed that those who acted as oppressors must be prepared to rethink their behaviour and examine their own role in oppression if real liberation were to take place: 'Those who authentically commit themselves to the people must re-examine themselves constantly' (op cit, p 47). Freire attached importance to literacy in an age and society where illiteracy was a powerful barrier to people's engagement.

A key concept that Freire developed was conscientisation – in the original Portuguese, *conscientização*. It's an essential part of Freire's idea of popular education. Here, the individual is supported (for example, by the adult educator/community development worker), to break through disempowering understandings of themselves and reality, imposed on them, through being involved in and reflecting on a process of action to bring about change. Thus:

> The process of conscientization involves identifying contradictions in experience through dialogue and becoming part of the process of changing the world. (Psychology Wiki, 2022)

This concept of *conscientisation* is closely connected with the idea of empowerment. Freire used it to mean a process of developing a critical awareness of one's social reality through self-reflection and social/political action. This embraces the two aspects of empowerment, of which more later, and is another reminder of the importance of both (Freire, 1971).

It's easier to explain the praxis of conscientisation from direct experience than solely by reference to philosophical writings. Thus, after I'd experienced what I'd describe as distress and madness and become a mental health service user, the only model I had for understanding was the dominant medicalised one through which the psychiatric system interpreted my experience and attached diagnostic labels to me. This chimes with Freire's exposition of the negative images we internalise of ourselves as marginalised groups, propagated by ruling institutions and their interpretations It was only when I got involved in a psychiatric system survivor-led organisation, *Survivors Speak Out* and was able to connect and discuss my experience with others in similar situations, who had come earlier to more social and liberatory understandings, that I could reinterpret what had happened to me, and see it as a starting point for collective action for change. This is what Freire meant when he wrote of critical consciousness as the ability to intervene in reality in order to change it (Freire, 2005). It's the route many survivors have taken and which has given rise to Mad Studies, a new social movement (NSM) which challenges individualistic, medicalised understandings of madness and distress (Beresford and Russo, 2022). Perhaps one difference between the ideas of empowerment and conscientisation is that the former emphasises that change comes from the understanding primarily of shared experience rather than an external influence.

Impact

Both these figures, Fanon and Freire, have had a wide impact. The influence of Fanon extended from the pioneers of the US Black Power movement, through Nelson Mandela, the ANC and Steve Biko in South Africa, to liberation and independence movements from Cuba to Palestine (Gibson, 2003; Hudis, 2015). The concept of conscientisation and Freire's work has had a powerful impact on many oppressed movements and a wide influence on liberatory education. This has extended to international adult literacy work and activist movements, the 1970s liberation theology movement, the South African Black Consciousness movement and the World Bank-funded Southern Highlands Rural Development Program's Literacy Campaign (Giroux, 2001).

The ideas of these two pioneers link with the concern for us to connect on equal and inclusive terms at the heart of this book. We see Frantz Fanon in his roles as both a humanistic psychiatrist and anti-colonial activist, committed to reconnecting people with their selves, relationships and worlds. We see his understanding of the importance of reuniting the political with the personal and a demand for politics which are personally liberating and egalitarian. Freire saw unequal social relations creating a culture of silence which instilled a negative self-image in oppressed people. He argued that learners therefore needed to develop a *critical consciousness* to recognise the oppressive aim of such a culture to resist it (CPUSA, 2022). The term conscientisation, which Friere went on to develop, originally derived from Frantz Fanon's coinage of a French term, *conscienciser*, in his book *Black Skins, White Masks* (1952, op cit). Freire saw conscientisation as a path to liberation that sought the humanisation of life. This process presupposed the elimination of oppression and also the overcoming of limiting situations in which human individuals were reduced. This exemplifies and points to the kind of reconceptualisation of formal politics with which we're concerned here through its reconnection with NSM pressures towards the equalisation of personal roles and relationships.

Learning from James Baldwin

There's one more influential figure who demands attention here. It's not coincidental that he was a writer like the three literary figures who first pointed us to the importance of 'connecting': Forster, Eliot and Hoggart. Indeed, he had his own comment to offer on the subject, highlighting its importance in his life:

> You think your pain and your heartbreak are unprecedented in the history of the world, but then you read. It was books that taught me that the things that tormented me most were the very things that connected me with all the people who were alive, who had ever been alive. (Baldwin, 1963a)

Baldwin, however, unlike his three predecessors was concerned with equality and inclusion as well as connection. This is hardly surprising given his identity as an outspoken Black gay American living through a time of great change and resistance as a writer, poet and campaigner (1924–87). It is probably unwise to have heroes among mere mortals, but for me, James Baldwin comes close. He bridges earlier discussions about connecting with the concerns we now have as a result of the impact of the NSMs – of which he was part – to address race, class, sexuality, diversity and equality in the process. This commitment to human and civil rights, which he discussed particularly with regard to being Black and gay liberation, is at the heart of all he did. Speaking of his realisation that he had to return to the US, his country of birth, from his sojourn in Paris, despite its violence and hate, he too highlighted the complexity of connection:

> But I missed my brothers and sisters and mothers ... I wanted to be able to see them, see their children ... I missed in short my *connections* (emphasis added). (Baldwin, 2016)

Like Fanon before him, he explored the destructive effects on oppressors, as well as oppressed, of discriminatory roles and relationships, saying:

> You cannot lynch me and keep me in ghettos without becoming something monstrous yourselves. And furthermore, you give me a terrifying advantage. You never had to look at me. I had to look at you. I know more about you than you know about me. (Baldwin, 2016)

As quoted at the head of this chapter, Baldwin also understood the worrying paradox of education. The aim of neoliberal education seems less to help us in our understanding of society, as he highlighted, and much more to keep the individual accepting of what is done to them (Baldwin, 1963b). The connections that Baldwin made are very much those that concern us here. Raoul Peck's film, *I Am Not Your Negro*, which explores the impact of Black activists Medgar Evans, Martin Luther King and Malcolm X and their assassinations, reminds us 'at the time of their deaths they had become increasingly interested in economic injustice and the class disparity' (Peck, 2017). What we also learn is that while we must all struggle determinedly to connect, the real responsibility lies with the oppressors.

Baldwin talked about his close friend, the young Black writer and activist Lorraine Hansberry, dead from cancer before she was 35, who had much to say both about her political struggles and gender inequity, highlighting, during her life and after her death, broader issues of identity and oppression (Marcus, 2022).

Baldwin, speaking to young Black people asked: 'How are you going to communicate to the vast heedless, unthinking, cruel white majority that you are here?' He answered his own question by putting the onus for change 'squarely on people in positions of power and privilege'. As he said:

Photograph 15.2: Malcolm X

Note: Was an African American revolutionary, Muslim minister, Black power leader and human rights activist in the US Black civil rights movement who was assassinated, 1925–65.
Source: Malcolm X, half-length portrait, facing right]/World Telegram & Sun photo by Ed Ford, Library of Congress, Prints & Photographs Division [reproduction number LC-USZ62–115058]

What white people have to do, is try to find out in their hearts why it was necessary for them to have a nixxxr in the first place. Because I am not a xxxxxx. I'm a man. If I'm not the xxxxxx here, and if you invented him, you the white people invented him, then you have to find out why. And the future of the country depends on that. Whether or not it is able to ask that question. (Buccola, 2019)

Conclusion

Baldwin recognised complex issues of marginalisation because of his own experience of intersectionality and inequality. We shouldn't forget this as we struggle for political and democratic reform, social justice and reconnection with each other. Clearly, education has a key role to play in equipping us all to understand and play a more active role in formal politics, to challenge inequalities regarding political access and to make it more possible for disadvantaged groups to have greater engagement with them. We need to understand ourselves and each other better – our different struggles and movements. This is a process that must start in childhood and not be left until adulthood to attempt some kind of catch-up or challenge. As we've seen, a very different approach to education from that which many of us have experienced at school is needed. As with Fanon and his peers, it draws on understandings that come from a series of related concepts and philosophies:

- critical pedagogy
- community development
- anti-poverty action
- empowerment
- consciousness-raising
- adult education
- critical race theory
- participatory learning and research
- decolonisation
- women's and queer studies

We can connect movements like Black Lives Matter and Queer Studies directly to pioneers like Baldwin and Hansberry. As well as needing to include much stronger elements enabling us to understand formal politics far beyond narrow traditional understandings of political education, this calls for opportunities for us all to have a better understanding of ourselves as citizens as well as people, as part of formal political processes rather than only as isolated individuals or market consumers. Next, we look at working together and how this can both engender and require more equal, inclusive ways of working.

16

Working together: building alliances, including everyone

> The state is not something which can be destroyed by a revolution, but is a condition, a certain relationship between human beings, a mode of human behaviour; we destroy it by contracting other relationships, by behaving differently.
>
> Colin Ward, *Anarchism: A very short introduction* (Ward, 2004)

Introduction

This book is about making change. The market has been deluged with such books, not least since times became much tougher for most people. Nevertheless, although the shelves are full of them and bookshops even now have whole sections devoted to the subject, with headings like 'Self Help' and 'Mind, Body and Spirit', the topic is generally the narrow one of trying to change *yourself*. Trying to change one person is likely to be a lot easier than trying to change the world! However, since the main reason most people seek change in themselves is to make their stay in this world more comfortable and positive, it's open to question how successful their efforts will ever be in isolation. In addition, most of these books tend to be based on one or another individualistic approach to self-development, so the sub-text is really more one of how you can improve your position in the unequal competition of life, rather than let's make things better for everyone. We may also wonder how helpful such a quest is in the context of the fundamental human desire at the heart of this book to 'connect'. Even beyond that, as Colin Ward reminds us at the beginning of this chapter, we may even have to subject taken-for-granted concepts like 'the state' to radical review (Ward, 2004).

Challenging individualised discourse about social change

In the world of popular self-improvement books, I've only encountered one that's the exception to this rule, one with which I can identify and that's England football international Marcus Rashford's guide for young people, *You Can Do It* (Rashford, 2022). He gained much wider visibility and was awarded the MBE through his serious efforts to do something about family and children's food poverty, intervening effectively to challenge Conservative government policy and influence understanding (Rashford, 2022). His approach is the antithesis of the 'fuck you' or 'don't give a fuck' book genre, emerging under neoliberalism, where the essential message is 'I am only interested in me' (Manson, 2017; Fuck You Books, 2023) – although significantly this has already come under direct attack through the theme of 'kindness' (Hamilton, 2024).

What's interesting about Rashford's handbook is that while it values the personal – looking after ourselves and thinking of others, it combines this with recognition of the socio-political. This extends to using the language of 'social justice', emphasising 'making a difference in the world' and recognising the importance of being a member of a *team*. Moreover, when he says this, he makes it clear he means more than a member of a sports team. It's about doing things *together*. Like many other sources of insight I've encountered writing this book, he brings an understanding of the importance of 'connecting' to his thoughts about 'finding a voice, making a difference'. As well as his commitment to connection being based on an understanding of the importance of inclusion and equality, it emerges as a thoughtfully nuanced one. He writes:

> You don't always have to be directly connected to someone for them to be your teammate. It doesn't have to be someone you see every day and it doesn't have to be someone you agree with all of the time. (op cit, p 163)

This really is an appreciation of 'connection' for the 21st century, which recognises the complex, changing nature of our lives, roles and relationships. It may take a village to bring up a child, but few of us globally live in villages now. Yet we may need to connect with many others to bring up that child; others with whom we don't necessarily have face-to-face contact, who we may only know briefly, and through other experience than familial ties, living locally or going to school with them. This is a helpful reminder that the nature of connection isn't fixed and we need to recognise this in our approach to formal politics as much as in our personal lives and in making sense of the two-way connections between them.

Working together – obstacles

In this chapter, we're focusing particularly on working together to achieve change and how we connect to do that. There's little doubt, as Rashford asserts, that we're likely to achieve much more together than individually and that's why this part of the book is so important. Few will disagree with this – historically, it has been movements and leaders with the ability to gather significant support around them (or at least neutralise opposition) that have led to the biggest changes – social, cultural and political.

Yet working together – how that actually operates in reality – is something which is often glossed over, or at least not given the attention it deserves. That's particularly true if we're concerned with working together based on egalitarian and inclusive principles. Perhaps this is because we've learned mistakenly to associate change-making more with cheering crowds or angry mobs rather than mass participation or active collectivities. This isn't surprising in a world that emphasises leadership and, as I have observed, often ignores its corollary – *followership* – but it's also unhelpful, especially in the context of any commitment to democratic politics. Working together is the obvious basis for democratic change. The less inclusive any change-making process is, the less likely that the outcome will be any more democratic. Thus, the 1917 Russian Revolution drew on widespread misery and discontent but was narrowly based and, for all the top-show, of 'elected soviets' and egalitarian language of 'citizens' and 'comrades', could never throw off the underlying reality it imposed, of an autocracy in charge of a vast, controlling bureaucracy. To make an impact for change, it looks as though we must work together with others. However, there are other issues here to take into account to get below the surface of this question and gain some real understanding of what that might mean and how to achieve it. We have to investigate the word 'work' just as much as the word 'together'.

Thinking about 'working'

For most of us in the 21st century, 'work' essentially means paid employment; that's to say, work in the public sphere to generate a livelihood. It hasn't always been so. Different economic systems impose different meanings on 'work'. Thus, in feudal agrarian societies it meant husbanding the land for the ruling lord who had some reciprocal responsibility and/or allowed you to keep some of what you produced. For women, it entailed all the tasks demanded by structures of social reproduction to secure the next generation and support the last. Under capitalism's social relations, men were the primary breadwinners in the labour market, with women subordinate, with primary responsibility for care and child rearing. More recently, there have been pressures as part of the quest for women's liberation to the equalising of care responsibility within the family, but with increasing time and economic pressures on both men and women to work within the formal economy. With the shift to neoliberal interpretations of capitalism, the trend has been one requiring wage earners to work for inferior pay and conditions, including longer hours.

This then is the primary modern understanding of what work means. Of course, it can mean other things, volunteering, caring, learning even getting involved in participatory activities, but paid employment is the defining meaning under capitalism and neoliberalism. With globalised economies, this extends beyond the Global North to the Global South. Working together in the labour market largely means operating in a hierarchy of unequal reward and recognition, often undertaking alienating and, increasingly, poorly paid and regulated tasks.

This is unlikely to offer us very helpful models of how to work together for change. Indeed, it may point us in a very different direction, with work's reform one of the key objectives of such activity. Yet for many of us, this is what work in the public sphere means – and work for political change inevitably takes us to the public sphere. At the same time, of course, women continue to have disproportionate demands made on them for so-called 'caring' work in the private sphere.

Thinking about 'working *together*'

Similarly, traditional ways in which people have worked together for change do not necessarily offer helpful ways forward. More often, they've reflected rather than broken with mainstream ways of doing things. They have often failed pioneer feminist Audre Lorde's test of avoiding using 'the master's tools', if the aim is 'to dismantle the master's house'. Thus, trades unions, the key vehicle that emerged for labour reform, have tended to reflect traditional mainstream structures and values and their hierarchies and inequalities, albeit typically bound by formal democratic procedures. The same has also often been true of traditional community-based approaches to collective working.

Often this last is depicted in quite simplistic and superficial ways. Anyone who has been seriously involved in any large scale or significant campaigning is likely to have some appreciation of how complex, multifaceted and contentious it can be. There are internal differences, competing aims and strategies, rival leaders and followers, different agendas and tactics, the media as ally, agent and sometimes enemy. If the assumption is that having a common cause would subordinate differences in our history, experience, cultures, identity and ambition, this is not necessarily the case.

We owe a big debt to new social movements (NSMs) for forcibly reminding us of this. What we have seen with such modern movements is a pattern of action shaped first by the desire to secure the rights and equality of some group or issue. Then the further struggles that take place as different groups within that overarching identity or experience struggle to secure equal valuing and understanding for their own particular standpoint. This has happened in relation to gender, race, sexuality, disability and so on in the civil rights, women's and other movements, as the particular oppression, for example, of Black or lesbian women, older or trans disabled people is asserted. This is intersectionality. Asserting and addressing it is an understandable and necessary part of the process of inclusive change but that doesn't mean it's necessarily comfortable or painless. Political struggles can be as difficult and stressful within, as they are confronting their external opponents. It's something we must remember and accept.

This is because such struggles are complex and can also serve different purposes. For some, they are the locus for a one-off challenge or lifetime concern. For others they are sites of political apprenticeship, single-issue activity or occupational advancement.

Working together for change can also be difficult. It can be a tough arena to operate in, with many people feeling reluctant to engage unless they reach a point where they feel they absolutely have to. That can help make it an increasingly vicious circle, with only the most determined or desperate prepared to engage. In addition, being involved in collective action, especially in individualising societies like advanced Western market societies is not everyone's cup of tea. Reluctance to get involved in formal politics is also often mirrored in reluctance to get involved in challenging it.

People seem much more prepared to get involved in hobbies and enthusiasms, volunteering/voluntary action that's not explicitly political than in campaigning and political activism. Perhaps this is because 'political' is still a dirty word in societies like the UK, and the former seems less contentious. It may also follow from the increasingly alienating nature of formal politics under neoliberalism. What this seems to mean is that a relatively small proportion of people get actively involved in campaigning and associated political activity, but are often involved intensely.

There are many disincentives from getting involved with others to achieve change. These need to be recognised if they're to be overcome. It's not just that the idea of 'working together' or 'collective working' may sound unfamiliar. From my own experience and the guidance I've gained over many years, I'd say it's a minefield!

Being an activist

To give readers some idea of my own background, I've been involved in many community-based, activist and campaigning activities. This has included local and international campaigns and organisations, from a neighbourhood tenants' organisation where I lived, to international mental health service users/survivors' and disabled people's organisations, and local and national trades unions. I've taken part in land-use and human rights struggles, save local amenity and services campaigns, strikes, pickets, demonstrations and marches, as well as producing pamphlets, exhibitions, painting graffiti and putting up posters. I've organised public meetings, been a spokesperson on radio, television and social media, and provided evidence for official inquiries. I've been involved in organising conferences, workshops, webinars and other online events. I've raised money for campaigns by rattling tins, selling publications and crowd-funding. I've been involved in a riot, witnessed violence done to a service user, received direct evidence of rape and sexual abuse of staff and service users in a homeless charity, as well as using false names and documents to investigate statutory services. I was a member of a community organisation that had been infiltrated by undercover police despite being committed to non-violent action within the law.

Such activities and experiences are campaigners' unremarkable stock-in-trade. I've valued what I've learned and probably wouldn't have it any other way. It might have been easier if I could have learned sometimes from other people's hard-earned experience! I've been involved in some collective action that's been so unpleasant that I've had to decide priorities and withdraw for self-preservation. This has usually been where power has been narrowly held, preparedness to share it minimal and participation correspondingly marginal. Then there have been others where real change has been achieved, with real participation, making it all worthwhile and life enhancing. Of course, one of the problems is that you rarely know which is going to be which!

An example of activism in relation to the COVID-19 pandemic

Sally Witcher is a disabled person at high risk of COVID-19, based in Scotland, who has long worked in the disability, equalities and inclusion fields. She talked with me about all the new issues that COVID-19 raised for her as someone personally and politically close to it and new ways of responding to them that people like her have been developing.

> Some very exciting and innovative things are happening using new technology, like Zoom. I've been very immersed in this personally and professionally especially because of all the equality and inclusion issues Covid and the (Conservative) government's failure to respond adequately have raised. A whole new grassroots community-led movement started to spring up, with lots of little groups who've come together, usually because they are either clinically at very high risk, or they're carers, or have long Covid.
>
> A lot of the organizing is necessarily distanced because the people are covid-cautious. What's also being done is build global as well as local communities. The World Health Network operates across the world with volunteers and communities. It's led by people who really know the science side and they've initiated what they call Covid Meet-Ups. So, people can set up their own groups, whether topic-based or local to a country or geographic area. I got involved with the Scottish group – people who before had never met ever in the flesh. They and other online groups have basically got me through this, these people, who I didn't know before. A real challenge is all the prejudice that's come out of the woodwork. The discrimination is more clearly out there now. I identify as somebody at exceptionally high risk from Covid but not in the way the government necessarily recognizes, because I have

multiple co-morbidities. Any additional damage is going to be a big problem for me. My GP put me on the original Shielding List (now defunct). But I still don't necessarily tick the official boxes. Many people at high risk don't. I had to engage with the reality that I was never going to feel safe outside my house again.

People pop up in different networks. There's a bunch in Edinburgh, they communicate with each just about every day on WhatsApp. The Scotland Group meet every Tuesday at 7pm. Often people share personal stuff. It's used for peer support – 'this rubbish thing happened to me today' – for organizing and sharing information, getting involved in action. Once there was a masked protest outside the Parliament, involving people from various online groups. The conversations can range from knitting, to I had a meeting with an official last week, or how capitalism doesn't seem to work, back to guinea pigs and pets. From the really personal to the political.

The Edinburgh group meet in person when the weather is ok, often in the local park, maybe eight or ten of us. We sit there in our masks, no doubt to the astonishment of some local people. We're all very careful, that gives you a lot of confidence. We've talked about having a masked flash mob!

In Scotland there have been mantras in relation to Covid like *Build Back Better* and we should create a *New Normal*. I talk about an *Inclusive* New Normal (#InclusiveNewNormal). I've tweeted a new strategy, looking abroad, checking out innovation and that's got picked up by mainstream media and politicians. It's now evolving into a constituted organization.

It was an existential seismic shock to society's structures when Covid came. People have started to see how we don't have good democracy. It's about learning how they covered up a pandemic, how they 'made it go away'. And it's being done globally – the clash between the current economic drivers alongside people's wellbeing, people not getting sick – and that clash has never been so acute. (Personal communication, 2023)

As Sally makes clear, in this approach to activism and collective action, the personal and political are intimately connected and interlocking. I've certainly learned many lessons from my own and others' experience of working together – what to do and, perhaps even more importantly, what not to do. These can perhaps best be summed up by the following heading.

The problems of ignoring differences in power and experience

Some of my earliest experiences of collective action related to what's categorised as community action and development. It quickly became apparent that the familiar, 'warm' term 'community' could conceal many difficulties for collective working. Not least that 'community' denotes exclusion just as often as inclusion, with some groups facing discrimination. Historically, there's tended to be an association of 'community' with geographic community – with definitions based on locality and assumptions made about the uniformity of people within such areas, particularly relating to the nature of housing, local economy and so on, associated with segregated poor and better-off areas. This has historically been the basis of area anti-poverty programmes in the UK and US. However, it can also reflect and conceal broader inequalities in society, with more confident, better-off people speaking and acting for others, white for Black and so on, while reasonably claiming to be locals, or outside professionals shaping the agendas of disadvantaged residents and so on. Both distort the process and outcomes of supposed 'collective working' (Beresford and Croft, 1986 and 1988).

As I have written elsewhere:

> From personal experience, this phenomenon of marginalized groups being drowned out in collective action, is common in community organizing, where much campaigning takes place. Here inequalities of power tend to mean that 'leaders' are more likely to have the political, status and cultural equipment (and even time and opportunity) to engage, than those who may be the most disadvantaged by the problems under consideration. This has also been reinforced by the professionalization of such activity (Beresford and Croft, 1988). Historically such campaigning has tended to reflect the exclusions and discriminations of the wider society, thus to be led by white middle-class professionals, rather than the poor, working class people who are most at the mercy of the social problems that such campaigns are ostensibly concerned with. (Beresford, 2021, p 101)

Related to this are the problems that arise when collective action based on common difficulties involves people with significantly different levels of experience and assertiveness in relation to existing power holders. Here a different difficulty emerges, where professionals and policymakers are able to manipulate the two in divisive and damaging ways, dismissing more experienced participants as 'professional activists' and their concerns as unjustified while playing on the inexperience of others. What is essential here is support for the latter. This is a problem that has discouraged me from prioritising involvement in mainstream structures for involvement which do not support people to gain the skills and confidence they need to be take part on truly equal terms.

This is where skill-development and education in its broader pedagogic, consciousness-raising sense we discussed in the last chapter come into play.

It's key to working together equally and inclusively and it's also one of the products of doing so. There's a two-way relationship between personal growth and change and collective action for change. The key concept that unites them is *empowerment* – we now explore this in more detail because of its crucial importance – both specifically to generate such change – and also because of its centrality in reuniting the political and the personal.

Empowerment: building block for change

The idea and practice of empowerment are crucial if we're to work effectively together. It's a concept that sums up this book's aim – to reunite the personal and the political in an emancipatory way. A lesson that NSMs have taught us is that shared experience is a powerful basis for collective action. This may not be of the same problem or barrier, but rather shared experience of oppression and discrimination. Across different issues and exclusions, this can be a shared experience which both helps us understand the predicament of others and takes priority over other motivations and backgrounds people have. Later we'll look more closely at why such shared understandings can have a special significance. First, we need to remind ourselves why empowerment has particular importance both in relation to NSMs and the present discussion.

The social work academic Robert Adams offered a helpful definition of empowerment as:

> the capacity of individuals, groups and/or communities to take control of their circumstances, exercise power and achieve their own goals, and the process by which, individually and collectively, they are able to help themselves and others to maximize the quality of their lives. (Adams, 2008, p xvi)

It's the NSMs which have particularly developed the praxis of empowerment. Every identity-based NSM has its particular expression of the idea, beginning with the US civil rights movement from the 1950s. That's no accident. It's because such movements build on the interrelation of the personal and political to challenge discrimination, working together on equal terms.

Empowerment is a crucial concept for unifying personal and political – as the NSMs seek to. That's why the two tend to be particularly linked – each giving force to the other. The emphasis of the identity-based NSMs on shared experience gives the praxis of empowerment further relevance. However, empowerment also has special resonance for this book. That's because of its concern with reconnecting the personal and political in order to transform formal politics and challenge the dominance of damaging and isolating neoliberalism. Empowerment offers many insights into how we can personalise the political as well as staying alert to the political relations of the personal.

Turning to empowerment, I'm particularly indebted to the approach pioneered by the US Black civil rights movement, although in general terms, this has been the consistent basis for empowerment in NSMs more generally. What's especially important about this idea is that it recognises the key importance of both personal development and collective action for successful change-making. In this, it extends the idea of conscientisation particularly associated with Paulo Freire, which we encountered earlier. However, it also, as he did implicitly, addresses the social and political in helping us make sense of the need for political action – in its broadest sense. Thus, empowerment explicitly addresses both agency, our capacity to make change, and structure, the broader structural issues and constraints we have to take on, and their interrelations.

So, the idea of empowerment is concerned with both the personal and political. *Personal* empowerment means engaging with ourselves – which means reflection and reflexivity in relation to ourselves – that's to say the examination of our own beliefs, judgements and practices, including our understanding of ourselves and how these may influence our views and actions. Personal empowerment also addresses how we may raise our confidence, expectations and skills to enhance our interactions with others and the social and political worlds we inhabit to achieve change.

So initially, empowerment is concerned with making personal change – change within us. However, crucially it doesn't stop there. The second part, which is recognised as conditional on such personal empowerment, is concerned with taking collective action for broader *political* change. Moreover, this is change based on what 'we' as a movement, having come together, come to recognise as the change needed to advance our rights and interests in broader contexts of social justice.

This is where empowerment's two elements – personal and *political* – converge and unify. The vehicle for bringing about personal empowerment is not some external leadership, hierarchy or external intervention. It's 'us' – a collective and continuing process of reviewing and renewing *ourselves*, enabled and supported by others with shared experience and comparable understandings, who similarly have come to question how they are understood in the world and how they might understand that world. This is how the disabled people's movement discovered the social model of disability and the philosophy of independent living – an organic model of the intellectual – where we are all each other's spur and support for reflexivity and renewed self-understanding. Just as we learn new ways of understanding ourselves and each other, rather than accepting the versions imposed on us by others, for example, as 'inherently inferior women' or 'pathological mental health service users', so we learn new ways of understanding policy and practice, research and theory, and are able to develop our own theories, ideologies and politics.

That's why there's an emphasis in empowerment discussions on *self-empowerment*. We can only do it for ourselves – singular and plural. Yes, we can be helped towards it by others perhaps, as professionals or without our lived experience, but we cannot be empowered by them. Our internal experiential knowledge is our starting point. It's what defines us and is a basis for trusting others who have taken similar journeys. It's not an external but internal task in the sense of happening within each of us as an individual, with the support and engagement of others with comparable and relevant experience. The politics inherent in such an understanding of empowerment is also a highly humanistic one, based on treating each other with kindness, respect and equality and, in a broader context, of rights and social justice.

Empowerment offers a way of uniting the political and personal in theory and action. It also offers us a *praxis* for reconnecting the political with the personal. It makes it possible for us to be part of political action where we know why we are there and what we are doing, and for that political action to take forms both in which we have some real say and involvement and which are directed to ends which we want and have identified. We've seen this develop in NSMs, and those NSMs then seek to influence and change formal politics in line with those goals and demands.

We've seen some organisations which originated with social goals take on more neoliberal values and structures. Thus, housing associations which now offer thousands of units of rented accommodation readily evict tenants and pay their CEOs very high wages. This was exemplified in 2022 by two-year-old Awaab Ishak's death as a result of mould in the 'social housing' where he lived, earlier reported by a health visitor, without remedial action being taken which would have saved him (Brown, 2022).

Self-organisation

Working together in our own organisations provides a valuable basis for building such self-determining change and changing our formal politics. By our own organisations I mean, for example, women's organisations controlled by women which support the full inclusion of women in all their diversity, with diversity valued and treated with equality. Or disabled people's organisations that are controlled by us, not by non-disabled leaders. There is, as we've seen, a large and growing literature about such movements and the self-run organisations that have been strongly linked with them (Bagguley, 1992; Castells, 2004; Todd and Taylor, 2004). What often distinguishes them in fact and aspiration is that:

- they don't operate on the basis of one (more privileged) group speaking for another, but with an emphasis on people speaking and acting for themselves;

- they place an emphasis on access and inclusion in terms of physical, communication and cultural access and addressing diversity on as equal terms as possible;
- they place an increasing emphasis on issues of intersectionality, seeking to recognise the rights of minorities within minorities; groups facing multiple discrimination and oppression within such groups;
- they are human, civil and social rights-based rather than starting from a narrow economistic approach;
- there is recognition of issues of reward and recognition – particularly in NSMs relating to health, social care, anti-poverty and other public policy;
- often, they value and are unified by shared, lived experience.
- they highlight equal roles and relationships and value the personal as well as the political, emphasising their interrelationships. (McAdam and Paulsen, 1993; Oliver, 1997; Nardini et al, 2020; Mackenzie, 2022)

Black civil rights and feminist/women's NSM organisations placed an early emphasis on exploring ways of working which challenged conventional hierarchies, were culturally appropriate and neither relied on formalistic democratic procedures nor ostensibly more informal approaches, both of which could conceal real power inequalities. Since then, disabled people's organisations, as we've seen with Shaping Our Lives, have highlighted issues of process that can disadvantage people, for example, who rely on different forms of communication, or need additional opportunities for advance preparation because of their impairments or learning difficulties.

We saw the kinds of barriers facing disabled people and people with long-term conditions in terms of having equal communication access. However, the barriers facing them working equally across the differences among and beyond them extend much further. They include barriers relating to:

- mobility
- vision
- Deafness and hearing
- energy
- cognition
- mental wellbeing
- fatigue
- pain and
- now more clearly recognised in relation to COVID-19 and long COVID, although long associated with ME, brain fog (Deane et al, 2019; Kings Fund and Disability Rights UK, 2022)

Shaping Our Lives over the years has developed some simple ground rules to encourage more equal and kind working together, to help make it a more positive experience. Following COVID-19 and lockdowns, they've developed a version for remote meetings. This is said aloud by a member of the group before all meetings and then agreed (SOL, 2022).

Shaping Our Lives and other disabled people's organisations have also highlighted the issue of payment for people directly involved in such user-led organisations (ULOs). This is based on the strong belief that service users are a group disproportionately restricted to lower incomes compared with others, and often reliant on welfare benefits because of the excluding nature of the labour market. Therefore, if service users do things that are the equivalent of paid work in their own organisations, it's only reasonable they should be paid for their skills and contribution. Campaigning and user involvement work is work like any other. Shaping Our Lives has long supported this principle, although people who don't want to be paid, or whose benefits might be adversely affected, can opt out. People need to know where they are as regards payment; it should be made speedily and appropriately and be comparable to that provided for others with comparable skills and experience.

Significantly, the operation of the UK Charity Commission generally does not allow for such payment. People who are trustees of registered charities are generally not permitted to be paid for work they do on behalf of them. This perpetuates a notion of 'them' and 'us' in charities' operation, reinforcing old regressive assumptions that there are two separate groups – those who give and those who receive charity. Despite the efforts of organisations like Shaping Our Lives to seek reform, this situation continues and is one reason why it became a community interest company *with charitable aims* rather than a registered charity. Another is the deliberate limit set to the 'political activity' of charities at a time when neoliberal ideology has greatly impacted on public provision, thus, restricting discussion about the merits of such reduced state intervention and an increasing responsibility being placed on charitable activity to combat poverty and material inequality.

At a time when, in line with neoliberal ideology, health, welfare and charitable services have become increasingly bureaucratic and hierarchical, NSMs have also encouraged an increasing interest in different forms of organisation and structure to encourage the more equal and inclusive relations associated with their values. So, we have seen the development of much flatter, more egalitarian structures and increased interest in more flexible ways of working and the provision of child care, paternity and bereavement leave, and more flexible working on the part of such NSM organisations in line with their values and as part of their broader approaches to service provision, campaigning and policy.

We've seen NSMs spearhead pressure for a living wage, choice of retirement age and between home and office working. This last has become a much broader concern since the introduction of distanced working during

COVID-19 lockdowns. They've been strongly associated with organisational structures based on more equal roles and relationships like:

- collectives
- collaboratives
- coproduction
- cooperatives

A workers' cooperative is one which is jointly owned by the workers, a collective an organisation that's managed by its members without formal hierarchy, each person having equal decision-making power. A co-op, on the other hand may be structured on a hierarchical basis. There are also co-ops controlled by their users. The general thrust of such organisations is towards more equal and democratic operation (Cathy, 2022).

Each in its different way has helped advance practice and understanding based on more equal, inclusive and humanistic work roles and relationships. These make possible different approaches to ownership, service provision and people's experience of human services and support. Twenty-five years ago, a big UK-wide project, funded by the UK Lottery, highlighted the benefits of user-led services from the viewpoints of their service users, user workers and governance. However, their expansion has still been very limited in a neoliberal political environment that has overly privileged privatisation and the market in health and social care, despite their long-evidenced deficiencies (Barnes et al, 2001).

We also sometimes see the benefits of more equal working in the mainstream system, when organisational accidents offer such opportunities. Thus, Suzy Croft, the palliative care social worker said:

> Healthcare tends to be very hierarchical. This isn't only because it's got very managerial, but because of the histories of the different professions involved. So, there's medics at the top with their quasi-military ranks from juniors to consultants and then nurses, 'allied health' and so on. My first job in palliative care wasn't like that. We essentially worked as an equal team. It was a wonderful experience – highlighting the massive benefits of more equal ways of working. We were a community-based team working out of a hospital but I was employed as a social worker by the council. We didn't include any consultants but we could call upon a couple in the hospital – and the rest of us for a time – and maybe this had something to do with it, were all women – social worker, nurses, administrator, we all just worked as an equal team – and it was really positive. We got on, valued each other's contribution and were left alone! Of course, it couldn't last and, when an ambitious consultant became involved, it ended. (Croft, Personal communication, 2022)

User-led, community-based and democratic organisations are not necessarily available in every locality to provide opportunities for empowerment and the strengthening of new approaches to more inclusive and democratic campaigning and service provider organisations. This is also significantly linked with the inferior access to funding which such organisations have. An alternative has been pioneered by Shaping Our Lives, supported by the UK Big Lottery. The aim has been to create two new services with and for disabled people and people who use health and social care services in a project called 'The Inclusive Involvement Movement' (IIM). This is to make it easier for them to be involved when health and social care policies and services are being designed, researched and improved so that their voices are heard and can make a difference. The new services are:

1. the *My Involvement Profile*, an involvement tool that will support service users to detail their lived experience and advocate for their own inclusive involvement, and;
2. *Involvement Mentors*, offering training and support to service users to implement a simple but effective involvement framework with local decision-makers that supports a national standard of meaningful involvement. These mentors work with organisations (health and social care services and universities) locally, using their local knowledge and connection with Shaping Our Lives to support inclusive involvement. (Shaping Our Lives, 2020)

The goal is to develop an additional approach to empowerment and conscientisation where people don't have access to a ULO locally.

The connection with coproduction

The idea and practice of coproduction is one of the most ambitious of current approaches to more participatory, equal and inclusive working. Indeed, some commentators suggest there are limits to its implementation so long as the prevailing political system continues to operate in an excluding and unequal way (Carr, 2018). Nonetheless, it has particular relevance in challenging such ideology and helping reconnect us and formal politics. Underpinning coproduction is a commitment to breaking down boundaries between consumers and producers, service users and providers, and expert and experiential knowledge. It's concerned with bringing participants together equally to coproduce better research, policy and practice. The editors of one text on COVID-19 and coproduction offer a helpful definition:

> central to our understanding of co-production are processes through which inequalities in power are acknowledged and addressed to facilitate

collaboration. So, co-production ... is about bringing together citizens, communities, patients, and/or service users with those working in health and social care research, policy, and practice, and attempting to form equitable partnerships. This extends to citizens, communities, patients, and/or service users making meaningful contributions to agenda setting and the formation of aims and objectives, not merely being 'involved' once these important decisions have been made by those who traditionally hold power. This draws otherwise excluded perspectives and understandings into strategic and procedural decision-making processes and makes the most of everyone's different skills, knowledge, experience, and abilities. (Williams et al, 2021, p 13)

Six principles for coproduction have been identified:

- Value all participants and build on their strengths.
- Develop networks of mutual support.
- Do what matters for all involved.
- Build trust.
- Share power and responsibility.
- People can be change-makers, and organisations enable this. (Blanluet, 2018)

What's perhaps particularly interesting is how the values of coproduction address and encourage the kind of egalitarian and inclusive values associated with NSMs and support ways of working together for change consistent with achieving more humanistic and inclusive policy and politics. Put another way, coproduction offers a particularly helpful way of making positive political change. It draws on equalising roles, relationships and diversity, consistent with the change-making approach we discuss here.

Conclusion

If people are to be inclusively involved in political processes that achieve change, then we'll need to work together. How we work together is key to making that possible. It means connecting the personal with the collective by engaging in structures that recognise and challenge inequalities of power, relationships, roles and experience, attaching more equal value to all of them. There needs to be a close two-way relationship between us and our approach to working together for change, if we are to be able to play an active and equal role, rather than just make up the numbers, as some kind of stage army. If we are all to be part of the political process, then some of us at least will need help to get involved to:

- know what to do;
- see it as possible;

- gain confidence;
- make the most effective contribution.

First, we gain understanding of ourselves and others from our own lived experience and review our views about both – specifically recognising and valuing the differences among us as well as what we have in common. Then we're likely to be in a better position to begin examining broader relations with other groups – other groups we are likely to need to ally with, if we're ever successfully to challenge the powerful minorities that have become even more economically and politically powerful under neoliberal ideology. In the next chapter, we look afresh at the idea of 'solidarity' and what it needs to mean where the aim is both to acknowledge diversity and treat it with equality.

17

Rethinking solidarity – extending connection

> Solidarity does not assume that our struggles are the same struggles, or that our pain is the same pain, or that our hope is for the same future. Solidarity involves commitment, and work, as well as the recognition that even if we do not have the same feelings, or the same lives, or the same bodies, we do live on common ground.
>
> Sara Ahmed, a British-Australian writer and scholar

Introduction: The massive contradiction

Something we've had to get used to under neoliberalism, for example, in the UK, is that institutions we've long valued, supported and defended, like the NHS and BBC, have become contradictory and ambiguous. We fight for the licence fee and public broadcasting because we know that without the BBC, UK broadcasting will suffer and it will be a free-for-all of destructive market forces and empire-building media moguls like Rupert Murdoch. However, we also weep over BBC news shifting to the right and becoming the amplifier of the neoliberal press. It failed miserably over issues like the decades-long Jimmy Saville sex abuse scandal, became over-bureaucratised, kow-towing to government. The NHS remains a jewel in the crown for many, but it's been hollowed out by privatisation, its staff overloaded and bullying endemic.

These realities highlight the issue at the heart of this book – the working through of the struggle now taking place between our personal politics and the formal politics they routinely challenge. As we saw during the pandemic, UK health and care workers struggled unto death – in too many cases – to do their jobs to the best of their ability, while for-profit organisations milked anti-COVID-19 budgets for billions. We saw the inspiring alliance between health researchers, workers and volunteers roll out the vaccination programme with speed, efficiency, kindness and caring, while politicians partied illegally.

This struggle between the values of our personal politics and the formal politics imposed on us is being worked through in most if not all of our institutions, including charities, schools, universities, professions, public bodies and so on, where the same pattern is repeated of:

- workers struggling to offset the hostile imperatives of neoliberalism in their work with people as customers and service users;

- values and structures of equality being constantly undermined by counter-forces coming down from the top;
- more and more of people's energy being absorbed in fighting to maintain prevailing personal values through activism and voluntary action in organisations like food banks for refugees, poor etc. challenging climate change and working for sustainability;
- where the protections afforded people by social rights legislation has been reduced, but the pressures on them increased, undermining physical and mental wellbeing.

This is reminiscent of the struggle highlighted by the UK campaign *In and Against the State* in the early1980s, but now at a far more extreme level, nationally and globally. In a pioneering new social movement (NSM) initiative, that group of socialists and feminists, identifying as 'socialist economists', raised the question of what the role of workers in the welfare state should be when the state's role in relation to capitalism was repressive (London Edinburgh Weekend Return Group, 1980; Beresford, 2016, pp 248–50). The question is even more important now. Later they wrote:

> It is essential to find ways of working for change from within our jobs and our private lives; ways of developing effective, organised oppositional action which comes directly out of the everyday oppression we experience. (http://libcom.org/library/acknowledgements-preface-second-edition, cited in Beresford, 2016, p 249)

This anticipates our present focus on transferring current progressive learning from the private/personal to the political sphere. The group prefigure some of the proposals here to recognise and challenge the way prevailing formal politics influence and damage our personal roles and relationships, for example:

- challenging 'individualisation' by strengthening collective and class identities through doing things together;
- rejecting misleading categories imposed upon us and building workers' own understandings of themselves and others, developing links and alliances;
- defining our problem/issue our way – as a basis for change, rather than accepting the analyses imposed upon us;
- refusing official procedure – working in more open, honest and equal ways with service users and other local people
(http://libcom.org/library/chapter-6-oppositional-possibilities cited in Beresford, 2016, p 249).

We can see people's present struggles under neoliberalism as a routine part of their daily lives, sapping energy, incurring defeats and achieving successes.

Most important, we see the NSMs impacting on the roles and relationships of more and more people as more of us turn to the movements that have been the vanguard for challenging neoliberal ideology, to challenge both our own disempowerment and that of others. This turn may be a sharp one of making the decision actually to get involved in them, or a subtler one, beginning to hear what they have to say, as it makes increasing sense in relation to our emerging realities and rising difficulties under neoliberalism.

There are many ways of representing the battle against neoliberalism, in traditional left/right terms, as personal struggle, altruism versus individual selfishness, for environmentalism against despoliation. Nevertheless, it's essentially a struggle over values about how we live and how we see and treat each other. It's the struggle between eternal and regressive, equalising and 'I'm alright, Jack', values.

Solidarity and NSMs

It's long been argued that the emergence of NSMs undermined the unity and solidarity that past class-based movements made possible. As a result, intentionally or not, they weakened and fragmented opposition to international capitalist and post-capitalist ideology. The dominance of the trade union and associated labour movement, the coherence generated from the 19th century by workers uniting and taking industrial and political action, the argument has gone, were dissipated and undermined.

As Andrew Heywood, the political writer observed, 'ideological developments have become increasingly fragmented' (Heywood, 2007, p 337), creating different, competing discourses, rather than unifying ideas and action. Broader concerns have been raised about fragmentation and lack of representation (Best, 2002). According to some commentators, these ideological developments have led to:

> Fragmentation, as the 'movement' of the 1960s splintered into various competing struggles for rights and liberties. The previous emphasis on transforming the public sphere and institutions of domination gave way to new emphases on culture, personal identity, and everyday life, as macropolitics were replaced by the micropolitics of local transformation and changes in subjectivity. (http://negotiationisover.com/2010/03/13/postmodern-politics-fragmentation-or-alliance/)

This has been seen as a weakening of solidarity, with campaigns and movements becoming preoccupied with their own issues. Such campaigns sometimes divert attention from broader social and economic forces. The discussion is narrowly framed in terms of particular groups struggling for their own rights, potentially at the expense of the collective whole, reflecting broader power inequalities and exclusions. Commentators like Frank Furedi have questioned how representative these forms of protest are. They've raised concerns about 'consumer activism' which undermines effective democratic opposition and social change (Furedi, 2004, p xvii). As Todd and Taylor observed:

> What mandate do NSMs have in a democratic society? Who do they speak for? Who provides legitimacy for the actions of such groups? Overall there is a concern that while NSMs may appear to enhance participation in politics … they do this in an inequitable way by furthering particularistic interests and not the interests of the collective body. (Todd and Taylor, 2004, p 20)

This is an argument still regularly raised, which needs further examination (for example, Winlow and Hall, 2022). Of course, powerful international movements developed on the old basis. They led to powerful left-of-centre political parties internationally in the Global North and encouraged the pressure for decolonisation in the Global South. They helped extend male suffrage and were an exemplar to women seeking the vote. Some of their leaders internationally, supported the causes of other oppressed groups and minorities. There are wonderful examples of this. For instance, in the UK, there were influential mass working-class meetings against the slave-owning Confederacy during the American civil war, and UK cotton workers went hungry to support the rights of Indian workers during the 1930's depression.

But we also saw:

- British trades unions backing the imperialist First World War, striking for higher wages, rather than opposing it;
- German working-class men supporting the racist, imperialist Nazi Party no less than the pro-Soviet Communist Party;
- UK trade unions supporting an end to Black Commonwealth immigration after the Second World War as well as the prioritising of male employment and women's return to the home;
- socialists internationally supporting eugenics into the 20th century, regardless of its application to disabled, distressed, poor and powerless people (Paul, 1984);
- trade unionists condemning casual and unskilled labour as strike-breakers, scabs and lumpen-proletariat, although such workers faced some of the worst contemporary poverty and deprivation.

Questioning the argument

So traditional labour/trade union movements had their limits when it came to supporting solidarity. These seemed to be significantly defined by an allegiance to nationalism and a similar criticism has been made of right-wing identity politics 'as homogeneous and uncompromisingly hostile to other identities: hence their politics of exclusion' (Berman, 2021). However, the broader argument suggesting the tendency of identity politics to lead to fragmentation, where 'tensions are playing out between appeals to commonality and the centrifugal forces of differentiation' (Berman, op cit) has been widely rehearsed and gained significant visibility and acceptance.

Yet, it doesn't necessarily sit comfortably with contemporary realities. First, it's an argument that's tended to be used by those critical of NSMs, who've not necessarily had the same commitment to inclusion that the latter have had, beyond rhetoric. They see determination to challenge colonialism by removing past celebratory statues and the teaching of ethnic studies or defence of trans rights as negative and divisive, when the latter's proponents make the case for them on the basis of inclusion and equality. The issue is perhaps rooted in conflicting understandings of who's being included in notions of solidarity and who may still be marginalised by traditional understandings. We should remember that the 'full employment' of Western economies post 1945, was one which marginalised and excluded women, disabled and Black and minoritised workers explicitly, and doubtless, out-LGBTQIA+ workers implicitly. Thus, as we've seen historically, 'community' was a term that as much delineated who was left out and not seen as part of the group, from disabled people to travellers and homeless people, so the same has implicitly been true in relation to notions of solidarity. Groups which have come to be associated with 'protected characteristics' under NSM-influenced approaches to social inclusion would not necessarily have even been included for consideration. If we overlook this, we may find ourselves comparing apples and pears rather than advancing any kind of helpful debate.

Challenging hierarchy

The NSMs have made something different possible. As we've begun to realise, and as intersectionality has reminded us, we're not a bunch of separate groups. We are actually locked into each other by our complex, intersecting identities and goals. Our mistake has been to ignore this. Instead, as so often happens when the power of one group is challenged by another, it isn't so much the imbalances of power that many seek to correct as their own place in the pecking order. This can result in a segregation of struggles and a hierarchising of oppressions. We have certainly seen this. However, we have also been seeing its antithesis – a commitment to equalising the relations between different oppressions and recognising the overlaps and shared experience of discrimination and damage between them.

This hierarchising of difference rarely does any of us any long-term good. Putting it crudely, at any time, one group may seem more devalued than another, more marginalised and oppressed. However, in the end, no group is a bit victimised, or more or less victimised than another. This is just another subtle manifestation of the realities of discrimination. Whenever it suits, the full force of hatred and prejudice can be expected to befall any out-group and all the efforts on its part to hide, conform or 'pass' are likely to count for very little when that happens.

That's another reason why it's preferable to opt for the proactive strategy of challenge rather than the defensive one of assimilation or integration. Because only then are we likely to be mistresses and masters of our own fates, rather than relying on any tolerance or 'goodwill' of others. This is rarely a reliable resource. One of history's lessons is that efforts to be like others rather than to be ourselves tend to rebound – if and when it suits. Ultimately, we can expect to come under attack for our difference in an inequitable world.

We should also remember that while the tendency is for groups to emphasise their differences, this is generally in order more effectively to fight for their common rights rather than because their goal is ultimately separatist. As a mental health service user/survivor, I support Mad Studies and highlight the difference of my experience, to argue for my right to be valued equally alongside other people. I don't do this because I see madness as an issue confined to a particular minority or pathological group, instead I highlight the overlaps with other people.

An evidenced case study

Here we have a chance to put this to the test. We've already referred to Shaping Our Lives, a UK ULO linked with the disabled people's/service user NSM. It was established to provide a direct voice for such service users, but it has always been committed to addressing broader issues of equality and inclusion to make sure that voice is as inclusive and diverse as possible. So, here, we can look more closely at this issue of solidarity in relation to the concern with diversity and inclusion of such NSMs. Disabled people's/ service user organisations have frequently come in for criticism for failing to address issues of diversity and inclusion adequately. Historically, the groups that such ULOs have sought to involve have been some of the most marginalised in society, as well as in formal politics and campaigning. A key aim of the international disabled people's movement has been to challenge the taken-for-granted exclusion of disabled people from political participation and counter pressures to segregate them (Charlton, 1998; Schalk, 2022).

Shaping Our Lives explored the relationship of diversity and solidarity. It drew on two national research projects it had undertaken to explore the relation between diverse involvement and supporting solidarity (Beresford and Branfield, 2012). Participants in these projects valued the involvement of a diverse range of service users. It meant people worked in different, more inclusive ways, sometimes acquiring new skills and understanding to do so. Shaping Our Lives concluded:

> Working together in this way strengthens solidarity because it challenges all forms of discrimination and external pressures to 'divide and rule'.

Typical feedback included comments like:

> You can feel comfortable at meetings. … There's support for people before meetings so they can take part properly. You can be open about who you are. I like being involved. The way we do things may seem slower. We try and make sure everyone knows what is going on and can say what they want. But you see that we get things done.

Shaping Our Lives concluded:

> Our experience is unquestionably that addressing diversity and working in more inclusive ways helps us strengthen our solidarity. It means that different movements work together and gain strength from each other. … We learn about the overlaps between service users and carers; service workers and users (which) encourages understanding and alliances – pointing us to a broader solidarity. (2012, op cit, pp 44–5)

Seeing beyond ourselves

Making the move from understanding our personal difficulties in individualistic terms, to recognising how they may be shared by others with similar experiences can be a giant step to take. But to recognise the commonalities between ourselves and others facing *different* difficulties can be a bridge too far.

In Shaping Our Lives, we learned that understanding our own oppression didn't necessarily mean we were better able to understand other groups'. Instead, what we found was that different groups had been encouraged to resent any advantage they could see one having over another. Why indeed should we assume that disempowered people have more insight than anyone else and have any better understanding of their oppression?

Neoliberal ideology has played on this with merciless skill; the ease with which disempowered people can be turned against each other is breathtaking. Therefore, it makes us, as insecure working-class people, fearful of Black and white refugees and asylum seekers. As people with increasingly insecure and inadequate employment, it generates suspicion and loathing of people on welfare benefits – and so on. There are two problems with falling for this trick. First, we can never really know what it's like to be in another's shoes, just as they can't know what it is like to be in ours. What we'll quickly see, if we allow ourselves to check, is that they too are misrepresented and scapegoated. Letting ourselves be divided is a recipe for isolation and defeat. Second, they may seem different from 'us', but what the groups identified as out-groups always have in common is the exclusion and oppression we all share. This in turn is a basis for shared struggle. Together we have strength in numbers. Unfamiliarity with another group doesn't mean there's need for suspicion. Nevertheless, it's an effective lever for the powerful to manipulate and keep us powerless.

What's interesting is the determination with which neoliberal administrations pursue such divisive policies, even, as in the case of seaborne refugees in the UK, when they rebound against them because they can't control the numbers as promised. Similarly, we see the wicked skill employed to convince people to accept hateful policies. Thus, the Nazi Himmler justifying the holocaust because 'the one decent Jew' every German knows [experience] simply disguises the fact that 'the others are swine' [ideology] (Vad Yashem, 1981).

As I wrote this, right-wing UK headlines, were reporting that national strikes by public service workers were creating chaos for *our* Christmas. We'll search in vain for the same headlines reporting the chaos caused by millions of cancelled operations because of the NHS's rundown, mass cuts in train services and fewer and fewer in need receiving social care support.

A first step to challenge dominant neoliberal politics is coming to recognise what we have in common with those we are taught to fear and loath. As Malcolm X, the human rights campaigner, first said: 'If you're not careful, the newspapers will have you hating the people who are being oppressed, and loving the people who are doing the oppressing.'

Recognising overlaps, building alliances

The findings from Shaping Our Lives offer some helpful insights. We can connect with people associated with other identities and experiences – if we're in situations supportive of that. We are capable of recognising broader overlaps between us.

Clearly, three things can help with this:

1. Gaining an understanding of intersectionality that allows us to see the links between our different experience and identities rather than just emphasising the differences.
2. Recognising the commonality of oppression, discrimination and exclusion.
3. Recalling, having or seeking any actual first-hand contact with any of them.

So long as we have an appreciation of the issues our own defining identity raises for us, then the likelihood is we won't be marginalised as isolated individuals, but we will *still* be in a minority – which can still be marginalised. However, if we can make the leap to recognise how many of us face some kind of barriers or discrimination – that's to say – are united by the wider oppressions we experience – then we have a chance of seeing ourselves as and becoming the *majority* we actually are. This isn't a modern Western-imposed idea. It's what people everywhere facing oppression have done since time began. Thus, the adage, 'United we stand, divided we fall.'

Groups facing oppression often come out particularly badly from some of the worst problems that can face us in the world, from war and natural disasters to threats like global warming. Early in the Ukraine-Russia war, we heard about Black people being forced away from safe borders and trains which were taking refugees out of the war zone (Akinwotu and Strzyzynska, 2022). The evidence also highlights that disabled people are at a particular disadvantage as regards climate change and related policy (Kosanic, 2022). Such instances highlight the commonality of different oppressive experiences, as well as the particular problems faced by marginalised populations.

Certainly, together we're in a majority under neoliberalism, where for so long it's been apparent that the ideology and regime serves the interests of only a tiny minority. That's why it's been inherent in the ideology and its associated politics, to keep us divided. That's why the breakthrough issue is to begin to recognise our common oppression and develop lines of action that build on this.

Our association with particular identities and experience does not have to be divisive, so long as we recognise the common oppression and denial of rights underpinning it. The lone teenage mother and refugee, the homeless person oppressed by the welfare benefits system and the trans person struggling to get through the bureaucratised gender reassignment process may not only be one and the same person, but they're also people with a crucial thing in common – and that's the discrimination they face under neoliberalism.

We need to let ourselves see what we have in common with each other – the hostile attitudes and material realities we face – as well as what we don't have in common with those who from their positions of power can create and perpetuate artificial divisions among us, often pretending they're on our side. They are the self-interested siren voices of populist neoliberalism and need to be outed as such.

That's not to say that some groups may not feel the oppression they face is much greater than that faced by others and that this needs to be more widely recognised. It's certainly not being suggested here that such differences and inequalities should be glossed over. They should be recognised and, from my experience, both intersectionalism and building links with other NSMs help in developing understanding and addressing such complexity.

We can't expect to undermine the inheritance of internalised and external oppression engendered over many years at the flick of a finger. However, more and more of us will be in a position to make a start once we can see these things for ourselves. That's been the lesson of every NSM, and developing strengthened relations and alliances between them will help reinforce this.

Building alliances doesn't just happen. We have to work for it. We have to develop contact with and confidence in each other. Intersectionalist overlaps are really helpful here. I speak from experience. Friends I made in the survivor movement were one of the key ways in which I and others worked to get closer to and build links with the disabled people's movement. And what distinguished those survivor friends was that mostly they were people with feet in both camps; one a survivor who was also blind, another a survivor who also had a physical impairment. They were trusted in both movements and that made it more straightforward. We need to see the whole of ourselves and not just be compartmentalised into one identity that others might want to see as our primary one.

Identities are complex and multifaceted. We're not just one thing, although often one aspect of our identity is seized upon in society to distort who we are and what connects rather than separates us. Historically, social policy tended to be a matter of one more privileged group intervening in the lives of other less powerful ones. Now, with the interest in participation in public policy, there are overlaps across the two sides of the welfare counter. Increasingly, service users' lived experience is being recognised in social work and related professions alongside other skills and aptitudes, and they are being recruited as workers, with their experiential knowledge recognised as an asset.

Anti-oppressive politics

So, what's sometimes dismissed by critics as 'identity politics' has the potential to be much more. Yes, it does begin by basing political agendas on particular identities or lived experience. However, 1) it does not have to stop there and 2) while these identities are diverse, they are united both by their overlaps and also their shared experience of discrimination and oppression.

The issue is not about separately jostling for our place in the sun, just highlighting what's special about *us* and how we're worse off than others, but while valuing difference, also recognising what we *share*. Moreover, what we crucially share as members of NSMs are:

- exclusion
- discrimination
- oppression
- stigmatisation

- hate crime
- barriers

Crucially we are much more powerful together than on our own. This is where the messages of the old and new movements converge:

- The people united will never be defeated.
- In unity is strength.
- United we stand, divided we fall.

Similarly, movements that unite with each other are likely to exert much more strength and solidarity than those that continue to plough a lone furrow. However, if these alliances are to be lasting and effective, then they will need to be genuine and transparent. They're unlikely to build trust or carry conviction if they're merely seen as tactical, marriages of convenience. It's one thing to form a traditional political partnership based on short-term shared interests, quite another when what's actually up for review are our world views and understandings of each other. This though is what NSMs demand in their challenge to traditional stereotypes, roles and relationships across all our diversity. They're based on more egalitarian attitudes and assumptions, and while, like all human activities, they will undoubtedly sometimes fall short of these, they're at the heart of their process and key to their demands. If we're to link and work with each other across experience and identities, then this has to be central to how we work and what we do. And dare I say it, a world where we begin to have trust in each other, understanding the different hands each of us has been dealt, is a better one (from my experience), than one served up with the hate and fear of a *Daily Mail* headline.

We talked earlier about the impact that NSMs have had. That isn't to say that their constituencies have been accepted on their own terms. Instead, there's been a mainstream tendency to value the latter merely in economistic terms – on the basis of their perceived market worth or net value to prevailing politics. Thus, the frequent talk of the pink, Black and purple pound and the enthusiasm to profit from the perceived market worth of the LGBTQIA+ and other 'communities'. What that says to me is that there's now at least some belated recognition of the consumerist value of groups facing discrimination, although this should not be confused with recognition of their equal rights and citizenship. There's a real difference between valuing us for what we're seen to be worth and valuing us and each other for who we are, what we have in common, our contributions and our shared values and principles of equality, inclusion, sustainability and kindness.

This almost grudging recognition undoubtedly has many expressions, but one recent one in the UK warrants singling out for mention. The

UK Department for Work and Pensions (DWP) is a key government department for disabled and older people, charged with responsibility for income maintenance. As we've seen, it's sometimes difficult to avoid concluding that it sees its essential role as restricting access to such benefits rather than ensuring the social security of those entitled to them (Pring, 2024). However, its preoccupation with cutting costs resulted in a major unintended and destructive consequence a few years back. As the disabled people's online organisation Spartacus reported, this was to damage the UK car industry through the DWP's arbitrary efforts to restrict disabled people's access to the Motability scheme. This scheme not only encouraged their mobility and supported them to live independent lives but also provided an important boost to the car industry (Butler, 2012), which the DWP failed to notice, such was its enthusiasm to constrain disabled people and impose supposed savings.

Prefiguring developments

The 1960s US Black civil rights movement was a fertile and multi-stranded NSM. One of its particularly interesting features is that while its more hard-line leaders are often remembered as separatist, violent and confrontational, some (in many cases the same people) prefigure the kind of alliance-building highlighted and advocated here. This is certainly true of both Malcolm X, the American Muslim minister and human rights activist (1925–65), and Fred Hampton, a leader of the US Black Panther Party (1948–69) both of whom were assassinated as major threats to the status quo. Both recognised the importance of alliance building, Fred pioneering it domestically, Malcolm internationally.

Malcolm X, in the latter part of his life, spent much time abroad, in Africa, the Middle East and Europe, developing strong relationships with and gaining support from anti-colonial leaders and the presidents of new nations escaping from colonialism. Long before that, as Malcolm X scholar Manning Marable noted, his sermons 'made increased references to events in Asia, Africa, and other [Global South] regions, and he emphasised the kinship Black Americans had with non-Western dark humanity' (Marable, 2011). He framed his struggle in terms of human, not only civil, rights to make it an international concern. While originally imbued with the Black leader Marcus Garvey's vision for Black freedom, the new Black African leaders in Ghana, for example, offered Malcolm 'a new idea of what Africa needed to unify against: the economic system of capitalism'. At the time of his death, he:

> was beginning to build the sort of Black united front his parents had raised him to believe in … to build a bridge between a unified Black

Photograph 17.1: Fred Hampton

Note: He was a leader of the Black Panthers and founder of the Rainbow Coalition, killed by the FBI and remembered as a powerful campaigner, speaker and alliance builder, 1948–69.
Source: CULR_04_0218_2449_001, Chicago Urban League Records, University of Illinois at Chicago Library. Available under creative commons CC BY-NC-ND 2.0 licence

America and a unified Africa, as his parents had dreamed of. And through Islam, Malcolm was even laying the hopeful foundations for the Afro-Asian solidarity that Marcus Garvey taught would overcome global White supremacy, and the colonialism and neocolonialism it supported. (Burnett, 2022)

In his teens, Fred Hampton identified with Global South socialist struggles as well as with communist revolutionaries. He began by organising Black African Americans and was attracted by the Black Panther credo which integrated Black self-determination with a Maoist class and economic critique and challenged sexism. Significantly, he and his associates were able to secure a non-aggression pact between Chicago's Black and other gangs, striving to develop an anti-racist, class-conscious, multi-racial alliance, emphasising that continuing conflict between them would only keep them impoverished. This led to a burgeoning 'Rainbow Coalition', which gained support from students and other local people. Their shared issues included poverty, anti-racism, corruption, police brutality and substandard housing.

The National Rainbow Coalition became a prominent political organisation raising public awareness of numerous political issues and consolidated a large voting bloc. The FBI initiated disinformation and other undermining tactics to challenge Hampton's skills building alliances and were ultimately implicated in the appalling murder that brought his activities to an end. What was truly revolutionary about his approach to activism was his effort to bring different groups together through a strategy of 'serving the community, [which] talked about breakfast programs, educating the people, community control of police' (Goodman, 2009).

Both Malcolm X and Fred Hampton showed their understanding that building alliances – *connecting* with other causes – was more than just a matter of short-term political convenience. As Malcolm X put it:

> We cannot think of uniting with others, until after we have first united among ourselves. We cannot think of being acceptable to others until we have first proven acceptable to ourselves. One can't unite bananas with scattered leaves.

For Fred Hampton too, the task of building solidarity meant much more than the traditional economistic approach – rather it was a melding of the principles of old and new social movements, anti-capitalism with inclusion and anti-discrimination, and positive redistribution with egalitarian roles and relationships. As he said:

> We got to face some facts. That the masses are poor, that the masses belong to what you call the lower class, and when I talk about the masses, I'm talking about the white masses, I'm talking about the black masses, and the brown masses, and the yellow masses, too. We've got to face the fact that some people say you fight fire best with fire, but we say you put fire out best with water. We say you don't fight racism with racism. We're gonna fight racism with solidarity. We say you don't fight capitalism with no black capitalism; you fight capitalism with socialism. (quoted in Jones, 2013, p 387)

A final point

There's perhaps one key point to reinforce here. In this chapter, we've tried to highlight that identities and experience can be complex. As we've stressed, few of us have one monolithic identity. We may have an identity that others tend to define us by, or we want to highlight in defining ourselves. As we learn from the study of intersectionality, we are also likely to have overlapping, cross-cutting identities, all of which can affect how we come at the world and how the world sees us. However, there is even more to the multifaceted nature of identity than this. Our identities will extend to more than we may realise and may not give us a choice in that. This is almost inevitable in a society where however much some ideologies might seek to deny it, we are all connected with each other and societal structures in complex ways. Thus, our pension funds may be invested in global corporations with poor human rights records. We may work for companies that have scant regard for environmental protection. We may not be able to afford to buy our clothes at retailers who maintain decent standards of employment in the Global South and who don't exploit children. Globalised neoliberal politics and economies make it very difficult for any of us – except the most privileged – to be choosy either as workers, consumers or savers, as well as conflicting with progressive values we may hold dear. It's helpful for us to remember this when we're trying to work out – as best we can – our own personal strategies for challenging the damaging and alienating aspects of the world in which we live – and the positive alliances we can develop in that context. The choice that may often face us is one of doing least harm, because of the complex ways in which we are interlocked into systems and structures we may actually oppose.

Conclusion

There's always been some alliance building between NSMs and some that have particularly highlighted intersectionality as a key basis for strengthening it and for building solidarity. However, we've reached a point where such alliance-building needs to be an explicit, worked-through key strategy given the scale and extent of marginalisation and the apparently unstoppable momentum of neoliberalism. We need to talk about this from our different perspectives, with our different needs, issues and demands, under the aegis of our common social, civil and human rights. We need to foreground this discussion. In this author's view, this is likely to be the most effective route to challenging the position of the 'overclass', offering the most helpful and unifying agenda to rally around. However, as has already been said, this needs to be an approach to building alliances and solidarity based on principle rather than opportunism. Thus, it needs to be based on:

- highlighting shared oppression, discrimination and exclusion;
- being honest about differences and past inequalities between us, about past relations and the impact of previous colonisation and the need for decolonisation;
- a philosophy of equality and social justice;

- being value-based and anti-oppressive;
- building these values from the bottom and recognising shared and broader experience;
- acknowledging the connections within us, as well as between us, some we may want, others thrust upon us;
- fully addressing issues of diversity, access and inclusivity;
- prioritising inclusive approaches to participation;
- rejecting a narrowly instrumental interest in other groups, instead valuing our commonality.

We can see how this is an expression at a high collective level of the concern to connect on equal terms that lies at the heart of this book and the participatory politics it favours. Such a strategy offers us a real prospect of building equal roles and relationships within and between us and a real counter to the alienating, divisive and anti-social formal politics we are now subject to. In the next and final chapter, we will try to draw together some of the learning from writing this book as well as key principles emerging both for understanding our collective situation and trying to change it.

18

Conclusion and next steps

> The most violent element in society is ignorance.
> Emma Goldman, anarchist, 1869–1940

> The measure of intelligence is the ability to change.
> Widely attributed to Albert Einstein, physicist, 1879-1955

Introduction

When I started writing this book, the problem was two-fold. Neoliberalism seemed a particularly destructive force, and yet there appeared no prospect of it being brought to a halt. The question was how's that to be achieved? There is now some suggestion that this question has been superseded. Has anything really changed over that time? I'm certainly not convinced, but there's another issue too. Even if we have seen the last of neoliberalism, does that really mean that something better is waiting in the wings? Looking generally at the rising conflict and uncertainty in the world and looking specifically at the scale of the extreme right vote in the UK and US in 2024, I personally, doubt it – unless we all become actors in making it happen. Let me explain.

An end of neoliberalism?

Since I started on this book, the political, economic and moral bankruptcy and anti-democratic nature of neoliberalism has increasingly been showing itself. In the US, we've seen an extremist president reduced to setting the mob on his own seat of government and then standing successfully to lead that government again, pardoning the offenders. Something similar has been happening in Brazil with attacks on its Congress. In the UK, a queue of short-lived prime ministers found the old right-wing game plan and its previously unstoppable rhetoric less and less effective in silencing their detractors. A mix of global pandemic and rising economic uncertainty has made matters worse. Some analysts though still seem to believe that neoliberalism's end may be in sight.

There's no question that it has failed economically, as some of its closest allies, the IMF and World Bank, have long been suggesting. Promised growth has been hesitant, and growing problems of poverty and inequality remain unresolved. The whole premise of economic growth has also come in for increasing criticism. Neoliberalism has long been over-promised and its failings repeatedly highlighted. However, that's not the same as its end being in sight. This is one dead man who seems to keep walking – on and on.

Neither UK, US nor European politics show any significant sign of breaking out of the neoliberal box, indeed, the opposite can be argued. That includes oppositions. There are still significant trends in the UK and Europe of retreat from traditional welfare statist politics and continuing interest in more extreme right-wing ones. Even more concerning, in its rush for deregulation, the UK government under prime minister Sunak recommitted itself even to reducing the economic safeguards that were set up in the wake of the 2008 financial crash (Makortoff, 2022). Voters for the Labour government that displaced him still await something different from their electoral choice.

It's not been difficult nonetheless to find commentators ready to tell us that neoliberalism is dead (Stiglitz, 2024). They've been increasingly talking up its demise (Meadway, 2021). In 2020, the *Financial Times* called for radical reforms (Financial Times, 2020). Since then, the historian Adam Tooze, like others, pointing particularly to the effects of the pandemic, suggested that neoliberalism's days were numbered, writing:

> It was hard to avoid the sense that a turning point had been reached. Was this, finally, the death of the orthodoxy that had prevailed in economic policy since the 80s? Was this the death knell of neoliberalism? As a coherent ideology of government, perhaps. (Tooze, 2021)

Dutch historian Rutger Bregman was even less qualified in his assertion that:

> the ideology (neoliberalism) that was dominant these last 40 years is dying. What will replace it? (Bregman, 2020)

In response to this question, each comes up with their own proposals for change, largely based on more state intervention, regulation and control. This is not so much a break with the past as a taken-for-granted return to it, with various elites offering their own prescriptions for the future. That, in fact, is where this book came in, because of the evident failure of such prescriptive approaches to policy change to date, to work and dislodge neoliberal politics. Perhaps it has just been another case of the wish being parent to the thought.

But how helpful would such a wish actually be? Relying on a process of change, essentially based on inequality, hardly seems progressive, even if it could help rid us of far-right ideology. Moreover, how likely would it be to do that? Where would the broad-based force for such change at the ballot box come from? Equally important, what kind of politics is likely to take over and get things back on track in the wake of neoliberalism's decline? No clear contenders are offered. More to the point, how would this return politics to a democratic path and enable the rest of us to have more say over our lives and politics and hope for a sustainable outcome?

This looks like more of the same, not a break with the past. It's the way it's long been – various elites offering their own proposals rather than making it possible for the rest of us to begin to have more control – which most politics and particularly neoliberal politics prevent. The only thing that is different here is some variation in the prescriptions on offer and the power behind them, but not the *process* adopted for change. As has already been highlighted, the most conspicuous political development in countries like the UK in recent years has been increasing popular support for extreme right politics from people who feel dispossessed. We are seeing this now writ even larger in Trump2 America. If there's one lesson to be gained over the history of neoliberal politics, it's that a successful challenge is only like to come from adopting a more participatory and inclusive approach to change, one in which people have some sense of ownership. There is already rising interest in this, particularly in the context of public/social policy (Williams, 2021) and increasing electoral enthusiasm for the Greens, who have highlighted participation.

Speculation on neoliberalism's status must also take into account how you define it. If it's, as this author would argue, a politics that includes:

- cutting state support for its citizens while being prepared to increase control over them;
- seeing state intervention's primary purpose as supporting the market and those most advantaged by it;
- maintaining regressively redistributive taxation;
- prioritising profit and seeing it as best safeguarded by deregulation, including over the environment;
- combining globalised economics freeing the movement of goods, while restricting the mobility of populations;

then it is difficult to see what's fundamentally changed and that its end is actually in sight. The road ahead for any politics looks rocky. There are no shortcuts. If we want a changed politics then we must work coherently for it.

We shouldn't forget that serious related global problems continue unabated: forced population movement; economic uncertainty and rising fears for public health; war raging in eastern Europe as well as beyond. Now the West is increasingly sabre rattling against both China and Russia – all benefitting the industry with the most comfortable current prospects globally – arms production.

This bodes badly for any future political strategy that doesn't take on the uncertain state of national and global democracy, diplomacy and economic policy. All are still based on global north/south inequality, environmentally unsustainable production and a balance of terror reliant on increasing levels of armed conflict.

World annual military expenditure has now passed the two trillion dollar mark for the first time (SIPRI, 2022). The financial cost of global warming and environmental damage is already unparalleled – the human costs incalculable. It's no use wringing our hands and saying 'something must be done'. After two world wars, innumerable proxy conflicts, many human-made 'natural' disasters, the lesson has to be that nothing is likely to be done except to make matters worse. Instead of imprecations for change, we must do things differently – and that's what this book's for.

Reconnecting with a new politics

A set of new principles is now required which foreground the values highlighted by the international new social movements (NSMs), which, paradoxically, have been emerging over the same period as the development of neoliberalism, but which offer both a counter-force and counter-philosophy to it. This, as we have said, is essentially a politics of *connection*. Here we can see a potential way forward for those century-long calls to '*only connect*'. The NSMs highlighting of the 'personal as political', also helps us develop a formal politics informed by the more inclusive and equal human roles and relations which they have helped us realise in our personal lives. These are principles that both build the means and highlight the ends needed for challenging division and hate and for unifying and sustainable change. They provide a basis both for us connecting with each other on equal and inclusive terms and for reducing the alienation that sets us apart and makes us fair game for the Machiavellian politics and ideology that continue to dominate.

They offer the best hope of equal connection. Means and ends here are inseparable. Both need to be based on the same inclusive and egalitarian values. That reality has been at the heart of this book and its emerging argument. It also extends to the participatory and emancipatory approaches to communication and education which we have discussed. We can't separate the how from the what and where – that's both this text's logic and structure. It's why we have addressed both means and ends throughout it. It's also why we have not prescribed the ends – beyond saving the planet and working to avert war, hate and division – since that is the goal of most and everyone's task, right and opportunity.

We will not gain a real say by others speaking for us. We won't challenge the oppression and discrimination against us and others unless we fight together for the rights and freedom to define and be ourselves, alongside all groups marginalised by identity and lived experience. We all live on the same planet and must join forces, whoever and wherever we are, to protect it and ensure it has a future. We can all play our part as best we can in our actions and through our values.

That's why we must have clear goals for our efforts and clear values for how we seek to achieve them. Of course, change is difficult and cannot be achieved in a day. At the same time, it's immensely helpful to have some way of indicating a serious shift in direction and some clear markers that this is the plan and the goal, even if it can't be the immediate reality. That's where the United Nations concept of 'progressive realisation' is helpful and can suggest a way forward. Essentially, what it means is that while a state might not be in a financial position to implement reform now, it commits itself to making that reform – policy or political – over an agreed and realistic timescale which takes account of the financial difficulties involved. As the United Nations puts it:

> The concept of 'progressive realization' describes a central aspect of States' obligations in connection with economic, social and cultural rights under international human rights treaties. At its core is the obligation to take appropriate measures towards the full realization of economic, social and cultural rights to the maximum of their available resources. The reference to 'resource availability' reflects a recognition that the realization of these rights can be hampered by a lack of resources and can be achieved only over a period of time. Equally, it means that a state's compliance with its obligation to take appropriate measures is assessed in the light of the resources – financial and others – available to it. Many national constitutions also allow for the progressive realization of some economic, social and cultural rights. (United Nations, 2007)

Principles for a new politics

The same kind of principles could be adopted first to encourage and pressure states to make the reforms proposed here and then for them to begin to demonstrate their commitment to supporting and advancing them. We have explored ten such principles for a humanistic and inclusive politics within these pages. They are principles of:

- participation
- empowerment
- inclusion and equality
- valuing lived experience and experiential knowledge
- equal alliance
- social understandings

- grassroots action – bottom-up action meeting top-down
- support for user-led organisations
- sustainability
- equal and inclusive connection

Probably half these principles are unlikely to be seen on the lists of what mainstream political theorists and ideologues see as significant issues. They're also a reminder that the current neoliberal political climate allows most of us little if any voice and doesn't even allow many of us the chance to be fully ourselves. Here at least we've been able to offer a forum to explore these principles and begin to focus on them. I outline what they should mean in the following sections.

Participation

Participation means prioritising effective and inclusive participation in all aspects of politics and policy development and operation, highlighting the need for a democratic rather than consumerist approach. Support for people to understand and engage in formal political life is provided through accessible whole-life learning from childhood onwards. Structures for participation are reconciled with those for representative democracy. The underpinning principle for participation is that everyone, unless proven otherwise, can express their preferences and make a difference, if they are provided with access and support to do so.

Empowerment

A core concept for change is that of empowerment, on the lines developed by the US Black civil rights movement. This has two interlocking strands: personal empowerment, building people's confidence and skills for involvement and political empowerment and supporting them to work together for social and political change. Critical is the interrelation of the two. A key resource for building empowerment is support for people's own self-organisation and lived experience, identity-based organisations and groupings.

Inclusion and equality

Anti-discriminatory approaches and safeguards need to be built into policy, political process and provisions for participation. These are based on recognition of wider discriminations operating beyond existing protected categories as well as the importance of intersectionality in recognising and combatting barriers and exclusions and challenging unequal roles and relations. This extends to indigenous populations and populations subjected to colonisation, and demands a rigorous and all-embracing approach to decolonisation. Full recognition needs to be given to learning, communication, environmental and cultural access.

Lived experience

Full and equal value needs to be given to lived experience alongside other forms of knowledge production and development. The contribution of emancipatory disability and survivor research and that of other user-led research approaches and principles should be recognised and treated with equality alongside traditional 'expert' knowledge based on experiment and professional perspectives. Equal funding and other support should be given to such innovative approaches to knowledge and evidence development. Relevant lived experience alongside other requisite skills and qualities should be valued as a basis for professional and occupational helping roles.

Equal alliance

NSMs have challenged the barriers and discriminations that particular experience and identity-based groups in society face to enable those groups to define their own identities and challenge those barriers. These groups are unified by the discrimination and oppression they face, but often they are hierarchised, which undermines unity and weakens them. It's important not only to develop solidarity within but also *between* them if the power of ruling minorities is to be challenged and intersectional issues fully acknowledged and addressed. This means starting new conversations, new connections, new beginnings and breaking out of old inequalities, prejudices and separations. We may now seek reconciliation between us, but where there is a history of inequality, we must be honest about this and address it. In social relations, as in personal and political relations, inequalities have to be worked through and cannot be left unresolved. Nevertheless, to harp on about them is to perpetuate a discourse of division rather than to help challenge it and offers no way forward. Building new alliances between us transforms minorities into a majority and spells the end of neoliberalism.

Social understandings

One of the defining characteristics of NSMs organised around identity and lived experience is the way they have developed social understandings of their subjects – themselves – which frame them in terms of the *oppression* that they tend to experience in society. Therefore, we're not being told about a deviant or pathological group, or a group marked out by its individual inadequacy or morbidity, but one which faces social and cultural barriers and prejudices in particular societies. Thus, the key principle of challenging the ruling pressure to individualise issues and causations, as the disabled people's movement did by defining disability as the negative and hostile reaction of society to people with (perceived) impairments, and the way that the difference of women, Black and minoritised people and LGBTQIA+ communities has been shown to be perceived and treated as deficiency rather than as an expression of diversity demanding an equal response. The problem is rooted in the society that identifies it, not in the individual who faces the resulting oppression.

Grassroots action

The development of democracy demands a continuing pressure through grassroots action to build and improve it. Until we live in very small, consensual or perfect societies, we're likely to rely at best on some mix of representative and participative democracy and we need to encourage diverse political activism to support both. We also need to do more to work out how better to reconcile bottom-up and top-down ways of working. Grassroots action needs to address issues of diversity and inclusion if everyone is to have an equal opportunity both to develop their political views and for them to make a difference. We've seen how neoliberal ideology has tended to centralise policy and politics. In the UK and some other neoliberal societies, we've also seen political pressure to restrict protest. Peaceful protest is key for a healthy and inclusive democracy and isn't an issue for party politics or police intervention. Building from the bottom should also encourage us to put an emphasis on the personal and on modelling campaigning process and goals on the more equal and inclusive personal values emerging in the 21st century.

Support for citizen and service user organisations

Political involvement and empowerment are collective as well as individual activities. Historically, the tendency has been for more advantaged groups to campaign and speak for other less advantaged ones. NSMs have challenged this tradition and encouraged people and groups to campaign on their own behalf. The concept of 'self-advocacy' has grown from that. Reflecting this, the disabled people's movement drew a distinction between organisations 'of' and organisations 'for', arguing the importance of shifting resources to those who spoke for themselves. The former are strongly linked with the NSMs. The evidence is that internationally their funding situation is still much less secure than that of traditional voluntary and charitable organisations. It's important to challenge this and equalise the distribution of resources and strengthen core funding, in line with the value that marginalised groups attach to their own organisations and self-organisation. These are key for local development and beyond, and essential to advance processes of personal and political empowerment and involvement.

Sustainability

Sustainability must be at the heart of everything – our personal, social and political goals and how we seek to achieve them. Put simply, based on the three recognised pillars of sustainability – environmental, economic and social – we must commit ourselves to sustainability in all we do, how we do it and why we do it. We are nowhere without our planet! UNESCO draws a distinction between sustainability as a long-term goal (that is a more sustainable world), while sustainable development refers to the many processes and pathways to achieve it. We have been exploring the two and their close interrelations through the whole of this book. This is clearly a massive task and one our existing politics, which rest on conflict, production and competition, are unlikely ever to achieve. It is a task which includes concern with climate change, the protection of species, forest, fauna and natural resources. We need to understand the difference between real progress and greenwashing, between penalising individuals for using plastic bags and straws and governments committing to structural change. We need to involve everyone, including children, in anti-paternalistic ways because they have the greatest investment and often the clearest understanding of these issues. We need to recognise that real commitment to this goal will mean change in almost everything we do, but that the cost is likely to be modest – next to its real-world alternative. It's difficult to see how neoliberalism with its preoccupation with consumerism and commodification can survive the need to shift to a world that challenges increasing production and consumption. It is not difficult to see how a world that recommits itself to the wellbeing of all that live on it might be rather better placed to do so.

Reconnecting

Sustainability is perhaps the greatest and most urgent argument for challenging neoliberalism and the best hope for working out a humanist alternative for the rest of us. Just the thought of that possibility – a safe, interdependent, kind and caring world for our children and grandchildren – could make anyone's heart leap. Even the idea of a world without nuclear threat, of wars without end and increasing natural disasters, seems almost beyond imagination. Just think what it would feel like if we could feel ourselves starting on such a journey, beginning that process of connecting with equality that generations now have hoped for. At a more mundane level, reconnecting with the personal provides a convincing argument for renewing public and social policy and restoring it to its original welfare state intention of advancing our physical, emotional and spiritual wellbeing, meeting our needs and securing our rights. An economy that prioritises looking after each other and the planet we live on also provides an alternative rationale and vision to replace the false vision of increasing production and generates a multitude of benign work and activities to make it possible.

…Above all connect

The British socialist thinker Raymond Williams developed an early intellectual framework for this during the latter part of the 20th century. He made contributions to drama, film, literary criticism, sociology, cultural and media studies and politics. He was committed to an educated, participatory democracy. He brings us back at a loftier level to the idea of connecting. He believed that making connections between politics, economics, education and culture was a continuing critical task (Eldridge and Eldridge, 1994).

Thus, reconnection is not only something we need to do with each other and ourselves but also with the world in which we live. This is the kind of harmony that humans have aspired to for millennia and which is embodied in the Zulu concept of 'ubuntu' meaning a person is a person through other persons. With variants across Africa:

> Ubuntu is predicated on the idea that personhood is attained through complex processes of interactive exchange between people and the totality of their environment – inclusive of the natural environment and other dimensions of living such as the living dead (ancestors) and unborn. (Eromosele, 2022, p 335)

This is a truly holistic and social approach to us as human, social and political beings. It highlights the importance of connection which lies at the heart of this book and whatever confidence we can have for the future. If we have got so far under the exclusionary and disempowering conditions of neoliberalism, imagine how far we can go as we envision and build more sympathetic circumstances, roles and relationships for such change. We are talking of a politics of *connection*, equality and inclusion. Here lies hope.

References

Adams, R. (2008), *Empowerment, Participation and Social Work*, New York, Palgrave Macmillan.

Adams, R. (2018), Sharp rise in pupil exclusions from English state schools, *The Guardian*, 19th July, https://www.theguardian.com/education/2018/jul/19/sharp-rise-in-pupil-exclusions-from-english-state-schools accessed 25th November 2022.

Adams, V. (2014), 'Nothing with nothing' – TS Eliot and the regeneration of Margate, *Kent Connections*, 19th August https://medium.com/kent-connections/nothing-with-nothing-t-s-eliot-and-the-regeneration-of-margate-5d534534dc62 accessed 8th June 2022.

Adler, K. (2024), How likely is France to wake up on Monday morning to a new far-right dawn?, *BBC News*, 7th July, https://www.bbc.co.uk/news/articles/c4ng03lnv0vo accessed 9th July 2024.

Ahmed, S. (2014), *The Cultural Politics of Emotion*, 2nd edition, Edinburgh, Edinburgh University Press.

Akinwatu, E. and Strzyzynska, W. (2022), Nigeria condemns treatment of Africans trying to flee Ukraine, *The Guardian*, 28th February, https://www.theguardian.com/world/2022/feb/28/nigeria-condemns-treatment-africans-trying-to-flee-ukraine-government-poland-discrimination accessed 7th February 2023.

Alldred, P. (1999), Not making a virtue of a necessity: Nancy Fraser on post-socialist politics, in Jordan, T. and Lent, A. (editors), *Storming The Millennium: The new politics of change*, London, Lawrence and Wishart, pp 127–39.

Allport, A. (2009), *Demobbed: Coming Home after the Second World War*, New Haven, Connecticut, Yale University Press.

Althusser, L. (2014), *On the Reproduction of Capitalism: Ideology and ideological state apparatuses*, trans. and ed. G.M. Goshgarian, London, Verso.

Althusser, L. (1971), *Ideology and Ideological Apparatuses, Lenin and Philosophy and Other Essays*, https://eclass.uoa.gr/modules/document/file.php/ENL555/Week%2010/Louis-Althusser.pdf accessed 2nd February 2022.

Amer, K. and Noujaim, J. (directors), (2019), *The Great Hack*, US released Netflix.

Anderson, S. (2012), *Languages: A very short introduction*, Oxford, Oxford University Press.

AP News (2022), Report: Ukraine war ups arms sales but challenges lie ahead, *AP News*, 5th December, https://apnews.com/article/europe-business-united-states-global-trade-stockholm-614c607fd8b25ab609cfdfdea617705c accessed 17th January 2023.

Axellson, P. (2020), Anthony Magnabosco; Street epistemology, *IntellectInterviews.com*, 13th July, https://intellectinterviews.com/2020/07/anthony-magnabosco-street-epistemology/ accessed 23rd January 2023.

Azhar, M. (2024), *Small Town, Big Riot*, BBC Documentary, Two Episodes, BBC Television, https://www.bbc.co.uk/iplayer/episodes/m0021k3x/small-town-big-riot accessed 28th September 2024.

Bagguley, P. (1992), Social change, the middle class and the emergence of 'new social movements': a critical analysis, *The Sociological Review*, February, Vol 40, Issue 1, pp 26–48.

Baird, V. (2023), Ex-victims' commissioner hits out at 'evil' in Met police amid David Carrick fallout, *The Guardian*, 17th January, https://www.theguardian.com/uk-news/2023/jan/17/met-police-chief-officers-removed-david-carrick accessed 17th January 2023.

Baldwin, J. (1962), *Another Country*, New York, Dial Press.

Baldwin, J. (1963a), The doom and glory of knowing who you are, *Life Magazine*, 24th May, cited in Grimes, S., *James Baldwin on Books and Connection*, https://medium.com/the-1000-day-mfa/unprecedented-in-the-history-of-the-world-49bc965a7305 accessed 24th November 2022.

Baldwin, J. (1963b), A talk to teachers, *New Yorker*, 16th October, https://www.zinnedproject.org/materials/baldwin-talk-to-teachers accessed 10th July 2024.

Baldwin, J. (2016), *I Am Not Your Negro*, Film, Directed by Raoul Peck, Velvet Films.

Ball, J., Borger, J. and Greenwald, G. (2013), Revealed: how US and UK spy agencies defeat internet privacy and security, *The Guardian*, 6th September, https://www.theguardian.com/world/2013/sep/05/nsa-gchq-encryption-codes-security accessed 7th July 2022.

Bank, D., Dimauro and D. Pehme, M. (2017), *Get Me Roger Stone*, Netflix.

Barber, A. (2021), *Consumed: The need for collective change; colonialism, climate change and consumerism*, London, Brazen.

Barham, P. (2023), *Outrageous Reason: Madness and race in Britain and empire, 1780–2020*, Monmouth, PCSS Books.

Barker, C. (2005), *Cultural Studies: Theory and practice*, London, Sage.

Barnes, C. and Mercer, G. (1997), (editors), *Doing Disability Research*, Leeds, The Disability Press, University of Leeds.

Barnes, C., Mercer, G. and Morgan, H. (editors), (2001), *Creating Independent Futures: Evaluation of services led by disabled people – Stage Three Report*, Leeds, Disability Press, University of Leeds.

Barnett, R.W. (2003), *Asymmetrical Warfare: Today's challenge to US military power*, Nebraska, Potomac Books.

Barr, C. and Topping, A. (2021), Fewer than one in 60 rape charges lead to charge in England and Wales, *The Guardian*, 23rd May, https://www.theguardian.com/society/2021/may/23/fewer-than-one-in-60-cases-lead-to-charge-in-england-and-wales accessed 25th September 2022.

Bazongo, G. (2021), I was a COP26 delegate: here are my thoughts, Blog, Tree Aid, https://www.treeaid.org/blogs-updates/reflecting-on-cop26/?gclid=EAIaIQobChMI35Hlja_P9QIVJO7mCh2XggJCEAAYAiAAEgJVhvD_BwE accessed 26th January 2022.

Baumberg, B., Bell, K. and Gaffney, D. with Deacon, R., Hood, C. and Sage, D. (2013), *Benefits Stigma in Britain*, Elizabeth FinnCare/University of Kent, https://www.turn2us.org.uk/T2UWebsite/media/Documents/Benefits-Stigma-in-Britain.pdf accessed 11th April 2022.

BBC Data Journalism Team (2023), Coronavirus Public Inquiry, *BBC Verify*, 5th July, https://www.bbc.co.uk/news/uk-51768274 accessed 13th January 2025.

BBC News (2021), Universities could face fines over free speech breaches, BBC *News*, 12th May, https://www.bbc.co.uk/news/education-57076093 accessed 25th July 2022.

BBC News (2022), Why your internet habits are not as clean as you think, smart guide to climate change, *BBC News*, https://www.bbc.com/future/article/20200305-why-your-internet-habits-are-not-as-clean-as-you-think accessed 7th July 2022.

BBC News (2023), The papers, 'Amazon uses monopoly to hurt shoppers, says US lawsuit', front page headline, *Financial Times*, 23rd September, https://www.bbc.co.uk/news/blogs-the-papers-66931628 accessed 27th September 2023

Beemyn, G. and Goldberg, A. (editors), (2021), *The Sage Encyclopedia of Trans Studies*, London, Sage.

Bell, E. (2006), Excluding the excluded: New Labour's penchant for punishment, *Observatoire De La Societe Britannique*, pp 191–204, https://journals.openedition.org/osb/550 accessed 11th February 2023.

Benner, E. (2024), *Adventures in Democracy: The turbulent world of people power*, London, Allen Lane.

Beresford, P. (2003), *It's Our Lives: A short theory of knowledge, distance and experience*, London, Citizen Press in association with Shaping Our Lives.

Beresford, P. (2006), Making the connections with direct experience: from the western front to user-controlled research, *Educational Action Research*, Vol 14, No 2, pp 161–9.

Beresford, P. (2010), *A Straight Talking Guide To Being A Mental Health Service User*, Ross-on-Wye, PCCS Books.

Beresford, P. (2012), The 'overclass' is the real threat to society, second thoughts, poverty, *The Guardian*, 3rd April, https://www.theguardian.com/society/2012/apr/03/overclass-threat-society accessed 2nd November 2021.

References

Beresford, P. (2014), Personal communication email to Miranda Fricker, 28th November 2014 and a paraphrase of her reply 30th November 2014.

Beresford, P. (2016), *All Our Welfare: Towards participatory social policy*, Bristol, Policy Press.

Beresford, P. (2019), Public participation in health and social care: exploring the co-production of knowledge, policy and practice review article, *Frontiers in Sociology*, January, https://www.frontiersin.org/articles/10.3389/fsoc.2018.00041/full accessed 1st June 2022.

Beresford, P. (2021), *Participatory Ideology: From exclusion to involvement*, Bristol, Policy Press.

Beresford, P. and Branfield, F. (2012), Building solidarity, ensuring diversity: lessons from service users' and disabled people's movements, in Barnes, M. and Cotterell, P. (editors), *Critical Perspectives on User Involvement*, Bristol, Policy Press, pp 33–45.

Beresford, P. and Croft, S. (1984), Welfare pluralism: the new face of Fabianism, *Critical Social Policy*, Issue 9, Spring, pp 19–39.

Beresford, P. and Croft, S. (1986), *Whose Welfare: Private care or public services?*, Brighton, Lewis Cohen Urban Studies Centre at University of Brighton.

Beresford, P. and Croft, S. (1988), Being on the receiving end – lessons for community development and user involvement, *Community Development Journal*, Vol 23, No 4, October, pp 273–9.

Beresford, P. and Croft, S. (1989), User-involvement, citizenship and social policy, *Critical Social Policy*, Issue 26, Autumn 1989, pp 5–18.

Beresford, P. and Russo, J. (editors), (2022), *The Routledge International Handbook of Mad Studies*, Abingdon, Routledge.

Beresford, P. and Slasberg, C. (2023), *The Future of Social Care: From problem to rights-based sustainable solution*, Cheltenham, Edward Elgar Publishers.

Beresford, P., Green, D., Lister, R. and Woodard, K. (1999), *Poverty First Hand*, London, Child Poverty Action Group.

Beresford, P., Fleming, J., Glynn, M., Bewley, C., Croft, S., Branfield, F. and Postle, K. (2011), *Supporting People: Towards a person-centred approach*, Bristol, Policy Press.

Beresford, P., Farr, M., Hickey, G., Kaur, M., Ocloo, J., Tembo, D. and Williams, O. (editors), (2021), COVID-19 and co-production in health and social care research, policy, and practice, *Volume 1: The Challenges and Necessity of Co-production*, Open Access e Book, Bristol, Policy Press.

Beresford, P., Golding, F., Hughes, M., Levin, L., Mohamed, O., Schon, U-K. and Unwin, P. (2023), Special issue title: Voice and influence of people with lived experience, *British Journal of Social Work*, Vol 53, No 3, April, https://academic.oup.com/bjsw/issue/53/3.

Bergen, R.K. and Bogle, K.A. (2000), Exploring the connection between pornography and sexual violence, *Violence and Victims*, Vol 15, Issue 3, pp 227–34.

Berlant, L. (editor), (1998), *Intimacy*, Chicago, University of Chicago Press.

Berlinski, C. (2011), *'There Is No Alternative': Why Margaret Thatcher matters*, New York, Basic Books.

Berman, R.A. (2021), Identity politics versus solidarity: comments on Thierse. *Teloscope*, 12th March, http://www.telospress.com/identity-politics-versus-solidarity-comments-on-thierse/ accessed 7th December 2022.

Bernard, R., Bowsher, G., Sullivan, R. and Gibson-Fall, F. (2021), *Health Security*, Vol 19, Issue 1, 18th February, pp 3–12, https://www.liebertpub.com/doi/10.1089/hs.2020.0038 accessed 14th January 2022.

Besley, A.C. and Peters, M.A. (2006), Neoliberalism, performance and the assessment of research quality, *South African Journal of Higher Education*, Vol 20, No 6, pp 814–32, https://journals.co.za/doi/pdf/10.10520/EJC37299 accessed 6th August 2022.

Best, S. (2002), *Introduction to Politics and Society*, London, Sage Publications.

Beveridge, A. (2003), The madness of politics, *Journal of the Royal Society of Medicine*, December, Vol 96, No 12, pp 602–4, https://www.ncbi.nlm.nih.gov/pmc/articles/PMC539664/ accessed 17th April 2022.

Bieler, A. (2011), Labour, new social movements and the resistance to neo-liberal restructuring in Europe, *New Political Economy*, Vol 16, No 2, pp 163–83.

Bjornberg, K.E., Karlsson, M., Gilek, M. and Hansson, S.O. (2017), Climate and environmental science denial: a review of the scientific literature published in 1990–2015, *Journal of Cleaner Production*, Vol 167, 20 November, pp 229–41.

Blair, M. (1998), The myth of neutrality in educational research, Connoly, P. and Troyna, B. (editors), *Researching Racism in Education*, Buckingham, Open University Press, pp 12–20.

Blake, J. (director), (2022), *Two Daughters*, BBC 2 TV, BBC iPlayer, https://www.bbc.co.uk/programmes/m0017x5x accessed 9th July 2024.

Blakeley, G. (2024), *Vulture Capitalism: Corporate crimes, backdoor bailouts and the death of Freedom*, London, Bloomsbury.

Bland, A. (2022), Monday briefing: reasons for optimism – and pessimism – after Le Pen, 1st Edition, *The Guardian*, 25th April, https://www.theguardian.com/world/2022/apr/25/first-edition-emmanuel-macron-victory-le-pen-france accessed 8th May 2022.

Blanluet, N. (2018), The five principles of coproduction illustrated, knowledge base, *Co-production Network for Wales*, 26th December, https://info.copronet.wales/the-5-principles-of-co-production-illustrated/ accessed 16th March 2023.

Blydenburgh, K. (undated), Always remember that you are absolutely unique, just like everyone else, *Lifehack*, https://www.lifehack.org/451335/always-remember-that-you-are-absolutely-unique-just-like-everyone-else accessed 26th March 2022.

Boaz, A. and Pawson, R. (2005), The perilous road from evidence to policy: five journeys compared, *Journal of Social Policy*, Vol 34, No 2, pp 175–94.

Booth, R. (2021), Coronavirus report warned of impact on UK four years before pandemic, *The Guardian*, 7th October, https://www.theguardian.com/politics/2021/oct/07/coronavirus-report-warned-of-impact-on-uk-four-years-before-pandemic accessed 11th September 2022.

Bourdieu, P. (1986), The forms of capital, chapter 1, in Richardson, J. (editor), *Handbook of Theory and Research for the Sociology of Education*, Westport, CT, Greenwood, pp 241–58.

Bregman, R. (2020), The neo-liberal era is ending: what comes next? *The Correspondent*, 14th May, https://thecorrespondent.com/466/the-neoliberal-era-is-ending-what-comes-next accessed 13th January 2023.

Bronte, C. (1992), *Jane Eyre*, London, Wordsworth Modern Classics.

Brooks, C., Nieuwbeerta, P. and Manza, J. (2006), Cleavage-based voting behavior in cross-national perspective: evidence from six postwar democracies, *Social Science Research* Vol 35, No 1 pp 88–128.

Brown, M. (2022), Landlord was warned of mould that killed toddler in Rochdale, Housing, *The Guardian*, 8th November, https://www.theguardian.com/society/2022/nov/08/landlord-was-warned-of-mould-that-killed-toddler-in-rochdale-flat accessed 5th December 2022.

Buccola, N. (2019), *The Fire Is Upon Us: James Baldwin, William F Buckley Jr and the Debate over Race in America*, Princeton, Princeton University Press.

Buchanan, I., Baker, C., Bolton, P., Kirk-Wade, E., Cracknell, R., Sturge, G. and Alen, G. (2024), *Women in Politics and Public Life, Research Briefing*, 6th March, London, House of Commons Library, https://commonslibrary.parliament.uk/research-briefings/sn01250/ accessed 15th January 2025.

Buechler, S.M. (1999), *Social Movements in Advanced Capitalism*, Oxford, Oxford University Press.

Bunning, K. (2022), Personal Communication, Associate Professor, Intellectual & Developmental Disability, School of Health Sciences University of East Angliahttps://theconversation.com/we-were-at-cop26-it-had-mixed-results-172558, 27th September 2022.

Burelli, T., Lillo, A., Campbell-Durifle, C. and Touchant, L. (2021), We were at COP26: it had mixed results, Blog, *The Conversation*, accessed 26th January 2022.

Burkell, J. and Regan, P.M. (2019), Voter preferences, voter manipulation, voter analytics: policy options for less surveillance and more autonomy. *Internet Policy Review*, Vol 8, No 4, https://doi.org/10.14763/2019.4.1438, https://policyreview.info/articles/analysis/voter-preferences-voter-manipulation-voter-analytics-policy-options-less accessed 3rd March 2022.

Burnett, L. (2022), The international Malcolm X, *Cross Cultural Solidarity: History in the Service of Solidarity*, https://crossculturalsolidarity.com/the-international-malcolm-x/ accessed 19th December 2022.

Burns, K. (2020), 9 Questions about trans issues you were too embarrassed to ask, *Vox* website, https://www.vox.com/identities/21332685/trans-rights-pronouns-bathrooms-sports accessed 30th May 2022.

Burrows, S., Green, G., Speed, E. and Thompson, C. (2021), *Access To Health Care for Travelling Communities in the East of England*, September 2021, University of Essex, https://arc-eoe.nihr.ac.uk/sites/default/files/uploads/files/Access%20to%20Health%20Care%20for%20Travelling%20Communities%20in%20the%20East%20of%20England%20September%20Update%202021_0.pdf accessed 25th October 2022.

Bustelo, M.G. (2016), Review, neoliberalism and terror: critical engagements, in Heath-Kelly, C., Baker-Beall, C. and Jarvis, L. (editors), *Global Policy*, 16th September, https://www.globalpolicyjournal.com/blog/16/09/2016/book-review-neoliberalism-and-terror-critical-engagements accessed 6th January 2022.

Butler, H. (1985), *Escape from the Anthill*, Dublin, Lilliput Press.

Butler, P. (2012), How the Spartacus welfare cuts campaign went viral, *The Guardian*, Disability, 17th January, https://www.theguardian.com/society/2012/jan/17/disability-spartacus-welfare-cuts-campaign-viral accessed 16th December 2022.

Butler, P. (2022), Care for UK's most vulnerable face 'collapse' as providers count Cost, *The Guardian*, 25th November, https://www.theguardian.com/society/2022/nov/25/care-for-uks-most-vulnerable-faces-collapse-as-providers-count-cost accessed 6th January 2023.

Calder, G. (2016), *How Inequality Runs in Families: Unfair advantage and the limits of social mobility*, Bristol, Policy Press.

Cameron, C. (2023a), Some Things Never Seem To Change: Further towards an affirmation model, *Disability & Society*, DOI: 10.1080/09687599.2023.2295799, https://doi.org/10.1080/09687599.2023.2295799 accessed 13th January 2025.

Cameron, C. (2024a), Some Things Never Seem to Change: Towards an affirmation model, *Disability & Society*, Current Issues, Vol 39, Issue 7, pp 1890–95, https://doi.org/10.1080/09687599.2023.2295799.

Cameron, C. (2024b), Sometimes I wish it was all over, *Disability & Society*, Current Issues, Vol 39, Issue 2, pp 506–11, https://doi.org/10.1080/09687599.2023.2275525.

Cannon, P. (2021), Tax evasion statistics UK 2018–20, Barrister at Law Website, https:// accessed 17th March 2022.

Carr, S. (2018), 'Who owns co-production?', in Beresford, P. and Carr, S. (editors), *Social Policy First Hand: An international introduction to participatory welfare*, Bristol, Policy Press, pp 74–83.

Casey, L. (2012), *Listening to Troubled Families: A report by Louise Casey CB*, Department for Communities and Local Government, July, London, Department for Communities and Local Government.

Castells, M. (2004), *The Power of Identity*, 2nd edition, Oxford, Blackwell.

Castells, M. (2017), *Another Economy Is Possible: Culture and economy in a time of crisis*, Cambridge, Polity Press.

Cathcart, B. (2000), *The Case of Stephen Lawrence*, London, Penguin.

Cathy (2022), What's the difference between cooperatives and collectives, meet Cathy, *Cooperative Development Institute*, https://cdi.coop/coop-cathy-coops-and-collectives-difference/ accessed 5th December 2022.

Chakrabarti, S. (2021), After Sarah Everard's murder, police powers need to be curbed not strengthened, *The Guardian*, 1st October, https://www.theguardian.com/commentisfree/2021/oct/01/sarah-everard-murder-police-powers-stephen-lawrence-judicial-inquiry accessed 5th October 2021.

Charlton, JI (1998), Nothing about us without us: Disability, *oppression and empowerment*, Oakland, CA: University of California Press.

Chaney, S. (2022), *Am I Normal?: The 200 year search for normal people – and why they don't exist*, London, Profile Books in association with Wellcome Collection.

Chomski, N. (2017), *Requiem for the American Dream: The 10 principles of concentration of wealth and power*, New York City, Seven Stories Press.

Chrisafis, A. (2024), Risk of far right gaining power has not gone away, warns French Green leader, *The Guardian*, 12th July, https://www.theguardian.com/world/article/2024/jul/12/risk-of-far-right-gaining-power-has-not-gone-away-warns-french-green-leader accessed 12th July 2024.

Clausen, J. A. (editor), (1968), *Socialization and Society*, Boston: Little Brown and Company.

Colder Carras, M., Machin, K., Brown, M., Martinnen, T.-L., Maxwell, C., Frampton, B. and Jackman, M. (2022), Strengthening review and publication of participatory mental health research to promote empowerment and prevent co-optation, special article, *Psychiatric Services in Advance*, https://ps.psychiatryonline.org/toc/ps/0/0 accessed 22nd August 2022.

Collinson, P. (2017), Four in 10 right-to-buy homes are now owned by private landlords, *The Guardian* 8th December, https://www.theguardian.com/society/2017/dec/08/right-to-buy-homes-owned-private-landlords accessed 23rd March 2022.

Conolly, P. and Troyna, B. (1998), *Researching Racism in Education: Politics, theory and practice*, Milton Keynes, Open University.

Conzo, P., Fuochi, G., Anfossi, L., Spaccatini, F. and Onesta, C. (2021), Negative media portrayals of immigrants increase ingroup favoritism and hostile physiological and emotional reactions, *Nature, Scientific Reports*, 11, article number 16407, https://www.nature.com/articles/s41598-021-95800-2#citeas accessed 11th April 2022.

Cowburn, A. (2020), Boris Johnson cabinet now two-thirds privately educated after reshuffle, compared to 7% of UK population, *The Independent*, 14th February, https://www.independent.co.uk/news/uk/politics/boris-johnson-cabinet-reshuffle-news-privately-educated-mps-a9335261.html accessed 20th October 2021.

CPUSA (2022), Revolutionary education and the breakthrough of Paolo Freire: education as a force to transform the world: the work of Paolo Freire, *Marxist Education*, 25th October, https://web.archive.org/web/20161025154727/http://tx.cpusa.org/school/classics/freire.htm accessed 23rd November 2022.

Cukor, G. (director), (1944), *Gaslight*, Film, Hollywood, MGM.

Curtice, J. (2023), England local elections 2023, *BBC website*, 5th May, https://www.bbc.co.uk/news/uk-politics-65475817 accessed 24th March 2024.

Dancy, M. (2004), The myth of gender neutrality, American Institute of Physics Conference Proceedings, 22nd September, Vol 720, No 31, https://aip.scitation.org/doi/abs/10.1063/1.1807247 accessed 22nd August 2022.

Dattari, C.P. (2022), Neoliberalism was born in Chile. Now it will die there, *OpenDemocracy*, 31st January, https://www.opendemocracy.net/en/oureconomy/neoliberalism-was-born-in-chile-now-it-will-die-there/ accessed 8th May 2022.

Davies, R.W. (2000), Carr's changing views of the Soviet Union, in Cox, M. (editor), *E.H. Carr: A critical appraisal*, Basingstoke, Palgrave Macmillan, pp 91–108.

Deane, K., Delbecque, L., Gorbenko, O., Hamoir, A.M., Hoos, A., Nafria, B., Pakarinen, C., Sargeant, I., Richards, D.P., Skovlund, S. and Brooke, N. on behalf of the PFMD Patient Engagement Meta-framework Co-creation Team (2019), Co-creation of patient engagement quality guidance for medicines development: an international multistakeholder initiative, *BMJ Innovations*, Vol 5, Issue 1, p 13, https://innovations.bmj.com/content/5/1/43 accessed 6th December 2022.

Deivanayagam, T.A., Lasoye, S., Smith, J. and Selvarajah, S. (2021), Policing is a threat to public health and human rights, commentary, *BMJ Global Health*, Vol 6, Issue 2, https://gh.bmj.com/content/6/2/e004582 accessed 6th October 2021.

Delboy, S. (2018), Neoliberalism and relationships, Blog, Fermata Psychotherapy, 15th July, https://www.fermatapsychotherapy.com/blog/2018/7/15/neoliberalism-and-relationships accessed 24th December 2022.

Department of Health (1999), *National Service Framework for Mental Health: Modern Standards and Service Models*, London, Department of Health.

References

Derbyshire, D. (2022), Social media damaging children, *Daily Mail Online*, 11th July, https://www.dailymail.co.uk/news/article-1153583/Social-websites-harm-childrens-brains-Chilling-warning-parents-neuroscientist.html accessed 11th July 2022.

Ditum, S. (2016), *Pimp State* by Kat Banyard review – the horrors of the sex industry, *The Guardian*, Review, 30th June, https://www.theguardian.com/books/2016/jun/30/pimp-state-by-kat-banyard-review accessed 9th January 2023.

Dodd, V. (2020), Mother of murdered daughters attacks 'toxic' Met police culture, *The Guardian*, 26th June, https://www.theguardian.com/uk-news/2020/jun/26/met-chief-dumbfounded-at-officers-alleged-photos-of-murdered-sisters accessed 4th October 2021.

Dodd, V. (2021), Sarah Everard: former prosecutor to lead inquiry into rape and murder by police officer, *The Guardian*, 22nd November, https://www.theguardian.com/uk-news/2021/nov/22/sarah-everard-former-prosecutor-to-lead-inquiry-into-and-by-police-officer accessed 10th January 2025

Dodd, V. (2021a), MPs rebuke police for 'systemic failure' to improve record on race, *The Guardian*, 30th July, https://www.theguardian.com/uk-news/2021/jul/30/mps-rebuke-police-for-systemic-failure-to-improve-record-on-race accessed 5th October 2021.

Dodd, V. (2021b), Metropolitan Police failed family of sisters watchdog finds, *The Guardian*, 25th October, https://www.theguardian.com/uk-news/2021/oct/25/metropolitan-police-to-apologise-to-family-of-murdered-sisters accessed 2nd November 2021.

Dodd, V. (2021c), Sarah Everard: former prosecutor to lead inquiry into rape and murder by police officer, *The Guardian*, 22nd November, https://www.theguardian.com/uk-news/2021/nov/22/sarah-everard-former-prosecutor-to-lead-inquiry-into-and-by-police-officer accessed 4th June 2022.

Dodd, V. (2023), Louise Casey's report on the Met police: The fall of an institution, *The Guardian*, 21st March, https://www.theguardian.com/uk-news/2023/mar/21/louise-caseys-report-on-the-met-police-the-fall-of-a-british-institution accessed 21st March 2023.

Dodd, V. (2024), Devastating report lays bare police failings over Sarah Everard killer, *The Guardian*, 29th February, https://www.theguardian.com/uk-news/2024/feb/29/killer-of-sarah-everard-should-never-have-joined-police-report-finds accessed 7th March 2024.

Dodd, V. and Haque, S. (2022), 80% of UK police accused of domestic abuse kept jobs, figures show, *The Guardian*, 17th March, https://www.theguardian.com/uk-news/2022/mar/17/80-percent-of-uk-police-accused-of-domestic-abuse-kept-jobs-figures-show accessed 4th June 2022.

Dorling, D. (2011), Underclass, overclass, ruling class, supernova class, chapter 8, in Walker, A., Sinfield, A. and Walker, C. (editors), *Fighting Poverty, Inequality and Injustice: A manifesto inspired by Peter Townsend*, Bristol, Policy Press, pp 153–74.

Dorling, D. (2018), *Peak Inequality: Britain's ticking time bomb*, Bristol, Policy Press.

Dorling, D. (2019), *Inequality and the 1%*, 3rd Edition, London, Verso.

Doyal, L. and Gough, I. (1991), *A Theory of Human Need*, Basingstoke, Macmillan.

Drakeford, M. and Butler, I. (2005), *Scandal, Social Policy and Social Welfare*, Revised 2nd Edition, Bristol, Policy Press.

Dreyer, J.S. (2017), Practical theology and the call for the decolonisation of higher education in South Africa: reflections and proposals, *HTS Theological Studies*, Vol 73, No 4, pp 1–7.

Durkheim, E. (2002), *Suicide: A study in sociology*, London, Routledge Press.

DWP (2021), *Fraud and Error in the Benefit System 2019 to 2020*, Department for Work and Pensions National Statistics, Gov.UK, https://www.gov.uk/government/statistics/fraud-and-error-in-the-benefit-system-financial-year-2019-to-2020-estimates/fraud-and-error-in-the-benefit-system-2019-to-2020 accessed 17th March 2022.

Eagleton, T. (2007), *Ideology: An introduction*, 2nd Edition, London, Verso.

Eagleton-Pierce, M. (2015), *Neoliberalism: The key concepts*, London, Routledge.

Eaton, G. (2021), How Tory dominance is built on home ownership, *New Statesman*, 12th May, https://www.newstatesman.com/politics/uk-politics/2021/05/how-tory-dominance-built-home-ownership accessed 21st March 2022.

Eddo-Lodge, R. (2017), *Why I Am No Longer Talking to White People about Race*, London, Bloomsbury.

Editorial (2022), The Guardian view on levelling up: a serious project meets a deeply unserious PM, Opinion Inequality, *The Guardian*, 8th June, https://www.theguardian.com/commentisfree/2022/jun/08/the-guardian-view-on-levelling-up-a-serious-project-meets-a-deeply-unserious-pm accessed 17th January 2023.

Edwards, A., Edwards, C., Wahl, S.T. and Myers, S.A. (2019), *The Communication Age: Connecting and engaging*, 3rd Edition, US, Sage.

Eggers, A.C. (2014), Partisanship and electoral accountability: evidence from the UK expenses scandal, *Quarterly Journal of Political Science*, Vol 9, No 4, pp 441–72. doi:10.1561/100.00013140.

EHRC (2021), *Protected Characteristics*, London, Equality and Human Rights Commission, https://www.equalityhumanrights.com/en/equality-act/protected-characteristics accessed 5th July 2023.

Eldridge, J.E.T. and Eldridge, E.J. (1994), *Raymond Williams: Making connections*, London, Routledge.

Electoral Commission (2004), *Delivering Democracy: The future of postal voting*, August, London, Electoral Commission, http://services.salford.gov.uk/solar_documents/annexb.pdf accessed 12th March 2022.

Elgot, J. (2022), The Shaming of Whitehall: how the Partygate scandal unfolded, *The Guardian*, 19th May, https://www.theguardian.com/world/2022/may/19/the-shaming-of-whitehall-how-the-partygate-scandal-unfolded accessed 29th May 2022.

Eliot, T.S. (1922), *The Waste Land*, New York, Boni and Liveright.

El Kaliouby, R. (2015), Sentimental advertising, Blog, *Affectiva*, 19th March, https://blog.affectiva.com/the-fine-line-of-sentimental-advertising accessed 5th January 2023.

Engels, F. (1949), Letter to F. Mehring, in Marx, K. and Engels, F., *Selected Works in Two Volumes*, Vol 2, Moscow, Foreign Language Publishing House.

Equality Trust (2019), *Billionaire Britain*, December, Briefing, London, The Equality Trust, https://equalitytrust.org.uk/resource/billionaire-britain accessed 20th October 2021.

Equality Trust (2021a), *How Has Inequality Changed?* Inequality Trust Website, London, The Inequality Trust, https://equalitytrust.org.uk/how-has-inequality-changed accessed 20th October 2021.

Equality Trust (2021b), *The Scale of Economic Inequality in the UK*, London, The Equality Trust, https://equalitytrust.org.uk/scale-economic-inequality-uk accessed 20th October 2021.

Erimosele, F. (2022), Madness, decolonisation and mental health activism in Africa, in Beresford, P. and Russo, J. (editors), *The Routledge International Handbook of Mad Studies*, London, Routledge, pp 327–9.

Ertman, M. and Williams, J.C. (2005), *Rethinking Commodification: cases and readings in law and culture*, New York, New York University Press.

Evans, A. (2018), Book Review, *Why I Am No Longer Talking to White People About Race*, Blog, *LSE*, 2nd March, https://blogs.lse.ac.uk/lsereviewofbooks/2018/03/02/book-review-why-im-no-longer-talking-to-white-people-about-race-by-reni-eddo-lodge/ accessed 14th July 2022.

Extinction Rebellion (2022), Website, https://extinctionrebellion.uk/the-truth/about-us/ accessed 30th May 2022.

Fanon, F. (1952), *Black Skin, White Masks*, New York, Grove Press.

Fanon, F. (1963), *The Wretched of The Earth*, New York, Grove Weidenfeld.

Farnsworth, K. (2013), Bringing corporate welfare in, *Journal of Social Policy*, Vol 42, No 1, pp 1–22.

Farnsworth, W. (2021), *The Socratic Method: A practitioner's handbook*, Boston, David R. Godine Publishers, https://www.amazon.co.uk/Socratic-Method-Practitioners-Handbook/dp/1567926851 accessed 23rd January 2023.

Featherstone, L. (2018a), Talk is cheap: the myth of the focus group, long read, *The Guardian*, 6th February, https://www.theguardian.com/news/2018/feb/06/talk-is-cheap-the-myth-of-the-focus-group accessed 25th March 2022.

Featherstone, L. (2018b), *Divining Desire: Focus groups and the culture of consultation*, New York, OR Books.

Felter, C. (2021), Will the world ever solve the mystery of Covid-19's origin?, *Council on Foreign Relations, Newsletter*, https://www.cfr.org/backgrounder/will-world-ever-solve-mystery-covid-19s-origin accessed 17th January 2022.

Ferguson, J. (2010), The uses of neoliberalism, *Antipode: A radical journal of geography*, Vol 20, No 1, pp 155–84.

Financial Times (2020), Editorial, Virus Lays Bare the Frailty of the Social Contract, Financial Times, 4th April, https://www.ft.com/content/7eff769a-74dd-11ea-95fe-fcd274e920ca accessed 15th January 2025.

Finnemore, M. and Jurkovich, M. (2020), The politics of aspiration, *International Studies Quarterly*, Vol 64, No 4, pp 759–69.

Fisher, M. (2009), *Capitalist Realism: Is there no alternative?*, Ropley, Zero Books.

Flinders, M. (2020), These Boris Johnson character flaws are not funny: they are profound, Blog, Political Studies Association, 19th October, https://www.psa.ac.uk/psa/news/these-boris-johnson-character-flaws-are-not-funny-they-are-profound accessed 7th February 2022.

Flood, T. and Kikabhai, N. (2018), Education (ignorance) addressing inclusive education: the issues and its importance from a participatory perspective, Ch 11, in Beresford, P. and Carr, S. (editors), *Social Policy First Hand: An international introduction to participatory social welfare*, Bristol, Policy Press, pp 103–6.

Fogel, A. and Garvey, A. (2007), Alive communication, *Infant Behavior and Development*, 19th February, No 30, pp 251–7.

Forster, E.M. (1910), *Howards End*, London, Penguin Classics.

Foster, D. (2016), The Tory landlord MPs who don't care if rented homes aren't fit to live in, *The Guardian*, 15th January, https://www.theguardian.com/housing-network/2016/jan/15/tory-landlord-mps-housing-bill-private-rented accessed 11th March 2022.

Foucault, M. (1995), *Discipline And Punish: The birth of the prison*, New York, Vintage Books.

Fox, F. (2018), A sex worker perspective, *Porn Studies*, Forum, Vol 5, No 2, pp 197–9.

Francis-Devine, B. (2020), *Income Inequality in the UK, Research Briefing*, 13th August, London, House of Commons Library, https://commonslibrary.parliament.uk/research-briefings/cbp-7484/ accessed 20th October 2021.

Frank, T. (2004), *What's The Matter with Kansas?: How the Conservatives won the heart of America*, New York, Henry Holt.

Freire, P. (1971), *Pedagogy of the Oppressed*, translated by Ramos, Myra Bergman, New York, Herder and Herder.

Freire, P. (2005), *Education for Critical Consciousness*, New York, Continuum International Publishing Group.

Fricker, M. (2007), *Epistemic Injustice: Power and the ethics of knowing*, Oxford, Oxford University Press.

Fuck You Books (2023), *GoodReads*, https://www.goodreads.com/shelf/show/fuck-you accessed 26th January 2023.

Fukuyama (1992), *The End of History and the Last Man*, New York, The Free Press.

Furedi, F. (2004), 'Foreword: reflections on some uncomfortable realities', in Todd, M.J. and Taylor, G. (editors), *Democracy and Participation: Popular protest and new social movements*, London, Merlin Press, pp viii–xviii.

Galbraith, J.K. (1958), *The Affluent Society*, Boston, Houghton Mifflin.

Garnett, D. (1938), *The Letters of T.E. Lawrence*, 579, Letter to Eric Kennington, writing as T.E. Shaw, London, Jonathan Cape, pp 870–1.

Gaventa, J. (1982), *Power and Powerlessness: Quiescence and rebellion in an Appalachian Valley*, Chicago, University of Illinois Press.

Gibson, L. (2014), Resilience or resistance? Time banking in the age of austerity, *Journal of Contemporary European Studies*, Vol 22, No 2, pp 171–83.

Gibson, N.C. (2003), *Fanon: The postcolonial imagination*, Oxford, Polity Press.

Gibson, S. and Klevin, S. (2022), *Orgasm Inc: The story of One Taste*, Netflix.

Gibson-Graham, J.K. (1996), *The End of Capitalism (As We Knew It): A feminist critique of political economy*, Oxford, Blackwells.

Giroux, H.A. (2001), Culture, power and transformation in the work of Paulo Freire, in Schultz, F. (editor), *Sources: Notable selections in education*, 3rd Edition, New York, McGraw-Hill Dushkin.

Glasby, J. and Beresford, P. (2006), Who knows best?: evidence based practice and the service user contribution, Commentary and Issues, *Critical Social Policy*, Vol 26, No 1, pp 268–84.

Gogan, J. (director), (2016), *Hubert Butler: Witness to the future*, Film, Netflix.

Goldin, F., Smith, D. and Smith, M. (2014), *Imagine: Living in a socialist USA*, New York, Harper Perennial.

Goodman, A. (2009), The assassination of Fred Hampton: How the FBI and the Chicago Police Murdered a Black Panther, *Democracy Now*, 4th December, https://www.democracynow.org/2009/12/4/the_assassination_of_fred_hampton_how accessed 19th December 2022.

Goodrew, G. (2019), Biopower, disability and capitalism: Neoliberal eugenics and the future of ART regulation, *Duke Journal of Gender Law and Policy*, Vol 26, pp 137–55.

Gorvett, Z. (2015), The hidden psychology of voting, *BBC Future*, https://www.bbc.com/future/article/20150506-the-dark-psychology-of-voting accessed 3rd March 2022.

Gouldner, A.W. (1980), *The Two Marxisms, in Alienation, From Hegel to Marx*, Oxford, Oxford University Press, pp 177–98.

Gov.UK (2010), Definition of disability under the Equality Act 2010, *HM Government*, https://www.gov.uk/definition-of-disability-under-equality-act-2010 accessed 26th September 2022.

Graham-Harrison, E. (2021), Police Clash with Mourners at Sarah Everard Vigil in London, *The Observer*, 13th March, https://www.theguardian.com/uk-news/2021/mar/13/as-the-sun-set-they-came-in-solidarity-and-to-pay-tribute-to-sarah-everard accessed 10th January 2025.

Gramsci, A. (1971), *Selections from the Prison Notebooks*, New York, International Publishers.

Gray, B. (2005), The ravages of second hand experience: Hubert Butler's perception of universalism and distance, *Nordic Irish Studies*, Vol 4, pp 29–36.

Green, R. and Kynaston, D. (2019), *Engines of Privilege: Britain's Private School Problem*, London, Bloomsbury.

Greenemeier, L. (2013), Cool it: is the internet too hot for data centers to handle?, *Scientific American*, Technology, Newsletter, April, https://www.scientificamerican.com/article/greening-the-internet/ accessed 17th January 2020.

Gregory, L. (2014), Resilience or resistance?: Time banking in the age of austerity, *Journal of Contemporary European Studies*, Vol 22, No 2, pp 171–83.

Greve, B. (2020), *Welfare Populism and Welfare Chauvinism*, Bristol, Policy Press.

Grey, C. (2021), *How Brexit Unfolded: How no one got what they wanted (and why they were never going to)*, London, Biteback Books.

Griffiths, S. (editor), (2007), *The Politics of Aspiration*, London, Social Market Foundation, https://www.smf.co.uk/publications/the-politics-of-aspiration/ accessed 19th March 2022.

The Guardian (2019), Editorial, *The Guardian* view on children and social media: a safeguarding failure by the state, *The Guardian*, 4th January, https://www.theguardian.com/commentisfree/2019/jan/04/the-guardian-view-on-children-and-social-media-a-safeguarding-failure-by-the-state accessed 11th July 2022.

The Guardian staff and agencies (2023), 90% of people in China province infected with Covid, says local health official, *The Guardian*, 9th January, https://www.theguardian.com/world/2023/jan/09/life-is-moving-forward-china-enters-new-phase-in-covid-fight-as-borders-open accessed 18th January 2023.

Guest, M. (2022), From protestant ethic to neoliberal logic: evangelicals at the interface of culture and politics, *Research in the Social Scientific Study of Religion*, Vol 32, pp 482–507.

Gutierrez, P., Clarke, S. and Kirk, A. (2021), Covid world map: which countries have the most coronavirus vaccinations, cases and deaths, *The Guardian*, 1st December, https://www.theguardian.com/world/2021/dec/01/covid-world-map-which-countries-have-the-most-coronavirus-vaccinations-cases-and-deaths accessed 10th January 2022.

Gye, H. (2023), Disciplinary-system changes could lead to firing of 2,000 police officers, *The I*, 5th July, p 4.

Hall, S. (2007), Richard Hoggart, the uses of literacy and the cultural turn, *International Journal of Cultural Studies*, Vol 10, No 1, pp 39–49, https://journals.sagepub.com/doi/10.1177/1367877907073899 accessed 9th June 2022.

Hallett, H. (2024), *The UK Covid-19 Inquiry: Module 1 report, the resilience and preparedness of the United Kingdom*, HC18, House of Commons, 18th July, https://covid19.public-inquiry.uk/reports/module-1-report-the-resilience-and-preparedness-of-the-united-kingdom/ accessed 23rd September 2024.

Halliday, J. (2021), Sarah Everard murder: police commissioner urged to resign over 'streetwise' comment, *The Guardian*, 1st October, https://www.theguardian.com/uk-news/2021/oct/01/sarah-everard-murder-police-commissioner-apologises-for-saying-women-should-be-more-streetwise accessed 6th October 2021.

Hamilton, D.R. (2024), *The Joy of Actually Giving a F*ck*, London, Hay House.

Hammond, P. (2021), *Dr Hammond's Covid Casebook: The collected pandemic columns of Private Eye's medical correspondent 'MD'*, London, Private Eye.

Hanisch, C. (2006), *The Personal Is Political*, the 1969 article reprinted with a new introduction, truthtellers@hvi.net, https://webhome.cs.uvic.ca/~mserra/AttachedFiles/PersonalPolitical.pdf accessed 23rd May 2022.

Hansard Society (2022), *Annual Audit of Political Engagement 2019*, London, Hansard Society, https://www.hansardsociety.org.uk/projects/audit-of-political-engagement accessed 13th March 2022.

Hanson, M. (2018), Teaching is on the road to hell – the story of the national curriculum proves it, *The Guardian*, 12th February, https://www.theguardian.com/lifeandstyle/2018/feb/12/teaching-is-on-the-road-to-hell-the-story-of-the-national-curriculum-proves-it accessed 2nd November 2022.

Harari, Y.N. (2023), Human nature, intelligence, power, and conspiracies, Lex Fridman Podcast, No 390, https://www.youtube.com/watch?v=Mde2q7GFCrw accessed 18th August 2023.

Hare, N. (1969), The challenge of the Black scholar, *Black Politics*, December, Vol 1, No 2, pp 58–63.

Harmes, A. (2012), The rise of neoliberal nationalism, *Review of International Political Economy*, Vol 19, No 1, pp 59–86.

Harrison, M. and Sanders, T. (editors), (2015), *Social Policies and Social Control*, Bristol, Policy Press.

Harvey, D. (2007a), *A Brief History of Neoliberalism*, Oxford, Oxford University Press.

Harvey D. (2007b), Neoliberalism as creative destruction, *The Annals of the American Academy of Political and Social Science*, Vol 610, NAFTA and Beyond: Alternative perspectives in the study of global trade and development, March, pp 22–44.

Harvey, F. (2022), What are the key outcomes of Cop27 climate summit?, *The Guardian*, 20th November, https://www.theguardian.com/environment/2022/nov/20/cop27-climate-summit-egypt-key-outcomes accessed 18th January 2023.

Hayek, F.A. (1944), *The Road to Serfdom*, Abingdon, Routledge.

Heath-Kelly, C., Baker-Beall, C. and Jarvis, L. (editors), (2016), *Neoliberalism and Terror: Critical engagements*, Abingdon, Routledge.

Henderson, A. (2018), Noam Chomsky: social media is 'undermining democracy', *Salon*, 24th December, https://www.salon.com/2018/12/24/noam-chomsky-social-media-is-undermining-democracy/ accessed 13th July 2022.

Herman, E.S. and Chomsky, N. (1995), *Manufacturing Consent: The political economy of the mass media*, New York, Vintage.

Hertz, N. (2021), *The Lonely Century: A call to reconnect*, London, Sceptre.

Hesse, H. (1919), *Demian*, London, Penguin Modern Classics.

Heywood, A. (2007), *Political Ideologies: An introduction*, 4th Edition, Basingstoke, Palgrave Macmillan.

Hill Collins, P. and Bilge, S. (2016), *Intersectionality, Key Concepts*, London, Wiley.

Hiller, J. (2016), Epistemological foundations of objectivist and interpretivist research, chapter 11, in Wheeler, B. (editor), *Music Therapy Research*, 3rd Edition, Barcelona, Barcelona Publishers, pp 99–127.

Hilson, S. (2021), What is stealth marketing? Is it an ethical strategy?, *RockContent*, 16th December, https://rockcontent.com/blog/stealth-marketing/ accessed 4th January 2023.

Hobbes, T. (2016), *Leviathan*, London, Penguin Classics.

Hobert, R. and Toft, E. (2021), COP26 explained: what to know about the UN Climate Change Conference, Blog, United Nations Foundation, 25th October, https://unfoundation.org/blog/post/cop-26-explained-what-to-know-about-the-un-climate-change-conference/?gclid=EAIaIQobChMIrNm5-pnP9QIV0trVCh03uwhIEAAYAiAAEgJFFPD_BwE accessed 26th January 2022, https://www.theguardian.com/society/2025/jan/13/lady-wilkins-obituary

Hoggart, R. (1971), *Only Connect: On culture and connection – the Reith Lectures*, London, Chatto and Windus.

Hoggart, R. (2009), *The Uses of Literacy: Aspects of working class life*, Penguin Modern Classics, London, Penguin.

Holloway, J. (2018), What on Earth is the fediverse and why does it matter?, *New Atlas*, 18th September, https://newatlas.com/what-is-the-fediverse/56385 accessed 13th July 2022.

HRA (2021), *Public Involvement in a Pandemic: Lessons from the UK Covid-19 public involvement matching service*, London, NHS Health Research Authority, https://s3.eu-west-2.amazonaws.com/www.hra.nhs.uk/media/documents/8948_Public_Involvement_in_Pandemic_Research_Report_V9_-_Accessible.pdf accessed 14th September 2022.

Hudis, P. (2015), *Frantz Fanon: Philosopher of the Barricades*, London, Pluto Press.

Hudson, B. (2021), *Clients, Consumers or Citizens?: The privatisation of adult social care in England*, Bristol, Policy Press.

Huemer, M. (2012), *The Problem of Political Authority: An examination of the right to coerce and the duty to obey*, Basingstoke, Palgrave Macmillan.

Huet, E. (2018), The dark side of the orgasmic meditation company, *Bloomberg UK*, 18th June, https://www.bloomberg.com/news/features/2018-06-18/the-dark-side-of-onetaste-the-orgasmic-meditation-company accessed 3rd January 2023.

Hughes, I. (2019), Three reasons why we need to talk about the mental health of political leaders, *The Conversation*, 1st November, https://theconversation.com/three-reasons-why-we-need-to-talk-about-the-mental-health-of-political-leaders-126217 accessed 9th February 2022.

Hughes, M., Golding, F., Levin, L., Beresford, P., Unwin, P. and Mohamed, O. (2024), BJSW special issue on the voice and influence of people with lived experience: our reflections one year on, *British Journal of Social Work*, Vol 54, Issue 5, July 2024, pp 1783–9, https://doi.org/10.1093/bjsw/bcae118.

Humphries, R. (2022), *Ending the Social Care Crisis: A New Road to Reform*, Bristol, Policy Press.

Hunter, M. (2017), What's with all the hype – A look at aspirational marketing, *Norway Global, The Nordic Page*, https://www.tnp.no/norway/global/3059-whats-with-all-the-hype-a-look-at-aspirational-marketing/ accessed 21st March 2022.

Iberdrola (2022), Digital divide: digital divide throughout the world and why it causes inequality, Newsletter, *Iberdrola*, https://www.iberdrola.com/social-commitment/what-is-digital-divide accessed 11th October 2022.

IIR News Team (2016), 'Dangerous' Casey, failing and blaming victims, *Institute of Race Relations*, https://irr.org.uk/article/dangerous-casey-failing-and-blaming-victims/ accessed 9th October 2021.

IPCC (2021) What causes global warming?, *Intergovernmental Panel on Global Warming website*, https://becauseipcc.thesuccession.ca/what-causes-global-warming/?gclid=Cj0KCQiAqvaNBhDLARIsAH1Pq53CLMSuNKZ53UHyhn2waTndMJfeiULcFnZu8_4mcVn4oHv6wjzf83YaAicdEALw_wcB accessed 21st December 2021.

Isakovic, N.P. (undated), Covid-19: *What has Covid-19 taught us about neoliberalism?*, Women's International League for Peace and Freedom, https://www.wilpf.org/covid-19-what-has-covid-19-taught-us-about-neoliberalism/ accessed 17th January 2022.

Jackson Lears, T.J. (1985), The concept of cultural hegemony: problems and possibilities, *The American Historical Review*, Vol 90, No 3, June, pp 567–93.

Jacobs, A. (1997), Only Connect (review of *Le Ton Beau de Marot: In praise of the music of language,* by D.R. Hofstadter, Basic Books, November, *First Things,* https://www.firstthings.com/article/1997/11/only-connect accessed 8th June 2021.

Jeffries, S. (2022), The big idea: is tourism bad for us, *The Guardian,* 7th March, https://www.theguardian.com/books/2022/mar/07/the-big-idea-is-tourism-bad-for-us-globalisation-flight-holiday accessed 29th August 2023.

Jipson, J. and Jitheesh, J.M. (2019), The neoliberal project is alive but has lost its legitimacy: David Harvey, *The Wire,* 9th February, https://thewire.in/economy/david-harvey-marxist-scholar-neo-liberalism accessed 12th May 2022.

John, T. (2021), Anti-trans rhetoric is rife in the British media: nothing is being done to extinguish the flames, *CNN London,* https://edition.cnn.com/2021/10/09/uk/uk-trans-rights-gender-critical-media-intl-gbr-cmd/index.html accessed 11th April 2022.

Jones, C.D. (2013), *Don't Call Me Black, Call Me American,* lulu.com, https://books.google.co.uk/books?id=EBKVAwAAQBAJ&pg=PA387&redir_esc=y#v=onepage&q&f=false accessed 19th December 2022.

Jones, G. (2018), Social media is driving young people to loneliness and despair, *TFN, News* (Third Force News), SCVO, 4th January, https://tfn.scot/news/action-needed-to-prevent-mental-health-storm accessed 11th July 2022.

Jones-Casey, M. (2022), How the internet is heating homes: the future of megaprojects, *Foresight Works,* 5th May, https://foresight.works/the-internet-is-heating-homes-heres-how/ accessed 16th July 2022.

Joppke, C. (2023), Explaining the Neoliberal Right in the Neoliberal West, *Societies,* Vol 13, No 5, p 110, https://doi.org/10.3390/soc13050110.

Jordan, T. and Lent, A. (editors), (1999), *Storming the Millennium: The new politics of change,* London, Lawrence and Wishart.

Jungherr, A., Gonzalo, R. and Gayo-Avello, D. (2020), *Retooling Politics: How digital media are shaping democracy,* Cambridge, Cambridge University Press.

Juren, A.J., Frohlich, J. and Ignaszewski, A. (2012), Commonplace to condemned: the discovery that tobacco kills, and how Richard Doll shaped modern smoking cessation practices, *British Columbia Medical Journal,* Vol 54, No 4, pp 183–8, https://bcmj.org/articles/commonplace-condemned-discovery-tobacco-kills-and-how-richard-doll-shaped-modern-smoking accessed 19th December 2021.

Kaveney, R. (2014), T.S. Eliot: Searching for sainthood amid hate speech and hurt, *The Guardian,* 31st March, https://www.theguardian.com/commentisfree/2014/mar/31/ts-eliot-sainthood-hate-speech-hurt-poetry accessed 6th July 2022.

Kendall, D. (2005), *Sociology in Our Times*, Belmont, California, Thomson Wadsworth.

Kidd, I.J., Medina, J. and Pohlhaus, G. Jr. (editors), (2017), *The Routledge Handbook of Epistemic Injustice*, 1st Edition, Abingdon, Routledge.

King, T. (2021), Empty words, no action: Cop26 has failed first nation peoples, *The Guardian*, 15th November, https://www.theguardian.com/commentisfree/2021/nov/15/empty-words-no-action-cop26-has-failed-first-nations-people accessed 15th November 2021.

Kings Fund and Disability Rights UK (2022), *Towards a New Partnership between Disabled People and Health and Care Services: Getting our voices heard*. London, The King's Fund, https://www.kingsfund.org.uk/publications/partnership-disabled-people-health-care-services#contents.

Kirchgaessner, S., Ganguly, M., Pegg, D., Cadwalladr, C. and Burke, J. (2023), Revealed: the hacking and disinformation team meddling in elections, *The Guardian*, 15th February, https://www.theguardian.com/world/2023/feb/15/revealed-disinformation-team-jorge-claim-meddling-elections-tal-hanan accessed 16th February 2023.

Kirk, G. and Okazawa-Rey, M. (2000), Neoliberalism, militarism and armed conflict, an introduction, introduction to special issue, neoliberalism, militarism and armed conflict, *Social Justice*, Vol 27, No 4, pp 1–17, http://www.socialjusticejournal.org/archive/82_27_4/82_01Intro.pdf accessed 5th January 2022.

Kornbluth, J. and Gilman, S. (directors), (2017), *Saving Capitalism*, Film documentary, Netflix.

Kosanic, S. (2021), What tensions exist between disability rights and climate change and environmental policy?, in Tidball, M. (editor), *Up to the Challenge: Does the National Disability Strategy do enough to address the twin crises of climate change and life post-COVID-19 pandemic?*, Emerging Issues in Disability Law and Policy Series, Report No. 01/22, Oxford, Oxford Disability Law and Policy Project and University of Oxford Faculty of Law, pp 23–5.

Kuper, S. (2022), *Chums: How a tiny caste of Oxford Tories took over the UK*, London, Profile Books.

Lakner, C., Yonzan, N., Mahler, D.G., Aguilar, R.A.C., Wu, H. and Fleury, M. (2020), Updated estimates of the impact of Covid19 on global poverty: the effect of new data, World Bank Blogs, World Bank, 7th October, https://blogs.worldbank.org/opendata/updated-estimates-impact-covid-19-global-poverty-effect-new-data accessed 25th October 2021.

Lancaster University (2023), Library of lived experience in the North, University of Lancaster, https://www.lancaster.ac.uk/health-and-medicine/research/spectrum/research/living-library/#:~:text=One%20way%20is%20to%20do,or%20they%20might%20be%20staff accessed 29th September 2024.

Lansley, S. (2021a), *The Richer, The Poorer: How Britain enriched the few and failed the poor. A 200-year history*, Bristol, Policy Press.

Lansley, S. (2021b), Britain will fail to reduce poverty until it reduces inequality, Transforming Society Blog, 15th October, Bristol, Policy Press, https://www.transformingsociety.co.uk/2021/10/15/britain-will-fail-to-reduce-poverty-until-it-tackles-inequality/ accessed 24th October 2021.

Larner, W. (2000), Neo-liberalism, policy, ideology, governmentality, *Studies in Political Economy*, Vol 63, No 1, pp 5–25.

Lawrence, T.E. (1955), *The Mint: A day-book of the RAF depot between August and December 1922 with later notes by 352087, A/C Ross*, London, Jonathan Cape.

Leff, J. (2001), Why is care in the community perceived as a failure?, *British Journal of Psychiatry*, Vol 179, Issue 5, pp 381–3, https://www.cambridge.org/core/journals/the-british-journal-of-psychiatry/article/why-is-care-in-the-community-perceived-as-a-failure/58A574C96241D2FC1845DA2895B8FAFE, accessed 11th February 2023.

Leith, S. (2014), George Orwell's Schooldays, *The Guardian*, 8th February, https://www.theguardian.com/books/2014/feb/08/george-orwell-such-such-schooldays accessed 29th October 2022.

Levitt, T. (2020), Covid and farm animals: five pandemics that changed the world, *The Guardian*, 15th September, https://www.theguardian.com/environment/ng-interactive/2020/sep/15/covid-farm-animals-and-pandemics-diseases-that-changed-the-world accessed 14th January 2022.

Li, Y. and Devine, F. (2011), Is Social Mobility Really Declining?: Intergenerational Class Mobility in Britain in the 1990s and the 2000s, Sociological Research Online, Vol 16, No 3, DOI: 10.5153/sro.2424 https://www.researchgate.net/publication/227599467_Is_Social_Mobility_Really_Declining_Intergenerational_Class_Mobility_in_Britain_in_the_1990s_and_the_2000s accessed 14 January 2025.

London Edinburgh Weekend Return Group (1980), *In and Against the State*, London, Pluto Books, http://libcom.org/library/preface-first-edition.

London Metropolitan University (undateda), Decolonising academia, London Metropolitan University *website*, https://www.londonmet.ac.uk/about/equity/centre-for-equity-and-inclusion/race/decolonising-academia/ accessed 28th June 2022.

London Metropolitan University (undatedb), What does decolonising mean?, *London Metropolitan University website*, https://www.londonmet.ac.uk/about/equity/centre-for-equity-and-inclusion/race/decolonising-academia/what-does-decolonising-mean/ accessed 30th May 2022.

Lorde, A. (2007), The master's tools will never dismantle the master's house (1984), *Sister Outsider: Essays and Speeches*, Berkeley, CA, Crossing Press, pp 110–14.

Losasso, M. (2018), 'On Margate sands I can connect nothing with nothing', *Plinth*, 7th February, https://plinth.uk.com/blogs/magazine/on-margate-sands-i-can-connect-nothing-with-nothing accessed 8th June 2022.

Loughran, T.L. (2016), Landscape for a good woman's weekly: finding magazines in post-war British history and culture, in Ritchie, R., Hawkins, S., Phillips, N. and Kleinberg, S.J. (editors), *Women in Magazines: Research, Representation, Production and Consumption*, London, Routledge, pp 40–52.

Lukes, S. (2004), *Power: A radical view*, 2nd Edition, Basingstoke, Palgrave Macmillan.

Machiavelli, N. (2003), *The Prince*, London, Penguin Classics.

Mackenzie, S. (2022), Social movement organizing and the politics of emotion: from HIV to Covid-19, *Sociology Compass*, Vol 16, Issue 5, https://compass.onlinelibrary.wiley.com/doi/full/10.1111/soc4.12979 accessed 2nd December 2022.

Madden, M. and Speed, E. (2017), Beware zombies and unicorns: towards critical public involvement in health research in a neoliberal context, *Frontiers in Sociology*, June, Vol 2, No 7, pp 1–6.

Makortoff, K. (2022), Jeremy Hunt's City deregulation plans are 'dangerous' mistake, warns expert, *The Guardian*, Financial sector, 9th December, https://www.theguardian.com/business/2022/dec/09/jeremy-hunt-sets-out-sweeping-reforms-to-financial-sector accessed 14th January 2023.

Malik, K. (2021), Can Covid death rates be reduced to a clash of values?: it's not so simple, *The Observer*, 8th August, https://www.theguardian.com/commentisfree/2021/aug/08/how-world-fought-covid-cant-be-reduced-to-glib-east-v-west-values accessed 10th January 2022.

Manson, M. (2017), *The Subtle Art of Not Giving a Fuck: A counter-intuitive approach to living a good life*, New York, HarperCollins.

Marable, M. (2011), *Malcolm X: A life of reinvention*, New York, Viking.

Marc, A. (2015), *Conflict And Violence in the Twenty First Century: Current trends as observed in empirical research and statistics, Fragility, Conflict and Violence*, Washington DC, World Bank Group, https://www.un.org/pga/70/wp-content/uploads/sites/10/2016/01/Conflict-and-violence-in-the-21st-century-Current-trends-as-observed-in-empirical-research-and-statistics-Mr.-Alexandre-Marc-Chief-Specialist-Fragility-Conflict-and-Violence-World-Bank-Group.pdf accessed 4th January 2022.

Marcus, E. (2022), Lorraine Hansberry, *Making Gay History, The Podcast*, Season 8, https://makinggayhistory.com/podcast/lorraine-hansberry/ accessed 25th November 2022.

Martin, G. (2004), in Todd, M.J. and Taylor, G. (editors), *Democracy and Participation: Popular protest and new social movements*, London, Merlin Press, pp 1–28.

Marx, K. (1847), Chapter One: a scientific discovery, in *The Poverty of Philosophy*, Marxists.org, https://www.marxists.org/archive/marx/works/1847/poverty-philosophy/ch01.htm accessed 3rd January 2023.

Maslow, A.H. (1943), A theory of human motivation, *Psychological Review*, Vol 50, No 4, pp 370–96.

Mason, R., Mohdin, A. and Sinmaz, E. (2023), Police in England and Wales to get new powers to shut down protests before disruption begins, *The Guardian*, 15th January, https://www.theguardian.com/world/2023/jan/15/police-to-get-new-powers-to-shut-down-protests-before-disruption-begins, accessed 27th February 2023.

Maughan, P. (2013), Mental health and Mrs Thatcher: 'All due to a lack of personal drive, effort and will – a discussion over dinner', *The New Statesman*, 8th May, https://www.newstatesman.com/politics/2013/05/mental-health-and-mrs-thatcher-all-due-lack-personal-drive-effort-and-will accessed 9th February 2022

Mayo, P. (1999), *Gramsci, Freire, and Adult Education: Possibilities for Transformative Action*, London, Zed Books.

McAdam, D. and Paulsen, R. (1993), Specifying the relationship between social ties and activism, *American Journal of Sociology*, No 99, pp 640–67.

McBride, E. (2021), *Dangers Inside and Out*, Stories, Wellcome Collection, 21st September, https://wellcomecollection.org/articles/YSZh_hEAAGTR0xn7, accessed 23rd December 2023.

McIntyre, N., Parveen, N. and Thomas, T. (2021), sExclusion rates five times higher for black Caribbean pupils in parts of England, *The Guardian*, 24th March, https://www.theguardian.com/education/2021/mar/24/exclusion-rates-black-caribbean-pupils-england accessed 15th January 2025.

McKiernan, J. and Miller, H. (2024), Who Are Westminster's newbie MPs?, *BBC*, 8th July, https://www.bbc.co.uk/news/articles/c727ny2jd84o accessed 9th July 2024.

McManus, M. (2018), Neoliberalism, technology and the creation of postmodern culture, *Krytyka Polityczna & European Alternatives*, 16th July, http://politicalcritique.org/opinion/2018/neoliberalism-technology-postmodern-culture/# accessed 18th January 2022.

Meadway, J. (2021), Neoliberalism is dying: now we must replace it, *OpenDemocracy*, Our economy analysis, 3rd September, https://www.opendemocracy.net/en/oureconomy/neoliberalism-is-dying-now-we-must-replace-it/ accessed 13th January 2023.

Media Monkey (2015), The moment students turned their backs on Katie Hopkins' hate speech, *The Guardian*, 26th November, https://www.theguardian.com/media/mediamonkeyblog/2015/nov/26/katie-hopkins-brunel-university-students-turn-backs-video accessed 15th July 2022.

Mény, Y. and Surel, Y. (2002), *Democracies and the Populist Challenge*, Basingstoke, Palgrave.

Meyer, D.S. (2021), *How Social Movements (sometimes) Matter*, Cambridge, Polity Press.

Microsoft (2019), Communication is a real problem for UK workers and their companies, Microsoft research reveals, Microsoft, 27th November, https://news.microsoft.com/en-gb/2019/11/27/communication-is-a-real-problem-for-uk-workers-and-their-companies-microsoft-research-reveals/ accessed 1st October 2022.

Miller, K. (2022), The true story behind Netflix's 'Orgasm Inc': all about OneTaste and allegations against the 'Orgasm Cult': a new doc explores the company's troubled past, *Women's Health*, 5th November, https://www.womenshealthmag.com/life/a41868591/orgasm-inc-onetaste-true-story/ accessed 3rd January 2023.

Millett, K. (1970), *Sexual Politics*, New York, Doubleday.

Mols, F. and Jetten, J. (2020), Understanding support for populist radical right parties: toward a model that captures both demand-and supply-side factors, *Frontiers in Communication*, Vol 5, DOI: 10.3389/fcomm.2020.557561, https://www.frontiersin.org/articles/10.3389/fcomm.2020.557561/full accessed 14th April 2022.

Mombiot, G. (2016), *How Did We Get Into This Mess?*, London, Verso.

Morgan, D. (2019), *Snobbery*, in association with the British Sociological Association, Bristol, Policy Press.

Moss, S. (2009), T.S. Eliot wrote the waste land in this Margate shelter, shortcuts, *The Guardian*, 9th November, https://www.theguardian.com/books/2009/nov/09/ts-eliot-waste-land-margate accessed 8th June 2022.

Muller, J.-W. (2017), *What Is Populism?*, London, Penguin.

Murphy, M. (2015), Feminist opposition to the sex industry has little to do with women's 'choices', *Feminist Current*, 11th March, https://www.feministcurrent.com/2015/03/11/feminist-opposition-to-the-sex-industry-has-little-to-do-with-womens-choices/, accessed 9th January 2023.

Murray, C. (1996), Charles Murray and The Underclass: The developing debate, London, Institute of Economic Affairs Health and Welfare Unit.

Murray, D. (2020), *The Madness of Crowds: Gender, race and identity*, London, Bloomsbury Continuum.

Nardini, G., Rank-Christman, T., Bubitz, M.G., Cross, S.N.N. and Peracchio, L.A. (2020), Together we rise: how social movements succeed, *Journal of Consumer Psychology*, 20th October, Vol 31, Issue 1, pp 112–45.

Nash, M. and Stewart, B. (editors), (2002), *Spirituality and Social Care: Contributing to personal and community well-being*, London, Jessica Kingsley Publishing.

Nature (2020), Time to revise the sustainable development goals, Editorial, *Nature*, No 583, pp 331–2, https://www.nature.com/articles/d41586-020-02002-3 accessed 25th October 2020.

Navarro, V. (2007), Neoliberalism as a class ideology: or, the political causes of the growth of inequalities, *International Journal of Health Services*, Vol 37, No 1, pp 47–62.

Neocleous, M. (2000), *The Fabrication of Social Order: A critical theory of police power*, London, Verso.

Newman, J. (2021), What actually is levelling up?: What we know about Johnson's agenda – and what we don't, *The Conversation*, 23rd July, https://theconversation.com/what-actually-is-levelling-up-what-we-know-about-boris-johnsons-agenda-and-what-we-dont-164886 accessed 5th November 2021.

Nicolescu, V.Q. and Neaga, D.E. (2014), Bringing the market in, letting the science out. Neoliberal educational reform in Romania, *Procedia Social and Behavioural Sciences*, No 142, pp 104–10, https://www.sciencedirect.com/science/article/pii/S1877042814045236?ref=cra_js_challenge&fr=RR-1 accessed 6th August 2022.

Nicholson, R. (2022), Two daughters review – a raw, devastating account of the murders of Bibaa Henry and Nicole Smallman, *The Guardian*, 29th May, https://www.theguardian.com/tv-and-radio/2022/may/29/two-daughters-review-the-murders-of-bibaa-henry-and-nicole-smallman-are-laid-bare-in-devastating-film accessed 18th September 2023.

NLT (2022), Adult literacy, *National Literacy Trust*, https://literacytrust.org.uk/parents-and-families/adult-literacy/ accessed 1st October 2022.

Norman, J.M. (2022), The Elementary Education Act mandates universal education of children between the ages of 5 and 12 in England and Wales, *Jeremy Norman's History of Information*, https://www.historyofinformation.com/detail.php?id=3232 accessed 27th October 2022.

Novick, L. and Burns, K. (directors), (2022), *The US and the Holocaust*, US, Public Broadcasting Service.

Oakley, A. (1979), *Becoming a Mother*, London, Martin Robertson.

Oakley, A. (1981), Interviewing women: a contradiction in terms, in Roberts, H. (editor), *Doing Feminist Research*, London, Routledge and Kegan Paul, pp 30–61.

Oakley, A. (2015), Interviewing women again: power, time and the gift, *Sociology*, Vol 50, Issue 1, 20th May, pp 195–213.

Observer Editorial (2023), The Observer view on the government's pointless voter ID scheme, *The Observer*, 26th February, https://www.theguardian.com/commentisfree/2023/feb/26/the-observer-view-on-the-governments-pointless-voter-id-scheme accessed 21st March 2023.

O'Dell, L. (2019), Deaf news: less than 1 in 10 Britons know more than two words in sign language, survey finds, *The Limping Chicken*, Deaf Blog, 3rd May, https://limpingchicken.com/2019/05/03/deaf-news-9-in-10-brits-do-not-know-more-than-two-words-in-sign-language-survey-finds/ accessed 27th September 2022.

Office for Disability Issues (2011), *Equality Act: Guidance on matters to be taken into account in determining questions relating to the definition of disability*, London, HM Government, https://assets.publishing.service.gov.uk/government/uploads/system/uploads/attachment_data/file/570382/Equality_Act_2010-disability_definition.pdf accessed 26th September 2022.

Oliver, M. (1996), *Understanding Disability: From theory to practice*, Basingstoke, Macmillan.

Oliver, M. (1997), The disability movement is a new social movement, *Community Development Journal*, June, Vol 23, Issue 3, pp 244–51.

Oliver, M. and Barnes, C. (2012), *The New Politics of Disablement*, Basingstoke, Palgrave Macmillan.

Onions, P., Machin, K. and O'Neill, R. (2018), Pat's Petition: the emerging role of social media and the internet, in Beresford, P. and Carr, S. (editors), *Social Policy First Hand: An international introduction to participatory social welfare*, Bristol, Policy Press, pp 332–5.

Orlowski, J. (director), (2020a), *The Social Dilemma*, Netflix documentary, see also: https://www.google.co.uk/search?q=the+social+dilemma&sxsrf=ALiCzsbTD-9-iLY7ywtSkMLOWIijB5443g%3A1657541656634&ei=GBTMYuWhJpnNgQbv07S4Cw&ved=0ahUKEwjljZPt5_D4AhWZZsAKHe8pDbcQ4dUDCA0&uact=5&oq=the+social+dilemma&gs_lcp=Cgdnd3Mtd2l6EAMyCgguELEDEIMBEEMyBAgAEEMyBAgAEEMyBAgAEEMyBQgAEIAEMgQIABBDMgUIABCABDIFCAAQgAQyBQgAEIAEMgUIABCABDoHCAAQRxCwAzoHCAAQsAMQQzoKCAAQ5AIQsAMYAToMCC4QyAMQsAMQQxgCOgQIIxAnOgQILhBDOhAIABCABBCHAhCxAxCDARAUOgsILhCABBCxAxCDATo HCC4Q1AIQQzoLCAAQgAQQsQMQgwE6BQguEIAEOgsILhCxAxCDARDUAjoLCC4QgAQQsQMQ1AI6BwguELEDEEM6CggAEIAEEIcCEBQ6CAguEIAEELEDOggILhCABBDUAjoLCC4QgAQQxwEQrwE6CAguEIAEELEDOg4ILhCABBDHARDRAxDUAkoECEEYAEoECEYYAVDNBFjjF2DoGWgBcAB4AYAB8wGIAbsNkgEGMTQuMy4xmAEAoAEByAERwAEB2gEGCAEQARgJ2gEGCAIQARgI&sclient=gws-wiz accessed 12th July 2022.

Orlowski, J. (2020b), We need to rethink social media before it's too late. We've accepted a Faustian bargain, *The Guardian*, Opinion, 27th September, https://www.theguardian.com/commentisfree/2020/sep/27/social-dilemma-media-facebook-twitter-society accessed 10th July 2022.

Orwell, G. (1949), *Nineteen Eighty-Four*, London, Penguin.

Ostry, J.D., Berg, A. and Tsangarides, C.G. (2014), *Redistribution, Inequality, and Growth, IMF Staff Discussion Note*, February, SDNI/14/02, Washington DC, International Monetary Fund, https://www.imf.org/external/pubs/ft/sdn/2014/sdn1402.pdf accessed 27th October 2021.

Ostry, J.D., Loungani, P. and Furceri, D. (2016), Neoliberalism: oversold? *Finance and Development*, IMF, June, Vol 53, No 2, https://www.imf.org/external/pubs/ft/fandd/2016/06/ostry.htm accessed 21st October 2021.

Oswald, M. (2017), *The Spider's Web: Britain's second empire*, independent documentary, https://spiderswebfilm.com accessed 9th October 2024.

PA Media (2022), Met police blocked from fresh challenge to Sarah Everard vigil ruling, *The Guardian*, 31st May, https://www.theguardian.com/uk-news/2022/may/31/met-police-blocked-from-fresh-challenge-to-sarah-everard-vigil-ruling accessed 4th June 2022.

Panorama (2024), Trump: a second chance? *BBC One*, 28th October, https://www.bbc.co.uk/iplayer/episode/m0024h6r/panorama-trump-a-second-chance accessed 31st October 2024.

Papoulias, C., Csipke, E., Rose, D., McKellar, S. and Wykes, T. (2014), The psychiatric ward as a therapeutic space: systematic review, *British Journal of Psychiatry*, September, Vol 205, No 3, pp 171–6.

Paul, D. (1984), Eugenics and the left, *Journal of the History of Ideas*, Vol 45, No 4, pp 567–90.

Peck, C. (2023), *Escaping Twin Flames*, Netflix documentary, https://en.wikipedia.org/wiki/Escaping_Twin_Flames accessed 13th November 2023.

Peck, R. (2017), 'I Am Not Your Negro', Film, screenplay, Peck/Baldwin, USA, Magnolia Pictures.

Pichardo, N.A. (1997), New social movements: a critical review, *Annual Review of Sociology*, Vol 23, pp 411–30.

Pine, L.N.N. (1996), *The Family in the Third Reich, 1933–1945*, PhD Thesis, Department of International History, London School of Economics and Political Science, https://etheses.lse.ac.uk/1410/1/U084457.pdf accessed 3rd January 2023.

Pisani, B. (2017), We are letting Amazon and Apple 'avoid taxes, invade privacy, and destroy jobs,' says NYU professor, *Trader Talks, CNBC*, 3rd October, https://www.cnbc.com/2017/10/02/scott-galloway-the-four-amazon-apple-google-facebook.html accessed 8th July 2022.

Pollock, A. (2021), Multinational care companies are the real winners from Johnson's new tax, Opinion, *The Guardian*, 14th September, https://www.theguardian.com/commentisfree/2021/sep/14/multinational-care-companies-new-tax-privatised accessed 6th January 2023.

Price, R. (2007), Tony Blair will be remembered as 'he most successful Labour leader of all time', 10th May, *News Wise*, University of Maryland, https://www.newswise.com/articles/tony-blair-will-be-remembered-as-the-most-successful-labour-leader-of-all-time accessed 8th May 2022.

Primoratz, I. (editor), (2007), *Politics and Morality*, London, Palgrave Macmillan.

Prince, R. (2018), *Comrade Corbyn*, updated new edition, London, Biteback books.

Pring, J. (2024), *The Department: How a violent government bureaucracy killed hundreds and hid the evidence*, London, Pluto Press.

Prospero (2017), The Human Library Organisation replaces pages with people, *The Economist*, 3rd November, https://www.economist.com/prospero/2017/11/03/the-human-library-organisation-replaces-pages-with-people accessed 29th September 2024.

Pühringer,S. and Ötsch, W. O. (2017), Right-wing populism and market-fundamentalism: Two mutually reinforcing threats to democracy in the 21st century, ICAE Working paper Series No 59, Johannes Kepler University Linz, Institute for Comprehensive Analysis of the Economy (ICAE).

Putzel, J. (2020), The 'Populist' Right Challenge to Neoliberalism: Social Policy between a Rock and a Hard Place, *Development and Change*, Forum, Vol 51, Issue 2, March, https://onlinelibrary.wiley.com/doi/full/10.1111/dech.12578 accessed 12 January 2025.

Psychology Today (undated), Projection, *Psychology Today Website*, https://www.psychologytoday.com/gb/basics/projection accessed 7th April 2022.

Psychology Wiki (2022), Conscientization, *Psychology Wiki*, https://psychology.fandom.com/wiki/Conscientization accessed 22nd November 2022.

Quijano, A. (2013), Coloniality and modernity/rationality, in Mignolo, W.D. and Escober, A. (editors), *Globalization and the Decolonial Option*, London, Taylor and Francis, pp 31–42.

Quinn, B. (2021), Far-right Covid conspiracy theories fuelling antisemitism, warn UK experts, *The Guardian*, 12th October, https://www.theguardian.com/world/2021/oct/12/far-right-covid-conspiracy-theories-fuelling-antisemitism-warn-uk-experts accessed 18th January 2023.

Rabin-Haft, A. (2022), *The Fighting Soul: On the road with Bernie Sanders*, New York, Liveright Publishing Corporation.

Rao, S. (2015), *Is the Private Sector More Efficient: A cautionary tale*, Singapore, UNDP Global Centre for Public Service Excellence.

Rashford, M. (2022), *You Can Do It: How to find your voice and make a difference*, London, Macmillan Children's Books.

Rathbun, G. and Turner, N. (2012), Authenticity in academic development: the myth of neutrality, *International Journal for Academic Development*, Vol 17, No 3, pp 231–42.

Reicher, S.D., Haslam, A. and Platow, M.J. (2014), Social psychology, in Rhodes, R.A.W. and Hart, P. (editors), *The Oxford Handbook of Political Leadership*, Oxford, Oxford University Press, pp 149–60.

Reynolds, L. and Szerszynski, B. (2012), Neoliberalism and technology: Perpetual innovation or perpetual crisis, in Pellizzoni, L. and Ylonen, M. (editors), *Neoliberalism and Technoscience: Critical assessments*, Farnham, Ashgate, pp 27–46.

RNID (2022), *Facts and Figures, Information and Support*, Peterborough, Royal National Institute for Deaf People, https://rnid.org.uk/about-us/research-and-policy/facts-and-figures/ accessed 27th September 2022.

Roberts, J. (2021), *Four Hours at the Capitol*, Documentary, HBO, https://www.hbo.com/documentaries/four-hours-at-the-capitol accessed 9th February 2022.

Rosa, S.K. (2023), *Radical Intimacy*, London, Pluto Press.

Rose, D. (2022), *Mad Knowledges and User-Led Research – The politics of mental health and illness*, Basingstoke, Palgrave Macmillan.

Rose, D., Fleischmann, P., Wykes, T., Leese, M. and Bindman, J. (2003), Patients' perspectives on electroconvulsive therapy: systematic review, *British Medical Journal*, 21st June, Vol 326, No 7403, p 1363.

Rose, S. and Rose, H. (1971), Social responsibility (lll): the myth of the neutrality of science, *Impact of Science on Society*, Vol 21, No 2, pp 137–49.

Rowntree, B.S. (1901), *Poverty: A study of town life*, London, Macmillan.

Runciman, D. (2010), Why do people vote against their own interests, Blog, *BBC News Channel*, 30th January, http://news.bbc.co.uk/1/hi/world/americas/8474611.stm? accessed 9th February 2022.

Russo, J. (2023), Psychiatrization, assertions of epistemic justice and the question of agency, *Frontiers in Sociology*, No 8 1092298, DOI: 10.3389/fsoc.2023.1092298, https://www.academia.edu/96592826/Psychiatrization_assertions_of_epistemic_justice_and_the_question_of_agency?email_work_card=view-paper accessed 21 February 2023.

Rutherford, M. (2022), *Control: The Dark History and Troubling Present of Eugenics*, London, W & N.

Ryan, F. (2022), To those who wish to penalise poor people, cold and hunger are signs of a perfect system, Opinion, *The Guardian*, 9th March, https://www.theguardian.com/commentisfree/2022/mar/09/poor-cold-hunger-media-benefits-claimants accessed 11th April 2022.

Ryan, J. (2022), *Reports of Misogyny and Sexual Harassment in the Metropolitan Police, Debate Pack CDP 2022/0046*, 1st March, London, House of Commons Library, https://researchbriefings.files.parliament.uk/documents/CDP-2022-0046/CDP-2022-0046.pdf accessed 4th June 2022.

Saad-Filho, A. (2007), Marxian and Keynesian critiques of neoliberalism, in Panitch, L. and Leys, C. (editors), *Socialist Register*, 2008, November, titusland%2C+SR_2008_saad-filho.pdf accessed 12th May 2022.

Sakellariou, D. and Rotarou, E.S. (2017), The effects of neoliberal policies on access to healthcare for people with disabilities, *International Journal for Equity Health*, Vol 16, No 199, https://doi.org/10.1186/s12939-017-0699-3.

Sanchez, E. and Deck, J. (2019), Why global citizens should care?, *Global Citizen*, 20th March, https://www.globalcitizen.org/en/content/ten-happiest-countries-in-the-world/?utm_source=paidsearch&utm_medium=ukgrant&utm_campaign=genericbrandname&gclid=CjwKCAiA0JKfBhBIEiwAPhZXDxr_HjIKugzYKL_dEtYzjmagdiPPYC5Xvp_VvZ4hZjVT1KVrD5bAsxoC16IQAvD_BwE accessed 9th February 2023.

Sarkis, S. (2019), Gender bias impacts communication and leadership, *Forbes*, 26th February, https://www.forbes.com/sites/stephaniesarkis/2019/02/26/gender-bias-impacts-communication-and-leadership/?sh=6ff97ae677ef accessed 25th September 2022.

Scambler, G. (2018), Heaping blame on shame: 'weaponising stigma' for neoliberal times, *The Sociological Review*, Vol 66, No 4, pp 76–782.

Schalk, S. (2022), *Black Disability Politics*, Durham and London, Duke University Press.

Schierup, C-U., Munck, R., Likic-Brboric, B. and Neergaard, A. (2015), *Migration and Labour under Neoliberal Globalization: Key issues and folder shared with you: 'governance and policies drafting' challenges*, Oxford, Oxford University Press.

Schimank, U. and Volkmann, U. (editors), (2012), *The Marketization of Society: Economizing the Non-Economic*, Bremen, University of Bremen.

Schoch, M. and Lakner, C. (2020), Global poverty reduction is slowing, regional trends help understand why, *World Bank Blogs*, 5th November 2020, https://blogs.worldbank.org/opendata/global-poverty-reduction-slowing-regional-trends-help-understanding-why accessed 25th October 2021.

Schuller, M. (2001), *Howards End by E. M. Forster: 'Only Connect!'*, Seminar Paper, GRIN, https://www.grin.com/document/44788#:~:text=The%20idea%20of%20'only%20connect,the%20past%20and%20the%20 accessed 8th June 2022.

Schwab, K. (2017), *The Fourth Industrial Revolution*, World Economic Forum, New York, Currency Press.

Schwartz, M. (2011), Military Neoliberalism: Endless war and humanitarian crisis in the twenty-first century, *Societies Without Borders*, Vol 6, Issue 3, pp 190–303.

Scott, A. (1990), *Ideology and the New Social Movements*, London, Unwin Hyman.

Selman, M. (2024), Labour to 'do more' on web safety after after charities attack Ofcom, *The Times*, 17th July, p 1, https://www.bbc.co.uk/news/articles/c147pvlx7njo accessed 17th July 2024.

Shaping Our Lives (2020), *Building Inclusive Communities, Shaping Our Lives, Stage Two Bid to the National Lottery Community Fund – Reaching Communities England*, January.

Sherborne, M. (2011), *H.G. Wells: Another kind of life*, London, Peter Owen.

Siddique, H. (2019), Impact of social media on children faces fresh scrutiny, *The Guardian*, 15th January, https://www.theguardian.com/media/2019/jan/15/impact-social-media-children-mental-health accessed 14th July 2022.

SIPRI (2022), World military expenditure passes $2 trillion for first time, *Stockholm International Peace Research Institute*, 25th April, https://www.sipri.org/media/press-release/2022/world-military-expenditure-passes-2-trillion-first-time accessed 30th January 2023.

Smith, K.I. (2021), The 81 women killed in 28 weeks, Blog, *The Guardian*, 2nd October, https://www.theguardian.com/society/2021/oct/02/the-81-women-killed-in-28-weeks accessed 4th October 2021.

Smyraios, N. (2016), L'effet GAFAM: Stratégies et logiques de l'oligopole de l'internet, *Communication and Languages*, Vol 2, No 188, pp 61–83, https://www.cairn.info/article.php?ID_ARTICLE=COMLA_188_0061# accessed 8th July 2022.

Sodha, S. (2022), Don't be taken in by that £50bn 'fiscal black hole'. It's just a dodgy Tory metaphor, *The Observer*, 13th November, https://www.theguardian.com/commentisfree/2022/nov/13/dont-be-taken-in-by-50bn-fiscal-hole-dodgy-tory-metaphor accessed 18th November 2022.

SOL (2022), Ground rules for remote meetings, *Shaping Our Lives*, https://shapingourlives.org.uk accessed 2nd December 2022.

Spencer, J.L. (2022), *Ricky Gervais Supernature*, TV Special, 24th May, Netflix.

Stanton, A. (1989a), *Invitation to Self-Management*, Ruislip, Dab Hand Management.

Stanton, A. (1989b), Citizens of workplace democracies, *Critical Social Policy*, No 9, September, pp 56–65.

Sweeney, A., Beresford, P., Faulkner, A., Nettle, M. and Rose, D. (editors), (2009), *This Is Survivor Research*, Ross-on-Wye, PCSS Books.

The Secret Welfare Rights Worker (2021), Realities of welfare reform under COVID-19 lockdown: what disabled and older people actually experience, in Beresford, P., Farr, M., Hickey, G., Kaur, M., Ocloo, J., Tembo, D. and Williams, O. (editors), (2021), *COVID-19 and Co-production in Health and Social Care Research, Policy, and Practice, Volume 1: The Challenges and Necessity of Co-production*, Open Access e Book, Bristol, Policy Press, pp 109–16.

Staples, S. (2000), Neoliberalism, militarism, and armed conflict, *Social Justice*, Winter, Vol 27, No 4 (82), pp 18–22.

Stewart, H. and Allegretti, A. (2022), Liz Truss under pressure as rivals steal march in Tory leadership race, *The Guardian*, 13th July, https://www.theguardian.com/politics/2022/jul/13/liz-truss-under-pressure-as-rivals-steal-march-in-tory-leadership-race accessed 1st August 2022.

Stiglitz, J. (2019), Three decades of neoliberal policies have decimated the middle class, our economy and our democracy, Opinion, *MarketWatch*, 13th May, https://www.marketwatch.com/story/three-decades-of-neoliberal-policies-have-decimated-the-middle-class-our-economy-and-our-democracy-2019-05-13 accessed 3rd November 2021.

Stiglitz, J. (2024), How Neoliberalism Failed, and what a better society could look like, Roosevelt Institute, 7th August, https://rooseveltinstitute.org/publications/how-neoliberalism-failed/ accessed 24th January 2025.

Stone, R. (2018), *Stone's Rules: How to win at politics, business and style*, New York, Skyhorse Publishing.

Stonewall (2019), *Improve Health and Social Care Services for LGBT People*, London, Stonewall, https://www.stonewall.org.uk/improve-health-and-social-care-services-lgbt-people?gclid=CjwKCAjw5remBhBiEiwAxL2M916v4xbikGU_uPJ7-WappTr4btRm-fzewoaAGvkNbIY_tHN-RmS8EBoC7UEQAvD_BwE accessed 5th August 2023.

Sorkin, A.R. (2010), *To Big to Fail: Inside the battle to save Wall Street*, New York, Penguin.

Tawney, R.H. (1913), *Inaugural Lecture on Poverty as an Industrial Problem Reproduced in Memorandum on the Problems of Poverty*, London, William Morris Press.

Taylor, C. (1992), The politics of recognition, in Gutmann, A. (editor), *Multiculturalism and the Politics of Recognition*, Princeton, Princeton University Press, pp 27–73.

Thomas, L. (2018), Gaslight and gaslighting, *The Lancet Psychiatry*, Vol 5, Issue 2, pp 117–18, https://www.thelancet.com/journals/lanpsy/article/PIIS2215-0366(18)30024-5/fulltext#%20 accessed 2nd August 2022.

Titcombe, R. (2015), The bucket theory of learning and behaviourism, *Roger Titcombe's Learning Matters: The truth about our schools*, 21st March, https://rogertitcombelearningmatters.wordpress.com/2015/03/21/the-bucket-theory-of-learning-and-behaviourism/ accessed 2nd November 2022.

Todd, M.J. and Taylor, G. (editors), (2004), *Democracy and Participation: Popular protest and new social movements*, London, Merlin Press.

Tooze, A. (2021), Has Covid ended the neoliberal era? The Long Read, *The Guardian*, 2nd September, https://www.theguardian.com/news/2021/sep/02/covid-and-the-crisis-of-neoliberalism accessed 12th January 2023.

Topping, A. and Dodds, V. (2023), Met police pay damages to women arrested at Sarah Everard's vigil, *The Guardian*, 14th September, https://www.theguardian.com/uk-news/2023/sep/14/met-police-pays-damages-to-women-arrested-at-sarah-everard-vigil accessed 16th September 2023.

Touraine, A. (1981), *The Voice and the Eye: An analysis of social movements*, Cambridge, Cambridge University Press.

Townsend, M. (2021), Crisis after Crisis: what is going wrong at the Met police?, *The Observer*, 18th July 2021, https://www.theguardian.com/uk-news/2021/jul/18/crisis-after-crisis-what-is-going-wrong-at-the-met-police accessed 6th October 2021.

Townsend, P. (1979), *Poverty*, London, Penguin.

Toynbee, P. (2021), Whatever Johnson's 'levelling up' means it isn't about Britain's shocking poverty levels, Opinion, Poverty, *The Guardian*, 28th May, https://www.theguardian.com/commentisfree/2021/may/28/johnson-levelling-up-poverty-levels accessed 4th November 2021.

Tracini, J. (2022), *Ten Things I Hate about Me: How to stay alive with a brain that is trying to kill you*, London, Trapeze.

Tuckwell, P. and Beresford, P. (1978), *Schools for All: Inclusive education for children with learning difficulties*, London, Mind and Values Into Action.

Turner, B.S. (2013), *The Religious and the Political: A comparative sociology of religion*, Cambridge, Cambridge University Press.

Tyler, I. (2014), *Revolting Subjects: Social abjection and resistance in neoliberal Britain*, London, Zed Books.

Uberoi, E. and Johnston, N. (2021), Political Disengagement in the UK: Who is disengaged, Briefing Paper, No CBP-7501, 25th February 2021, London, House of Commons Library, https://commonslibrary.parliament.uk/research-briefings/cbp-7501/ accessed 8th March 2022.

UNDESA (2020), *World Social Report 2020, Inequality in a Rapidly Changing World*, New York, United Nations Department of Economic and Social Affairs.

United Nations (2007), *Report of the United Nations High Commissioner for Human Rights, Economic and Social Council, Social and Human Rights Questions: Human rights*, Geneva, United Nations Social Council, 25th June, E/2007/82, https://www.ohchr.org/sites/default/files/Documents/Issues/ESCR/E_2007_82_en.pdf accessed 1st October 2024.

Unwin, P., Meakin, B. and Jones, A. (2020), *Including the Missing Voices of Disabled People in Gypsy, Roma and Traveller Communities: Final report*, November, Worcester, University of Worcester, https://shapingourlives.org.uk/wp-content/uploads/2021/08/Missing-Voices-Report.pdf accessed 25th October 2022.

UPIAS (Union of the Physically Impaired against Segregation)/Disability Alliance (1976), *Fundamental Principles of Disability: Being a summary of the discussion held on 22nd November, 1975 and containing commentaries from each organization*, London, The Union of the Physically Impaired Against Segregation and the Disability Alliance.

Vad Yashem (1981), Evacuation of the Jews: from a speech before senior SS officers in Poznan, 4th October 1943, *Shoah Resource Centre*, https://www.yadvashem.org/odot_pdf/Microsoft%20Word%20-%204029.pdf accessed 29th January 2023.

Varoufakis, Y. (2017), *And the Weak Suffer What They Must?: Europe, austerity and the threat to global stability*, London, Vintage.

Vera-Grey, F. (2021), If we're serious about ending violence against women, we need to talk about culture, *The Guardian*, 4th October, https://www.chron.com/news/article/The-most-searched-porn-term-in-America-will-not-6865633.php accessed 9th January 2023.

References

Virnoche, M. and Marx, G.T. (2024), 'Only Connect' – E. M. Forster in an Age of Electronic Communication: computer-mediated association and community networks, *Sociological Inquiry*, 22nd October, Vol 67, No 1, pp 645–50.

Vitrale, A.S. (2017), *The End of Policing*, London, Verso.

Vohland, K, Weißpflug, M. and Pettibone, L. (2019), Citizen science and the neoliberal transformation of science – an ambivalent relationship, *Citizen Science: Theory and Practice*, Vol 4, No 1, p 25.

Walker, P. (2024), Voter ID rule may have stopped 400,000 taking part in UK election, poll suggests, *The Guardian*, 8th July, https://www.theguardian.com/politics/article/2024/jul/08/voter-id-rule-may-have-stopped-400000-taking-part-in-uk-election-poll-suggests accessed 11th July 2024.

Ward, C. (2004), *Anarchism: A very short introduction*, Oxford, Oxford University Press.

Ward, S.C. (2014), *Neoliberalism and the Global Restructuring of Knowledge and Education*, London, Routledge.

Warner, M. (2011), *Fear of a Queer Planet: Queer politics and social theory*, Minnesota, University of Minnesota Press.

Warren, K.J. and Cheney, J. (1991), Ecological feminism and ecosystem ecology, *Hypatia*, Vol 6, No 1, pp 179–97.

Waterson, J. (2021), Society of Editors withdraws claim UK media is not racist, *The Guardian*, 18th August, https://www.theguardian.com/media/2021/aug/18/society-of-editors-withdraws-claim-that-uk-media-is-not-racist accessed 11th April 2022.

Watts, J. (2016), Margaret Thatcher's role in securing controversial £42bn arms deal with Saudi Arabia revealed, *The Independent*, 23rd August, https://www.independent.co.uk/news/uk/politics/margaret-thatcher-arms-deal-saudi-arabia-uk-fighter-jets-sale-files-a7205521.html accessed 18th October 2021.

Weale, S. (2020), System for children with special needs in England 'riddled with inequalities', *The Guardian*, 6th May, https://www.theguardian.com/education/2020/may/06/education-system-for-children-with-special-needs-in-england-riddled-with-inequalities accessed 25th November 2022.

Weinberg, J. (2020), *Who Enters Politics and Why?: Basic human values in the UK Parliament*, Bristol, Bristol University Press.

Welbourne, T. (2022), Emotional advertising: how and why brands use it to drive sales, *The Drum*, 14th February, https://www.thedrum.com/opinion/2022/02/14/emotional-advertising-how-and-why-brands-use-it-drive-sales accessed 4th January 2023.

Welshman, J. (2012), Troubled families: the lessons of history, 1880 1912, paper based on a presentation at a History and Policy seminar for the Department for Education on 24th November 2011, *History and Policy*, www.historyandpolicy.org/papers/policy-paper-136.html

Welshman, J. (2013), *Underclass: A history of the excluded since 1880*, 2nd Edition, London, Bloomsbury.

Whitfield, D. (2001), *Public Services Or Corporate Welfare: Rethinking the nation state in the global economy*, London, Pluto.

Wike, R. and Castillo, A. (2018), *Many around the World Are Disengaged from Politics*, 17th October, Washington DC, US, Pew Research Center, https://www.pewresearch.org/global/2018/10/17/international-political-engagement/ accessed 14th March 2022.

Wikipedia (2022), Philosophy of education, *Wikipedia*, https://en.wikipedia.org/wiki/Philosophy_of_education accessed 21st November 2022.

Wikipedia (2022), Big tech, *Wikipedia*, https://en.wikipedia.org/wiki/Big_Tech accessed 8th July 2022.

Wikipedia (2023a), Sentimentality, *Wikipedia*, https://en.wikipedia.org/wiki/Sentimentality accessed 5th January 2023.

Wikipedia (2023b), Illegal drug trade, *Wikipedia*, https://en.wikipedia.org/wiki/Illegal_drug_trade accessed 9th February 2023.

Wikipedia (2024), 'List of incidents of violence against women', *Wikipedia*, https://en.wikipedia.org/wiki/List_of_incidents_of_violence_against_women accessed 17th December 2024.

Wikipedia (2025a), *Occupy Movement*, https://en.wikipedia.org/wiki/Occupy_movement accessed 10th January 2025.

Wikipedia (2025b), *Demographic History*, https://en.wikipedia.org/wiki/Demographic_history accessed 11th January 2025.

Wilde, O. (1905), *De Profundis*, original manuscript, London, British Library Collection, https://www.bl.uk/collection-items/manuscript-of-de-profundis-by-oscar-wilde accessed 5th January 2023.

Wilkinson, R. and Pickett, K. (2010), *The Spirit Level: Why equality is better for everyone*, London, Penguin.

Williams, F. (2021), *Social Policy: A critical and intersectional analysis*, Cambridge, Polity Press.

Williams, O., Tembo, D., Ocloo, J., Kaur, G., Hickey, M., Farr, M. and Beresford, P. (editors), (2021), *COVID-19 and Co-production in Health and Social Care Research, Policy, and Practice, Volume 2: Co-production: Methods and working together at a distance*, Open access ebook, Bristol, Policy Press.

Winlow, S, and Hall, S. (2022), *The Death of the Left: Why we must begin from the beginning again*, Bristol, Policy Press.

Wolfe, N.D. (2011), *The Viral Storm: The dawn of a new pandemic age*, London, Penguin.

Wolfson, S. (2018), Amazon's Alexa recorded private conversation and sent it to random contact, *The Guardian*, 24th May, https://www.theguardian.com/technology/2018/may/24/amazon-alexa-recorded-conversation accessed 7th July 2022.

Wood, J. (2024), *The Kindness Fix: How and why we must build a more compassionate society*, Bristol, Policy Press.

World Bank (2020), *Reversals of Fortune: Poverty and shared prosperity 2020*, Washington DC, The World Bank, https://www.worldbank.org/en/publication/poverty-and-shared-prosperity accessed 25th October 2021.

World Bank (2021), Bringing mobile phones and internet to rural Niger, Feature, *World Bank*, 8th January, https://www.worldbank.org/en/news/feature/2021/01/08/bringing-mobile-phones-and-internet-to-rural-niger accessed 7th July 2022.

Wykes, T., Csipke, E., Williams, P., Koeser, L., Nash, S., Rose, D., Craig, T. and McCrone, P. (2018), Improving patient experience of mental health inpatient care: a randomised controlled trial, *Psychological Medicine*, Vol 48, No 3, pp 488–97.

Wylie, C. (2019), Mindfuck: Inside Cambridge Analytica's Plot To Break the World, London, Profile Books.

Yaojun, L. and Devine, F. (2011), Is social mobility really declining? Intergenerational class mobility in Britain in the 1990s and the 2000s, *Sociological Research Online*, August, Vol 16, No 3, https://journals.sagepub.com/doi/abs/10.5153/sro.2424 accessed 27th October 2022.

Yeates, N. and Holden, C. (editors), (2009), *The Global Social Policy Reader*, Bristol, Policy Press.

Yudkin, J. (2012), *Pure, White and Deadly: How sugar is killing us and what we can do to stop it*, London, Penguin Books.

Zaman, T. (2014), Political Islam in neoliberal times, *OpenDemocracy*, 17th November, https://www.opendemocracy.net/en/north-africa-west-asia/political-islam-in-neoliberal-times/ accessed 10th February 2023.

Zerilli, J. (2021), *A Citizen's Guide to Artificial Intelligence*, Cambridge, MA, MIT Press.

Zuboff, S. (2022), Surveillance capitalism or democracy? The death match of institutional orders and the politics of knowledge in our information civilization. *Organization Theory*, Vol 3, Issue 3, https://doi.org/10.1177/26317877221129290 accessed 22nd July 2024.

Index

References to photographs appear in *italic* type.

A

Adams, Robert 213
advertising 88
Age of Enlightenment 175, 176
ageism 112
Ahmed, Sara 80
Ailes, Roger 105
air travel, subsidised 32, 40
alienation 48, 51, 63, 118, 185, 198
 Marx on 56–7
 from ourselves 70–5
 and private/public schools 194
 see also disconnection; divisiveness
alliance building 152, 230–5, 236–7, 244
Althusser, Louis 43
Alt-tech 147
Amazon 141
American Dream 72
Andrew, Prince 63
animals, treatment of 38–9
anti-vax movement 55
Appadurai, Arjun 83
arms trade 35–6
Army Education Corps 58
artificial intelligence (AI) 33–4
aspirational branding 71
aspirational politics 60, 62, 70–1, 74
 gap between people's reality and hopes 71–2, 73–4
 self-aspiration 71
 snobbery 74–5
asylum seekers 81, 228
asymmetrical warfare 37
Attlee, Clement 58

B

Baldwin, James 76, 77, 201–4
banking model of learning 197
Banksy (street artist) 84
barriers model of disability *see* social model of disability
BBC 222
benefit fraud 73
Bennett, Alan 194
Beresford, Peter 183–4, 184–5, 189, 212, 223
Berlant, Lauren 93
Bernard, Rose 39

Big Tech 140–3, 145–6
 dependence on 146
 regulation of 148
 social networks, alternatives to 147
Biko, Steve 201
biological warfare 39
Black consciousness 198
Blair, Tony 98–9, 102, 195
Braille 166
Bregman, Rutger 239
Brexit 45, 51, 55, 64, 66, 72, 80, 81, 116, 152
British Sign Language (BSL) 166
Brown, Tom 194
bucket theory 197
Buckley, Helen 167–8, 169–70
Buechler, S.M. 109
Bunning, Karen 156
Bush, George 35
Butler, Hubert 60–1, 65

C

Cambridge Analytica 45–6, 80
Cameron, David 71, 129
Campbell, Jane 165
capital account liberalisation 21
Casey Review 16, 29
Center for Humane Technology (United States) 147
Chaney, Sarah 175, 176
charities 217
Charity Commission 217
child-led education 197
China 16, 39, 81, 240
Churchill, Winston 71
civil rights movement 109, 213, 214, 233, 243
Clausen, John 195
climate change 2, 32, 230
 COP26 (Conference of the Parties) 40–1
 Paris Agreement 40
Clinton, Bill 46
Clinton, Hilary 46, 102
collective emotions 81
collective experiential knowledge 188–9
collective working 206–7, 208–9
 activism related to COVID-19 pandemic 210–11
 and community action 211–12
 coproduction 219–20

and differences in power and
  experience 211–13
 empowerment 213–15
 meanings of work 207–8
 new social movements 208
 reluctance in involvement 209
 self-run organisations 215–19
colonialism 17, 35, 176, 177, 198, 226
commodification
 of emotions 88
 exchange relationships 86–8
 of healthcare 87
 of housing 23, 24, *86*
 of needs 83–5, 89
 of public services 25
communication 139
 across groups 152
 attunement 157
 challenging discrimination 152–3
 complexity of 156–7
 connection between different movements 153
 and COVID-19 pandemic 157–8, 162–4
 developments 131
 digital divide 161
 electoral 159
 equalizing relationships 151
 first-person contact 149–50, 151
 Gypsy, Roma and Traveller communities 161–2, 166, 171
 and ideology 158–9
 inclusive 148–9, 155–72
 and inequalities 157–8, 159, 160, 161
 intention 157, 170
 and language 156
 ownership of 140–1
 and people with disabilities 164–6
 personal, interference in 140
 personal changes related to 149
 political 156, 158, 159–60, 165
 reconnecting with each other 149–50
 regulation 148–9
 Shaping Our Lives 167–72
 strategy, new 148
 and technology 139–40, 146–7, 160–1
 see also Big Tech; connection/reconnection; social media
community 226
 and collective working 211–12
 community care 64
 and divisiveness 63–4
compassion in public life 120
connection/reconnection 3, 31, 76, 78, 125–6, 149–50, 157, 202, 206, 241, 246–7
 between different movements 153
 Eliot on 126, 127–8, 130
 equalizing relationships 151
 and e-technology 146–7

Forster on 126–7, 128, 130
Hoggart on 128–30, 131
 inclusive approach to 130, 152, 153
 between personal and political 111–12, 197, 213, 215, 241
 and social media 143–5
 white privilege and decolonisation 132–5
 see also communication; intimacy
Connelly, Cyril 194
conscientisation 200–1, 214
consumer activism 225
COP26 (Conference of the Parties) 40–1
coproduction 85–186, 179, 219–20
Corbyn, Jeremy 69, 102–3, 104
corporate welfare 28
council homes 58, 73, 83
counter-terrorism 38
Couzens, Wayne 12, 15
Covid Meet-Ups (World Health Network) 210–11
COVID-19 pandemic 38–9, 43, 53, 55, 104, 217–18, 222
 activism related to 210–11
 and communication 157–8, 162–4
 and knowledge 180–1
 partygate scandal 69, 116
 and politics of disconnection 68–9
 and poverty 23
Crick, Bernard 106
critical consciousness *see* conscientisation
Croft, Suzy 218–19
cultural hegemony 42–3
culture wars 81
Curtice, John 97

D

Daedone, Nicole 94
decolonisation 35, 117, 132, 134–5, 176, 198, 225, 244
democracy 2, 44
 and collective working 207
 and communication 160
 and connection 51
 and grassroots action 245
 lived experience of 106
 and new social movements 122
 and populism 50
 and social media 143–5, 147
 see also participation
democratisation 198
 of Big Tech reforms 148
 of knowledge 189–90
Department for Work and Pensions (DWP), United Kingdom 63, 233
deplatforming *see* no-platforming
deregulation 17, 25, 26, 28, 141, 239
Dick, Cressida 13
Dickens, Charles 1
digital divide 161

285

disabilities, people with 25, 63, 90, 230
  and alienation 72
  collective working of 216–17
  and communication 164–6
  and COVID-19 pandemic 210–11
  definition of disability 164–5
  emancipatory disability research 178
  and epistemic injustice 187
  Pat's Petition 145
  Shaping Our Lives 167–72, 216–17, 219, 227–8, 229
disabled people's movement 165, 187, 189, 214, 227, 231, 245
disconnection 50–1, 93–4, 125–6
  beyond formal politics 56–7
  divisiveness 59–66, 67
  from the origins of everything 66–9
  from ourselves 70–5
  political disengagement 51–6, 67
  and political socialisation 57
  and private/public schools 194
  professionalisation of politics 52
  and social media 144
discrimination 80, 109, 193, 227
  challenging 132–5, 152–3
  and communication 160
  and community action 212
  double 184
  and experiential knowledge 183–4
  knowledge 181, 186–7
  and Metropolitan Police (United Kingdom) 14, 29
  of older people 112, 165
disinformation campaigns 39
distributed social networks 147
distrust in politics 52, 55
diversity 245
  and new social movements 112, 122
  and solidarity 227–8
  see also inclusion
divisiveness 59, 73, 126, 230
  and community 63–4
  culture of fear and suspicion 60–1
  between disempowered groups 228–9
  eugenics 65
  and exclusion 63, 64, 65
  and hate 60, 61–2
  hostility between 'us' and 'them' 62–3
  and individualisation of responsibility 67
  narrative 65–6
  and negative mindset about ourselves 60
  othering 60, 64
  and social media 143
  and tourism 59
  underclass 64–5
Doll, Richard 32
double discrimination 184
Durkheim, Emile 79

E

ecological feminism 123
Eddo-Lodge, Reni 152
education 192, 204
  and Baldwin 201–4
  bucket theory 197
  and change 192–3
  child-led 197
  decolonisation of 117
  and Fanon 198, *199*, 201
  and Freire 198, 199–201
  inclusive 196
  liberatory approaches to learning 197–201
  meritocratic 195
  progressive 197
  reform, and neoliberalism 193–5
  and socialisation 195–6
  theories and philosophies of 196–7
electoral manipulation 45–6, 50, 88, 132
Eliot, T.S. 126, 127–8, 130, 159
emancipatory disability research 178
emotional advertising 88
emotions
  collective 81
  commodification of 88
  effects of neoliberalism on 80
  and exchange relationships 88
  happiness 88, 89
  individual expressions of 81
  manipulation of 79–80, 88
  needs, commodification of 84
  neoliberal response to emotional world 82–8
  and politics 82
  sentimentality 88–9
  see also intimacy
empowerment 243, 245
  and collective working 213–15
  and connection between personal and political 213–14, 215
  and conscientisation 200, 201, 214
  definition of 213
  self-empowerment 199, 215
Engels, Friedrich 42
environmental movement 123–4
epistemic injustice 186–7
Epstein, Jeffrey 63, 105
Equalities Act 2010 (United Kingdom) 164
equality 17, 19, 108, 112, 131, 155, 202, 206, 215, 243–4, 246
eugenics 65, 133, 225
European Union 2, 17
Everard, Sarah 4, 11–13, 14, 15, 29
exchange relationships 86–8
exclusion 57, 121, 225, 226, 229
  and community 63, 64
  and community action 212

and digital divide 161
and eugenics 65
racist 132–5
school 196
experiential knowledge 110, 174, 178, 181–3, 190, 231
collective 188–9
and empowerment 215
and epistemic injustice 186–7
individual 188
revaluing 183–4, 187–8
Extinction Rebellion 118

F

Facebook 144
Facebook/Cambridge Analytica scandal 45–6, 143
false consciousness 42
Fanon, Frantz 133, 198, *199*, 201
Farnsworth, Kevin 28
fear 60–1, 82, 162, 229
Featherstone, Liza 55–6
Federal Trade Commission (United States) 141
femicide 4, 11–13, 14, 29
feminism 111, 113–14, 118–20, 123, 178
first-person contact (communication) 149–50, 151
Fisher, Mark 97
Floyd, George 12
focus groups 55–6
Forster, E.M. 94, 126–7, 128, 130, 159
Frank, Thomas 48
Fraser, Nancy 110
freedom 19, 105, 241
Freire, Paolo 198, 199–201, 214
French presidential elections (2022) 98
Fricker, Miranda 186–7
Fukuyama, Francis 16, 100
Furedi, Frank 225

G

Galbraith, J.K. 25, 27
Galloway, Scott 141
Garvey, Marcus 233, 234
gaslighting 173–4
gated communities *22*, 25
general election (2019), United Kingdom 132
Gervais, Ricky 20, 158
Get Me Roger Stone (documentary) 46
global financial crisis (2008) 28–9, 40, 239
Global South 26, 38, 40, 41, 59, 114, 225, 234
globalisation 17, 26, 30, 59
and Big Tech 143
and conflict 35
and culture of fear and suspicion 60–1
and militarism 36

Gramsci, Antonio 42
grassroots action 245
Green, Philip 63
Grenfell Tower fire (2017) *85*
guide dogs for the blind 166
Gypsy, Roma and Traveller (GRT) communities 161–2, 166, 171

H

Hall, Stuart 128
Hampton, Fred 233, 234–5, *234*
Hanisch, C. 111
Hansberry, Lorraine 203
happiness 88, 89
Harari, Yuval Noah 33
Hare, Nathan 177
hate
and divisiveness 60, 61–2
hate speech 153–4
Hayek, Friedrich 79
healthcare
commodification of 87
reforms of Obama 47–8
and travelling communities 161–2
user-led organisations 218
Heath-Kelly, Charlotte 37
Hegel, Georg Wilhelm Friedrich 56
Henry, Bibaa 14
hermeneutical injustice 187
Hertz, Noreena 94, 131
Hesse, Hermann 60
Heywood, Andrew 224
hierarchisation of difference 153, 226–7
high streets *142*, 145
Higher Education (Freedom of Speech) Act 2023 (United Kingdom) 153–4
Himmler, Heinrich 229
Hitler, Adolf 61
Hobbes, Thomas 44
Hoggart, Richard 128–30, 131–2, 159
home ownership for council tenants 73
homelessness *86*
Hopkins, Katie 154
horse-and-sparrow theory 27, 195
housing
associations 215
commodification of *23*, *24*, *86*
council homes 58, 73, 83
Rowton houses 25
Howard's End (Forster) 126–7
hyper-capitalism 17

I

I Am Not Your Negro (film) 202–3
identity 231, 235–6
and aspirational politics 70–1
and new social movements 109, 110, 111
politics 226, 231–2

white privilege and decolonisation 132–5
see also intersectionality
ideological apparatuses of the state (ISA) 43
ideology 175
 and communication 158–9
 definition of 43
 and focus groups 56
 fragmentation of ideological developments 224–5
 and public participation 44
 see also neoliberalism
illegal drug trade 89
inclusion 130, 190, 202, 206, 241, 243–4, 245, 247
 and collective action 207
 and community 64
 and connection 130, 152, 153
 inclusive communication 148–9, 155–72
 inclusive education 196
 and knowledge production 190
 and solidarity 226, 227–8
Inclusive Involvement Movement (IIM) 219
income inequality, and neoliberalism 20, 21
independent living, philosophy of 214
individualisation of responsibility 67–8
Industry 4.0 33
inequality 14, 40, 72, 75, 206, 212, 244
 and communication 157–8, 159, 160, 161
 and coproduction 186
 and digital divide 161
 and education 196–7
 and exchange relationships 87
 and femicide 11, 12
 levelling up policy 27
 and neoliberalism 19–21, 26, 27–8, 40, 130
 and new social movements 110, 114
 reduction of 24
 and scientific knowledge 177
Intergovernmental Panel on Climate Change (IPCC) 32
International Monetary Fund (IMF) 17, 21, 26, 101, 238
International Telecommunication Union (ITU) 161
international tourism 59
interpretivism 179–80
intersectionality 208, 236, 243
 and communication 153, 165, 166
 and new social movements 109, 111–12
 and solidarity 226, 229, 230, 231
intimacy 76–8, 93–4
 effects of neoliberalism on emotions 79
 emotional manipulation 79–80
 neoliberal response to emotional world 82–8

OneTaste 92, 93, 94
pornography 91–2, 93
 as a private/public nexus 93
 social care 90–1, 93
 and totalitarian politics 82
Involvement Mentors (Shaping Our Lives) 219
Ishak, Awaab 215
isolation 82, 229
 and COVID-19 pandemic 162, 164
 and digital divide 161
 and neoliberalism 64, 66, 94, 97, 131
 of older people 165
 and social media 146
 see also disconnection

J

Jacobs, Alan 126
Johnson, Boris 19, 27, 50, 65, 100, 150, 174

K

Kant, Immanuel 66
Kendall, D. 111
Kennington, Eric 131
King, Colin 132–5
Kirk, Gwynn 36
knowledge
 approaches to involvement 185
 challenge to traditional research 177–8
 coproduction 179, 185–6
 decolonisation of 176
 democratisation of 189–90
 devaluing of lived experience 181–3
 discrimination 181, 186–7
 distance between experience and interpretation 184–5
 double discrimination 184
 experiential 110, 174, 178, 181–5, 186–9, 190, 215, 231
 and gaslighting 173–4
 manipulation 173
 and neoliberalism 174–5
 production of 176–7, 179, 185
 scientific 175, 176–7, 182–3
 sharing and dissemination of 190–1
 see also research

L

language 156, 166
Lanier, Jaron 143, 147
Lansley, Stewart 21, 22
Lasswell, Harold 106
Lawrence, Stephen 13
Lawrence, T.E. 131
Le Pen, Marine 98
learning difficulties, people with 182, 196
levelling up policy 27
liberalism 18–19, 79
 see also neoliberalism

Index

Lincoln, Abraham 49
lived experience 80, 134, 151, 164, 174, 181–3, 187, 188, 189, 190, 198, 231, 244
 see also experiential knowledge
local elections (2023), United Kingdom 97–8
Lorde, Audre 118–20, *119*, 122, 146, 208
Losasso, Mae 127–8
Loughran, Tracey 128
Lukes, Steven 159

M

Machiavelli, Niccolo 44–5, 47
Macron, Emmanuel 98
Mad Studies 110, 188, 201, 227
Magnabosco, Anthony 150
Makaton 166
Mandela, Nelson 201
Marable, Manning 233
market fundamentalism 50
Marx, Gary 127
Marx, Karl 56, 83, 101
mass media 33, 60–1, 62, 80, 150, 174
Maxwell, Ghislaine 63
Meakin, Becki 168, 170–1
mental health
 of children, impact of social media on 145–6
 community care 64
 service users, knowledge of 181–2
meritocratic education 195
Merrill Lynch 28
Metropolitan Police (United Kingdom) 13–16, 29
Middle East, conflict in 35, 36
militarism 36–7
military-industrial complex 35–6
Millett, Kate 118, 123
Monbiot, George 27
Montessori approach 197
morality 105–6
 personal 45
 political 45, 97
 and underclass 64
Morgan, Daniel 13
Morgan, David 75
Motability scheme 233
Murdoch, Rupert 222
Murray, Charles 21, 22, 64
My Involvement Profile (Shaping Our Lives) 219

N

national curriculum 194, 197
National Health Service (NHS) 58, 68, 87, 90, 99, 103, 157, 222, 229
Nazis 82, 229
Neill, A.S. 197

Neocleous, Mark 15
neoliberalism 1, 2–3, 16–18, 42, 44, 49, 97, 105, 222, 223
 acceptance of 98–100
 and alienation 57
 as an anti-personal ideology 25–6
 and Big Tech companies 141
 commodification *23*, *24*, 25, 83–8, *86*, 89
 and conflict of values 106, 107, 117
 consumer involvement 122–3
 and disconnection from ourselves 70–5
 and disconnection from the origins of everything 66–9
 and divisiveness 59–66, 67, 73, 126
 and educational reform 193–5
 effects on emotions 79
 effects on research 177
 efficiency of economic system 83
 electoral manipulation 45–6, 50, 88, 132
 emotional manipulation of 79–80
 end of 238–41
 exchange relationships 86–8
 failure of 26–7, 101, 238–9
 financialisation 40
 focus groups 55–6
 gap between ideology and practice 18
 and globalisation 17
 and inequality 19–21, 26, 27–8, 40, 130
 and intimacy 78–94
 and knowledge 174–5, 185, 190
 levelling up policy 27
 overclass 22, 105, 236
 and political disconnect 44–5
 and political disengagement 54, 55–6, 67
 populist 46–8, 49, 50–1, 230
 and poverty 19–21, 22–3, 24, 26
 production methods 40
 and proposals for change 239–40
 redistributive reality of 27–9
 reliance on grand theory/ideology for opposing 100–2
 response to emotional world 82–8
 role in creating hostility between disempowered groups 228
 and snobbery 74–5
 and social/personal roles and relationships 107–8
 and state 17, 19, 79, 101, 175
 trickle-down effect 27
 underclass 21, 64–5
 welfare state-based responses to 102–4
 and work 207
 see also Big Tech; new social movements (NSMs)
neoliberalism, consequences of 30–1
 artificial intelligence 33–4
 causation 31–2
 climate change 32

interconnection between issues 39–40
pandemics 38–9, 40
scale of human impact 31
technological change 32–4
war, conflict and terrorism 35–8
new social movements (NSMs) 3, 5, 64, 76, 78, 81, 94, 104, 116–17, 149, 157, 160, 190, 191, 223, 241
  alliance building between 230–1, 232, 244
  and Big Tech 145
  changes inspired by 117–18
  characteristics of 110
  and connection 129, 130
  connection between different movements 153
  connection between personal and political 111–12, 215, 241
  criticism on 111
  different forms of organisation/structure of 217–18
  and diversity 112, 122
  and empowerment 213, 214
  and experiential knowledge 183, 188, 189
  focus and goals of 109
  and gap between personal and formal politics 116, 117, 124
  impact of 113–15
  learning from personal roles/relationships 118–20
  and neoliberalism 109, 118, 122–3
  participation 121–3
  pattern of action 208
  recognition of consumerist value of groups 232
  and research 177–9, 180
  significance of 108–11
  social understandings of subjects 244–5
  and solidarity 112, 153, 224–5
  sustainability 123–4
1984 (Orwell) 82, 142
non-binary people 118
no-platforming 94, 153–4

O

Oakley, Ann 178
Obama, Barack 35, 46, 47
Occupy movement (2011) 20
Ofsted 197
Okazawa-Rey, Margo 36
older people 90
  disabled 165
  discrimination of 112
  view on community 63
  voting behaviour of 54
Oliver, Mike 178
OneTaste 92, 93, 94
Orgasm Inc. (documentary) 92

Orlowski, Jeff 143, 147
Orwell, George 82, 99–100, 142, 160, 194
othering 60, 64
overclass 22, 105, 236

P

pandemic *see* COVID-19 pandemic
Paris Agreement 40
parliamentary expenses scandal (2009), United Kingdom 54
participation 243
  of Big Tech users 148
  and ideology 44
  and new social movements 121–3
  political 51–6, 160
  and research 185
  see also political disengagement
partygate scandal 69, 116
Pat's Petition 145
Peck, Raoul 202
personal morality 45
Pine, Lisa 82
Piven, Frances Fox 17
police 13–15
  concerns about 14
  history of 15
  and murder of Bibaa Henry and Nicole Smallman 14
  and murder of Sarah Everard 13, 29
  relationship with government/state 15
political allegiance, changing 58
political communication 156, 158, 159–60, 165
political disengagement 51–6, 67
political morality 45, 97
political socialisation 57
politics, definitions of 106–7
politics of envy 62–3, 72
Pollock, Allyson 90
populism 2, 46–8, 49, 50–1, 55, 57, 60, 61–2, 81, 97, 103, 107, 230
pornography 91–2, 93
positivism 177, 179, 181, 182, 183, 184
post-war reconstruction 35
poverty 40, 72
  and education 192–3
  global, estimates of 23
  and neoliberalism 19–21, 22–3, 24, 26
  reduction of 23, 24, 140
  see also inequality
power 80, 105, 128, 226
  of Big Tech companies 141
  and collective working 212
  and communication 159
  and cultural hegemony 42
  and divisiveness 62
  and experiential knowledge 183
  and femicide 11, 12
  and ideology 43, 44, 45, 159

and intersectionality 112
and new social movements 122
and politics 123
and research 185
Prime Minister's Questions (PMQ), United Kingdom 50
private education 194
privatisation 17, 25, 28, *85*, 218, 222
professionalisation of politics 52
progressive education 197
progressive realisation 242
protected characteristics 52, 129, 197, 226
public, patient involvement (PPI) 185
public involvement in politics 51–4
public school system 193, 194–5

Q

queer studies 177
queer theory 177
Quijano, Anibal 176

R

racism 14, 132–5, 152
Rainbow Coalition 235
randomised controlled trials (RCTs) 179, 180
Rashford, Marcus 205–6
Reagan, Ronald 27, 46, 159–60
refugees 81, 104, 156, 228, 229, 230
Reich, Richard 41
Reicher, Stephen 71
Reith Lectures (Hoggart) 129
remote work 162, 217–18
repressive state apparatuses (RSA) 43
research
  approaches to involvement in 185
  coproduction 179, 185–6
  emancipatory disability research 178
  and experiential knowledge 183–5
  feminist 178
  interpretivism 179–80
  neutrality in 184
  positivism 177, 179, 181, 182, 183, 184
  relationship between researcher and researched 178–9
  traditional, challenge to 177–8
  see also knowledge
right-wing populism 50, 60, 61–2, 107
Roma *see* Gypsy, Roma and Traveller (GRT) communities
Rosa, Sophie 94
Rowton houses 25
Rubio, Mario 144
Runciman, David 47–8
Russia 81, 144, 240
  conflict with Ukraine 35, 36, 105, 116, 230
  neoliberal economics in 16
  Russian Revolution (1917) 207

S

sadvertising 88
Sanders, Bernie 102–3
Saville, Jimmy 222
scientific knowledge 175, 176–7, 182–3
Scotland Yard 29
second-wave women's movement 111
self-advocacy 245
self-aspiration 71
self-empowerment 199, 215
self-run organisations 215–19
sentimentality 88–9
service user organisations 78, 227, 245–6
Service User Research Enterprise (SURE) 180
Shaping Our Lives 167–72, 216–17, 219, 227–8, 229
short-termism 34, 117
signing/sign language 166
small state 17, 18, 24–5, 43, 67, *85*, 99, 104, 180
Smallman, Nicole 14
Smith, John 99
Smyrnaios, Nicos 141
snobbery 74–5
social care 19, 28, 90–1, 93, 219
social justice 206, 214
social media 46, 64, 140–1
  and behaviour modification 143
  and connection 143–5
  dependence on 146
  and divisiveness 143
  impact on children 145–6
  no-platforming 153–4
  paradox of 141–3
  and politicisation of personal 147
social mobility 70, 126, 193
social model of disability 165, 214
socialisation
  definition of 195
  and education 195–6
  political 57
socialism 100, 101
Socratic method 150
Sodha, Sonia 160
solidarity 244
  alliance building 230–5, 236–7, 244
  anti-oppressive politics 231–3
  and hierarchisation of difference 226–7
  and hostility between disempowered groups 228–9
  identity politics and fragmentation 226
  and NSMs 112, 153, 224–5
  recognising overlaps 229–31
  Shaping Our Lives 227–8, 229
  understanding other disempowered groups 228, 232

special education 196
spoken language 156
Staples, Steven 36
state 107
  and neoliberalism 17, 19, 79, 101, 175
  relationship with police 15
  small state 17, 18, 24–5, 43, 67, *85*, 99, 104, 180
  state socialism 101
  subsidies 28
  welfare state 102–4
state schools 194
Steiner schools 197
Stone, Roger 46, 47
summer riots (2024), United Kingdom 81
Summerhill School 197
Sunak, Rishi 239
Survivors Speak Out 200
suspicion 60–1, 131, 228, 229
sustainability 123–4, 246
Sustainable Development Goals 24, 26, 70, 124
systematic reviews 179, 180

T

Tawney, R.H. 22–3
Taylor, Charles 110
Taylor, G. 225
technology
  and communication 139–40, 146–7, 160–1
  suspicions of 131–2
  technological change 31, 32–4
  see also Big Tech
terrorism 37–8
testimonial injustice 187
Thatcher, Margaret 18, 19, 35, 58, 61, 64, 73, 99, 100, 133
third way (New Labour, UK) 99, 195
Todd, M.J. 225
Tooze, Adam 239
totalitarianism 82
tourism 59
Tracini, Joe 187–8
trade unions 208, 224, 225
transgender people, issues of 117–18
transgender studies 177–8
traveller communities *see* Gypsy, Roma and Traveller (GRT) communities
trickle-down effect 27, 195
Trump, Donald 2, 45, 46, 50, 51, 55, 97, 102, 150, 174
Truss, Liz 27, 71, 174
trust 54, 80, 112, 232
Turing, Allan 33, 117
Twin Flame Universe (TFU) 92
Twitter/X 144, 154

U

ubuntu 247
Ukraine–Russia conflict 35, 36, 105, 116, 230
underclass 21, 64–5
United Nations 24, 26
  Climate Change Conference *see* COP26 (Conference of the Parties)
  Department of Economic and Social Affairs 21
  International Telecommunication Union (ITU) 161
  progressive realisation 242
  Sustainable Development Goals 24, 26, 70, 124
  UNESCO 246
United States 26, 81, 89, 102–3, 128, 238
  American Dream 72
  Capitol attack (2021) 46–7
  civil rights movement 109, 213, 214, 233, 243
  commodification of healthcare in 87
  Get Me Roger Stone (documentary) 46
  military intervention policy of 35
  Obama health reforms 47
  police killings 12, 13
  presidential election (2016) 144
user-led organisations (ULOs) 215–19, 227–8
  see also Shaping Our Lives
Uses of Literacy, The (Hoggart) 128–9

V

Virnoche, Mary 127
Von Mises, Ludwig 79
voter turnout 53–4

W

war
  biological warfare 39
  communication during 158
  and neoliberalism 35–7
  Ukraine–Russia conflict 35, 36, 105, 116, 230
  World War II 117, 195
War Office Selection Boards (Wosbees) 195
Ward, Colin 205
Waste Land, The (Eliot) 127–8
wealth inequality 20
Weber, Max 107
Weinstein, Harvey 105
welfare benefits 19, 73, 157, 158, 217, 228
welfare chauvinism 104
welfare corporatism 27–8
welfare pluralism 99
welfare state 79, 102–4, 223
Wells, H.G. 193

white privilege 132–5
Wilde, Oscar 89
Williams, Raymond 247
Witcher, Sally 210–11
Wolfe, Nathan 38
women
  caring work of 207, 208
  femicide 4, 11–13, 14, 29
  underrepresentation in politics 51–2
  women's movement/feminism 109, 111, 113–14, 118–20, 123
Women's Temperance Movement 151
Wood, Jason 120
Woolf, Virginia 74
World Bank 17, 23, 26, 35, 101, 140, 238
World Health Network 210–11
World Health Organization 12
World Trade Organization 26
World War II 117, 195

X

X, Malcolm *203*, 229, 233–4, 235

Y

You Can Do It (Rashford) 205–6

www.ingramcontent.com/pod-product-compliance
Lightning Source LLC
Chambersburg PA
CBHW051529020426
42333CB00016B/1843